THE MACEDONIAN QUESTION

OXFORD HISTORICAL MONOGRAPHS

Editors

R. J. W. EVANS   J. HARRIS

J. ROBERTSON

R. SERVICE   P. A. SLACK

B. WARD-PERKINS   J. WATTS

The Macedonian Question

Britain and the Southern Balkans
1939–1949

DIMITRIS LIVANIOS

OXFORD
UNIVERSITY PRESS

OXFORD
UNIVERSITY PRESS

Great Clarendon Street, Oxford OX2 6DP

Oxford University Press is a department of the University of Oxford.
It furthers the University's objective of excellence in research, scholarship,
and education by publishing worldwide in

Oxford New York

Auckland Cape Town Dar es Salaam Hong Kong Karachi
Kuala Lumpur Madrid Melbourne Mexico City Nairobi
New Delhi Shanghai Taipei Toronto

With offices in

Argentina Austria Brazil Chile Czech Republic France Greece
Guatemala Hungary Italy Japan Poland Portugal Singapore
South Korea Switzerland Thailand Turkey Ukraine Vietnam

Oxford is a registered trade mark of Oxford University Press
in the UK and in certain other countries

Published in the United States
by Oxford University Press Inc., New York

British Library Cataloguing in Publication Data

Data available

Library of Congress Cataloging in Publication Data

Data available

Typeset by Laserwords Private Limited, Chennai, India
Printed in Great Britain
on acid-free paper by
the MPG Books Group

ISBN 978–0–19–923768–5

3 5 7 9 10 8 6 4 2

στη μητέρα μου, για όλα

Acknowledgements

This study, a revised version of my doctoral dissertation, owes much to the support of a number of scholars. First, I should like to thank Professor Richard Clogg, my supervisor. I am particularly indebted to him for the invaluable guidance he has offered me, and his insightful comments. I am also extremely grateful to the 'Grand Old Man' of Greek anthropology, Dr John Campbell. Not only did he read a substantial part of my work with a sharp eye, but he was also an important source of support during my stay in Oxford. Dr Richard Kerr Kindersley and Professor Thanos Veremis read drafts of my thesis, and offered valuable suggestions. Professor Stefan Troebst also deserves my thanks for his constructive criticism of a final draft of this work.

The publication of a thesis normally offers the author the pleasant duty to record a number of intellectual debts that have been accumulated over many years. I should like to express, however inadequately, my gratitude to Professor John Koliopoulos, who has guided me during my studies at Aristotle University of Salonica, and first introduced me to things Macedonian. I am indebted to him for his unfailing encouragement. Dr Evangelos Kofos generously gave me the benefit of his scholarly expertise and kindness. Professor Basil Gounaris, a long-standing friend and mentor, deserves my thanks for our 'Macedonian conversations' over the years. I would also like to thank Professor Basil Kondis for his advice on Foreign Office material. A special word of thanks is also due to Dr Dimitris Portolos, Ms Katerina Haritatou, and Mr Giannis Petsopoulos for their discreet, but decisive, support. My stay in Oxford was made possible by the generosity of Mr and Ms Fitch. Without their financial support I could not have pursued my studies. I owe to them heartfelt thanks for the unique opportunity they have offered me.

Anna, a scholar of Italian humanism, was forced to live with the Macedonian revolutionaries for far too long. Her good nature and steady nerve allowed her to react to their raids in our daily life with good cheer. I shall always be grateful to her for her support. Regrettably, this book came too late to be placed in the hands of the person who most deserved to see it published. My gratitude to my mother is beyond words, and this work is dedicated to her.

D. L.

Contents

Note on Transliteration

Transliteration from Balkan languages has presented scholars with much trouble, not least because consistency and accuracy has to be tempered with an attempt to avoid unwarranted pedantry. I list below the transliteration schemes that are used in this book, but I have silently overlooked them whenever there are forms (including phonetic or historical) that have been established in English publications. So there is 'Mihailov', instead of 'Mihaylov', King 'Alexander' of Yugoslavia has remained so, but Protogerov's first name became 'Alexandŭr'. For Greek, I have rendered the 'η' as 'i', and therefore 'resistance' has been rendered as 'antistasi' and not 'antistase'. For Serbo-Croat, I have used its own version of the Latin alphabet (the *Latinica*). Given that many authors writing in English have also used the *Latinica* for the rendering of Macedonian names, I have followed this practice, and consequently 'Kolishevski' has become 'Koliševski' and the 'Antifascist Assembly' (of the National Liberation of Macedonia—ASNOM) has been rendered as 'Antifašističko Sobranie', and not as 'Antifashistichko'.

TRANSLITERATION SCHEMES

a) Bulgarian

а—a
б—b
в—v
г—g (hard)
д—d
е—e
ж—zh
з—z
и—i
й—y
к—k
л—l
м—m

b) Greek

α - a
β - v
γ - g
δ - d
ε - e
ζ - z
η - i
θ - th
ι - i
κ - k
λ - l
μ - m
ν - n

н−n	ξ - x
о−o	ο - o
п−p	π - p
р−r	ρ - r
с−s	σ - s
т−t	τ - t
у−u	υ - y
ф−f	φ - f
х−h	χ - ch
ц−ts	ψ - ps
ч−ch	ω - o
ш−sh	
щ−sht	αυ, ευ−af, ef or av, ev
ъ−ŭ	μπ - b if initial, mb if not
ю−iu	ντ - d if initial, nd if not
я−ya	γκ−g if initial, ng if not
	ου−ou

Abbreviations

ASNOM	*Antifašističko Sobranie na Narodnoto Osloboduvanje Na Makedonija*/Antifascist Assembly of National Liberation of Macedonia
AVNOJ	*Antifašističko Veće Narodnog Oslobođenja Jugolsavije*/Antifascist Council of National Liberation of Yugoslavia
BANU	Bulgarian Agrarian National Union
BCF	Balkan Communist Federation
BCP	Bulgarian Communist Party
BHQ	Balkan Headquarters
BLO	British Liaison Officer
BMORK	*Bŭlgarski Makedono-Odrinski Revoliutsionni Komiteti*/Bulgarian Macedo-Adrianopolitan Revolutionary Committees
CC	Central Committee (of Communist parties)
CD	Central Department (of the Foreign Office)
Cominform	Communist Information Bureau (also Informbureau), 1947–56
Comintern	Communist (Third) International, 1919–43
CPA	Communist Party of Albania
CPM	Communist Party of Macedonia
CPY	Communist Party of Yugoslavia
DAG	Democratic Army of Greece
EAM	*Ethniko Apeleftherotiko Metopo*/National Liberation Front (Greece)
EDES	*Ethnikos Dimokratikos Ellinikos Syndesmos*/National Republican Greek League
ELAS	*Ellinikos Laikos Apeleftherotikos Stratos*/Greek People's Liberation Army

IMRO	See **VMRO**
IMRO (United)	See **VMRO (obedinena)**
JGHQ	Joint General Headquarters (Greece)
KKE	*Kommounistiko Komma Elladas*/Communist Party of Greece
MRO	Macedonian Revolutionary Organization
NOF	*Naroden Osvododitelen Front*/National Liberation Front
OF	*Otechestven Front*/Fatherland Front (Bulgaria)
OSS	Office of Strategic Services (USA)
OZNA	*Odeljenje za Zaštitu Naroda*/Department for the Defence of the People (Yugoslavia)
PRM	People's Republic of Macedonia
SEKE	*Sosialistiko Ergatiko Komma Elladas*/Socialist Labour Party of Greece
SNOF	*Slavomakedonski Naroden Osvoboditelen Front*/Slav-Macedonian National Liberation Front
SOE	Special Operations Executive (Britain)
SRPJ (k)	*Socijalistička Radnička Partija Jugoslavije (komunista)*/Socialist Workers' Party of Yugoslavia (communist)
TMORO	*Tayna Makedono-Odrinska Revoliutsionna Organizatsiya*/Secret Macedo-Adrianopolitan Revolutionary Organization
UNRRA	United Nations Relief and Rehabilitation Administration
UNSCOB	United Nations Special Commission on the Balkans

VMRO	*Vŭtreshna Makedonska Revoliutsionna Organizatsiya*/Internal Macedonian Revolutionary Organization
VMRO (Obedinena)	*Vŭtreshna Makedonska Revoliutsionna Organizatsiya (Obedinena)*/Internal Macedonian Revolutionary Organization (United)

PART I

WEAVING THE NESSUS SHIRT, 1870–1939

1

Introduction

MACEDONIAN ILLUSIONS

'Le mot Macédoine fait illusion.'[1] Thus, Jacques Ancel in 1930. Few students of the Macedonian Question would be prepared to contest the ability of Macedonia, as a word or an entity, to provide ample opportunity for diehard illusions. There is hardly an aspect of this problem that can be taken for granted without provoking intense debate, while the enormous amount of printed material devoted to it was undertaken to defend conflicting national causes, rather than to serve Clio. The uncertainties appear even in the very name 'Macedonia', since it has never had the same geographical and national connotations for every ruler or contender concerned. Although it is widely accepted that, as a territorial designation from the late nineteenth century onwards, the term Macedonia refers to the region contained within the three Ottoman *vilayets* of Salonica, Monastir, and Kosovo, the Ottomans generally avoided that name, using instead the term *Rumeli* (the land of the Romans).[2] On the other hand the Bulgarians frequently excluded from Macedonia the area south of the 'Greater Bulgaria' created by the Treaty of San Stefano in 1878,[3] some Greek scholars argued that the *vilayet* of Kosovo should not be considered Macedonian territory,[4] while the Serbs often considered the northern part of that *vilayet* as an integral part of Serbia and denounced any geographical 'enlargement' of

---

[1] Jacques Ancel, *Peuples et nations des Balkans: Géographie politique* (Paris, 1930), 74.

[2] For most scholars, the geographical boundaries of Macedonia are the Šar mountains to the north, the lakes of Ochrid and Prespa to the west, the Pindus range, Mount Olympos and the Aegean Sea to the south, and, to the east, the Rila and Rhodope mountains and the river Nestos. Douglas Dakin, *The Greek Struggle in Macedonia, 1897–1913* (Salonica, 1966), 3.

[3] Richard von Mach, *The Bulgarian Exarchate: Its History and the Extent of its Authority in Turkey* (London and Neuchâtel, 1907), 43.

[4] See V. Colokotronis, *La Macédoine et l'Hellénisme: Étude historique et ethnologique* (Paris, 1919), 607.

Macedonia as a Bulgarian 'machination'.[5] Unsurprisingly, the 'national' affiliations of the population of that unfortunate land have provoked a much more heated debate than the designation of its borders, an issue plagued by mutually exclusive national rivalries, invented historical legacies, and local as well as international politics.

First, it should be stressed that the maps and statistics produced by various Balkan quarters in the late nineteenth and early twentieth centuries were at best prejudiced and unbalanced and at worst constituted little more than a paper war, since their principal objective was to influence foreign powers, legitimize territorial claims, and vindicate state policies.[6] In the eyes of contemporary European observers, Ottoman statistics were equally unreliable: in some cases their registers included—or made a serious effort to count—only males, they referred to the vague notion of the 'household', while the 'divide and rule' policy which the Porte followed in the early twentieth century has also to be taken into consideration.[7] However, the most significant element contained in their statistics, namely the classification of the population according to religious affiliation, and not on a linguistic or 'ethnic' basis, merits some analysis, for this feature reflects an Ottoman reality which points to the limited analytical value of 'national' or 'ethnic' categories in Balkan history prior to the rise of nationalism in the region.

The priority of religion in the shaping of Ottoman society led to the emergence of the *millet* system, a classification of the subjugated populations according to religion, which cut across social, regional, ethnic, and linguistic barriers. Originally, the *millet* system covered the Jews, the Orthodox Christians, and the Armenians (the 'peoples of the book'), but in the course of the eighteenth and nineteenth centuries the *millets* multiplied chiefly through the fragmentation of the empire's Orthodox Christian community. By the end of the nineteenth century the Ottomans had recognized no less than twelve *millets*, while a Vlach

---

[5] T. R. Georgević, *Macedonia* (London, 1918), 2–6.

[6] For an interesting aspect of this paper warfare, the function of ethnological maps, see a rich collection in H. R. Wilkinson, *Maps and Politics: A Review of the Ethnographic Cartography of Macedonia* (Liverpool, 1951).

[7] For the shortcomings of the Ottoman statistics see Carnegie Endowment for International Peace, *Report of the International Commission to Inquire into the Causes and Conduct of the Balkan Wars* (Washington DC, 1914), 28. Regarding the Ottoman political aims and their relation to the statistics see the letter of Hilmi Pasha, inspector general for the Macedonian *vilayets* in 1904, concerning the census of that year in Bulgarian Academy of Sciences, *Macedonia: Documents and Materials* (Sofia, 1978), 491.

millet was established in the early twentieth century.[8] The Orthodox *millet* was called *Millet-i Rum* (i.e. the 'Roman' Millet) and was placed under the spiritual, and to some extent temporal, leadership of the Patriarch of Constantinople, which was its *millet bashi* (head of the millet).[9]

The Orthodox *millet* was Greek in outlook: the Patriarch and many of the bishops were Greeks (or thoroughly Hellenized) and Greek was widely, although not exclusively, used for church services. In Macedonia, however, under this supranational cover there were Albanian-, Greek-, Vlach-, and Slav- speakers, the last claimed by all three principal contenders for the entire area: Serbs, Bulgarians, and Greeks. Any attempt to calculate the numbers of these groups is fraught with difficulty, but a descent to the statistician's den is inevitable.[10] At the beginning of the twentieth century, within the Macedonian

[8] See Anthony O' Mahony, 'The Christian Communities of Jerusalem and the Holy Land: A Historical and Political Survey', in id. (ed.), *The Christian Communities of Jerusalem and the Holy Land: Studies in History, Religion and Politics* (Cardiff, 2003), 7–8, for a catalogue of the Ottoman *millet* communities at the end of the 19th cent. For the Vlach *millet*, established in 1905, see H. N. Brailsford, *Macedonia: Its Races and their Future* (London 1906), 188–9. For the origins and evolution of the *millet* system see Kemal Karpat, *An Inquiry into the Social Foundation of Nationalism in the Ottoman State: From Social Estates to Classes, from Millets to Nations* (Princeton, 1973); Bernard Lewis and Benjamin Braude (eds.), *Christians and Jews in the Ottoman Empire: The Functioning of a Plural Society, i. The Central Lands* (New York, 1982).

[9] For the Orthodox *millet* and its functions see Richard Clogg, 'The Greek Millet in the Ottoman Empire', in Lewis and Braude (eds.), *Christians*, i. 185–207; Paraskevas Konortas, 'From Tai'fe to Millet: Ottoman Terms for the Ottoman Greek Orthodox Community', in Dimitri Gondicas and Charles Issawi (eds.), *Ottoman Greeks in the Age of Nationalism: Politics, Economy and Society in the Nineteenth Century* (Princeton, 1999), 169–80; id., *Othomanikes Theoriseis gia to Oikoumeniko Patriarcheio: Veratia gia tous Prokathemenous tis Megalis Ekklisias, dekatos edvomos—arches eikostou aiona* [Ottoman Views of the Ecumenical Patriarchate: Berats for the Leaders of the Great Church, from the Seventeenth to the Beginnings of the Twentieth Century] (Athens, 1998).

[10] For statistical accounts see Carnegie Endowment for International Peace, *Report of the International Commission,* 28, 30. More details in the chart at the end of G. M. Terry, 'The Origins and Development of the Macedonian Revolutionary Movement, with Particular Reference to TMORO from its Conception in 1893 to the Ilinden Uprising of 1903,' (unpublished M.Phil. thesis, Nottingham, 1974). For Bulgarian ethnographic estimates see Iordan Ivanoff, *Les Bulgares devant Le Congrès de la Paix, Documents historiques, ethnographiques et diplomatiques* (2nd edn., Berne, 1919), 294–304, but mainly Vasil Kŭnchov, *Makedoniya: Etnografiya I Statistika* (Sofia, 1900). Kŭnchov's work, a laboriously researched account, is undoubtedly the best of its kind. For the Greek point of view, Colokotronis, *La Macédoine,* 603–19. See also the maps in Wilkinson, *Maps.* For comparative estimates based on Balkan, Ottoman, and European accounts see Vemund Aarbakke, *Ethnic Rivalry and the Quest for Macedonia, 1870–1913* (Boulder, Colo., 2003), 6–24. It should be stressed that the discrepancies noted in the statistics were due not only to the criteria, linguistic or religious, used for classification, but

vilayets the Muslims constituted roughly a third of the population. This group was composed mainly of 'Turks', approximately 400,000 in 1912, and 'Albanians', about 120,000, while the whole Macedonian population at that time was about 2,280,000.[11] Apart from these groups, the Macedonian Muslims included a number of Bulgarian-speaking Pomaks, who were concentrated mainly in Thrace, the Greek-speaking Valaades in south-western Macedonia, a small number of Gypsies, and the Salonica Dönme (Jews who had converted to Islam).[12] It should be noted that the Ottomans made a concerted effort to inflate the numbers of Muslims in the Macedonian *vilayets* by administrative manipulation. Thus, the addition of the overwhelmingly Albanian *sanjaks* of Elbasan and Prizren in the *vilayets* of Monastir and Kosovo respectively produced a Muslim majority in these units.[13]

The numerically predominant group in the region was the Slav-speakers, approximately half of the Macedonian population, and especially strong in the rural areas. The Greek-speaking population was confined largely in towns and large villages; they could be found mostly in the southern parts of the region, especially along the Aegean coastline, and they were predominant in the Chalkidiki peninsula. The Vlachs, mainly transhumant shepherds speaking a Latin-based language, formed scattered enclaves mainly in southern and south-western Macedonia; they were fairly numerous in the Pindus range, in mountain villages and in cities as, for instance, in Monastir.[14] There was also a small number of Christian Albanians. However, if the focus is shifted from language to religious affiliation the picture changes dramatically. From 1870

also to the fact that different accounts employed different geographical delimitations of Macedonia.

[11] These figures and terminology are drawn from contemporary British sources. FO 371/10667, C15185/2332/7, memorandum on 'The Macedonian Question and Komitaji Activity' by the CD of the FO dated 26/11/1925. This memorandum is discussed in Miranda Paximadopoulou-Stavrinou, 'To Foreign Office kai to Makedoniko to 1925' [The Foreign Office and the Macedonian [Question] in 1925], *Valkanika Symmeikta*, 10 (1998), 225–42. The Ottoman census of 1904 gave a Muslim population of more than 1,500,000, which appears to be an exaggerated estimate. Ivanoff, *Les Bulgares*, 298.

[12] For the Dönme see Mark Mazower, *Salonica, City of Ghosts: Christians, Muslims and Jews, 1430–1950* (London, 2004), 65–79. For the Gypsies and the Jews of Macedonia see also Brailsford, *Macedonia*, 81–5.

[13] Richard von Mach, *Bulgarian Exarchate*, 43.

[14] The British account mentioned in n. 11 gives a number of about 300,000 Greek- and 200,000 Vlach-speakers in the three *vilayets*, compared to 1,150,000 Slavs around 1912. The number of the Vlachs is exaggerated, probably reflecting a pro-Greek bias, or Greek sources.

onward, when the Bulgarians were granted ecclesiastical autonomy and established the Exarchate,[15] the Greeks considered only the Exarchists as Bulgarians, and viewed the Patriarchists, who remained loyal to the Ecumenical Patriarchate, as Greeks. According to the Ottoman census of 1904 there were in Macedonia 648,962 Patriarchists and 557,734 Exarchists.[16] Evidently, the criteria used to define the various groups varied wildly. For Bulgarian scholars and publicists, what mattered was not religious affiliation, as the Slavs were split between the Exarch and the Patriarch, but language, and consequently Bulgarian statistics are based on exclusively linguistic criteria, thus allowing for a depression of the number of both Greeks and Serbs. The exact opposite method was employed by Greek sources, which make no reference to language and focus instead on religious affiliation and what they call 'commercial language' of the population. Following this classification, the number of Greeks rises conveniently.[17]

Clearly, the main issue at stake in Ottoman Macedonia was the loyalties and perceived 'national orientation' of the Slav-speaking population, and this calls for some examination of the reasons that prompted the Slav-speakers to opt for the Exarch or the Patriarch after 1870. To begin with, a major distinction should be made between the vast majority of peasants—as were most of the Slavs—and the small but extremely vocal minority of Greek, Bulgarian, and Serbian schoolteachers, priests, and government officials of the Balkan countries in Macedonia.[18] This element was clearly nationalist in orientation and its main aim had been the awakening of the 'sleeping beauty' of Greek, Bulgarian, and Serbian nationalism. Given that theirs was the

[15] The establishment of the autonomous Bulgarian Church, a major turning point in Macedonian politics, will be treated in greater detail below.

[16] Colokotronis, *La Macédoine*, 606. As was frequently the case with the statistics, there are two sources which provide figures for the statistics of 1904. One is the Turkish paper of Salonica *ASR* (no. 994) and the other is the Austrian paper *Politische Korrespondenz* (18/3/1904). The discrepancies in the numbers given are quite noticeable, with the latter being more favourable to the Greeks. In both cases the Patriarchists outnumber the Exarchists but in the version given in *ASR* it appears also that a classification rested on language, which gives 896,496 Bulgarians, including both Exarchists and Patriarchists; 307,000 Patriarchist Greeks; 99,000 Vlachs; and 100,717 Serbs. For this version see Ivanoff, *Les Bulgares*, 298.

[17] See Aarbakke, *Ethnic Rivalry*, 9–13, 162–83, for Greek and Bulgarian statistical accounts.

[18] Fostering the nationalist spirit in Macedonia and the Balkans in general through education produced astonishing side effects. According to British sources, in 1912 there was less illiteracy in Bulgaria than in Italy. FO 371/10667, C15185, memorandum of the CD of the FO dated 26/11/1925.

role of flying the nationalist flag, the subsequent analysis will focus on the peasants, who found themselves caught in a much more confusing situation.

It is now widely accepted that nationalism in the modern sense of the word is not inborn. As Ernest Gellner eloquently put it, 'nations, like states, are a contingency, and not a universal necessity'.[19] It is unlikely that such a contingency existed in the Macedonian *vilayets* prior to the establishment of the Bulgarian Church in 1870. It should be noticed that the key element for the understanding of the Orthodox Greek *millet* is the word Orthodox rather than Greek. This frequently missed aspect can be applied to a certain extent even to the Greek clergy, and was painfully discovered by Greek nationalists, who pointed out, not without resentment, that 'Prelates of the church are not Greeks, they are Christians'.[20] Inevitably, the Patriarchate drew much more fire from other quarters: Bulgarian, but also European, accounts have repeatedly accused the post-Byzantine patriarchs of acting as agents of 'denationalization' and 'Hellenization' of the Balkan Slavs, citing particularly the abolition of the two medieval Slavonic sees, the Patriarchate of Peć and the Archbishopric of Ochrid, in 1766 and 1767 respectively. The suppression of these churches brought Serbs and Bulgarians under the direct ecclesiastical jurisdiction of the Patriarchate and led to an increase in the number of Greek bishops, and to widespread use of Greek in church services. There is evidence to suggest, however, that patriarchal motives had little to do with the imposition of 'Greek' rule over the Slavs, and much more with a concerted effort to stem the advances of Catholicism in those areas. Apart from the fact that by then both sees were already administered largely by Greek prelates, they faced grave financial problems. The local synods petitioned the Patriarch to revoke their autocephaly, a request to which the 'Great Church' responded, in an attempt to safeguard not 'Hellenism', but Orthodoxy.[21]

The absence of the 'ethnic' factor can also be confirmed by developments occurring at about the same time in distant Ottoman Syria: after a

[19] Ernest Gellner, *Nations and Nationalism* (Oxford, 1988), 6.

[20] This statement carries additional weigh since it was made by Ion Dragoumis, an active participant in Macedonian affairs. He was vice-consul in Monastir from 1902 to 1904 and formed an extensive organization to counteract the activities of the Bulgarian Comitadjis. His statement is quoted from Thanos Veremis, 'From the National State to Stateless Nation, 1821–1910', in id. and Martin Blinkhorn (eds.), *Modern Greece: Nationalism and Nationality* (Athens, 1990), 21.

[21] Paschalis Kitromilides, 'Balkan Mentality: History, Legend, Imagination', *Nations and Nationalism*, 2/2 (1996), 182.

large segment of the Arab Orthodox flock of the Patriarchate of Antioch became Uniate, including the Arab patriarch Cyril Al-Tanas himself, the Ecumenical Patriarchate intervened directly in 1725 and started appointing to Antioch only Greek clerics. In the 1760s, at the time of the suppression of the Slavonic sees in the Balkans, the Patriarchate of Constantinople appointed in Antioch a Greek, dismissing an Arab candidate 'lest some one of the Arabs come in and . . . extinguish the bright flame of Orthodoxy'.[22] Clearly Arab candidates were suspect, but only because they could endanger Orthodoxy by passing to Catholicism and to the Uniate Church. It was largely a defensive concern, namely the protection of the Orthodox flock and perceptions of an imminent Catholic onslaught, that led Constantinople to tighten its grip over both the Arabs of Antioch and the Slavs of the Balkans at the end of the eighteenth century.

Turning from the clergy to their Balkan Slav flock, the prevalence of religion is equally pronounced. In early twentieth century, some Slav-speaking children from a village near Ochrid who had been asked to identify their ancestors, responded that 'they weren't Turks, they were Christians'.[23] Another fairly typical answer could be 'Greek'. A French traveller in the late nineteenth century was told by a Slav in the town of Resna that 'our fathers were Greeks and none mentioned the Bulgarians'.[24] A literary translation of the word 'Greek' used above might well be 'Christian', for these two terms were inseparably linked, given that most Macedonian Slavs remained deeply immersed in the pre-modern religious identity of the Orthodox *millet*, and had available to them education mostly in Greek.[25] It quickly became apparent to the apostles of nationalism in Macedonia that the peasants could simply not understand the word 'nation' in the way their 'national leaders' did. The use of the word 'Bulgarian' is another illuminating example,

---

[22] Robert M. Haddad, *Syrian Christians in Muslim Society: An Interpretation* (Princeton, 1970), 63, quotation on p. 66.

[23] It is worth quoting this often-cited short dialogue in full. 'Who built this place [a medieval fortress]?' I asked them. The answer was significant: 'The free men'. 'And who were they?' 'Our grandfathers.' 'Yes, but were they Serbs or Bulgarians or Greeks or Turks?' 'They weren't Turks, they were Christians.' Brailsford, *Macedonia*, 99.

[24] Victor Bérard, *La Turquie et l' Hellénisme contemporain* (Paris, 1897), 125.

[25] Before the establishment of the Exarchate, Greek education in Macedonia, despite its many problems, was virtually unchallenged. After 1870, however, the Bulgarians made a determined effort and at the turn of the century they had 843 schools with 31,719 pupils, while the Greeks had 1,000 schools with 70,000 pupils. Dakin, *Greek Struggle*, 20; Carnegie Endowment for International Peace, *Report of the International Commission*, 27.

as it had in many cases social rather than ethnic connotations. It was used to denote the hard-working peasant, the poor and the illiterate, irrespective of language, something that Serbian and Greek accounts were all too happy to acknowledge for their own reasons.[26] The fluidity of ethnic terms in the Balkans was not, of course, a novelty, as the word 'Serv-alvanito-vulgaro-vlachos' (Serb-Albanian-Bulgaro-Vlach), used by a Greek chronicle of the fifteenth century, clearly suggests.[27]

The establishment of the Bulgarian Exarchate signalled a period of fierce antagonism in Macedonia, which is mainly seen as a manifestation of 'national' consciousness of the Bulgarians in Macedonia.[28] Although the growth of Bulgarian nationalism since 1870, supported by a rapidly expanding educational network, was considerable, adherence to the Bulgarian national cause was far from being the only or, in many cases the most important, consideration for abandoning the Patriarch and opting for the Exarch. A closer examination reveals a far more complex situation. What is not open to doubt is a tendency of many Slavs to have church services in their language. The Exarchate was not the first to consider and finally to exploit this need. What Orthodox sources refer to as 'the Uniate propaganda', but also Catholicism, owed much of its modest success in Macedonia to the use of Slavonic.[29] This wish, along with a determination to break with oppressive bishops, prompted a large segment of the Slav-speakers into the fold of the Exarchate.[30] Such motives were by no means confined to the Slavs. In the early twentieth

---

[26] Cf. e.g., Jovan Cvijić, *Remarques sur l'ethnographie de la Macédoine* (Paris, 1907), 22. Cvijić, however, was not an impartial observer. Cf. p. 13.

[27] Cited in Ivo Banac, *The National Question in Yugoslavia: Origins, History, Politics* (Ithaca, NY and London 1988), rep. 328.

[28] For a general discussion of the relationship between nationalism and religion see George Arnakis, 'The Role of Religion in the Development of Balkan Nationalism', in C. and B. Jelavich (eds.), *The Balkans in Transition: Essays on the Development of Balkan Life and Politics since the Eighteenth Century* (Berkeley and Los Angeles 1963), 115–44, esp. 133–40.

[29] An inscription in a Catholic church in Macedonia commemorated the date of conversion as follows: 'On March 1858 we recovered our national tongue'. Cited in Thomas Meininger, *Ignatiev and the Establishment of the Bulgarian Exarchate 1864–1872: A Study in Personal Diplomacy* (Madison, 1970), 22.

[30] According to a native of Veles, 'the citizens of Veles did not begin to take an interest in the church struggle until 1860. It is possible that even then they might not have joined in the church struggle but for the fact that at that time the Suffragan-Bishop of Veles was Greek. Antim by name . . . made himself so unpopular in Veles and in the eparchy of Veles-Debar, that the agents of the Bulgarian propaganda won over the whole of Veles to the church struggle for the Bulgarian Exarchate.' Georgevitch, *Macedonia*, 235.

century, some Vlachs from Monastir petitioned the Patriarchate to use 'Roumanian' in their church. The Patriarchate refused, and this led many Vlachs to join the Exarchate which proved to be willing to accommodate their request.[31]

By the end of the nineteenth century Bulgarian guerrilla bands, some of them local and connected with the Macedonian Revolutionary Organization, but others including men from the Bulgarian principality, roamed the Macedonian *vilayets* of Monastir and Salonica and terrorized the peasants in order to send petitions to the Ottomans for permission to join the Exarchate.[32] Thus, merciless terror became a decisive factor in shaping the alleged national preferences of the peasants and provided the Exarchate with a commanding stronghold in many Macedonian areas.[33] In 1904 the Greek consul reported from Salonica that 'only a few [Slav-speakers] dare to remain Greeks'.[34] The Greeks, defeated in the Graeco-Turkish war of 1897 and preoccupied with the Cretan issue, had other foreign policy priorities, and were latecomers in practising 'the politics of terror'. Their first systematic attempt to form bands and send them to Macedonia was made in 1904 and ended with the outbreak of the 'Young Turk' revolution in 1908.[35]

Generally speaking, during the period under consideration (1870–1908) most of the Macedonian villages were 'mixed', i.e. contained an Exarchist and a Patriarchist 'faction', although in most cases both factions spoke Bulgarian dialects, with schoolteachers, priests, or chieftains as their local leaders. The rest of the population was rather passive and indifferent. Surrounded as they were by an extremely hostile environment, the main concern of the peasants was to safeguard their life and

---

[31] See the letter of the British Consul General Biliotti to the British chargé d'affaires Whitehead, Salonica, 26 Jan. 1903, reprod. in Basil Gounaris et al. (eds.), *The Events of 1903 in Macedonia as Presented in European Diplomatic Correspondence* (Salonica, 1993), 29–30.

[32] According to Article 10 of the Firman of 1870, which established the Exarchate, it was stated that a locality has the right to join the Bulgarian Church, if two-thirds of the population approved it. The Firman can be found in Bérard, *La Turquie*, 184–7, Article 10 at 186–7. For the MRO see below.

[33] For the activities of the Bulgarian Comitadjis (Committee men) see Dakin, *Greek Struggle*, 44–70.

[34] Archeion Ypourgiou Exoterikon (Archives of the Ministry for Foreign Affairs), AYE 1904/Proxeneion Thessalonikis, Nikolaos Eugeniadis to the foreign minister Athos Romanos, 28/2/1904, Protocol Number 107.

[35] For the Greek 'Makedonikos Agonas' ('Macedonian Struggle') see Dakin, *Greek Struggle*. For the Bulgarian bands in Macedonia see Aarbakke, *Ethnic Rivalry*, 124–8.

their modest property by keeping this game of terror out of their villages. This was a demanding task, not least because both Greek and Bulgarian bands included brigands, whose attraction to plunder and cattle-stealing was rarely tempered by 'national' or other considerations.[36] Naturally, when a Greek or a Bulgarian chieftain entered a village and asked 'What are you, Greeks or Bulgarians?'[37] he was provided with the answer he wanted to hear rather than a manifestation of 'national feelings'. As a consequence a village could shift its allegiance overnight, and very often the peasants decided to accommodate both Exarchist and Patriarchist bands to prevent reprisals. Many of these 'Comitadjis' (Committee men) who tried hard from 1893 to 1908 to transfer the loyalties of the Slav-speakers to the Exarchate can hardly be classified as nationalists of any particular cause. They were armed irregulars who became involved in that struggle for a variety of reasons, and not least because they saw in the Bulgarian organization the only way to shake off the Ottoman yoke. Given that the Macedonian Revolutionary Organization was the first to offer this option it won over the most daring and revolutionary elements in Macedonia, a reality their Greek adversaries regreted bitterly. Thus, many of those who manned the Bulgarian bands had been recruited primarily as Christians to fight against the Turks, and not as 'Bulgarians'. The relatively low presence of nationalism was further highlighted by the fact that some Exarchist Comitadjis later joined the Greek bands and ended up as fervent Patriarchists, when pecuniary motives prompted them to do so, an attraction that also brought to the Greek cause the services of many Macedonian brigands.[38]

Furthermore, socio-political dimensions of ethnicity have also to be taken into consideration. In some cases the scheme Exarchists vs

[36] For a lucid analysis of the brigands' role in the Greek struggle for Macedonia see John S. Koliopoulos, *Brigands with a Cause: Brigandage and Irredentism in Modern Greece 1821–1912* (Oxford, 1987). For an account of the Greek guerrilla warfare in 1904–8 in Macedonia see Dimitris Livanios, 'Conquering the Souls: Nationalism and Greek Guerrilla Warfare in Ottoman Macedonia, 1904–1908', *Byzantine and Modern Greek Studies*, 23 (1999), 195–221.

[37] Numerous examples illustrating this situation can be found in the memoirs of the various Greeks chieftains. See Vassilis Stavropoulos (Korakas), 'Apomnimonevmata' [Memoirs], in *O Makedonikos Agonas: Apomnimonevmata* [The Struggle for Macedonia: Memoirs] (Salonica, 1984), 383–465; K. I. Mazarakis-Ainian (Akritas), 'Anamniseis' [Reminiscences], *ibid.* 249.

[38] See Dakin, *Greek Struggle*, 119–32. According to a Greek source involved in that struggle Bulgarian chiefs joined the Greek organization believing that the Greeks would pay for their services. See D. Kakavos, *Apomnimonevmata* [Memoirs] (Salonica, 1972), 88.

Patriarchists was nothing more than a cover for deeper social cleavages.[39] In the Karadjova region, for instance, in central Macedonia, there were isolated fanatically Patriarchist villages encircled by fairly numerous Exarchist ones. However, the fact that the inhabitants of the former villages were not indigenous but relatively newcomers in the area, suggests that since the indigenous element was Exarchist the hostility between them and the newly arrived peasants made it almost imperative for the latter to opt for the Patriarch. Local politics reveal another aspect of this question, as bitter political struggles among the notables of a village or a town could lead the rival factions to use the local Greek and Bulgarian organizations for their own political ends, and in order to pay off old–political or personal—scores. According to a protagonist of the Greek armed struggle, the Bulgarian movement in Macedonia arose from 'hatred among the village councils. The opposition sided with the Bulgarians and proselytized the illiterate peasants.'[40] Although this is clearly a sweeping generalization, and comes from an anti-Bulgarian source, it nevertheless does reflect a reality, which is very often neglected. In other cases the contravention of traditional moral values committed by a Patriarchist or an Exarchist notable might well have prompted the conservative peasants to transfer their loyalty. In 1905 a prominent Patriarchist *prokritos* (notable) in the village of Goumenissa in the *vilayet* of Salonica, delayed his wedding due to financial difficulties. This issue provoked the opposition of the whole village and forced the Greek Consul General of Salonica, Lambros Koromilas, to ask the Ministry for Foreign Affairs to allocate funding for the wedding. The fact that this would restore the credibility of the Greek 'party' in the village clearly indicates the importance of these factors in the rural areas of Macedonia.[41]

All in all, the effort of extracting a clear-cut national conscious-ness out of the Macedonian Slav-speaking peasantry proved a difficult task. Their loyalties remained attached mostly to their land, family, and religious affiliation and to some extent their language. Although

[39] See Basil Gounaris, 'Social Cleavages and "National Awakening" in Ottoman Macedonia', *East European Quarterly*, 29/4 (1995), 409–26.

[40] Mazarakis, *Anamniseis*, 203. Mazarakis, an officer of the Greek army, had a thorough knowledge of the situation in Macedonia in the early 20th cent. He had worked in the Greek Consulate in Salonica in 1904 and had travelled extensively in Macedonia. He also become in 1905 a guerrilla leader. See Dakin, *Greek Struggle*, 232–6. I am grateful to Basil Gounaris for bringing to my attention the case of Karadjova.

[41] AYE 1905/Proxeneion Thessalonikis, A.A.K./B, Koromilas to the Ministry for Foreign Affairs, 30/9/1905, No. 665.

none of these features, if taken separately, could articulate a clearly defined national identity, the Balkan nationalists tried to do so, with varying degrees of success. Thus the Greeks capitalized on the religious factor and the Bulgarians on the linguistic one. Both movements, however, were based on the assumption that 'nations too are products of the primordial ties of race, ancestry, religion, language and territory'.[42] In Macedonia, as elsewhere,[43] this was not the case. National consciousness had to be constructed—and often to be imposed—by others than the people concerned. As for the peasants themselves, they seemed to evade the whole issue and stressed instead what contemporary observers derided as 'opportunism', determined by more 'real' and less 'imagined' considerations: the main problem is not to be 'under the Turk'. 'Our fathers were Greeks and none mentioned the Bulgarians. By becoming Bulgarians we have won, the Turk respects us and Europe supports us. If we have to be Serbs, it is not a problem, but for the time being it is better to be Bulgarians.'[44]

There was one term, however, absent from the above list: the 'Macedonians'. That was not surprising, for most Slavs who did not choose to call themselves 'Bulgarians' would have opted for 'Greek' or 'Christian' instead. The use of the term 'Macedonians', of course, was not unknown, either to the Slavs or to the wider world, although few would use it in a 'national', as opposed to a regional, sense to denote a Slavic group distinct from Serbs and Bulgarians, and the influence of those who did was not significant. The most celebrated case of 'Macedonianism' at the turn of the century was that of Krste Petkov Misirkov, who published in 1903 a book *On Macedonian Matters* defending the existence of a Macedonian nation and calling for the use of a Macedonian language. The book was published in Sofia, but it did not reach its intended audience, as Bulgarian police confiscated and destroyed all copies. Misirkov himself did not prove to be an ardent supporter of his own claims, as he expressed strong pro-Bulgarian views

---

[42] A. Smith, *The Ethnic Origins of Nations* (Oxford, 1985), 452.

[43] See e.g. the slow and difficult process of transforming 'peasants' into 'Frenchmen', described by Eugene Weber, *From Peasants into Frenchmen: The Modernization of Rural France 1870–1914* (Stanford, 1976).

[44] *Nous autres, pourvu que nous ne soyons plus sous le Turc, il nous soucie bien de Serbie ou de Bulgarie! Nos pères etaint Hellènes, et personne ne parlait alors de Bulgares. En devenant Bulgares, nous avons gagné que le Turc nous respecte et l'Europe nous soutient. S'il faut être Serbes rien n'empêchera, mais pour l'heure Bulgares vaut mieux.* Bérard, *La Turquie*, 125.

shortly afterwards, and continued to oscillate between Bulgarian and Macedonian nationalism.[45]

Misirkov and the small circle of intellectuals who professed a Macedonian consciousness, however inconsistently, were not the only source of Macedonianism. Serbian politicians and scholars, such as Stojan Novaković, for instance, also acknowledged at about the same time the existence of a separate Macedonian group, but they did so in an attempt to deny those Slavs to Bulgarian nationalism, thus safeguarding the 'historic rights' of Serbia in the region. The most important case in point was the respected Serbian geographer Jovan Cvijić, in whose ethnological maps the 'Macedo-Slavs' figured prominently. They did not have a concrete national consciousness, he argued, and could be assimilated by both Serbs and Bulgarians. He did not fail to add, however, that they 'preserved some traces of historical Serbian traditions'.[46] The Macedo-Slavs featured in many other maps of the Balkans, including pro-Greek ones, but mostly with the same aim: to erect as many barriers as possible between them and the Bulgarians, whose claim on the loyalty of the Macedonian population was considered by both Serbs and Greeks as the most menacing.[47]

THE BALKAN 'NESSUS SHIRT':[48] THE POLITICS OF THE MACEDONIAN QUESTION, 1870–1939

From a political point of view the Macedonian Question was an integral part of the Eastern Question, which in the Balkan context consisted

[45] His book was published in an English trans. in Skopje in 1974. On Misirkov and his career see Aarbakke, *Ethnic Rivalry,* 120–1; for his pro-Bulgarian views see Kyril Drezov, 'Macedonian Identity: An Overview of the Major Claims', in James Pettifer (ed.), *The New Macedonian Question* (London, 1999), 58; for a pro-Macedonian account see Andrew Rossos, 'Macedonianism and Macedonian Nationalism on the Left', in Ivo Banac and Katherine Verdery (eds.), *National Character and National Ideology in Interwar Eastern Europe* (New Haven, 1995), 227–8.

[46] Jovan Cvijić, 'The Geographical Distribution of the Balkan Peoples', *Geographical Review,* 5/5 (1918), 345–61, at 358; id., *Remarques.* On Cvijić and Serbian geography in the context of the Macedonian Question see Banac, *The National Question,* 307–28. On Serbian attempts to use 'Macedonianism' against the Bulgarians see Evangelos Kofos, 'National Heritage and National Identity in Nineteenth- and Twentieth-Century Macedonia', in Veremis and Blinkhorn (eds.), *Modern Greece,* 113; Bulgarian Academy of Sciences, *Macedonia: Documents and Materials* (Sofia, 1978), 407.

[47] See Wilkinson, *Maps,* 146–53, and the maps on fig. 84.

[48] The 'Nessus shirt', a quite telling characterization, was proposed by the British ambassador to Sofia Sidney Waterlow. FO 371/14135, C2490/82/7, 27/3/1930.

chiefly of the management of the gradual Ottoman withdrawal from the peninsula by the Great Powers according to their competing strategic interests. Against that background, the struggle of the Bulgarian bishops in the nineteenth century to create a Bulgarian Church independent of the Greek Patriarchate of Constantinople marked the emergence of the Macedonian Question in modern times.

In their struggle against the Patriarchate the Bulgarians found in Count Nikolai Pavlovich Ignatiev, the most senior panslav in the Russian foreign ministry, a powerful ally.[49] Although the Russians remained initially rather distant observers of the Greek–Bulgarian controversy, Ignatiev came as Russia's envoy to Constantinople in 1864 with a twofold aim: to help the Bulgarians 'without breaking with the Greeks' and thus to consolidate Russian influence in the area.[50] His delicate task, however, was rendered impossible, for neither the Bulgarians nor the Patriarchate were prepared to find any common ground: extreme nationalists eventually dominated the Bulgarian side and rejected proposals for reconciliation coming from the Patriarchate, despite the fact that some of these had met with Ignatiev's open approval.[51] On the other hand it became apparent that the Patriarch would not favour any extension of Bulgarian ecclesiastical jurisdiction south of the Balkan mountains. When the negotiations reached a deadlock in 1868, Ignatiev decided to choose Slavdom rather than Christendom and pressed for an independent Bulgarian Church. In many respects, that was a defeat for Ignatiev, for the ensuing Greek–Bulgarian schism demonstrated that Russian policy 'failed to guide the struggle for a Bulgarian church along the channels they desired'.[52]

The Ottomans intervened in 1870, and established the Bulgarian Exarchate, provoking the reaction of the Patriarchate, which excommunicated the Bulgarian bishops in 1872, and accused them of introducing the concept of 'phyletism' (that is, nationalism) in the Orthodox

[49] Michael Boro Petrovich, *The Emergence of Russian Panslavism, 1856–1870* (New York and London 1956), 258–69; Ignatiev '[b]rilliantly aided by his seductive wife, himself combining great physical energy, unabashed self-confidence, ingratiating charm, jocular brusqueness, and unappeased talent for intrigue . . . could feel that he was deservedly styled "*le vice-Sultan*"'. B. H. Sumner, 'Ignatyev at Constantinople, 1864–1874', *Slavonic and East European Review*, IV 32 (1933), 571.

[50] Meininger, *Ignatiev*, 28.

[51] Evangelos Kofos, *O Ellinismos stin Periodo 1869–1881* [Hellenism during the Period 1869–1881] (Athens, 1981), 21.

[52] B. H. Sumner, *Russia and the Balkans 1870–1880* (Oxford, 1937), 113.

Church.[53] Moreover, it will be remembered that the firman of 1870 stipulated that a village could opt for the Exarch, provided that two-thirds of the population desired to do so, a provision set to generate much friction between the two sides.

Although the establishment of the Exarchate was widely viewed as a victory for the Bulgarian national cause in Macedonia, the greatest hour of the emerging Bulgarian nationalism was yet to come. The Russo-Turkish war of 1877–8–a consequence of the Eastern Crisis (1875–8)–and the subsequent Treaty of San Stefano created the *Tselokupna Bŭlgariya* (Undivided, or complete, Bulgaria), which included most of the Macedonian provinces but not the port of Salonica. These developments provoked intense fears of Russian domination of the Balkans in the European capitals, an anti-Slav delirium in Greece, and profound dismay in Serbia. But the Russian victory was as spectacular as it was short-lived. A European congress, held in Berlin a few months later, eradicated the Bulgarian gains in Macedonia and retained Ottoman sovereignty over the region.[54] The powers confined the newly born Bulgarian principality between the Danube and the Balkan mountains. Eastern Rumelia, an autonomous province under Ottoman suzerainty, was established to the south of the new state.

As the prospects for shaking off the Ottoman yoke seemed to be bleak in 1878, secret Bulgaro-Macedonian *druzhestvi* (societies) began to be formed mainly by chieftains and intellectuals devoted to San Stefano's 'Greater Bulgaria'. This led to some violent incidents committed by isolated guerrilla bands. The Bulgarian premier Stefan Stambolov (1887–94), however, opted for 'peaceful penetration' and more bishops for the Exarchate rather than armed raids, and sought to dissolve the most active of those societies.[55] Nevertheless the seeds of revolutionary activity had been already sown.

In Salonica, in November 1893, four teachers, a bookseller, and a physician founded the most famous Macedonian organization. Its exact

[53] Paschalis Kitromilides, 'Imagined Communities' and the Origins of the National Question in the Balkans', repr. in id., *Enlightenment, Nationalism and Orthodoxy: Studies in the Culture and Political Thought of South-Eastern Europe* (Aldershot 1994), study xiii.

[54] For the Congress of Berlin see Sumner, *Russia*, 501–53. W. N. Medlicott, *The Congress of Berlin and After, 1878–1880* (London, 1938). For British policy see Richard Millman, *Britain and the Eastern Question, 1875–1878* (Oxford, 1979).

[55] For the early revolutionary activity in Macedonia (1878–93) and the attitude of Stambolov see Duncan Perry, *The Politics of Terror: The Macedonian Liberation Movement, 1893–1903* (Durham, NC 1988), 35.

name is disputed. Initially it was called Macedonian Revolutionary Organization (MRO), but in 1896 it assumed the title *Bŭlgarski Makedono-Odrinski Revoliutsionni Komiteti* (Bulgarian MacedoAdrianopolitan Revolutionary Committees—BMORK) and membership was open to 'any Bulgarian' who desired to serve the 'cause', namely liberation from the Turkish yoke and the political autonomy of Macedonia.[56] The much-praised autonomist solution must not be taken at face value; autonomy meant preservation of the territorial integrity of Macedonia which could eventually lead to incorporation of the region into Bulgaria. A convenient precedent had been already established by the annexation of Eastern Rumelia to Bulgaria in 1885. Besides, any proposal for direct annexation of Macedonia would have met with the refusal of the Great Powers. According to Christo Tatarchev this was the reason which forced them to put forward the idea of 'autonomy' instead of 'annexation'.[57] Shortly after its formation BMORK started setting up a clandestine network, which included guerrilla bands—manned by the Comitadjis—to prepare the ground for an armed rebellion.

The Bulgaro-Macedonian revolutionary movement was not unanimous in supporting autonomy. In Sofia, in January 1895, another organization was formed called *Makedonski Komitet* (Macedonian Committee), which became in December the *Vŭrhoven* (Supreme) *Makedonski Komitet*. The *Vŭrhovisti* (Supremists), as they were usually called, very soon established close links with the Bulgarian government and army, and favoured outright annexation of Macedonia. Not surprisingly, the Supreme Committee was at loggerheads with BMORK and the efforts of the former to subjugate the latter led not only to mutual distrust but also to armed clashes between the rival Comitadji bands.[58]

This antagonism along with the conviction that autonomy was the only sensible and viable solution to the Macedonian Question prompted BMORK to manifest more openly its autonomist orientation. In 1902 the adjective 'Bulgarian' was erased and the

[56] See the 1896 statutes in Bulgarian Academy of Sciences, *Macedonia*, 419. The founders were Damyan (Dame) Grouev, Petar Poparsov, Anton Dimitrov and Christo Batandzhiev (teachers), Ivan Hadzhinikolov (bookseller), and Christo Tatarchev (physician). Nadine Lange-Akhund, *The Macedonian Question, 1893–1908 from Western Sources* (Boulder, Colo., 1998), 36. See also Aarbakke, *Ethnic Rivalry*, 97. Banac, *National Question*, 314.

[57] Bulgarian Academy of Sciences, *Macedonia*, 622. Cf. Fikret Adanir, 'The Macedonians in the Ottoman Empire, 1878–1912', in Andreas Kappeler, Fikret Adanir, and Alan O'Day (eds.), *The Formation of National Elites* (New York, 1992), 171.

[58] Dakin, *Greek Struggle*, 47–51; Perry, *Politics of Terror*, 43–52.

organization was renamed *Tayna Makedono-Odrinska Revoliutsionna Organizatsiya* (Secret Macedo-Adrianopolitan Revolutionary Organization—TMORO) A few years later, however, it obtained its final name, under which it became legendary to some, notorious to others, but famous to all: *Vŭtreshna Makedonska Revoliutsionna Organizatsiya* (Internal Macedonian Revolutionary Organization—IMRO.) Despite the fact that those changes were accompanied by an effort to widen the appeal of the organization among the non-Slavs, its influence on the Greeks and the Vlachs remained insignificant.

In the early twentieth century IMRO had established a commanding stronghold in the Macedonian provinces. According to a popular saying, 'the day was to the Turk the night to the Comitadji'.[59] In 1903, however, it was dealt a severe blow. Following an abortive rising in the Dzhumaya and Razlog areas, organized by the Supremists Yankov and Tsontsev in the autumn of 1902, some IMRO leaders began to think of a large-scale rebellion in Macedonia.[60] Urged by fears that the Ottomans might uncover the clandestine organization, they decided after much wavering at a congress held in the village of Smilevo in April 1903 to launch an uprising. During the congress Boris Sarafov, a former Supremist, 'swore the Bulgarian army would help them'.[61] Thus the uprising, ill-prepared and ill-timed, broke out in August, on St Elijah's day (Ilinden in Slavonic) and was confined mainly in western Macedonia. By the beginning of September the 'Ilinden Revolt' had been crushed by the Turks with ferocity.[62] In the 1940s it became one of the most potent foundation myths of Macedonian nationalism which considered the uprising, as it still does, as the most significant manifestation of Macedonian national consciousness.[63]

Despite the suppression of the revolt, rifles did not fall silent. From 1904 to 1908, as has already been noted, Greek and Bulgarian bands engaged in an unconventional guerrilla struggle to command the hotly disputed loyalties of a population largely indifferent to the sirens of nationalism. Gradually the Greek bands, organized by the local

---

[59] FO 371/14317, C5316, FO memorandum, dated 1/6/1930.

[60] Richard Crampton, *Bulgaria 1878–1918: A History* (New York and Boulder, Colo., 1983), 283.

[61] Joseph Swire, *Bulgarian Conspiracy* (London, 1939), 99.

[62] For the revolt see Nadine Lange-Akhund, *The Macedonian Question*, 118–30; Dakin, *Greek Struggle*, 98–106.

[63] For the significance of Ilinden in modern Macedonian nationalism see Keith Brown, *The Past in Question: Modern Macedonia and the Uncertainties of Nation* (Princeton, 2003).

Greek consuls and mainly by the Consul General in Salonica, Lambros Koromilas, managed to check the Bulgarian terrorist activity, often by equally ruthless means. The Young Turk revolution in 1908 raised great expectations that the rule of law could have a chance in the Ottoman Empire. The Greek and Bulgarian bands displayed a surprising readiness to lay down their arms and in some cases manifestations of fraternization took place. Initially the omens were favourable. Elections were held, in which both rivals participated, and the new parliament was opened on December 1908. That interval proved to be very short. After an abortive conservative coup against the revolution in mid-1909, the Young Turks started to resemble the old ones, in the eyes of their Christian subjects. The Balkan actors of the Macedonian drama, keen to advance their nationalist agendas, perceived the new policy of 'Ottomanism' as an attempt at Turkification, and euphoria was replaced by frustration.[64]

Once the failure of the Young Turks to provide Macedonia with a sensible administration became apparent, the various contenders began to consider more radical solutions. They had many reasons for doing so. The annexation of Bosnia by the Dual Monarchy in 1908 had put the Serbs in an awkward position, and obliged them to look for compensation to the south. A slice of Macedonia, not to mention an outlet to the Aegean Sea, could meet some of their needs for security and economic growth. Serbian educational propaganda had penetrated Macedonia since the 1860s but its progress has been modest and uncertain. In 1886 the St Sava society was formed to make a stand for the interests of Serbia in Macedonia, but it was dissolved in 1891, although Serbian efforts to spread their national ideology in the province continued.[65] In general, the Serbian claim was based on historical grounds, as the Serbian Empire, which reached its peak under Stefan Dušan ('the Mighty'), had ruled over Macedonia in the thirteenth and fourteenth centuries; on the existence in some parts of Macedonia of the traditional Serbian custom of the 'Slava'; and on linguistic grounds.[66]

Bulgaria was also increasingly concerned about the future of Macedonia, and became much more so when the situation in that area

[64] For the impact of the Young Turks on Macedonia, see Dakin, *Greek Struggle*, 378–408.

[65] Perry, *Politics*, 16.

[66] For accounts defending Serbian claims see Pavle Popović, *Serbian Macedonia: A Historical Survey* (London, 1916); T. R. Georgević, *Macedonia* (London and New York, 1918).

deteriorated as a result of the Young Turks' policies. The dream of a Greater Bulgaria could not be easily abandoned. The Bulgarian premier Ivan Geshov (1911–13) epitomized the prevailing trend in Bulgarian politics, when he stated that 'after the union of Eastern Rumelia with Bulgaria, the latter had no other ideal except to restore her San Stefano frontiers, or . . . to obtain for Macedonia and Thrace an autonomous government'.[67] The Greeks were similarly ill-disposed towards the Ottomans. The troubles caused by the Cretan Question, the humiliation of Greece in 1897, as well as some economic disputes, were solid reasons for such a development.[68]

The Italo-Turkish war of 1911 over Tripoli gave considerable impetus to the feeling, already existing in the Balkans, that the time to settle with the Turks once and for all had come.[69] Meanwhile Greece, Bulgaria, and Serbia began to learn, not without difficulty, that only Balkan unity offered some guarantee of Ottoman expulsion from the region. On March 1912 the Serb–Bulgarian Treaty of Friendship and Alliance was signed. Russia, or at least its ministers in the Balkans, poured considerable energy into that process and eventually succeeded in persuading Sofia and Belgrade to combine their strength.[70] At that time, agreement was also reached regarding the partition of Macedonia. The territory to the east of the river Struma (Strymonas) and the Rhodope mountains was to be ceded to Bulgaria, while Serbia should receive the area to the north and west of Šar mountains. The ultimate decision on the fate of the remaining Macedonian territory was left to the Russian tsar.[71] At about the same time negotiations between Greece and Bulgaria were under way, and a Treaty of Defensive Alliance was concluded on May 1912. No mention, however, was made of Macedonia.[72]

The tiny kingdom of Montenegro, also part of the Balkan League, declared war against the Ottomans on October 1912 despite the Powers' call for moderation, and very soon Greece, Serbia, and Bulgaria

---

[67] Ivan Gueshoff, *The Balkan League* (London, 1915), 1–2.

[68] The Greek economy was dealt a blow by the Turkish decision not to link up the Greek railway system with that of Macedonia. FO 371/14317, C5316, FO memorandum, dated 1/7/1930. Further details in Basil Gounaris, 'Greco-Turkish Railway Connection: Illusions and Bargains in the Late Nineteenth Century Balkans', *Balkan Studies*, 30/2 (1989), 311–32.

[69] For the Italo-Turkish war (1911–12) see M. Anderson, *The Eastern Question 1774–1923: A Study in International Relations* (New York, 1978), 287–91.

[70] For the role played by Nekludov and Hartwig, Russian ministers in Sofia and Belgrade respectively, see Gueshoff, *Balkan League*, 33–4; Dakin, *Greek Struggle*, 430–1.

[71] The text is given by Gueshoff, *Balkan League*, 114–17.   [72] Ibid. 127–9.

followed suit. Within two months the allied forces had won an easy
victory and the Turks were forced to sign a truce in December. By
the Treaty of London (May 1913) Turkey lost all of her European
territory and ceded Crete to Greece. Balkan unity, however, proved
to be fragile. Serbia desired, and had already occupied, a much larger
slice of the Macedonian pie than it had initially agreed with Bulgaria;
Greece had occupied Salonica hours before a Bulgarian detachment,
and Romania demanded a part of the Bulgarian province of Dobrudja
if it was to remain neutral. As a consequence, considerable nervousness
was evident in Sofia: the Bulgarians had fought bravely, and pushed
the Ottomans towards Constantinople, but their territorial gains were
considered totally unsatisfactory. By the summer of 1913 the prospects
for a peaceful settlement among the allies had been diminished. On
June 1913 Bulgaria crossed the Rubicon. She attacked both Greece and
Serbia without a declaration of war. The results were disastrous. Greeks
and Serbs advanced rapidly; the Romanians seized the opportunity to
enter the struggle and advanced towards Sofia, while the Ottomans
recaptured Adrianople. Bulgaria had no choice but to surrender. The
Treaty of Bucharest (August 1913) gave Greece the lion's share of
Macedonia—more than a half of the region; Serbia acquired the
central-western part of it, which included Skopje and Ochrid; while
Bulgaria had to content herself with only 10 per cent of the Macedonian
territory. The severe setback that Bulgaria suffered gave rise to strong
'revisionist' attitudes, which influenced her foreign policy for years to
come.[73] The Bulgarian premier Vasil Radoslavov (1913–18) described
accurately the state of feeling prevailing at that time in his country when
he admitted that a sense of revenge was predominant.[74]

The Great War was, as far as Macedonia was concerned, the realization
of Bulgarian revenge; or so it seemed. Both camps tried in 1915 to win
it over and both had been eager to offer large parts of Macedonia as a
lure. The Central Powers made the most tempting offer and, given that
in the summer they took the upper hand in the war, the Bulgarians took
their side.[75] Serbian Macedonia and parts of eastern Greek Macedonia
were the gains. That success did not last long. In the Treaty of Neuilly
(November 1919) Serbia not only regained her part of Macedonia but

[73] For the diplomatic background of the Balkan wars see E. C. Helmreich, *The Diplomacy of the Balkan Wars* (Cambridge, Mass., 1938). Also Carnegie Endowment for International Peace, *Report of the Commission*, 38–69; Dakin, *Greek Struggle*, 446–71.

[74] Crampton, *Bulgaria*, 425.

[75] Ibid. 441–2. Anderson, *Eastern Question*, 327–9.

also achieved a strategic adjustment of its frontiers by obtaining the Bulgarian districts of Strumitsa, Tsaribrod, and Bosilegrad. Bulgaria was also deprived of an outlet to the Aegean Sea by ceding western Thrace to an Allied force. In 1920 it was transferred to Greece.[76]

In light of the above it is hardly surprising that the Macedonian Question continued in the 1920s to be the main cause of bitterness between Bulgaria and her neighbours. The newly born Kingdom of Serbs, Croats, and Slovenes was the most vulnerable.[77] Burdened by deeply rooted national, religious, historical, linguistic, and socio-economic differences, Yugoslavia could hardly afford the problems caused by the perpetuation of the Macedonian issue. Nonetheless, her domestic policy in the Yugoslav part of Macedonia, which was officially styled 'Southern Serbia', was an utter failure. As has been already noted, Serbian influence on the Macedonian Slavs had never been particularly strong. Thus a forceful policy of 'Serbianization' was launched, Serbian colonists were encouraged to settle in Macedonia, and an educational campaign was initiated, for children should learn that 'I am a true Serb like my father and my mother'.[78] Their 'fathers and mothers', however, had been lost to the Yugoslav state. According to Bulgarian accounts this happened because the population was overwhelmingly Bulgarian and strongly resisted the Yugoslav 'denationalization' process.[79] But such views tend to neglect some important dimensions of the problem.[80]

Although the strength of Bulgarian nationalism among the population should not be underestimated, especially in the eastern part of the region along the Yugoslav-Bulgarian border, the majority of the Slav peasants appeared to be rather indifferent to questions of nationality. According to British observers, what definitely alienated them from Serbian rule was mainly the extremely low standard of administration, the attitude of the incompetent and short-sighted civil servants who applied the

[76] Ibid. 358–9.

[77] In 1929 in line with King Alexander's effort to unify his country the state was renamed Kingdom of Yugoslavia (Jug meaning south). For the sake of simplicity, however, the term Yugoslavia will be used here from 1919 onwards.

[78] Kostadin Paleshutski, *Makedonskiyat Vŭpros v Burzhoazna Iugoslaviya, 1918–1941* [The Macedonian Question in Bourgeois Yugoslavia] (Sofia, 1983), 49. In 1929 'Southern Serbia' was renamed 'Vardarska Banovina'.

[79] A typical example is Paleshutski's work cited above. See also Bŭlgarska Akademiya na Naukite [Bulgarian Academy of Sciences], *Makedonskiyat Vŭpros: Istoriko-Politicheska Spravka* [The Macedonian Question: Historical and Political Information] (Sofia, 1968).

[80] It should be added that 'Southern Serbia' included not only the Yugoslav part of Macedonia but also the predominantly Albanian districts of Kosovo and Metohija.

Serbianization policy, and, last but not least, the economic crisis which the peasants suffered, particularly after the reduction in the prices of important local products subjected to state monopoly.[81] Apart from anti-Serbianism, the prevailing mood called for stability, not upheaval, for years of fighting and insecurity had clearly taken a heavy toll among the peasantry. In 1920, a Macedonian peasant had this to say to the Bulgarian minister in Belgrade, Kosta Todorov: 'for God's sake, don't liberate us any more. We have been liberated of everything we possessed. If anyone begins liberating us again, we shall be the first to take up arms against him.'[82] Developments in the area after 1945, as shall be seen, were to demonstrate that such assessments had much basis in fact, and confirm the view that the 'Bulgarophile' tendencies of the population during the interwar years were due more to brutal Serbian rule than to Bulgarian national sentiments. Be that as it may, the Macedonian policy of the Yugoslav governments did not create 'true Serbs' but a permanent state of unrest throughout the interwar period. Paradoxically, it was Tito, and not a traditional Serbian politician, who would undertake the thankless task of mending the troubled relations between Belgrade and Skopje caused by the interwar Serbian failure in Macedonia. If the Slavs refused to offer their loyalty to 'their' state, the fairly numerous Albanians of the area did not even bother to tackle the question. According to the British vice-consul in Skopje, the peasants in the Albanian-inhabited areas thought of Macedonia as 'a foreign country as might be Denmark or Spain and the centres of political action . . . are Tirana and Constantinople rather than Sofia or Belgrade'.[83]

As far as Greek Macedonia is concerned, the exchange of populations between Bulgaria and Greece ('voluntary', 1919 onwards) and between Turkey and Greece (compulsory, 1923 onwards), provided for by the Treaties of Neuilly and Lausanne respectively, dramatically altered the ethnographic picture of that area.[84] More than 600,000 Greek refugees

    [81] FO 371/12092, C9610, report on 'Southern Serbia in 1927', by the British vice-consul in Skopje, D. J. Footman, dated 23/11/1927. For the conditions in Yugoslav Macedonia see Stephen Palmer and Robert King, *Yugoslav Communism and the Macedonian Question* (Hamden, Conn., 1971), 12. Banac, *National Question*, 320.

    [82] Kosta Todoroff, 'The Macedonian Organization Yesterday and Today', *Foreign Affairs*, 6/3 (1928), 481.

    [83] FO 371/12092, C16431, report by the British vice-consul in Skopje, D. J. Footman, dated 19/12/1927.

    [84] On these exchanges see Stephen Ladas, *The Exchange of Minorities: Bulgaria, Greece and Turkey* (New York, 1932); Dimitri Pentzopoulos, *The Balkan Exchange of Minorities and the Impact upon Greece* (Paris, 1968).

were settled in Macedonia, mainly in its eastern part, while over 50,000 Slavs left Greece. Before 1923, the Greeks were a minority in their own northern province, but after the coming of the refugees the Hellenization of Greek Macedonia became reality. According to the Greek census of 1928, there were about 80,000 Slav-speakers in northern Greece, which is undoubtedly a gross underestimate, for Greek archival sources give a much higher number: about 200,000. According to the same sources, however, the majority were just peasants, while the 'Bulgarians', that is those who displayed a Bulgarian national consciousness, were about 80,000.[85] Despite the Slav exodus from Greek Macedonia, a by-product of population exchanges, fear, and oppression on the part of the Greek state, solid Slav enclaves remained in the Greek province, and particularly in the districts of Florina, and Kastoria, in Greek west Macedonia.[86]

Officially they were just 'locals', 'Slavophones', or 'Slavophone Greeks', who had lost their 'mother tongue', but had retained their 'ancestral religion'. For contemporary Greek observers, many factions could be found among them, according to manifestations of what they perceived to be a Greek or Bulgarian 'national consciousness'. But for many of them a reasonable economic position and freedom to speak their language would go a long way in making their life tolerable, as their loyalties were confined to their village and family rather than to 'nations'. Even those who referred to themselves as Macedonians in the 1940s, probably under the influence of Macedonian agitation of pro-Titoist guerrillas, valued their peace more than anything else: with disarming honesty, an elderly Slav told an English liaison officer in 1944 that 'we have had so many different masters that now, whoever comes along, we say (placing his hands together and smiling pleasantly and making a little bow) "kalos orisate" [welcome]'. Another Slav did not fail to stress that all he wanted was 'to know that what I work for, what I sweat for, will at the end be mine'.[87] The Greek state, however, often

[85] George Mavrogordatos, *Stillborn Republic: Social Coalitions and Party Strategies in Greece 1922–1936* (Berkeley and Los Angeles, 1983), 274.

[86] For estimates of the number of Slav-Macedonians in Greek Macedonia see Phillip Carabott, 'Aspects of Hellenisation of Greek Macedonia, ca. 1912–ca.1959', *κάμπος: Cambridge Papers in Modern Greek*, 13 (2005), 30–5. For the districts of Kastoria and Florina, see John S. Koliopoulos, *Plundered Loyalties: World War II and Civil War in Greek West Macedonia* (London, 1999), 38–9.

[87] FO 371/43649, report by Captain P. H. Evans entitled 'Report on the free Macedonia movement in area Florina 1944', dated 1/12/1944. The report has been published by Andrew Rossos: 'The Macedonians of Aegean Macedonia: A British Officer's Report, 1944', *Slavonic and East European Review*, 69/2 (1991), 282–309.

applied a quite naive reductionism, conditioned by the state of Greek nationalism at the time, which demanded the overlapping of national sentiment with the spoken language. Thus, the use of the Bulgarian language was equated with 'Bulgarianism'.

Especially during the dictatorship of Ioannes Metaxas (August 1936–January 1941) a policy of vigorous assimilation was initiated, an authoritarian Greek version of similar processes which occurred at that time in many other Eastern European states. The use of Bulgarian was prohibited and police persecution reached its peak.[88] In the 1920s, the influx of refugees had created another salient cleavage in Macedonia, as the dichotomy between the Slavs and the Greeks became part of a much wider antagonism between the indigenous element and the refugees over the possession of land.[89] As a result, economic and linguistic grievances, coupled with indiscriminate persecution by overzealous gendarmes, forced a large number of Slav-speakers to lose any respect for the Greek state. Not unlike the Yugoslav case, the Greeks did not have long to wait before facing the consequences of their interwar conduct. During the Second World War, most of these Slav-speakers opted (initially) for the Bulgarian Lion, only to end up (after 1943) wearing the Yugoslav Red Star.

Bulgaria had other problems to deal with in the interwar years. Peasant unrest and internal collapse caused by the 'national catastrophe' of 1918 brought into office Alexandŭr Stamboliiski, leader of the Bulgarian Agrarian National Union (BANU).[90] The Agrarian premier diverged sharply from his predecessors in both foreign and domestic policies, boldly stated in the Bulgarian *Sŭbranie* (Assembly) that he was neither Bulgarian nor Serbian but South Slav, and tried to reach a modus vivendi with the Yugoslavs.[91] Stamboliiski's policy provoked the wrath of a revived IMRO, which intensified its raids into Yugoslav territory in a desperate effort to keep the Macedonian Question open.[92] IMRO was led at that time by Todor Alexandrov, greatly admired by the Bulgar-Macedonians, who affectionately called him *Stario* (Old Man); he favoured autonomy for the area, but, had this solution been rendered impossible, Macedonia

---

[88] Carabott, '*Aspects*', 47–52.

[89] On this issue see Mavrogordatos, *Stillborn Republic*, 249.

[90] On Stamboliiski's Agrarian regime see John D. Bell, *Peasants in Power: Alexander Stamboliski and the Bulgarian Agrarian National Union 1899–1923* (Princeton, 1977).

[91] For an account of Stamboliiski's foreign policy see Bell, *Peasants*, 184–207.

[92] A list of raids made by IMRO into Yugoslav Macedonia is given by A. Reis, *The Comitadji Question in Southern Serbia* (London, 1927).

could have been placed under the protection of a Great Power, perhaps Britain. Alexandrov himself was given the chance to bring that solution—and himself—to the attention of international opinion by giving an interview to the London *Times* on 1 January 1924.[93]

The Niš Convention between Bulgaria and Yugoslavia, signed in May 1923, was the last straw for IMRO. The convention provided strict frontier control to prevent bands from entering Yugoslav territory. A month later Stamboliiski was overthrown by a coup in which IMRO played an active part. IMRO's men, gifted practitioners of the art of sensational killing, assassinated him, after staging a macabre theatre: they cut off his ears and nose, ridiculed him, forced him to dig his own grave, and did not neglect to cut off the 'hand that signed the Niš Convention'.[94]

From 1924 onwards IMRO established a state-within-a-state in the south-western part of Bulgaria, around the districts of Kiustendil and Petrich. Its control over the district was complete and indisputable. IMRO had its own police, controlled the local representatives to the *Sŭbranie*, and issued stamps featuring the founding fathers and chiefs of the organization, notably the legendary IMRO leader Gotse Delchev. Even the personal life of the peasants was closely watched. A single man could only walk out twice in the company of an unmarried girl. If he continued doing so, a letter from IMRO, asking for marriage or separation, would certainly prompt him to revise his tactics.[95] Apart from being the guardian of peasant values, however, the organization also catered for less moral pursuits: it secured a solid financial basis by imposing taxes upon the population, and engaged in drug trafficking.[96] After the assassination of Alexandrov in 1924,[97] however, internal strife broke out between the pro-left 'Federalists' who wanted the movement to be linked with the Comintern, and the right wing of the organization.[98]

[93] The article gave a rather favourable picture of 'Alexandrov of Macedonia'. Idyllic scenery was also present. 'In winter he lives in some humble peasant cottage; in summer he sleeps in the open air.' FO 371; C195, 4/1/1924.

[94] Swire, *Bulgarian Conspiracy*, 168.

[95] For a vivid (and sympathetic) account of IMRO's rule over Petrich see Stoyan Christowe, *Heroes and Assassins* (London, 1935).

[96] According to British sources, in 1933 alone, IMRO derived a revenue of 2,500,000 *leva* from traffic in raw opium. This number is given by Sir Nevile Henderson, British minister to Yugoslavia. PRO FO 371/19489, R520, 19/1/1935.

[97] This incident will be treated in greater detail below.

[98] Leaders of the former faction were Dimitar Vlahov, Todor Panitsa, Petŭr Chaulev, and Philip Atanasov. Their rivals were Alexandŭr Protogerov and Ivan Mihailov. See Elisabeth Barker, *Macedonia: Its Place in Balkan Power Politics* (London, 1950), 39–43.

At that time, Ivan (Vancho) Mihailov was the champion of the latter. A man of conflicting qualities, and impatient with the Federalists, Mihailov launched a spectacular campaign of assassinations. Mencha Karnicheva, a Vlach woman from Kruševo, made her mark in this game of terror by assassinating in cold blood her former lover Todor Panitsa, a leading Federalist, at the Vienna opera. She later married Mihailov. This algebra of death continued until 1928, and counted many prominent Macedonians of every description. That year, however, after finishing with the left, Mihailov turned against the other senior IMRO figure: the ageing General Alexandŭr Protogerov. The respected general was assassinated in July 1928, leaving Mihailov the sole leader of the organization. From that month, and until the organization's suppression in 1934, Protogerovists and Mihailovists killed each other in the streets of Petrich and Sofia, in a fratricidal struggle that marked the decline of the organization.[99]

During the 1920s and 1930s IMRO established connections with almost every single anti-Yugoslav quarter. It was funded by Italy, developed ties with the Croatian *Ustaša* led by Ante Pavelić, and trained its gunmen in Hungarian camps. The interwar Bulgarian governments adopted a passive attitude towards IMRO with varying degrees of tolerance, although its raids in Yugoslavia were a constant cause of international embarrassment. The governments of Alexandŭr Tsankov and Andrei Liapchev (1923–6 and 1926–31 respectively) had been particularly close to the Macedonians. Their protégé was General Vŭlkov, minister of war in both cabinets. At that time the IMRO paper *Svoboda ili Smŭrt* (Freedom or Death) was often published at the printing press of the Geographical Institute of the Ministry of War.[100]

The end of the 1920s, however, brought some encouraging prospects of a normalization in Bulgar–Yugoslav relations. King Alexander assumed dictatorial power in 1929 in a rather desperate and ultimately unsuccessful effort to shape up the process of unification of the Yugoslav lands after a decade of fierce Serb-Croat rivalry which culminated in 1928 when the leader of the Croatian Peasant Party Stjepan Radić was shot in the Yugoslav *Skupština* (Parliament) by a Montenegrin deputy. The Yugoslav king—with the constant encouragement of the British—came to realize that only a rapprochement with Bulgaria and

---

[99] A wealth of information about these cruelties can be found in two accounts: Swire, *Bulgarian Conspiracy* and Cristowe, *Heroes*.
[100] FO 371/14315, C2298, Henderson to FO 18/3/1930.

the subsequent curtailment of IMRO's activity could provide him with valuable time in order to keep his divided house in order. Following his initiatives a mixed commission met at Pirot on 25 February 1929 to deal with frontier incidents and in early 1930 an agreement was reached on frontier control. But this semblance of reconciliation was dealt a severe blow by bomb outrages committed by IMRO and the spectre of mutual mistrust rose again.

During the 1930s major developments in Balkan politics occurred which placed Bulgar–Yugoslav relations in a different perspective. Three Balkan states—Greece, Yugoslavia, and Romania—along with Turkey moved towards the formation of a collective security system in the region, which aimed to safeguard the preservation of the status quo against the menace of revisionism. After four Balkan conferences, held in Athens (1930), Constantinople (1931), Bucharest (1932), and Salonica (1933), the Balkan Pact was finally concluded in 1934. Although from the very beginning the signatories made strenuous efforts to include Bulgaria in the pact, the latter's refusal to repudiate her revisionism—no matter how utopian or 'theoretical' this revisionism had become—rendered this prospect impossible.[101]

The much-celebrated 'Balkan Entente' quickly started to falter in the face of Balkan realities, for it became apparent that collective security was to succumb rapidly to individual and conflicting objectives. Different priorities therefore drove a wedge between the members of the alliance. A rapprochement with Bulgaria had always ranked high in the Yugoslav foreign policy agenda. IMRO's liquidation in 1934, by the government of Kimon Georgiev,[102] provided King Alexander with a new opportunity. In September the Yugoslav king visited Sofia, where he was warmly received. The tragedy which followed a month later, when he was assassinated in Marseilles, failed to end the normalization of Bulgar–Yugoslav relations, despite the fact that it was committed by an IMRO gunman. That process was also facilitated by a major transformation which occurred in Yugoslavia's foreign policy after 1934.

---

[101] For the Balkan Pact see: Robert Kerner and Harry Howard, *The Balkan Conferences and the Balkan Entente 1930–1935* (Berkeley and Los Angeles, 1936). Further details in Zdravka Micheva, 'Balkanskiyat Pakt i Bŭlgaro-Iugoslavskite Otnosheniya 1933–1934' [The Balkan Pact and Bulgar–Yugoslav Relations], *Istoricheski Pregled*, 4 (1971), 3–30.

[102] On 19 Mar. 1934, Kimon Georgiev and Colonel Damyan Velchev carried out a coup against the Mushanov's government. The swift suppression of IMRO by the Bulgarian government was interpreted by many as a clear sign that IMRO's strength had completely evaporated.

Prior to that date Yugoslavia rightly perceived Italy as a major foe. Rome did everything she could to embarrass the weak kingdom. The conflicts over the Italo-Yugoslav frontier, the support Italy gave to IMRO[103] and to Croatia's *Ustaša*, as well as Italy's prominent role in Albania, were the principal causes for the friction between the two Adriatic rivals.[104] In order to satisfy her need for security Yugoslavia sought to secure France's protection and actively participated in the French-inspired Little Entente.[105] However, the coming to power of Milan Stojadinović (1935–8) signalled a new era. Stojadinović tried to reach a modus vivendi with Italy and diverged from the traditionally pro-French orientation of Yugoslav foreign policy.[106] Thus his drift towards Rome produced a treaty with Italy in 1937. As expected, the ease of tension between Italy and Yugoslavia gave impetus to the latter's reconciliation with Bulgaria, and a Treaty of Perpetual Friendship was signed on 1 January 1937. On the eve of the Second World War, the politics of the Macedonian Question had reached a precarious stalemate, which left much room for disquiet. It can be said that the only concrete result of the 1937 treaty, apart from alarming Yugoslavia's allies and fanning unfounded fears about the emergence of a Slavic block in the Balkans, was Bulgaria's success in ending its diplomatic isolation, which had not been at all splendid. Be that as it may, developments were to prove very soon that the word 'Perpetual', used in that treaty, was just another instance of wishful thinking.

THE DISCREET CHARM OF NATIONALISM: COMMUNISM AND THE MACEDONIAN QUESTION, 1894–1935

Just as extreme Shi'ite Muslims hold that Archangel Gabriel made a mistake, delivering the Message to Mohammed when it was intended for Ali, so Marxists

---

[103] For IMRO's connections with Italy see Stefan Troebst, *Mussolini, Makedonien und die Mächte 1922–1930: Die 'Innere Makedonische Revolutionäre Organisation' in der Südosteuropapolitik des Faschistischen Italiens* (Cologne, 1987).

[104] PRO FO 371/318, C575/141/92, 'Memorandum Respecting Italo-Yugoslav relations', dated 20/1/1930. For Italy's Albanian adventures see E. H. Carr, *International Relations since the Peace Treaties* (London, 1940), 69–71.

[105] Carr, *International Relations*, 38–43.

[106] See J. B. Hoptner, *Yugoslavia in Crisis 1934–1941* (New York and London, 1962).

basically like to think that the spirit of history or human consciousness made a terrible boob. The awakening message was intended for classes, but by some terrible postal error was delivered to nations.[107]

It is certainly more than an intriguing coincidence that the Balkan communist movement appeared as incompetent as the 'bourgeois' regimes in providing any kind of solution to the Macedonian Question, over which they remained divided throughout the interwar period. Such failure was not only due to miscalculated political manoeuvres, but also to the appeal that the 'discreet charm' of nationalism exercised upon them. The preponderance of this 'charm' over the much-praised slogan of proletarian internationalism created a tradition of mutual mistrust among the Balkan communists, which was to resurface with a vengeance during the wartime period.

The communists were not the first to clash over this issue, for an intense struggle between the Balkan social democratic parties had already broken out in the early twentieth century. Although the socialists had advocated a Balkan socialist federation as the only way to prevent war and friction in the area, the fate of Macedonia emerged again as a focal point of conflict.[108] Already in 1894, a Balkan socialist conference in Paris had declared the establishment of an autonomous Macedonian state within a Balkan federation as the only viable solution to the problem.[109] However, in the twentieth century, opinions diverged: the Bulgarian socialists, and especially the reformist 'Broad' faction,[110] claimed all Macedonian Slavs to be Bulgarians, and Sakŭzov himself defended Bulgaria's 'legitimate rights' in Macedonia in 1913.[111] At the same time, the prominent Greek socialist Platon Drakoulis, in an article published in the *Asiatic Review*, emphatically stressed that 'Salonica will remain undoubtedly an integral part

---

[107] Ernest Gellner, *Nations and Nationalism* (Oxford, 1988), 129.

[108] For the attitude of the Balkan socialists towards the national question, and the concept of Balkan Federation, see Joseph Rothschild, *The Communist Party of Bulgaria: Origins and Development, 1883–1936* (New York, 1959), 205–22; Leften Stavrianos, 'Balkan Federation: A History of the Movement Towards Balkan Unity in Modern Times', *Smith College Studies in History*, 30/14 (1942).

[109] Stavrianos, *Balkan Federation*, 151.

[110] The Social Democratic Party of Bulgaria was founded in 1891 by Dimitŭr Blagoev, and split in 1903 in two factions. The 'Narrow' wing, under Blagoev, was strictly Marxist and revolutionary, while the 'Broad' faction, under Yanko Sakŭzov, remained reformist and social democratic.

[111] Rothschild, *Communist Party*, 212.

of Greece'.[112] The attitudes of Balkan socialists towards the Balkan Wars (1912–13) also revealed divided opinions. The Bulgarian 'Narrows' denounced the wars as 'imperialist', and continued to advocate a Balkan federation, while the Greek socialists refused to do so.[113] There was, however, a notable exception: the predominantly Jewish socialist organization *Federasion* of Salonica held a strong anti-war position and took the view that Macedonia should be granted autonomy, a view that was shared by wider segments of Salonica's Jewish community.[114]

During the Great War the task of bridging the opposing views proved to be a very difficult undertaking. In Stockholm in 1917, at the sessions of a committee charged with the preparation of a socialist conference of the belligerent countries, the Bulgarian delegation openly favoured Bulgaria's national aspirations in Macedonia, arguing that the region was inhabited by Bulgarians and that its annexation was necessary for economic reasons. The Serbs put forward two proposals. Initially they suggested autonomy for Macedonia, but later they proposed a condominium of Greece, Serbia, and Bulgaria for Salonica. The latter was accepted by the committee. The Greeks, however, who had not participated in these deliberations, were furious. The most fierce reaction came from Drakoules, who wrote that this decision was 'dictated by the Bulgarian bourgeoisie'.[115]

It quickly became apparent that both the Broad Bulgarians and most of their Greek comrades found in nationalism their vulnerable spot. The Narrows and the Jewish socialists of Salonica on the other hand remained devoted to a vaguely defined concept of a Balkan federation, but for different reasons. The former considered the population of Macedonia to be Bulgarian, and as a consequence it can be said that had autonomy been achieved within a federation, Macedonia might have become a second Eastern Rumelia. In this connection, it should be noted that the social democratic groups in Skopje and Veles were part of the Bulgarian socialist movement, and merged with the Serbian socialist party only

[112] Giorgos Leontaritis, *To Elleniko Sosialistiko Kinima kata ton Proto Pangosmio Polemo* [The Greek Socialist Movement during the First World War II], (Athens, 1978), 64.

[113] Stavrianos, *Balkan Federation*, 189–90.

[114] Kentro Marxistikon Erevnon, *I Sosialistiki Organosi Thessalonikis Federasion 1909–1918* [Centre for Marxist Studies, The Socialist Organization of Salonica Federasion] (Athens, 1989), 257. See also Paul Dumont, 'Une organisation socialiste ottomane: La Fédération ouvrière de Salonique', *Études Balkaniques*, 11 (1975), 76–88.

[115] Leontarites, *Sosialistiko Kinima*, 108–15.

after 1913.[116] The Serbs wavered greatly, and their positions oscillated mainly between partition and autonomy. As far as the nationality of the Macedonians was concerned, they asserted that Macedonia was neither Bulgarian nor Serbian, but a mosaic of nations. According to the official newspaper of the Serbian Social Democratic Party, *Radničke Novine*, Macedonia was inhabited, in 1923, by 'Bulgarians, Serbs, Turks, Albanians, Greeks, Vlachs, and others'. Similar views had been expressed also by Macedonian socialists.[117]

Shortly after the foundation of the Communist Third International (Comintern) in March 1919, the Balkan communist parties initiated a process of transformation into 'pure' communist ones following the Bolshevik model. In Belgrade, a congress of unification of the various Yugoslav socialist parties was held in April 1919. The party that emerged was labelled *Socijalistička Radnička Partija Jugoslavije (komunista)* (Socialist Workers' Party of Yugoslavia [Communist]), and immediately joined the Comintern. It was renamed Communist Party of Yugoslavia (CPY) a year later; the Serbian Sima Marković became its first secretary general. Interestingly, the party was called 'Yugoslav' almost a decade before the country itself adopted the same name. The Narrow wing founded the Bulgarian Communist Party at about the same time, while the Socialist Labour Party of Greece (SEKE) affiliated itself with the Comintern in its second congress, held in Athens on 18 April 1920.[118] This almost instinctive rush of the Balkan communists to join the Comintern had far-reaching repercussions for all of them, but especially for the Greeks and the Yugoslavs. Much to their resentment, they would soon realize that decision-making was a luxury to be exercised rarely, if at all.

By the beginning of the 1920s the communists appeared as divided over the national question as their socialist predecessors had been, for

---

[116] Kostadin Paleshutski, *Iugoslavskata Komunisticheska Partiya I Makedonskiyat Vŭpros, 1919–1945* [The Yugoslav Communist Party and the Macedonian Question] (Sofia, 1985), 11.

[117] Ibid. 13–16.

[118] For the history of the Balkan communist parties, and of their relations with the International see Ivan Avakumović, *History of the Communist Party of Yugoslavia* (Aberdeen, 1964); for its beginnings see Ivo Banac, 'The Communist Party of Yugoslavia during the Period of Legality, 1919–1921', in id., (ed.), *The Effects of World War I: The Class War after the Great War: The Rise of Communist Parties in East Central Europe* (Brooklyn, NY, 1983), 188–230; Dimitrios Kousoulas, *Revolution and Defeat: The Story of the Greek Communist Party* (London, 1965). For the Bulgarian case, see Rothschild, *Communist Party.*

each party had been shaped, as well as burdened, by the specific situation prevailing at the time in their respective countries. In the case of the Communist Party of Yugoslavia this point weighed particularly heavily. From the very beginning of its existence the party adopted a strong 'unitarist' position, and the establishment of Yugoslavia was warmly received. Serbs, Croats, and Slovenes, they argued, were 'one nation with three names', and, consequently, Bosnians, Macedonians, and Montenegrins were classified as Serbs.[119] To many observers, including the Bulgarian communists, such views meant that the CPY had already passed under the control of the Serbs. In general, the party leadership considered the Macedonian Question a 'constitutional' issue, which could be solved by a democratic revision of the Vidovdan constitution. Although this 'centralist' view had been strongly criticized by the non-Serbian elements of the party, it remained its official line until 1923.[120]

At that time, SEKE—which was renamed Communist Party of Greece (KKE) in 1924—had not worked out a detailed programme on these issues. The party's early resolutions spoke vaguely of a 'Balkan Democratic Federation', with no specific reference to Macedonia.[121] Nevertheless, as shall be seen, the Greeks would soon find themselves suffering for a cause they did not want to fight for. The Bulgarian communists, however, were neither torn by internal quarrels, nor did they want to bypass the national question. In an effort to capitalize on the Macedonian Question to further its own political ends, the Bulgarian Communist Party (BCP) put forward the slogan for 'Independent Macedonia and Thrace' within a communist Balkan federation, and spared no effort to impose it on the Greeks and the Yugoslavs. If they could manage to do so, the Bulgarians could win many victories. First, they would take the wind out of IMRO's sails, for this powerful organization also favoured an autonomous Macedonia. Secondly, advocating Macedonian autonomy could provide them with a commanding stronghold among the fairly numerous Bulgaro-Macedonian

[119] Stephen Palmer and Robert King, *Yugoslav Communism and the Macedonian Question* (Hamden, Conn. 1971), 20–1; Kostadin Paleshutski, 'Iugoslavskata Komunisticheska Partiya I Natsionalniyat Vŭpros 1924–1934' [The CPY and the National Question], *Izvestia po Istoriya na B.K.P.*, 45 (1981), 121. For a balanced discussion of the 'roots of Communist unitarism' see also Ivo Banac, *The National Question In Yugoslavia: Origins, History, Politics* (Ithaca, NY and London 1988), 3303–36.

[120] Paleshutski, *Natsionalniyat Vŭpros*, 122–4. Cf. Richard Burks, *The Dynamics of Communism in Eastern Europe* (Princeton, 1961), 109, 111.

[121] Evangelos Kofos, *Nationalism and Communism in Macedonia*, 63.

refugees from Greek and Yugoslav Macedonia.[122] What was also of great importance, was that the BCP enjoyed the open backing of the Comintern, since Moscow had realized very soon the 'revolutionary potential' of the Macedonian Question, and it was quick to take advantage of it.[123]

Soviet support to the BCP was not only due to tactical reasons. Foreign policy objectives were also involved, for Moscow considered Yugoslavia a fragile multinational state, and an important link in the French-sponsored 'Little Entente'. Thus, supporting the BCP, instead of the Yugoslav party, was a sound foreign policy. Besides, the BCP was by far the strongest Balkan communist party, and prominent Bulgarian communists, like Georgi Dimitrov, enjoyed considerable prestige. Moreover, from the ideological point of view, the Bulgarians were closer to Soviet perceptions of a true Marxist party, since the time of Blagoev's activity in Russia.[124] Greece, on the other hand, seemed to be beyond the vital Soviet strategic space, while the KKE was too weak to be counted upon.

The Bulgarians wasted no time. In January 1920, they took the initiative in founding the Balkan Communist Federation (BCF). This organization, in which all the Balkan communist parties participated, remained under firm Bulgarian control, and become little more than a tool for imposing their solutions of the Macedonian Question. In fact, the period 1920–4 witnessed a strenuous effort on the part of the BCP to force its Balkan comrades to accept the break-up of Greece and Yugoslavia, by adopting the slogan of an 'autonomous Macedonia'.[125] In the Fourth Conference of the BCF, held in Sofia on 10 June 1922, Vasil Kolarov raised this issue for the first time, but the Greek delegate, Giannis Petsopoulos, refused to accept it, arguing that 'the Balkan Communist parties can not adopt the slogans that had been propagated by the Bulgarian bourgeois governments since their defeat in 1913'.[126]

---

[122] According to the secretary of the Macedonian National Committee of Sofia, in 1934, there were in Bulgaria 480,000 refugees. FO 371/18370, R6757, 24/11/1934.

[123] Elisabeth Barker, *Macedonia: Its Place in Balkan Power Politics* (London, 1950), 48–9.

[124] Rothschild, *Communist Party*, 246.

[125] For details on the position of the BCF towards the Macedonian Question see Tanya Turlakova, 'Balkanskata Komunisticheska Federatsiya I Natsionalniyat Vŭpros na Balkanite, 1920–1931' [BCF and the National Question in the Balkans], in *Problemi na Politikata na Balkanskite Komunisticheski Partii po Natsionalniyat Vŭpros* [Problems of the Policy of the Balkan Communist Parties on the National Question] (Sofia, 1987), 5–75.

[126] Kousoulas, *Revolution*, 55.

In the same conference, the Bulgarians urged the Balkan parties to 'support actively the national liberation movements in the Balkans'. This was the first, albeit indirect, reference to IMRO, and revealed the intention of the BCP and the Comintern, to establish contacts with it. The Yugoslav representative, however, Moša Pijade, firmly opposed such a proposition.[127]

These early skirmishes were soon to be followed by a real battle. At the Sixth Conference of the BCF, held in Moscow in November 1923, the Greeks and the Yugoslavs were forced to accept the autonomist solution for Macedonia. Moreover, both parties were severely reprimanded for not following the 'correct' line on the national question. The Yugoslavs were criticized particularly heavily, and were again pressed to exploit the national tensions in their country, and form a 'united front 'with all who fight for the self-determination of nations'—a clear reference not only to IMRO but also to the Croatian Peasant Party of Stjepan Radić. The conference was also important from another perspective: in his speech, Vasil Kolarov raised the issue of a separate Macedonian nationality, which 'Bulgarians, Turks, Greeks, Serbs and other national groups desire to form'.[128] Although his interpretation of the desires of so many peoples was not included in the resolution of the BCF, and remained in limbo for many years, it signalled the beginning of a process which culminated in 1934, when the Comintern officially recognized the existence of the Macedonian nation.

As might be expected, the other Balkan communists reacted strongly. The Greek representative, Nikolaos Sargologos, who had signed the resolution without the authority of the Central Committee, thought it wise not to come back to Greece, and fled to the United States. The party refused to accept the resolution, and sent a letter of protest to the BCF.[129] The CPY split badly. In its Third Conference, in Belgrade (December 1923), the 'centralist' group, under Sima Marković, clashed with the 'leftists', who also suggested recognition of Macedonian nationality. Finally, the party declared that 'only the establishment of an autonomous Macedonia and Thrace and their union with the other Balkan countries in a federal Balkan Republic, will establish lasting

---

[127] Turlakova, *Komunisticheska Federatsiya*, 19.
[128] Turlakova, *Komunisticheska Federatsiya*, 33–7; cf. Paleshutski, *Makedonskiyat Vŭpros*, 98.
[129] For Greek reactions see Evangelos Kofos, *Nationalism and Communism in Macedonia* (Salonica, 1964), 73.

peace among the Balkan peoples'. No mention, however, was made of Macedonian nationality.[130]

In 1924, it became apparent that the Macedonian Question was a focal point in a much wider policy of the Comintern, aiming at (*a*) exploiting national friction in the Balkans and especially in Yugoslavia, and (*b*) enlisting in the communist cause two powerful allies: the Croat Peasant Party and IMRO. That year, the erratic Stjepan Radić visited Moscow for negotiations that might lead to his party joining the Green International, a communist-controlled organization of peasant parties. Nothing substantial, however, came out of this spectacular trip.[131] The idea of harnessing nationalist horses to the communist chariot was officially articulated in the Fifth Congress of the Comintern, held in Moscow in the summer of 1924. The slogan calling for an independent Macedonia and Thrace was endorsed as 'wholly correct and truly revolutionary', while the 'revolutionary struggle of the Macedonian and Thracian peoples'—i.e. IMRO's activity—was openly praised.[132] At the same congress, the accusations against the Greeks and the Yugoslavs on the national question were stronger than ever. After a fierce attack from Dimitri Manuilski, the Greek representatives Dimitris Pouliopoulos and Serafim Maximos, as well as their Yugoslav counterparts, finally succumbed to the pressures and signed the documents.

These were officially approved by the two parties after extensive purges, and only with the constant 'help' of the Comintern. In November 1924, the Third [Extraordinary] Congress of the KKE adopted verbatim the Comintern resolutions, only to suffer police persecution and to provoke hysterical anti-communist sentiment. The prominent communist intellectual Giannis Kordatos reflected the feelings of many of his comrades, when he stated in 1927 that 'communism acted as an ally of Bulgarian chauvinism'.[133] The Yugoslavs also experienced a severe blow. The subsequent party congresses, held in Vienna (June 1926) and Dresden (April 1928), conceded the break-up of the Yugoslav state, by generously granting the right of self-determination to every 'oppressed' nationality in the country; the 'assimilation of the Macedonian people'

---

[130] Palmer and King, *Yugoslav Communism*, 32–4.
[131] Joseph Rothschild, *Eastern Europe between the Two World Wars* (Seattle and London, 1990), 222.
[132] Barker, *Macedonia*, 58.
[133] As cited in Kofos, *Nationalism and Communism*, 81.

was also condemned.[134] These congresses were also characterized by determined Comintern efforts to purge from the party all those who continued to challenge the 'correct' line on the national question. This process culminated in 1928, when Marković was forced to resign.

In the mid-1920s, negotiations between IMRO and the communists got under way. It was high time indeed, for many overtures had been made to the Macedonians since the early 1920s. Each party, however, viewed this rapprochement of nationalism and communism from a different perspective. IMRO was adversely affected in 1924 by the Italo–Yugoslav Pact and the (temporary) cutting off of Italian subsidies. Apart from the search for another source of money, Tsankov's decision to maintain the Niš Convention led to a rapid deterioration in the relations between the Macedonians and the Bulgarian government. Moscow, on the other hand, had its own aims—mainly to detach IMRO from the Bulgarian bourgeois regime, thus helping the BCP to gain ground. Moreover, the combined weight of IMRO and the CPY might seriously weaken Yugoslavia, which was considered by Moscow as the principal 'reactionary' state in the Balkans.[135]

The mediator between the Soviets and IMRO was Dimitar Vlahov, a member of the pro-Communist 'Federalist' wing of the organization. It seems that IMRO took the initiative in starting these deliberations. Negotiations had been started in Moscow in August 1923 between Vlahov and Soviet officials, and were continued in Vienna the following year. After some wavering, Moscow decided to conclude an agreement, and in May Alexandrov and Protogerov signed, together with Petŭr Chaulev and Vlahov, a 'Manifesto to the Macedonian People'.[136] This declaration conceded that Macedonia was inhabited by an 'ethnically diverse' population, and went on to reveal the new loyalties of the organization, by stressing that 'the revolutionary fight for the freedom of Macedonia can only count on the extreme progressive and revolutionary movements of Europe'.[137]

---

[134] Palmer and King, *Yugoslav Communism*, 42; Adam Ulam, *Titoism and the Cominform* (Harvard, Mass., 1957), 16; Burks, *Dynamics*, 111–12.

[135] Rothschild, *Bulgarian Communist Party*, 182–3.

[136] For details see Dimitar Vlahov, *Govori i Statii, 1945–1947* [Speeches and Articles] (Skopje, 1947), 156–68 [references to a Greek mimeographed translation, deposited at the Institute for Balkan Studies, Salonica]. Vasil Vasilev, 'Maiskiyat Manifest na Ts.Ka. na V.M.R.O. ot 1924g: Obstanovka, Pregovori, i Posleditsi' [The May Manifesto of the Central Committee of IMRO of 1924: Setting, Negotiations and Consequences], *Istoricheski Pregled*, 5 (1980), 39–63.

[137] See extensive parts of the manifesto in Barker, *Macedonia*, 55–7.

This communist victory proved short-lived. In June, Alexandrov repudiated the May Agreement, and instructed Vlahov, from Bulgaria, not to publish it. Vlahov refused to obey the 'Old Man', and the document appeared in the communist journal *Fédération balkanique* a month later. The turmoil caused by this publication led to Alexandrov's assassination in August. Although the reason behind the murder is still a matter of speculation, the fact that his assassins were closely related to the pro-communist IMRO chief Aleko Vasilev (alias Aleko Pasha—the 'King of Pirin'), makes it probable that there was a communist connection to this murder. This was also the opinion of Mihailov, which carried substantial weight, for, as has already been seen, he decided to assassinate most of the prominent Federalists. Aleko Pasha, Chaulev, and Panitsa were soon dead, while many unsuccessful attempts were made against Vlahov.[138] The Federalists, however, were determined to throw in their lot with Moscow, and, shortly afterwards, Vlahov founded IMRO (United) (VMRO (Obedinena)), which remained under firm communist control.[139] It never became a mass organization, and therefore its influence in the Balkan communist movement was insignificant. Its role, however, in Macedonian politics was disproportionate to its modest size in two respects. First, it advocated consistently and forcefully the existence of a Macedonian nation, and popularized it through newspapers, societies, and clandestine political work.[140] IMRO (United) became a major conveyor belt of nationalism, a role that a century before was served by the national churches; an institution, of course, the Macedonianists never had.[141] In a very real sense, IMRO (United) assumed the role of a secular Macedonian exarchate: just as the Bulgarian Exarchate had 'Bulgarized' the Macedonian Slavs since the 1870s, the IMRO (United) initiated a similar process for Macedonianism, albeit on a much smaller scale, and with much poorer results. The second important function of the organization concerned Titoist Yugoslavia: IMRO (United) trained a number of cadres, who eventually found their way into the CPY during the 1940s. This pool

---

[138] Stoyan Cristowe, *Heroes and Assassins* (London, 1935), 193, 197, 210.

[139] For this organization, which was dissolved in the mid-1930s, see Vlahov, *Govori*, 166–8; Barker, *Macedonia*, 42.

[140] For the role of IMRO (United) as conveyor belt of Macedonianism see Andrew Rossos, 'Macedonianism, and Macedonian Nationalism on the Left', in Ivo Banac and Katherine Verdery (eds.), *National Character and National Ideology in Interwar Eastern Europe* (New Haven, 1995), 238–41.

[141] Ibid. 240.

of men, who had the advantage of being both Macedonian nationalists and committed communists, suited nicely Tito's own agenda on the issue and provided the People's Republic of Macedonia, after 1944, with many prominent personalities. Vlahov himself, as shall be seen, emerged from his long sojourn in Russia (1935–44) at the end of the war, to become Tito's most senior Macedonian figure, a vice-president of the Federal National Assembly, and president of the People's Front of Macedonia.

From 1924 to 1935, the Balkan communist parties continued to advocate Macedonian autonomy, albeit with varying degrees of intensity and sincerity. The rise of the Nazi threat, however, led to a dramatic revision in communist tactics. Their first priority in the 1930s became the containment of the menace that Nazism represented for the future of Europe. Thus, the Balkan parties were urged by the Comintern, during its seventh Congress in 1935, to abandon the isolationist and sectarian tendencies of the previous decade, and to found 'United Fronts' with the Social Democrats and the peasant parties. The strategy on the national question had to be reconsidered accordingly. Instead of granting autonomy to all who might had wanted it, the communists were instructed to fight for 'equal rights for the minorities', within the boundaries of the existing states.[142] As should be expected, the Greeks and the Yugoslavs did not miss the opportunity. The *Front Narodne Slobode* (Front for the People's Liberation), founded by the CPY, declared promptly that secession from Yugoslavia 'serves only the imperialist fascists', while at the same time the Greeks, in their sixth Congress, suddenly realized that due to 'the change in the ethnographic composition in the Greek part of Macedonia' and to the necessities of the 'anti-fascist struggle' the slogan of autonomy had to be replaced by 'full equality for the minorities'.[143]

If Macedonian autonomy was left to die a quiet death, the controversy over the nationality of its inhabitants resurfaced. In February 1934, the Balkan secretariat of the Comintern issued a resolution which officially acknowledged the existence of the Macedonian nation. The resolution, which was published two months later in the IMRO (United) paper *Makedonsko Delo*, was drafted by a Pole. He did not seem to have expert

---

[142] For this reversion see Kofos, *Nationalism and Communism*, 90–4; Barker, *Macedonia*, 75.

[143] Charles Zalar, *Yugoslav Communism: A Critical Study* (Washington DC 1961), 44. Kofos, *Nationalism and Communism*, 91.

knowledge of the issue, and, therefore, Vlahov came to the rescue.[144] As the decade was coming to its close, the CPY, under the leadership of Tito, endorsed this decision, and tried to implement the new 'line'.[145] The ramifications of the 'Polish' resolution were to become apparent very soon indeed. Yet again, the Second World War proved the catalyst.

[144] For Vlahov's help see Paleshutski, *Makedonskiyat Vŭpros*, 222–3. Cf. Ivo Banac, *The National Question in Yugoslavia: Origins, History, Politics* (Ithaca, NY and London, 1988), 328.

[145] Paul Shoup, *Communism and the Yugoslav National Question* (New York and London, 1968), 51–2.

2

Tampering with the 'Sleeping Dogs': Britain and Macedonia 1878–1935

FROM SAN STEFANO TO THE GREAT WAR, 1878–1918

If for Bismarck the Balkans were not worth the bones of a single Pomeranian grenadier, for Britain the region hardly deserved the bones of a sturdy Liverpudlian sailor. In the first half of the nineteenth century Britain's involvement in the Balkans was due to fears of Russian domination of the peninsula, fears that were almost always misplaced and grossly exaggerated. The British had no vital interest in the region except the containment of the Russians. Were the Russians to be allowed to control the region, the argument ran, they would then proceed to capture Constantinople and from there they could march to India, and snatch the jewel from the British imperial crown. It was this paramount fear of Russia that led them to reject the Russian 'right' to 'protect' the Orthodox of the Empire, an 'obligation' the Russians sincerely, albeit wrongly, believed was accorded to them by the Treaty of Küçük Kaynarca in 1774;[1] nor were the British prepared to accept in the middle of the century that the 'sick man' was nearly as sick as Tsar Nicholas would like them to believe.[2] At any rate, sick or not, the Ottoman Empire should be allowed to stand on its feet, for if it did die, then the Russian scramble for filling the vacuum could seriously jeopardize British interests. Consequently, Britain firmly supported the territorial integrity of the Ottoman Empire, and sought to counteract any sign of possible Russian descent on the peninsula.

---

[1] For the motives of Russia's Balkan policy see Barbara Jelavich, *Russia's Balkan Entanglements, 1806–1914* (Cambridge, 1991).

[2] Cf. the famous conversations of Tsar Nicholas I with the British minister Sir George Hamilton Seymour in 1853, quoted in J. A. R. Marriott, *The Eastern Question: An Historical Study in European Diplomacy* (Oxford, 1967) 257–8.

British intervention in the Greek revolution of 1821 therefore, was largely prompted, apart from restoring security for British trade in the eastern Mediterranean, by the need to restrain the impatient and far-reaching Russian hand.[3] Similarly, in Crimea (1854–6) the British did not fight 'a war to give a few wretched monks the key of a grotto', as Thiers famously declared, but to check decisively Russian unilateral interference in the internal affairs of the Sultan.[4] This policy went hand in hand with a sustained effort to cool the irredentist ardour of the newly born states of Greece and Serbia, which were keen to seize the moment during an international crisis and attack the empire in order to 'unredeem' their brethren still under the Ottoman 'yoke'. Such an attempt by Greece during the Crimean War, ill-advised and badly organized, brought British warships to the country's principal port of Piraeus, in a humiliating blockade that ended well after the end of the war.[5]

The fate of Macedonia came first to preoccupy Britain during the eastern crisis of 1875–8, and in particular during the international convulsion produced by the San Stefano treaty. Prior to these events, the British public knew little about Macedonia, and cared even less. But in the last quarter of the century the traditional British policy of maintaining the status quo in the Balkans was dying a slow death. The departure from their pro-Ottoman policy was necessitated by many reasons: a continuing, and for the British frustrating, Ottoman inability to offer their Christian subjects some semblance of decent administration, the revulsion against 'the unspeakable Turk' due to the 'Bulgarian atrocities', the suspension of the repayments of loans in 1876 that alarmed British financiers, and the growing German influence and economic presence in Constantinople.[6] Given this shift, the British would be prepared to acquiesce cautiously to the creation of more autonomous states in the peninsula, without however giving Russia a free hand to pursue her interests unimpeded.

The presence of Ignatiev in Constantinople further complicated the situation, for he gave flesh and bones to a spectre that haunted the British for far too long: a committed panslav, willing to use his immense power

---

[3] For British policy towards the question of Greece see C. W. Crawley, *The Question of Greek Independence, 1821–1833* (Cambridge, 1930).

[4] Thiers's quotation as cited in Marriott, *Eastern Question*, 249.

[5] Domna Dontas, *I Eellas kai Ai Dynameis Kata ton Krimaikon Polemon* [Greece and the Powers during the Crimean War] (Salonica, 1973).

[6] G. D. Clayton, *Britain and the Eastern Question: From Missolonghi to Gallipoli* (London, 1971), 121–3.

in the Ottoman government to create a huge Slav block in the Balkans to
the detriment of the other Balkan states and to British security interests
in the eastern Mediterranean. During the Crimean War it was the British
ambassador to the Porte, Viscount Stratford (Canning) de Redcliffe,
who was the kingmaker, forcing the Russian envoy Prince Menshikov to
complain bitterly about the 'internal dictatorship of this Redcliffe'.[7] But
in the 1870s this role was played skilfully and persuasively by the 'Vice-
Sultan' Ignatiev. The important fact, however, that Ignatiev himself
was more powerful in Constantinople than in the Russian Ministry
Foreign Affairs, did little to assuage British fears about the prospect of
Russian domination of the Balkans and Constantinople. The Treaty of
San Stefano was Ignatiev's own creation, opposed by both Gorchakov
and Shuvalov, the Russian ambassador in London, who called the treaty
'the greatest act of stupidity we could have committed', and Ignatiev's
Bulgaria 'a nonsense'.[8] For Britain Ignatiev had clearly gone too far.
He had had ample warning, however, that his grandiose plans about
Bulgaria would be firmly resisted by Britain. During the Conference
of Ambassadors at Constantinople in December 1876, Ignatiev and
Salisbury had discussed the fate of Macedonia: Ignatiev had proposed a
large Bulgarian state stretching up to Lake Ochrid, and having access
to the Aegean at Dedeagatch (Alexandroupolis). But Salisbury (and
Austria), fearing that such a state would precipitate the collapse of the
Ottoman Empire, was prepared to accept the creation of two entities,
having as southern frontier a line connecting Adrianople and Monastir,
without an outlet to the Aegean. Of these two units, 'the Eastern would
remain in the hands of non-Slav population'.[9] Ignatiev had disregarded
all these stipulations, and consequently Britain had to call for radical
revisions: 'Greater Bulgaria' had to be scrapped, and Macedonia should
be returned to the Ottomans. The results of the Congress of Berlin,
therefore, came as little surprise.

Although Britain clearly preferred Ottoman control of Macedonia to
a thinly veiled Russian one under Igantiev's terms, the Ilinden Revolt
(August–September 1903), coupled with Ottoman excesses during its
suppression, and the campaign of terror waged by Bulgarian, Greek,
and to a lesser extent Serbian bands during the 'struggle for Macedonia'
(1904–8), forced upon them the necessity of implementing serious and

---

    [7] Clayton, *Britain and the Eastern Question,* 106.   [8] Ibid. 144.
    [9] Mihailo Stojanovic, *The Great Powers and the Balkans, 1875–1878* (Cambridge,
1939), 130–1.

far-reaching reforms if the province was to become remotely safe for its inhabitants. Even before Ilinden, however, the British had reached the conclusion that the Ottomans were incapable not only of enforcing law and order in the province, but also clearly of restraining even their own troops. Britain recognized, of course, that Austria and Russia would be the main protagonists in introducing plans for reform: Russia's interest was self-evident, while Austria had emerged after Berlin as the only Great Power with Balkan possessions, as she was allowed to 'administer and occupy' Bosnia and the Sanjak of Novi Pazar (*Novopazarski Zandžak*), and had interests that could reach up to Salonica. At the time, Britain did not have a vital stake to defend in the Balkans: it was the Persian Gulf and Mesopotamia that commanded their attention, and not the banks of the Vardar river.[10] The preservation of the status quo in Macedonia was desirable, as it prevented the eruption of Great Power friction, and safeguarded that nothing would change either in Constantinople or in the Straits and Suez. So Britain was prepared to let Russia and Austria take the lead in Macedonia. Lansdowne, the foreign minister, conceded to the Austrian ambassador in January 1903 that Britain 'recognised that Austria and Russia were specially interested in the matter', and were in a 'specially advantageous position for dealing with it', but at the same time he refused to offer them carte blanche: Britain, he added, attached 'immense importance . . . to the question', and had an 'earnest desire to contribute . . . to its satisfactory conclusion'.[11] Consequently, Britain supported the Austro-Russian plan for reforms in Macedonia, the so-called 'Vienna Scheme', which was presented to, and accepted by, the Ottomans in February 1903. The reforms called for the appointment of an inspector general of the three *vilayets* for three years, whose instructions the three Valis of the Ottoman *vilayets* should follow *strictement*; the inclusion of Christians in the gendarmerie and the police; a reorganization of the finances of the three *vilayets*; and an armistice for all who had been involved in 'political' activities but had not been convicted of any common-law crime.[12] Any delay in

[10] For British interests in the Ottoman Empire, see Marian Kent, 'Great Britain and the End of the Ottoman Empire, 1900–1923', in ead. (ed.), *The Great Powers and the End of the Ottoman Empire* (London, 1984), 172–205.

[11] Lansdowne to Sir F. Plunkett, 6 Jan. 1903. G. P. Cooch and Harold Temperley (eds.), *British Documents on the Origins of the War, 1898–1914*, v. *The Near East: The Macedonian Problem and the Annexation of Bosnia, 1903–1909* (London, 1928), 50.

[12] For the Vienna reforms see Dakin, *Greek Struggle*, 86–91. For the attitude of the Powers to the reforms see Mason Whiting Tyler, *The European Powers and the Near East,*

reforms, Lansdowne thought, 'might be fraught with the most disastrous consequences'.[13] The Ottomans, keen to keep foreign influence at bay, had already appointed Hilmi pasha, the governor of Yemen, as inspector general of the Macedonian *vilayets*, but the Powers saw no visible sign of improvement.

The continuing deterioration of public order in Macedonia as a result of Comitadji activity and the ferocity of Ottoman reprisals, highlighted the necessity of reforms. At that stage, the British emerged as a forceful advocate of the overhaul of the reform schemes, which they considered to be too narrow and ineffective. In particular, Lansdowne called for more direct foreign control, arguing that 'no scheme is likely to produce satisfactory results which depends for its execution upon a Mussulman Governor entirely subservient to the Turkish Gov[ermen]t and completely independent of foreign control'. The Powers, therefore, should propose the appointment of a Christian governor 'unconnected with the Balkan Peninsula' or the Great Powers. Failing that, 'European assessors' should be allowed to help a Muslim governor in his duties. Equally important were the appointment of European officers in the Macedonian gendarmerie, and the withdrawal of the Ottoman reserve forces ('Redifs and Ilavehs'). Finally, Lansdowne regretted that 'the two Powers', i.e. Russia and Austria, refused to support sending European military attachés to the Ottoman units stationed in Macedonia, aimed at 'restraining' the Turks and sending the Powers 'trustworthy information'.[14] Such proposals were considered too far-reaching by both Austria and Russia, and would certainly cut very little ice with Constantinople. Consequently the second reform attempt, which was concluded during the meeting of the Russian tsar with the Austrian emperor at Mürzsteg, in October 1903, was an attempt at compromise: the governor would continue to be a Muslim, but assisted by two 'civil agents', one Austrian and one Russian; European officers should control and reorganize the gendarmerie, and the borders of the three *vilayets* should be rectified to take into account the nationality of their inhabitants, to the extent, of course, that this was possible.[15]

1875–1908 (Minneapolis, 1925), 193–203. Further details in Steven Sowards, *Austria's Policy of Macedonian Reform* (Boulder, Colo., 1989).

[13] Cooch and Temperley (eds.), *British Documents*, 53.
[14] Ibid., Lansdowne to Plunkett, 29 Sept. 1903, 63.
[15] Dakin, *Greek Struggle*, 112–16.

These proposals were accepted by the Ottomans, but only when they realized that there was a united European front behind them, and at any rate did little to ameliorate the situation in the three *vilayets*. The spectre of new major disturbances was never far beneath the surface, and the raids of Bulgarian, Serbian, and Greek bands continued to increase. The British continued to push for the implementation of the reforms agreed at Mürzsteg, and often expressed to the other Powers their frustration at their slow pace. At the same time, it was realized that should the system of reforms collapse entirely, a proposition that did not seem unlikely, then Britain 'would be expected to intervene', and to propose alternative solutions. At that juncture, two of them became apparent: 'Macedonia might either be joined to Bulgaria, or given an autonomous regime under a Governor virtually independent of the Sultan'. But the former would be unacceptable to all Great Powers, including, of course, Britain. San Stefano, after all, was not that far away. Autonomy, however, could prove to be a viable proposition.[16] Elaborating on this scheme, Lansdowne suggested that the Powers should be able to agree on a platform of autonomy for Macedonia with a governor appointed by the Sultan but recommended by the Powers. The finances of the province, he added, 'should be placed under some form of international control'.[17] In the event, nothing came out of the autonomy plan, for no major revolt broke out, and the Powers were not forced to take a new position concerning the fate of the province. As for the British proposal concerning the control of Macedonia's budget by an international commission, the Sultan accepted it in December 1905, but only after all six Great Powers staged a naval demonstration.[18]

But the situation in Macedonia continued to be bleak. Neither the Ottomans nor the Balkan states, and in particular Greece and Bulgaria which had the most numerous bands in Macedonia, were prepared to take the British advice for reform and restraint respectively to heart. Both Athens and Sofia refused to accept that band activity was officially supported, and the Ottomans continued to manifest a profound inability to suppress them. Throughout the period leading to the Young Turk revolt of 1908, Britain repeatedly attempted to press the Balkan states to prevent the bands from entering Macedonia,

[16] Lansdowne to Monson, 20 Feb. 1904, Cooch and Temperley (eds.), *British Documents*, 68.
[17] Ibid., Lansdowne to Bertie, 23 Feb. 1904, 69.
[18] The sequence of events can be followed, ibid. 76–99.

while the British ambassador in Constantinople, Sir Nicholas O'Conor, tried to impress upon the Ottoman government the need to implement with greater speed and efficiency the agreed reforms in Macedonia. But Abdul Hamit, his position strengthened by German support, remained unimpressed, and shifted the blame to Athens, Belgrade, and Sofia: if the Powers, he told O'Conor during yet another audience over the subject, 'made as energetic representations at those capitals as at Constantinople it would suffice'.[19] But the British kept up the pressure and in 1908 they embarked on their last attempt to give the reforms a new lease of life: taking advantage of the recent Anglo-Russian understanding over Persia and Afghanistan[20] they proposed to the Russians that the governor of Macedonia be approved by the Powers, and that the Ottomans reduce their forces in Macedonia, with the Powers guaranteeing the integrity of the three *vilayets*, so as to allow the Ottomans to accept their proposals. Isvolskii, the Russian foreign minister, accepted the former, but sternly rejected the latter stipulation, either because he did not want to antagonize too forcefully the Ottomans, or because he wanted to keep all possible options open.[21] The new plan was announced during a meeting of King Edward with Tsar Nicholas at Reval in June 1908. The timing, however, was not ideal: a few days later the Young Turk revolt broke out, and the whole issue of reform in the Ottoman Empire was to take an entirely different twist.

In the period preceding the Balkan Wars of 1912–13, Britain saw in the various reform schemes a way of pacifying Macedonia without having to resort to far-reaching solutions. This was an important consideration, for maintaining the Powers' 'concert' over the subject was uppermost in British thinking about the Balkans. They were seriously interested in the reforms, and attempted to use their influence to enforce them. For Britain true reform meant wide-ranging and active European participation, with a governor approved by the Powers, and a gendarmerie trained and supervised by European officers. The less the Ottomans had to do with it, the better. They understood full well that such an attitude would not be to the Ottomans' liking, to say the least, but that was

---

[19] Cooch and Temperley (eds.), *British Documents*, O'Conor to Sir Edward Grey, 7 Dec. 1907, 219.

[20] Anderson, *Eastern Question*, 272.

[21] 'They [i.e. the Russians] do not like to postpone the fulfillment of Bulgarian aspirations for a fixed period of seven years', was the suspicion of Charles Hardinge, who together with Isvolskii drafted the reform plan. Cooch and Temperley (eds.), *British Documents*, 236.

a price worth paying to ensure that no serious revolt broke out again. Failing that, of course, autonomy could be suggested, but the precedent of Eastern Rumelia must have taught them that an autonomous Macedonia might well gravitate towards Bulgaria, resurrecting the spectre of a new San Stefano. During the Balkan Wars, however, the initiative concerning the fate of Macedonia was lost to the British.

Throughout the nineteenth century, the pattern that had emerged was fairly straightforward: Balkan action of some sort was followed quickly by European intervention, and in the end the new settlement was sealed by a European congress or treaty. IMRO was well aware of that pattern, and such considerations certainly influenced their decision to launch the Ilinden Revolt. In the twentieth century this was to change. It will be remembered that the Powers had advised moderation in the Balkan capitals before the first Balkan war broke out. But although London became during the wars the centre of European diplomacy on the issue, the ultimate solution to the Macedonian Question—the partition of the Ottoman province between Greece, Bulgaria, and Serbia—was a Balkan decision determined by the relative strength, and in Bulgaria's case weakness, of the Balkan actors themselves. That the initiative belonged to them became apparent very quickly: as the first war was unfolding, Cartwright emphasized that 'England wished to keep out of Balkan complications, and, above all, desired to maintain concert of Europe intact'.[22] Consequently, although the British did not initiate the partition of Macedonia, they were forced to accept it as the only solution that the situation called for. After the Balkan nationalist fever reached boiling point during the second Balkan war, which broke out in June 1913, with the Bulgarians attacking their former allies, the Foreign Office would come to the conclusion that the partition of Macedonia was not only the sole, but also a most beneficial, solution: The old British idea of autonomy was now pronounced clinically dead. 'An autonomous Macedonia', minuted Arthur Nicolson in July 1913, 'would merely mean a return to the old state of things of continuous massacres etc. It is to be hoped that such a project will not be put forward.'[23] That partition was accepted, however, should not mean to imply that it was also considered as just: in an oft-quoted passage, Grey

[22] Cooch and Temperley (eds.), *British Documents,* ix. *The Balkan Wars, pt. ii, The League and Turkey* (London, 1934), Sir F. Cartwright to Sir Edward Grey, 12 Nov. 1912, 137.
[23] Minute by Nicolson attached to Sir F. Cartwright to Sir Edward Grey, 22 July 1913, ibid. 928. For more details on British policy during the Balkan Wars see Richard

himself argued that 'the settlement of the second Balkan War was not one of justice but one of force. It stored up inevitable trouble for the time to come.'[24]

Only during the Great War would an attempt be made by Britain to gain the initiative and use Macedonia as a bargaining tool. The issue at stake was Bulgaria. With the country wavering between the Central Powers and the Entente, the offer of Macedonian lands to Sofia became the carrot that could conceivably tip the balance in favour of the British. Many such offers were made to Sofia in late 1914 and again in 1915, aimed either at keeping Bulgaria neutral, or at luring her to the Entente by inducing her to attack Turkey. In a most generous offer made in August 1915, the Allies offered Bulgaria substantial Macedonian lands right up to Ochrid in the west, the remaining portion of Ottoman Thrace, and the Greek port of Kavala.[25] These offers came to nothing, for the military situation in the summer of 1915 and the defeats of the Russian army seemed to demonstrate beyond doubt that the Allies were clearly on the defensive, and no sensible politician in Sofia would attach the fate of Bulgaria to the losing side of the war. Bulgaria, after all, had no reason to hurry matters: she accepted a similar offer from the Central Powers and occupied large parts of Serbian and Greek Macedonia. Apart from being ineffective, these offers profoundly angered both Greece and Serbia, who felt that they were unfairly treated by being asked to surrender to Bulgaria lands they considered inalienably theirs by right of both war and treaty. That situation prompted an exasperated Nikola Pašić to suggest in August 1915 that the allies were 'treating Serbia like an African tribe'.[26] Venizelos, the Greek premier, was scarcely less irritated: indeed, in 1915 he had agreed under British pressure to cede the port of Kavala to the Bulgarians, but he did so 'against his better judgment as a forlorn hope of preventing Bulgaria entering the war against us'.[27] He was not prepared to repeat that experiment, but the British continued to press him to do so. In 1917, further overtures to

Crampton, *The Hollow Détente: Anglo-German Relations in the Balkans, 1911–1914* (London, 1979), 55–74, 97–111.

[24] Keith Robbins, 'British Diplomacy and Bulgaria, 1914–1915', *Slavonic and East European Review*, 49/117 (1971), 564.

[25] For these offers, and their fate see Robbins, 'British Diplomacy', 560–85. For a Bulgarian view see Ivan Ilcev, 'Great Britain and Bulgaria's Entry into the First World War, 1914–1915', *Bulgarian Historical Review*, 10/4 (1982), 29–48.

[26] Robbins, 'British Diplomacy', 580.

[27] As cited in George Leontaritis, *Greece and the First World War: From Neutrality to Intervention, 1917–1918* (Boulder, Colo. 1990), 302.

Bulgaria would be made, this time in order to induce her to conclude a separate peace. In the course of these attempts, slices of Greek and Serbian Macedonia were again put on display to entice Bulgaria to detach herself from the Central Powers.[28] But the customer was not in a position to accept the goods. For Britain, as shall be seen, this was 'salient ingratitude', and Bulgaria would have to pay dearly for it. Not only did she lose her Aegean outlet, which was transferred to Greece, but she would never again be able to count on British support for her Macedonian claims. Some twenty-five years later, during the Second World War, Britain would have to face the Bulgarian predicament again, but by that time they were no longer in a position, nor had they the will, to make similar offers.

It should be stressed at this juncture that during the 1912–18 period the fate of Macedonia was approached by Britain from a purely strategic viewpoint, and her position was determined by political considerations, not sentiment. There were groups, however, consisting of openly pro-Serbian, pro-Bulgarian, and pro-Greek sympathizers, both within and outside the Foreign Office, which attempted to influence the course of events. The pro-Serbian lobby was probably the weakest of the three, although it included important personalities, such as the eminent historian Professor Seton-Watson. The pro-Greek camp, nourished by the diminishing but still strong philhellenic sentiment of the early nineteenth century, was substantial, and, apart from well-connected figures of the Greek community in London, included Professor Ronald Burrows, the principal of King's College London, and William Pember Reeves, the director of the London School of Economics; both were founding members of the 'Anglo-Hellenic League', dedicated to promoting the 'just claims and honour of Greece', in Macedonia and elsewhere.[29] The pro-Bulgarian circle, on the other hand, which counted among its numbers *The Times* Balkan correspondent J. D. Bourchier, a forceful defender of the 'Bulgarian character' of 'the Macedonian rural population', was chiefly represented by the 'Balkan Committee'. This organization had a distinguished membership, and was almost unanimous in supporting the Bulgarian claim to Macedonia.[30] All three

---

[28] For these attempts and Greek reactions see ibid., 251–320.

[29] Richard Clogg, *Anglo-Greek Attitudes: Studies in History* (London, 2000), 40.

[30] For Bourchier see Robbins, 'British Diplomacy', 561–2; for the pro-Serb group: ibid. 574–5. The Balkan Committee was formed after the Ilinden Revolt of 1903, with Lord Fitzmaurice as its president. Among its members were H. N. Brailsford, author of *Macedonia: Its Races and their Future*, (London, 1906), Noel Buxton, a tireless supporter

groups argued passionately and loudly in defence of their pet causes, and although it is quite difficult to measure their actual strength and political clout, it is arguably fair to say that most Balkan pundits in England at the time favoured a pro-Bulgarian solution to the Macedonian Question.[31] They did so not only because they believed that the satisfaction of the Bulgarian nationalist aspirations was a sound foreign policy move, as it would lure the country to the side of Britain, but also because, in their view, the Macedonian Slavs were true Bulgarians. The course of events, it will be remembered, proved them wrong on their first point. As for the second, they had to wait until the Second World War to see that there, too, they were wrong. Be that as it may, it should be emphasized that despite the outpouring of parliamentary questions, memoranda, and articles, the actual influence of all these groups in the shaping of British policy towards the Macedonian Question was minimal. British policy was simply, and supremely, pro-British.

INFLUENCE FOR MODERATION: BRITAIN AND MACEDONIA IN THE INTERWAR PERIOD

After the end of the Great War the partition of Macedonia between Serbia, Greece, and Bulgaria was reconfirmed, with Bulgaria suffering further loss of land: Thrace was transferred to Greece, and Strumitsa, Tsaribrod, and Bosilegrad were awarded to Yugoslavia. Tensions between Sofia and Belgrade were running high, and consequently throughout the interwar period the British found themselves again involved in the Bulgar–Yugoslav controversy over Macedonia.[32] The

---

of Bulgarian rights in the Balkans, and the politician and scholar James Bryce. For a selection of pro-Bulgarian writings (mostly on the 'Bulgarian character' of Macedonia) by British and American politicians and scholars of the period, see Constantine Stephanove, *The Bulgarians and Anglo-Saxondom*, (Berne, 1919); For the Balkan Committee see ibid. 187.

[31] Cf. Leontaritis, *Greece*, 253.

[32] Some aspects of British involvement in the Macedonian Question during the interwar years are covered in Andrew Rossos, 'The British Foreign Office and Macedonian National Identity, 1918–1941,' *Slavic Review*, 53/2 (1994), 369–94, who offers the Macedonian perspective on the subject. On the other hand, Vasil Vasilev, in his 'Velikobritania i Makedonskiyat Vŭpros, 1924–1929g.' [Great Britain and the Macedonian Question, 1924–9], *Istoricheski Pregled*, 5 (1985), 20–41, naturally emphasizes the role of pro-Bulgarian British politicians and organizations. Noel Buxton, 'a great friend

potentially explosive nature of that problem gave them serious cause for concern, while the enormous amount of mistrust between the two Balkan rivals, and the inability of the Bulgarian governments to eradicate IMRO, frequently frustrated the British officials, who had to keep abreast of the developments in the Balkans. And with good reason. Strictly speaking, there were no vital British interests at stake in these countries, apart from a modest volume of trade, which was greatly reduced in the 1930s as a result of German economic penetration. Politically, Bulgaria was an ex-enemy state with strong Italian, and later German, connections, while Yugoslavia, until Stojadinović's drift towards Italy, remained an almost exclusively French preserve.[33] It was felt, therefore, that among the Great Powers Britain was best placed to undertake the role of 'disinterested' and 'unprejudiced' mediator between Bulgaria and Yugoslavia. For the Foreign Office, Britain's was a role of a 'go-between', aiming only at the preservation of peace and stability.

It was precisely Britain's unequivocal devotion to the status quo, and her firm belief that only the maintenance of the Treaty of Neuilly could guarantee 'peace in their time', that obliged her to interest herself in the Macedonian intrigues of the Balkan Slavs. When Rowland Sperling, the British minister in Sofia, argued in 1928 that 'if the Balkan races could scrap with one another without disturbing the rest of the world, we should only be mildly interested in their proceedings', few would contest his views. 'Quite so,' replied Sir Orme Sargent. He was quick, however, to remind Sperling that, due to the Franco-Italian rivalry in the Balkans and 'our League obligations', it was 'impossible to isolate a Balkan war'. Sperling was not the only one to lose his temper over Macedonia. Two years later, in 1930, Sidney Waterlow, his successor, become so disappointed with Bulgarian inability to suppress IMRO that he suggested the withdrawal of the British Legation, and the disassociation of Britain with 'the fate of Bulgaria'. Sargent was obliged to spell out again the reasons for British involvement in the Macedonian Question: 'It is not from any love of Bulgaria or Yugoslavia that we concern ourselves with this troublesome question.' It was, rather, a fear

of Bulgaria', for example, and the Balkan Committee figure prominently in his article. See also Miranda Paximadopoulou-Stavrinou, 'To Foreign Office kai to Makedoniko to 1925' [The Foreign Office and the Macedonian [Question] in 1925], *Valkanika Symmeikta*, 10 (1998), 225–42.

[33] See Ch. 1.

that 'any disturbance might spread to the rest of Europe'.[34] In fact, the Bulgar–Yugoslav controversy, and the activities of IMRO, had made their common frontier one of the most turbulent spots in Europe, risking a conflagration impossible to contain. Moreover, Bulgarian irredentism, even in its peaceful version, presented a challenge to the sacrosanct peace settlements that the British endeavoured to maintain. Britain, therefore, could not afford to wash her hands of Macedonia. She had to make her presence felt, and to use her influence in the interest of peace.

   Having thus defined the preservation of the status quo as the only vital British interest in the Balkans, the Foreign Office devised a policy on the Macedonian Question, which was premissed upon four main propositions: (*a*) that existing boundaries should be respected, (*b*) that the Bulgarian governments should do their best to become 'masters in their own house', by curtailing the activities of IMRO, (*c*) that the Yugoslavs should 'meet the Bulgarians half way', by ceasing to support the exiled Agrarians,[35] and by improving the administration in 'Southern Serbia', and (*d*) that the Macedonian Question should be prevented from becoming an issue in international politics. As a result of this last point, no British encouragement should be given to attempts to raise the issue in the League of Nations.[36] Other important issues, however, were closely connected with, and approached in the context of, these basic guidelines. Prominent among them was the question of the nationality of the inhabitants of Yugoslav Macedonia, as well as the desirability and the practical value of the recognition of a 'Bulgarian' minority in Yugoslavia. Moreover, the question regarding whether or

[34] PRO FO/800, vol. 272, Private Papers of Sir Orme Sargent [Counsellor at the FO (1926–33), Assistant Under-Secretary of State (1933–9), Deputy Under-Secretary (1939–46), Permanent Under-Secretary (1946–9)], Letter to Sperling, dated 2/3/1928. FO/371/14316, C3687, Waterlow to Sargent, dated 5/5/1930, and minute by Sargent attached.

[35] After the 1923 coup against Stamboliiski's regime, many pro-Yugoslav Agrarians left the country, found shelter in Yugoslavia, and, led by Staboliiski's minister in Belgrade Kosta Todorov, became engaged in subversive activities against the Tsankov and Liapchev governments. Todorov, who believed that 'only in the atmosphere of Bulgar-Jugoslav fraternity can the Macedonian question be solved', became a passionate enemy of IMRO. He saw in it a serious obstacle in achieving a Bulgar–Yugoslav 'natural union'. See his 'The Macedonian Organisation Yesterday and Today', *Foreign Affairs*, 6/3 (1928), 482. See also his autobiography, *Balkan Firebrand: The Autobiography of a Rebel, Soldier, and Statesman* (Chicago, 1943).

[36] FO 371/14317, C5316, memorandum by the CD, dated 2/7/1930 (hereafter 1930 memo), on 'The Origins of the Macedonian Revolutionary Organisation and its History since the Great War'. A draft version of that memorandum can be found in FO 371/14316, C4470, dated 10/5/1930.

not the present solution of the Macedonian Question was a just and lasting one, was also addressed and sometimes fiercely contested within the Foreign Office. As far as the means of British intervention in the Bulgar–Yugoslav dispute were concerned, it was agreed that 'friendly advice', urging moderation and restraint, should be given to both governments along the lines mentioned above, while stronger language was to be used when it seemed that the situation was getting out of hand, in order to prevent the outbreak of a military incident.

Before discussing these issues, it should be stressed that such a policy was devised, and strongly supported, by the officials of the Central Department—and, after 1933, the Southern Department—which was ultimately responsible for the formulation of Britain's Balkan policies. The Foreign Office, however, was a much wider world, including the British political representatives in Bulgaria and Yugoslavia. British ministers, apart from reporting political developments in these countries, also communicated their views and perceptions to the Central Department, and frequently made suggestions regarding the general policy that Britain should follow in the Balkans.

If seen from a long-term perspective, this distinction appears to be an important one, for, as shall be seen, in many cases the view of those on the ground in Sofia, did not coincide with the view from London or from Belgrade, for that matter. More often than not, a divergence of opinion could be discerned between the 'centre' and the 'periphery' of the Foreign Office, and between the British diplomats in Belgrade and Sofia. Sometimes, the differences were over mere nuances, or clarifications of a given 'line' with no wider ramifications. There were numerous cases, however, when serious disagreements arose over the fundamental tenets of British policy. In these debates, swords were crossed, while accusations of pro-Yugoslav or pro-Bulgarian 'bias' were fired off from Sofia or Belgrade, compelling the Central Department—and mainly Sir Orme Sargent—to inflict upon them argumentative despatches, sometimes in the form of a private letter, in order to save them from the embarrassment of being 'at cross-purposes' with the policy as seen 'from here'. Sargent was eminently qualified to defend British policy, for he was one of the very few British diplomats who spent their entire careers exclusively within the confines of the Foreign Office, without having to endure a stint abroad. Within this context, an understanding of this 'triangular' interaction (Foreign Office–Sofia–Belgrade) not only provides a more balanced appreciation of British policy, but also offers a caveat against 'selective' use of archival sources, which tend to overestimate the weight or the impact of one angle, thus obscuring the whole picture.

It has already been noted that the British had conferred upon themselves the role of impartial but concerned mediator between the two sides in Macedonia; that they had no protégé to support and no foe to punish was a deeply entrenched belief in the Foreign Office. A united and strong Yugoslavia was, of course, a principal British desideratum,[37] but this proposition derived its legitimacy from the necessity of maintaining the peace settlements, and not from fond memories of the First World War. According to this resonance, Bulgaria had to be treated fairly, and the bitter memories of the past must not be allowed to influence decision-making. In a Central Department memorandum, written in 1924, although it was admitted that Bulgaria's decision to side with Germany was 'salient ingratitude', it was emphasized that Britain had treated her leniently and 'with great generosity'. Bulgaria had been tacitly allowed to violate the harsh military clauses of the Treaty of Neuilly, while her reparation payments amounted to less than 5 per cent of her budget. Moreover, the Bulgarians had been offered an economic outlet to the Aegean, under the treaty, but 'their own obstinacy' prevented them from accepting it.[38] This perception of a lack of sentimentalist bias, although not universally shared among British officials, enabled the Central Department to balance the scales even between Belgrade and Sofia. Moreover, it was felt that this 'impartiality' and 'sincerity' afforded the British a fair amount of prestige, which neither the Italians nor the French could match.[39]

The turbulent state of Bulgar–Yugoslav relations presented the British with many opportunities to implement their 'influence for moderation' policy. Constant pressure on the Bulgarians to curtail the activities of IMRO, was a permanent theme of this policy. A series of 'advice', alternating with 'representations', began in February 1924, when information from an unnamed source reached the Foreign Office, indicating that the IMRO leader, Todor Alexandrov, had been preparing his bands

[37] Cf. the assertion of Henderson, minister at Belgrade from 1929 to 1935, that 'Peace and security in the Balkans can only be assured by means of a united and strong Yugoslavia'. FO 371/16859, C768, 26/3/1931.

[38] FO 371/9719, C16914, 'Bulgaria', in a series of memoranda on Britain's relations with the European states, dated 7/11/1924.

[39] It is interesting in this respect to note that Henderson argued in 1933, that British prestige in Yugoslavia was of better quality than the French, which was based solely on 'politics and material advantages'. FO 371/16830, C747, 15/1/1933.

for a large-scale terrorist campaign in Yugoslavia. William Erskine, the British minister, was accordingly instructed to 'make the most serious representations' to the Bulgarians, urging them to prevent the raids. The Bulgarian foreign minister, Kalfov, replied that he was already aware of the danger, and had asked the frontier authorities to take the necessary measures. Shortly afterwards, Erskine informed London that Alexandrov had sent a circular, calling off action.[40] As to the relations of IMRO with the government, Erskine was inclined to believe, perhaps because of the moderate Kalfov, that 'the government is not using' the Comitadjis, for they realize the danger of doing so. In the Central Department, however, mistrust prevailed. It was commented that the government was using Alexandrov in order to provoke harsh Serbian reprisals, which would enable them to appeal to the League of Nations, and to internationalize the issue. 'We must know', a minute read, 'that the Bulgarians display peasant cunning, self-pity, and obstinacy'.[41]

After a short interval, however, IMRO's armed raids in Yugoslavia were resumed. These were mainly the work of determined fighters (usually in groups of three, the *troyka*), who penetrated Yugoslav Macedonia from the Bulgarian frontier, threw a couple of bombs in a central café, and fired some shots at the local gendarmes, before withdrawing into Bulgaria. Yugoslav patience was growing very thin because of these incidents, and, naturally, put the blame on the Bulgarians, who turned a blind eye to Comitadji activity. In July 1926, after a spate of attacks, the Foreign Office learned that the Yugoslav foreign minister, Momčilo Ninčić, was considering invading Bulgaria in order to 'punish the offenders'. Fearing an outbreak of hostilities, the Foreign Office swiftly instructed Howard Kennard in Belgrade, and Erskine in Sofia, to call for moderation. The Yugoslavs were reminded of the Greek invasion of Petrich, from which they gained nothing, and which ended in them paying a substantial fine. On the other hand, the Bulgarians were warned about 'the risk they were running' by allowing IMRO to commit outrages in Yugoslavia.[42] Adding some muscle to their warnings, Erskine was told to inform the government that, if tough measures were not taken, the refugee loan to Bulgaria would be endangered.[43] The

---

[40] FO 371/9659, C3163 (representations to Kalfov), 25/2/1924; FO 371/9659, C3353 (on Alexandrov's circular), 27/2/1924.

[41] FO 371/9659, C3163, 20/2/1924, and minutes attached.

[42] FO 371/11221, C3163, 29/7/1926, and FO telegrams to Sofia and Belgrade, dated 3/8/1926.

[43] FO 371/11221, C7262, 24/6/1926.

escalation of terrorism in 1927, however, which resulted in the murder of the Serbian military commander of Štip, General Mihailo Kovačević, called for stronger action. Thus, at the initiative of the British, Erskine, together with his French and Italian counterparts, made joint representations to Atanas Burov, the foreign minister, asking for some definitive action against the IMRO.[44] Although the Italian representations were markedly milder than those made by the British or the French, Andrei Liapchev was obliged to show some determination, So, he imposed martial law in the districts of Kiustendil and Petrich, but this was more of a facade rather than a serious attempt to break up IMRO. The organization was left intact and none of its leaders was arrested. As the furious Serbs closed the border, the British stepped up the pressure on Liapchev. The Bulgarians, the British thought, should understand 'the folly of their present inaction'. Consequently Erskine, along with the French minister, but without their Italian opposite number, renewed their strong representations to Burov. Yet again, nothing concrete came out of this action, for, apart from the internment of some agitators, IMRO's hold on Petrich remained unchallenged.[45]

It is interesting to note that the British, while making these moves in Sofia, fully appreciated the enormous difficulties of the Liapchev government, regarding the eradication of IMRO. They were aware of the close links that IMRO maintained with both the government and the army, and understood that a wholesale crackdown on the organization would not only be extremely difficult to achieve, but it would elevate their fallen men into heroes of the movement, and give them much publicity. It is significant, in this respect, that Erskine was told to ask the Bulgarians not to 'suppress IMRO in a day', but to 'do something with determination'. At the same time, the British were careful not to let the Yugoslavs believe that they were absolutely in the right. They were, therefore, constantly reminded that they should keep calm, avoid any action that could make the position of Bulgaria more difficult, and, significantly, improve the quality of their administration in Southern Serbia.[46] Mediating between the Slavs, however, was not without its problems. In early 1928, the Yugoslavs informed the

---

[44] 1930 memo.
[45] FO 371/12091, instructions to Erskine, 21/10/1927, attached to C8542; Erskine's talk with Burov, C8671, 25/10/1927. Annual Report on Bulgaria, FO 371/12864, C4652, 17/6/1928.
[46] Annual Report on Bulgaria, FO 371/12864, C4652, 17/6/1928. British views on Southern Serbia will be discussed in greater detail below.

British of the whereabouts of various Macedonian terrorists, which they hastily passed over to the Bulgarians. The latter discovered the provenance of the information, and questioned the wisdom of choosing 'this roundabout way' to communicate intelligence, causing the British considerable embarrassment. Howard-Smith and Sargent swiftly agreed that, if Britain was to keep her 'impartiality', they should be more careful in the future.[47]

By the end of the 1920s the Foreign Office had become the recipient of many reports pointing to increasing internal strife within IMRO. After the murder of its indisputable leader, Todor Alexandrov, in 1924, it will be remembered, a violent struggle broke out between two rival factions, headed by Ivan Mihailov and Alexandŭr Protogerov. This internecine feud, which marked the organization's degeneration, culminated in the murder of Protogerov in July 1928.[48] Given IMRO's apparent decline, the British thought that the time had come for definitive steps to be taken. Erskine doubted the effectiveness of yet another representation, for the government, in his view, was 'under the thumb' of the Macedonians, but the Foreign Office believed that Liapchev would do nothing, unless 'goaded into' it by the Powers. Thus, the French and the Italians were again approached for collective action, while Erskine was instructed to use 'the most forcible language' in order to persuade the Bulgarians that the situation was ripe for vigorous measures. The Italians, however, torpedoed the British initiative, partly because they perceived it as an outcome of Serbian pressure, but, mainly, because they were tacitly using the Macedonians as a weapon against Yugoslavia.[49] Italy's abstention, coupled with the fact that she rushed to make the representations 'public property', reduced their effect. The only result was the removal from the Cabinet of the minister of war, General Vŭlkov, a prominent IMRO sympathizer, who, as it has already been noted, allowed the printing facilities of his ministry to be used for the officially banned IMRO paper *Svoboda ili Smŭrt* (Freedom or Death). The dismissed minister did not fare too badly,

---

[47] FO 371/12856, C1139, 9/2/1928, and minutes attached.   [48] See Ch. 1.

[49] FO 371/12856, C5549, and minutes by Sargent and Howard-Smith, dated 20/7/1928 and 17/7/1928 respectively; on Italy's refusal, FO 371/12856, C6253, 16/8/1928, and C6177, 12/8/1928. It should be added that the French proposed more 'vigorous action', suggesting that the behaviour of the Bulgarians should be linked with the issue of the stabilization loan. The British, however, disagreed, arguing that the loan was vital for Bulgaria's economy, would strengthen the position of the government, and, therefore, should not be made 'dependent upon the settlement of a political problem'.

though: he found some solace in Rome, where he was appointed ambassador.

At the turn of the decade there were some encouraging signs of an improvement in Bulgar–Yugoslav relations, and a new opportunity for Britain to ensure that a cautious rapprochement would survive the mutual mistrust and suspicion. In early 1929 Yugoslavia, now under the royal dictatorship of King Alexander, announced that she had opened the border, which had been closed after the murder of General Kovačević, and called on the Bulgarians to meet at Pirot in order to discuss measures for the prevention of future incidents, as well as the question of 'double proprietors', i.e. those who lived on the one side of the border, but owned property on the other. The Bulgarians replied favourably and in March a joint communiqué was issued, which provided for the formation of a permanent Bulgar-Yugoslav commission to deal with the frontier traffic. Although no agreement was reached regarding the liquidation of the 'double properties', the Pirot Conference definitely shed a ray of hope.[50]

The Bulgarians ratified the Pirot resolutions in May, but a month earlier the Macedonians had done their best to rock the boat. In April, the Committees of Macedonian Emigrants, an IMRO stronghold, warmly welcomed in Sofia the Croat separatist leader Ante Pavelić. The presence of the *Ustaša* leader, who had strong links with IMRO, was a major embarrassment for Liapchev and infuriated the Yugoslavs, who retaliated by closing the border and refusing to ratify the Pirot resolutions. Once more, Britain put strong pressure on Belgrade to temper their anger, and Kennard, seconded by the French minister, urged the acting Minister for Foreign Affairs (the foreign minister, Vojislav Marinković, was away) to ratify the agreement. The pressure proved to be effective and the Yugoslavs returned to the negotiating table.[51] After protracted negotiations, an agreement on the liquidation of 'double properties' was reached, while on 1 February 1930 another agreement was signed, which stipulated the establishment of a permanent Bulgar–Yugoslav commission to enforce law and order in the frontier.[52] For a brief moment, the British could congratulate themselves, and Waterlow, in an optimistic mood, informed the Foreign Office from

---

[50] 1930 memo.

[51] FO. 371/13571, C4087, 3/6/1929. In Nov. 1929, Marinkovič admitted to Sir Eric Drumond that his decision to put the agreement into force was due to the Anglo-French representations. PRO FO 371/13573, C8616, 4/11/1929.

[52] The text can be found in FO 371/14314, C1119, 10/2/1930.

Sofia that, during a dinner party at the Legation, both Burov and the Yugoslav minister expressed their 'fervent gratitude' for Britain's good offices.[53]

Other quarters, however, harboured much less optimism about the Pirot Agreement. Certainly, IMRO could not bear the prospect of another Niš Convention,[54] and employed its usual tactics to embarrass the Bulgarian government. Hardly had the ink dried on the agreements, when two Macedonian gunmen threw four bombs in Pirot in early March, killing one man and wounding twenty-five. Shortly afterwards, another bomb was thrown in Strumitsa, killing a municipal guard. The Yugoslav minister in Sofia, considered by the British as a moderate, confided to Waterlow that these outrages were the work of Italy, which viewed with suspicion the recent rapprochement, but Marinković and King Alexander could hardly conceal their irritation; in their view, Bulgaria was solely responsible for these incidents, since no serious measures were taken to prevent them or to punish the perpetrators. The situation became critical in mid-March, as the British learned that the king was contemplating taking 'the law into his hands'. Thus, the British found themselves again obliged to coordinate international action. This time, the Italians decided to join in, apparently in an effort to avoid embarrassment which the support of IMRO would cause them, and, together with the more eager French, the usual 'strong language' was used by the ministers in Sofia. After the customary pattern, Henderson was instructed to urge the Yugoslavs to 'exercise calm and patience'. Moreover, the British, aware of the activity of the Bulgarian Agrarians in Yugoslavia, asked Belgrade to stop them creating trouble, which included armed raids in Bulgaria, and to restrict their movement.[55]

As has already been pointed out, 'holding the scales even' between the two Balkan states, and giving advice 'equally and simultaneously', was deemed necessary by the Foreign Office, not only because neither party had entirely clean hands, but also because it could best guarantee British 'impartiality' and, consequently, prestige. This policy, however, came under increasing attack from the British ministers in the Balkan capitals, who frequently accused the Foreign Office of taking sides in the dispute. In this respect, Sir Nevile Henderson, undoubtedly the

---

[53] FO 371/14314, C1118, 3/2/1930.

[54] As has been seen, Stamboliiski paid with his life for the Niš Convention of 1923, which aimed at preventing IMRO's raids.

[55] FO 371/14315, C2571, 24/3/1930; 1930 memo.

most pro-Yugoslav British minister in Belgrade, was a forceful critic of the Foreign Office.[56] 'It is unjustifiable and unfair' he noted in repeated letters to the FO in February and March 1930, to give 'advice' for moderation to the Yugoslavs, every time IMRO thought it nice to throw some bombs in Macedonia. Only after IMRO's suppression, he argued, should the Yugoslavs be asked to improve their own conduct. Making clear where his own sympathies lay, Henderson argued that Yugoslavia sincerely wanted a rapprochement, but the Bulgarians, 'a race whose instincts are chiefly communistic and bloody murder', had rendered this impossible by failing to eradicate IMRO. While complaining of London's anti-Yugoslav bias, Henderson spared neither the British press, especially the *Manchester Guardian* and *The Times,* nor the 'British public' in general, for their hostile attitude towards Yugoslavia.[57]

The view from the British Legation in Sofia was equally critical, although less outspoken. In 1928, Sperling accused London of treating the Serbs as a 'mother's pet', while Waterlow argued that the Yugoslavs should be blamed for the tension in the Balkans, for they allowed the Agrarians to carry attacks in Bulgaria, and stubbornly refuse to alleviate the position of the inhabitants of Southern Serbia. He even hinted that the outrages of 1930 might have been a Yugoslav provocation, as the incidents happened 'far from the border'. Therefore, according to Waterlow, Yugoslavia should be the first to break 'the vicious circle'.[58] It was Sargent's duty to take on the thankless task of administering a caveat to his critics. He repeatedly assured them that 'sentimental bias is not our philosophy', and that Britain's involvement in the Macedonian Question was due solely to the need of maintaining the Treaty of Neuilly, which, far from being fair 'or even just', offered the only ray of hope for peace 'in present time'. There was, of course, a certain amount of sympathy for Bulgaria in Britain—the activities of the Balkan Committee and some articles published in the *Near East* can testify to that—but the Foreign Office could discount this sentiment as

[56] Henderson's stout pro-Yugoslav feelings were no secret to his colleagues in London, who did not fail to make ironic comments about his sympathies. See his own account, *Water under the Bridge* (London, 1945), 115.

[57] For his eloquence see FO 371/14314, C2149, 14/3/1930; FO 371/14315, C2367, 20/3/1930; FO 371/14316, C3274, 22/3/1930. His complaints about the 'biased', and 'anti-regime' articles of *The Times* are recorded in FO 371/15273, C11312, 26/2/1931, and FO 371/15273, C1311, 20/2/1931.

[58] Sperling's remarks contained in Sargent's letter to him cited in n. 34. For Waterlow's views see FO 371/14315, C2318, 24/3/1930.

little more than the traditional British sympathy 'for the underdog'. As far as policy was concerned, Sargent emphasiszed, Britain had neither a 'pet' to look after, nor an unjustly punished Bulgaria to protect.[59]

Throughout the 1920s the British had tried to prevent IMRO's outrages from triggering a 'hot' war between Bulgaria and Yugoslavia, and had played their part in promoting a spirit of understanding and reconciliation. In this, and to the extent that their influence made the Balkan Slavs cool their ardour, they succeeded, for the frontier incidents, despite the sound and fury they aroused in Yugoslavia, failed to bring about the developments desired by their perpetrators. By the turn of the decade, they hoped that the increasing level of internal strife within IMRO, which had intensified after the murder of Protogerov in 1928, would be violent enough to cause its self-destruction. As the rival factions began to litter the streets of Sofia with the corpses of their opponents in the early 1930s, the Foreign Office become increasingly confident that internal feuds would do the job the Bulgarian governments were so unfit for. This would give them some comfort, for, as the Macedonians were exterminating each other at a rate that peaked to five murders a day in Sofia alone, the inability of the Mushanov government (1931–4) to deal them a definitive blow infuriated and dispirited them. Waterlow, who kept London fully informed of the Macedonian algebra of death, noted in 1932 and 1933 that the government was completely 'irresponsible' and incapable of doing anything, beyond some face-saving house searches for arms, and the rounding up of the 'usual suspects', which, of course, always excluded Mihailov.

There was, however, some good news as well. These nasty feuds, according to many sources available to the Foreign Office, had alienated the population of both Yugoslav and Bulgarian Macedonia from IMRO. In 1931, the population in Skopje was reported to be 'distant' from the organization; and a considerable decrease in the subsidies locally drawn was cited as a reliable indicator. Thus, despite Bulgarian impotence, the British tended to believe that IMRO's days were numbered, and that the 'Balkan pest' would sooner rather than later die a 'natural death'. This death, which eventually came in 1934, was not as natural as the

---

[59] Sargent's remarks in his letter to Sperling, cited in n. 34. The Balkan Committee, its chairman Sir Edward Boyle, and its president Noel Buxton, kept the FO busy by overloading them with memoranda, articles, and parliamentary questions, suggesting concessions to the 'Bulgarian minority' in Yugoslavia, and intervention by the League of Nations. These issues will be discussed below.

British had expected it to be, but, nevertheless, IMRO's almost bloodless suppression confirmed the view that the population had become heartily sick of the Macedonians.[60]

Fully fledged war, however, was only one way to 'internationalize' the Macedonian Question. Unfortunately for the British, who had done their best to keep this issue out of the international agenda, there were others as well, among whom the intervention of the League of Nations figured prominently. The League could intervene in the Bulgar–Yugoslav dispute either by bringing to an end an armed con-flict — as was the case with the Greek invasion of Bulgaria in 1925 — or by being asked to investigate a minority issue-in this case, the position of the Bulgarian minority in Yugoslav Macedonia. Consequently, the British, while using their influence to prevent armed conflicts, had also to deal with a fundamental question; namely, whether there was a Bulgarian minority in Yugoslav Macedonia, which required protection under the minority treaties. This, in turn, requires an examination of British views on Southern Serbia.

First, it should be noted that the Foreign Office approached the minority question from a purely political viewpoint. Whatever the politicians-turned-ethnographers of both sides might have said about the nationality of the Macedonians, the British were determined to keep Yugoslavia a strong and unitary state, for any exercise of revi-sionism, no matter how modest or limited it could be, would unravel an uncontrollable wave of demands, reducing Eastern Europe to a battlefield. The centrepiece of the British attitude was to deny the exis-tence of a Macedonian or Bulgarian minority in Yugoslavia. 'Indeed, once the existence of a Macedonian nationality is even allowed to be presumed, there is the danger that the entire Peace Settlement will be jeopardised by the calling into question not merely of the frontiers between Yugoslavia and Bulgaria, but also of those between Yugoslavia and Greece and between Yugoslavia and Albania.'[61] Therefore, Bal-four concluded, 'H.M.G. refuse to recognise a distinct Macedonian nationality requiring either independence or absorption by Bulgaria, or else a degree of autonomy, which Yugoslavia would not willingly concede.'[62]

---

[60] For British views on IMRO see Balfour's minutes in FO 371/14314, C723, 5/2/1930, and FO 371/15173, C8171, 27, 10/1931. See also FO 371/15895, C925, 21/1/1932; FO 371/15896, C8000, 17/9/1932; FO 371/16649, C5898, 1/7/1933.

[61] 1930 memo.   [62] Memorandum, dated 29/8/1930. FO 371/14318, C6756.

It seemed, however, that there was no contradiction between British political considerations and their actual views on the nationality of the Macedonians. For the Foreign Office, the Macedonians had no national affiliations whatsoever, nor would they be able to choose one, even if asked to do so. 'The majority of the Slavs . . . do not care to what nationality they belong', read a memorandum of 1925, adding that 'it is incorrect to refer to them as other than Macedo-Slavs. To this extent both the Serbian claim that they are Southern Serbs and the Bulgar claim that they are Bulgars are unjustified'.[63] 'The inevitable conclusion', according to the Foreign Office, was that 'a large part of the inhabitants of Macedonia do not have any particular national aspiration but would be perfectly content under any government which granted them reasonable freedom and protection from the "Comitadjis" who make life in the country a misery.' As a result, no plebiscite was needed, for there were no national sentiments to be found.[64] The absence of clear-cut national loyalties among the Macedonians was so entrenched in the Foreign Office that the clerks did not hesitate to comment on scholarly works which aimed at giving the Macedonians a nationality: in 1926 from Belgrade, Howard Kennard, sent London a summary of a book by the Serbian author Jovan Erdeljanović, entitled *Makedonski Srbi*, which epitomized the Serbian case. 'The truth is', an official wrote in a minute, that 'they are neither the one nor the other but just Macedonian Slavs. No more no less.'[65]

Much of the information available to the Foreign Office was derived from reports which followed tours of the area by various officials, mostly the vice-consuls in Skopje. These reports, which covered a wide range of issues, tended to confirm the views held by the Foreign Office. The language of the Macedonian Slavs was nearer to Bulgarian than Serbian, and until 1913 they 'called and considered themselves Bulgarians'; but the only thing that dominated their minds was a 'firm just and enlightened administration'. 'Nationalism', reported the vice-consul in Skopje, D. J. Footman, in 1925, was of 'minor importance'.[66] In 1927, the same official reported after another tour, that the Macedonians appeared to be 'indifferent alike to Serb and Bulgar pretensions', apart from the local intelligentsia, which remained to 'a fair proportion'

[63] FO 371/10667, C15185, memorandum on 'The Macedonian Question and Comitaji Activity', dated 26/11/1925.
[64] 1930 memo.   [65] FO 371/11221, C1940, 10/2/1926, and minute attached.
[66] FO 371/10793, report attached to C9288, 6/7/1925, and dated 30/6/1925.

pro-Bulgarian.[67] In their efforts to decipher the sentiment of the Macedonians, the British encountered a population which just wanted to be left in peace, and looked neither to Belgrade nor to Sofia for protection. 'No love for Bulgars is lost', asserted Rodney Gallop, secretary of the Belgrade Legation, after a tour in Macedonia in 1926, due to 'their brutality during the war'. Hostility to the Serbs, however, was much more in evidence. 'The Macedonians are not mixing with the Serbs . . . [and] they insist to be called neither Serbs nor Bulgars but Macedonians'. A Serbian colonist, whom he interviewed near Tetovo, told him that he was anxious to return to his motherland, for he felt that he lived 'in a foreign country'. The population, nevertheless, had no desire for an independent Macedonia: 'it was all the same for them who ruled them, they said, so long as they are not oppressed or neglected'. Thus, he concluded, Belgrade was faced 'with economic problems not political', for discontent stemmed from economic deprivation. 'A prosperous Macedonia will be a contented one.'[68] That the Serbs were considered conquerors rather than brothers, was no secret to the British. The population regarded them as 'invaders and unwelcome foreigners', the Belgrade vice-consul, Blakeney, noted in 1930; and with good reason, for as far as 'language, customs and sympathies' were concerned they were 'Bulgarians'. The vice-consul, who had a command of Slavic languages, asked many peasants for their nationality, but they declined to say more than a simple 'I come from these parts', perhaps out of fear of Serbian persecution. According to Blakeney, they might have preferred to be ruled by the Bulgarians, but 'if the Serbs could offer them good administration, and could relax their punitive and violent methods, they could accept Yugoslav domination'.[69]

On the basis of this information, the Foreign Office came to the conclusion that Macedonia was a national 'no man's land', 'just like Alsace: one of those parts of Europe which has no real nationality'.[70] A pro-Bulgarian feeling was evident, especially in Bitolj and among the thin layer of local intellectuals, but this was neither strong nor deep enough to appeal to the majority of the population. Consequently, there was no Bulgarian minority in Yugoslav Macedonia. Few would

[67] FO 371/12092, memorandum on 'Southern Serbia in 1927', attached to C9610, 23/11/1927.

[68] FO 371/11405, report by Rodney Gallop [secretary in Belgrade (1923–6), then in Athens; from 1940 at the FO], attached to C5052, 21/4/1926, and dated 19/4/1926.

[69] FO 371/14316, report attached to C3840, 19/5/1930.

[70] FO 371/14317, minute attached to C6037, dated 23/7/1930.

disagree with King Alexander, who in 1924 told the British minister in Belgrade, Sir Alban Young, that 'a Macedonian could become a Bulgar-Macedonian, or a Serbian-Macedonian with equal facility', according to the advantages which he could get from 'his selection'.[71] Definitely not Henderson: 'the Macedonians', he argued, 'have got to be either Yugoslavs or Bulgars. They had better be the former than the latter.'[72]

Indeed they had, for otherwise the British would have been obliged to put up with demands for minority rights, and even for rectification of borders, which could threaten the integrity of Yugoslavia. Making a 'good Yugoslav' out of a Macedonian, however, was a quite difficult task, and the British knew all too well that Belgrade was not up to the job. The extremely poor quality of the Serbian administration of the province was a persistent leitmotiv in all the reports dealing with this issue. IMRO's raids and the cold shoulder of the population forced Belgrade to maintain order 'with the big stick', visible more or less throughout the interwar years, which was handed to poorly paid, corrupt, and chauvinist Serbian gendarmes. The presence of almost 55,000 armed men in Macedonia—including the gendarmerie, frontier guards, armed villagers, and divisions of the Yugoslav army—was necessary in order to resign the population to the idea that the province was Yugoslav and would remain so.[73] Despite the improvement of security, however, the excesses of short-sighted gendarmes—which included beating up peasants for wearing hats resembling those of the Comitadjis—did nothing to reconcile the population with Belgrade's rule. Every time IMRO killed a gendarme, noted Footman, the murder was received with a 'quiet satisfaction'.[74]

The incompetence of the gendarmerie, matched only by the corruption of the entire Serbian administration, was only one aspect of Macedonian misery. Footman, who wrote a list of suggestions for the improvement of the situation, noted that the 'most crying grievance' was the tobacco monopoly, which fixed prices at a very low level. This

[71] FO 371/9719, C15558, 24/1/1924. Surprisingly enough, the views of the Yugoslav king were echoed by a Bulgarian prelate with good knowledge of the conditions in Bulgarian Macedonia. In 1932, Archimandrite Joseph, an assistant of the bishop of Nevrokop, confided to Waterlow that the Macedonians lacked the qualities 'which create national consciousness'. They transfer their loyalties 'for a small pecuniary consideration'. FO 371/15896, C5454, 30/6/1932.

[72] FO 371/15173, C1636, 10/3/1931.

[73] FO 371/14316, report by Major Oxley, military attaché of the British Legation, attached to C3840, 19/5/1930.

[74] FO 371/12092, report by Footman, dated 19/12/1927, attached to C16431.

unpopular measure not only considerably decreased production, but meant that the Macedonian peasants earned half as much as the Greeks. According to the vice-consul, the abolition of the monopoly would send the price of tobacco sky-rocketing, allowing the peasants to earn 300 million dinars for their crop, instead of a mere 40 million (at 1927 prices). Moreover, he suggested that if the officials had their jobs guaranteed by the state, instead of relying on party patronage, the quality of the administration would be greatly improved. Thus, he hoped, 'some Croat and Slovene' officials would come to Macedonia, slowing down the process of Serbianization: 'they,' he argued, 'being sure of their superiority, will not display it against the Macedonians, as the—more insecure—Serbs do'.[75] In 1927, the same official concluded that the whole process of Serbianization had produced no 'perceptible results'. Some progress had been made in education, with 'twice as many children attending school as in Turkish times', but lack of funding and of teachers made the pace very slow; nor was the colonization with Serbian shelters making the desired headway, due to the 'official mismanagement' of the settlement schemes.[76]

It is interesting to note, however, that successive British ministers in Belgrade persistently tried to emphasize the more positive aspects of these reports and to assure the Foreign Office that Yugoslavia would eventually digest the sour Macedonian salad. When the Skopje vice-consul A. Monck-Mason reported in 1924 that 'it is idle to pretend that Macedonia is treated with impartial justice', Sir Alban Young stepped in to provide some context: there was corruption, he admitted, but it was not confined to Macedonia: 'it is rife throughout the Kingdom'.[77] Howard Kennard was no exception to this rule. He firmly believed that the Macedonians were neither Serbs nor Bulgars. 'Only the Exarchate Bulgarised them.' So they would be Serbianized 'just as efficiently in a few years' time'. Administration was of course of a low standard; but 'this is the Balkans'.[78] In order to further strengthen his view, he toured Macedonia in 1926. From his report, an idyllic picture emerged: Skopje and Tetovo appeared to be 'relatively affluent', the condition of the roads was 'distinctly superior to everything in the Belgrade area', and schools could be found everywhere. He even attended a class in Ochrid,

[75] FO 371/12856, memorandum by Footman, attached to C1955, 6/3/1928.
[76] See his reports for 1927 and 1925 in FO 371/12092, C9610, 23/11/1927, and FO 371/10793, C9288, 6/7/1925.
[77] FO 371/9659, C2378, 7/2/1924.   [78] FO 371/12091, C8807, 26/10/1927.

where he found the teaching of French and history 'of a higher standard than in England'. It is not difficult, however, to discover the reason behind the sudden flourishing of French in an area where the majority of the population could not even read in its own language.[79] Kennard's visit, as he himself admitted, was official and 'under the aegis of the local authorities'.[80]

By the turn of the decade, however, the Foreign Office had become the recipient of more information, pointing to the increasing improvement of the administration in the province. Kennard reported in 1929 that efforts had been made for the replacement of corrupt officials with a 'certain number of Croats and Slovenes', while in 1931 and in 1933, following tours in the area by the military attaché Major Oxley and T. D. Daly, it was concluded that 'Southern Serbia is gradually becoming resigned to the Yugoslav idea'.[81] These reports delighted Henderson. 'The Macedonian', he wrote confidently, 'will settle down to become as good a Yugoslav as any citizen.'[82]

Yet again, despite the optimistic reports, it was realized that the Macedonian Question would not easily be solved within the framework of a centralized Yugoslavia. Kennard hesitantly admitted that 'the fairest solution' would be an autonomous Macedonia, including all three parts of this region. But he was quick to correct himself: 'it cannot be done for 1,500,000 Greek refugees have swamped the Saloniki region. It [i.e. Macedonia] must therefore be either Yugoslav or Bulgarian, and as it had become Yugoslav by the decision of arms and treaty, the most we can do is to insist on the enlightened regime.'[83] Others were not prepared to go that far. Footman regarded Serbian dominance of

---

[79] In 1929, *Politika* published statistical data on illiteracy in Yugoslavia. Southern Serbia had the dubious privilege of being the most illiterate province (84%). The national average was 52%. FO 371/13710, C899, 29/1/1929.

[80] FO 371/11405, C6187, 26/5/1926.

[81] FO 371/13571, C4589, 17/6/1929; FO 371/16828, C4601, 15/5/1933; FO 371/15173, C3943, 9/6/1931.

[82] Comments by Henderson on the 1933 report, FO 371/16828, C4601, 15/5/1933. It should be noted that the FO derived much information on the situation prevailing in Macedonia from an unnamed 'usual secret source', which was frequently quoted and was regarded as 'extremely reliable'. According to this 'source', in the beginning of the 1930s IMRO's influence in Yugoslav Macedonia was in considerable decline, while the assimilation process was making gradual but steady progress. Cf. FO 371/15174, C8858, 25/11/1931; FO 371/15173, C3411, 14/5/1931.

[83] FO 371/13710, C7093, 10/9/1929. Cf. his view, in 1928, that 'a real solution would be an autonomous Macedonia, but this would involve tearing up the peace treaties'. FO 371/12855, C939, 31/1/1928.

Yugoslavia as the major obstacle to any progress in the area, and argued that 'a remedy can be local autonomy' in a future government, where the Croats and the Slovenes would be in a preponderant position.[84] Even Sir Orme Sargent, who was always careful enough, felt that the only way for the alleviation of the situation in Macedonia was 'some sort of local autonomy . . . which the centralised Yugoslav government cannot contemplate'.[85] Since Belgrade could not tolerate even the idea of local autonomy, the most Britain could do was to press for administrative improvement; and so they did, on many occasions.[86]

If the ministers in Belgrade insisted that the assimilation of the Macedonians would eventually be achieved, those in Sofia had more doubts. Being closer to the Bulgarian viewpoint, they felt that more radical measures should be taken, if the Macedonian Question were ever to be solved. The proposed remedies threatened the cornerstone of British policy, and, therefore, provoked a heated debate. In 1928 Sperling, running out of patience with this intractable question, let the Foreign Office know that 'I hold no brief for the Macedonians, the Bulgarians or any of the other semi-civilised races inhabiting the Balkan peninsula. Sentiment is out of place in dealing with these races.' Having thus declared his impartiality, he asserted that 'nothing will make the Macedonians abandon their aspirations'. As a result, instead of asking Belgrade to improve the administration in the area, the British should consider 'some frontier rectification'. Sargent's reply was unequivocal: 'you may prove to be a true prophet, but I fear that you would suffer the fate of all prophets in their own country'. The treaties should be respected, he added, not because they are perfect, but because 'in this naughty world they offer the best means of preserving peace'.[87]

This short reply, however, did not deter Sperling from raising again the issue, referring to the needs of the 'Macedonian minority' in Yugoslavia, and asking for a survey by the League of Nations. This time he had gone too far, and the Central Department did not mince their words. Sperling's attempt to substantiate his arguments were a 'dismal failure', minuted C. H. Bateman. The Macedonians might have called themselves so, but 'they have no political consciousness. Prior

[84] FO 371/12856, C1311, 16/12/1928.
[85] FO 371/12855, minute attached to C730, dated 2/2/1929.
[86] FO 371/12856, C1955, 6/3/1928, for Kennard's advice to the Yugoslavs to improve their administrative record.
[87] FO 371/12856, C2670, 22/3/1928, and Sargent's minute, attached to C2670, 5/4/1928.

to the war they called themselves Greeks, Bulgars, or Serbs according to the circumstances.' On racial grounds, he concluded, there was no 'Macedonian' minority in Yugoslavia. Sargent attempted a more thorough, but no less argumentative, response. 'What is a Macedonian minority', he wrote, is a question that Sperling had failed to answer. 'Some of them call themselves Macedonians, but why we should consent to give them a name which coincides with a territory, which has been the bone of contention and has not been an autonomous entity for a 1,000 years.' Moreover, he argued that the term Macedonia refers to a region which the Slavs alone should not be allowed to appropriate. He reminded Sperling that there were also Turks, Albanians, Greeks, and Vlachs in Macedonia. 'They also could have the right to be called Macedonians.'[88]

Sidney Waterlow voiced similar arguments. The Bulgaro-Macedonians were an oppressed minority, which had been forcefully Serbianized. This was not a question of bad administration. 'I do not share the department's view', he wrote in 1930, 'that Macedonia had never been a geographical or racial entity.' He suggested, consequently, a 'united and independent Macedonia' which could serve as 'a link between their Serb and Bulgarian brothers'. The ultimate solution of this intractable problem should be nothing less than a Bulgar–Yugoslav federation with Macedonia as a unit. 'What blessing that would be.' Waterlow's 'solutions' were not confined only to Macedonia. After a visit to the districts of Tsaribrod and Bosilegrad—lost to Yugoslavia after the war—he was of the opinion that they should be incorporated into Bulgaria. This revisionist outburst was not left unanswered by the Foreign Office. An autonomous Macedonia was not 'a logical idea', minuted John Balfour, for the Greeks would oppose it, and the Albanians might claim 'their part', risking a general conflagration. Besides, a 'Bulgaro-Macedonian consciousness' was not entrenched among the population. It could be found 'here and there', but the majority 'just wanted to be left in peace'. As far as rectification was concerned, even the idea horrified the Central Department. A greater Bulgaria would certainly whet the Hungarian appetite, noted Balfour. Sargent's reaction, however, was the most telling: 'For heaven's sake, don't let us butt in.'[89]

---

[88]　The debate is recorded in FO 371/12856, C7743, 10/10/1928, and C7743.

[89]　FO 371/14316, C4187, Waterlow to FO, 21/5/1930, and minute by Balfour [in the FO (1929–32), chargé d' affaires in Sofia (1932–5) and in Belgrade

Needless to say, the Foreign Office found in Henderson a forceful ally who persistently argued that the Macedonians could not be regarded as a minority; they were only linguistically closer to Bulgaria.[90]

So, according to most British there was no Bulgarian minority in Yugoslav Macedonia: Macedonians and Serbs were classified as 'first cousins',[91] and the British officials were instructed to mind their language when referring to these relatives. 'In public', insisted Balfour in 1932, the term 'Macedonian' should be used instead of 'Bulgarian'. The used of the latter 'prejudges the issue', while 'Macedonia is an accepted geographical term and not open to political misconstruction'.[92] As a result, the League of Nations had no reason to invent a non-existent minority, nor should it be allowed to internationalize the whole issue. The conflicting interests of the Great Powers would hardly fail to produce deadlock and friction, causing, thus, irreparable damage to the prestige of the organization. The British had learned the lesson of the League's intervention in the Balkans, following the Greek invasion of Bulgaria in 1925, very well. In that case, the Greeks were to blame beyond any doubt, and unanimity was easily achieved, without causing any dissension.[93] In the Bulgar-Yugoslav dispute, however, France and Italy, stood on opposite sides of the fence. Moreover, neither party had absolutely clean hands. The Yugoslavs were maltreating the Macedonians, and harbouring the Bulgarian Agrarians. The Bulgarians, on the other hand, tacitly allowed IMRO to carry on its terrorist attacks, and had been allowing notorious personalities, such as Ivan Mihailov and his gunmen, to stroll Sofia's streets, obliging politicians to be accompanied by a half-dozen bodyguards when walking about. There was no chance, therefore, of the League solving the Macedonian Question. Any attempt to raise the problem in this 'wider international arena, could hardly fail to defeat its own ends by arousing such fierce passions and prejudices that the Council of the League would

(1935–6); after 1940, in the FO] attached. FO 371/14317, C5989, Waterlow to FO, 22/7/1930, and minutes by Sargent, and Busk. FO 371/14318, C7382, Waterlow to FO, 22/9/1930, and minute by Balfour. FO 371/14318, C8171, Waterlow to Henderson, 30/10/1930.

⁹⁰ FO 371/14315, C2507, 31/3/1930.

⁹¹ Balfour made this comment on Slavic kinship in a minute in FO 371/14318, minute attached to C7382, 22/9/1930.

⁹² FO 371/15896, C4930, 14/6/1932, memorandum by Balfour. He had, nevertheless, to wait for 12 years to realize that he was not that good a prophet.

⁹³ For the settlement of this question by the League see James Barros, *The League of Nations and the Great Powers: The Greek–Bulgarian Incident of 1925* (Oxford, 1970).

scarcely be able to achieve the unanimity necessary to impose a final settlement'.[94]

This view, however, was not universally shared, and the Foreign Office was frequently obliged to put up with demands for League intervention. Coming from a wide variety of quarters, these demands were put forward by all those who, by conviction or position, held the view that the Bulgarian population of Yugoslav Macedonia was being subjected to a harsh process of denationalization. Their common denominator was that they stressed the need for an inquiry, sponsored by the League, to investigate Yugoslav policy towards the 'Bulgarian minority'. Naturally, IMRO was a vocal advocate of such a measure: if bombs failed to attract international attention, they had every reason to hope that an international investigation would do so. Thus, many petitions were sent to the League, lodged by individuals with strong links with IMRO, asking for minority rights and the introduction of the Bulgarian language in the schools and churches of Yugoslav Macedonia. A former *député de parlement Yugoslave,* G. Anastasov, and a former *maire de Skopje,* D. Challev, were quite energetic in this direction.[95] In the Foreign Office, it was unanimously agreed that these petitions should not even be discussed in the League. The raising of this issue to the League 'will give life to MRO', argued Balfour.[96] Sargent fully agreed: 'the longer the League avoids to pronounce on the matter the better'. Moreover, the Macedonians could not claim minority rights, for they had no nationality: the idea of a 'separate Macedonian nationality', he minuted, was 'against the obvious trend of political evolution in the Balkans'. It will obstruct the 'natural . . . and inevitable tendency of the Slavophone population to be assimilated by the more masterful and expanding Yugoslav race'.[97] Thus, the petitions should not be brought to the council. Commenting on the 1931 petition, Alexander Cadogan was quite clear, and even graphic: 'It might be better to strangle it at birth and declare

[94] 1930 memorandum Cf. C. H. Bateman's memorandum on 'Minorities in the Balkans' in FO 371/12092, C9803, 23/11/1927. League's involvement, it was stated, 'will create bitterness, and will do nothing to alter the fundamental conditions in Macedonia'.

[95] In 1931 and in 1932, they lodged two petitions with the League. For the texts (in French) see FO 371/15173, C7413, 30/9/1931; FO 371/15895, C3763, 29/4/1932.

[96] It should be noted that the IMRO paper *Svoboda ili Smŭrt,* gave much publicity to the petitions, which 'have caused great pleasure'.

[97] See FO 371/15173, Balfour's memorandum, and minute by Sargent attached to C8388, dated 11/11/1931.

it non-receivable, if we can honestly do so.'[98] They could. The petition was examined by a committee of three representatives, including
a Briton, which promptly agreed with the official Yugoslav argument that the petitioners maintained *liaison spéciales . . . avec certaines
organisations terroristes* (that is, IMRO). Consequently it was declared
non-receivable. Many more petitions, asking for similar concessions,
were lodged with the League, only to follow the same short cut into
oblivion.

Despite the Foreign Office's determination to 'strangle' any attempt
to involve the League in the Macedonian imbroglio, others remained
undeterred. Noel Buxton and the Balkan Committee, for instance,
appeared to be tireless. From 1924 onwards, Buxton had repeatedly
asked the Foreign Office to reconsider its view on the issue, and,
although he always received polite but firm answers, he continued
to fire off memoranda, private letters, and parliamentary questions,
urging them, among other things, to grant minority rights to the
'Bulgaro-phone population' of Yugoslavia and Greece. His reputation
as a 'notorious Bulgarophil' was well known in the Foreign Office, but
his tendency to consider 'politeness as concurrence' irritated them. As
he seemed to ignore their replies to his enquiries, Cadogan decided
in 1929 that he should receive no more: 'It has been acknowledged',
he minuted on the last vintage of memoranda by Buxton; 'that is
sufficient.'[99]

If Buxton's demands could easily be dealt with, much more effort
was needed to restrain the Balkan Slavs. Every time the Macedonian
Question raised the local temperature, normally following a serious
IMRO raid, the Yugoslavs were quick to warn Sofia that they would
call upon the League to investigate the ties of the organization with
the Bulgarian government. The Bulgarians, on the other hand, were
no less keen on inviting the League to alleviate the treatment of
the 'Bulgarian minority' of Southern Serbia. Caught in this irritating
crossfire, the British spared no effort to cool their ardour. 'The only
way is moderation in both sides,' minuted Sargent in 1930. The League
would open a question it could not close again, and, therefore, its

[98] Minute by Cadogan [Counsellor at the FO, Permanent Under-Secretary of State
for Foreign Affairs (1939–46)], in FO 371/15173, dated 2/9/1931.
[99] For Buxton's activities see FO 371/9659, C3719, 29/3/1924 (memorandum),
FO 371/12091, C8852, 2/11/1927 (memorandum by the Balkan Committee), FO
371/12092, 15/11/1927 (parliamentary question), FO 371/13572, C5973, 5/8/1929
(memorandum by the Balkan Committee), and Cadogan's minute attached.

prestige would be damaged. So, 'let the sleeping dogs lie'.[100] Both sides, however, had been repeatedly upsetting them, or threatening to do so. As a result the British ministers often gave them stern warnings, reminding them of the risks involved if Pandora's box was opened in Geneva.[101] As the 1920s were coming to a close, it appeared that the British were achieving all their objectives. The Yugoslav threats to 'take the law into their hands' never materialized, the tension provoked by IMRO failed to trigger a large-scale military incident, and neither party appealed to the League of Nations. 'The sleeping dogs' of the Macedonian Question, despite some occasional barking, were left in peace.

As has already been seen, the British had always stressed the need for a rapprochement between Bulgaria and Yugoslavia. Developments in the mid-1930s, however, clearly demonstrated that a serious effort for cooperation might bring the two countries too close for Britain's comfort. The suppression of IMRO in 1934 greatly facilitated a hesitant rapprochement, which survived the Marseilles murder, and led to the conclusion of the 'Pact of Perpetual Friendship' in 1937.[102] This dramatic change in Bulgar–Yugoslav relations, although it left much to be desired, prompted the British to consider its possible ramifications. They were not alone. In July 1933—as the first signs of a rapprochement emerged in Sofia and Belgrade[103]—the anxious Greeks rushed to communicate to the Foreign Office their fear that a sudden South Slav understanding might unduly strengthen their hand, allowing them to pursue a more 'aggressive policy' towards Greece.[104]

What particularly concerned the British was whether the new twist could be seen as the forerunner of a South Slav union. The suspicion, to say the least, of a solid Slav bloc, extending from the Adriatic to the Black Sea, had never been absent from the Foreign Office. By emphasizing the

---

[100] FO 371/14314, minute by Sargent, attached to C1992, 12/3/1930.

[101] The Yugoslavs threatened to appeal to the League after the murder of General Kovačević in 1927, and after the outrages in Pirot and Nish, in 1930. It appeared, however, that they were not always prepared to do so. FO 371/14317, C5045, 18/6/1930, Henderson to FO. In any case, Kennard and Henderson, while giving their usual 'advice' for moderation, missed no opportunity to dissuade the king from considering a formal appeal (see above). The same course of action was followed by the British ministers in Sofia.

[102] See Ch. 1.

[103] From April onwards, a wave of visits was exchanged between prelates, businessmen, and groups of students (Yugoslav 'Sokols' and Bulgarian 'Yunaks'). FO 371/18373, C2627, Annual Report for Bulgaria in 1933.

[104] FO 371/16775, C7031, 21/7/1933, recording Greek concerns by the acting foreign minister.

common South Slav stock of Bulgarians, Macedonians, and Serbs, the British tended to regard the Bulgar–Yugoslav feuds as manifestations of 'family quarrels'. Consequently, the fear that kinship would eventually extinguish the flames of history and politics was ever present. In 1925 Erskine had sent London an IMRO resolution calling for an autonomous Macedonia in a Balkan federation, and in his comment upon this possibility, painted a picture that was destined to haunt the Foreign Office for years to come: 'An autonomous Macedonian state from Kavalla to Ochrid and from Uskub [Skopje] to Salonika will one day be evolved.' Bulgaria would follow suit; then 'a vast Slav state will exist. This will not be wholly to our advantage but clearly we can do nothing to prevent it.'[105] In 1934 the spectre of a Slav federation flickered again, and sparked off a significant debate. The framework for this debate was provided by a long and thoughtful memorandum by Sir Nevile Henderson, written in March.[106] Henderson, after a thorough review of the question of Bulgar–Yugoslav relations—in which the racial affinities of the Balkan Slavs were given much prominence—emphasized that it was a 'fundamental error' to believe that a Bulgar–Yugoslav union would maintain peace in the Balkans. 'Peace', he argued, 'ends where Serb, or rather Yugoslav-Bulgar, union begins . . . With the Balkan states as at present constituted, the balance of power is fairly well distributed. But this is at once altered if Bulgaria unites with Yugoslavia.' Romania, Greece, and Turkey would all feel the pressure of a united 'Yugoslav'—i.e. 'South Slav'—state of more than 20,000,000 people. In assessing the possibilities for such a gloomy prospect, Henderson was cautious but no less alarmist. Although 'actually union would be premature', he felt that 'time is an asset and not a drawback. Nevertheless, as a question of reality it is appreciably nearer than it was two years ago.'[107]

These conclusions did not fail to make a deep impression in the Foreign Office. Rodney Gallop fully shared Henderson's fears, and added another important dimension: 'we have to apprehend another eventuality at some future date when Soviet Russia has got over her growing pains, i.e. a strong pan-Slav bloc in Eastern Europe, threatening our own interests in the Middle East'. A Balkan federation, therefore, 'would

[105] FO 371/10667, C3734, 2/3/1925, Erskine to FO, and minute by Nicolson attached.
[106] FO 371/18369, R1543, 'A Memorandum on the Influence of the Yugoslav Ideal on Balkan Politics', enclosure in Henderson to FO.
[107] Ibid.

emphatically *not* be in our best interests'.[108] The other British ministers in the Balkans voiced similar views. Waterlow, now in Athens, also pointed to future complications: 'the problem of the future is the tendency of the South Slavs to coalesce', he told the Foreign Office. He argued, however, that if Slav unity was achieved it 'would be jelly rather than granite'. From Sofia, Sir Charles Bentinck thought that the question was 'somewhat hypothetical', but he agreed that the ultimate aim of a Balkan federation would be access to the Aegean.[109] Thus, suspicion lingered in the Foreign Office, but the Yugoslavs, who had got wind of British fears, categorically dispelled them. In September 1934, a senior Yugoslav official told a member of the British delegation to the League of Nations, that his country desired neither a federation, nor a revision of borders. Yugoslavia, he stated, would never support Bulgarian designs against Greece, nor would she allow the rapprochement with Bulgaria to jeopardize her links with the Little Entente. These assurances were received with relief tempered by scepticism: 'all to the good', minuted Gallop, 'although they may be conveniently forgotten in a few years' time'.[110]

Yet again, the British continued to watch closely what they perceived as an unfolding battle between blood and politics. In 1936 John Balfour, in a memorandum on 'Integral Yugoslavia', remarked that despite 'a hereditary tradition of enmity . . . it is not possible to draw a fundamental distinction of blood, religion or language between Bulgarians and Serbs'. Given this racial background, a Balkan federation might be formed, with Salonica and the Aegean as its 'natural outlets'. He could derive some comfort, however, from the fact that Prince Paul entertained no plans of this sort. He just wanted 'national consolidation', while a Balkan union was favoured only by the Croats, and some Belgrade intellectuals and journalists.[111] The following years, however, were to show that Balfour's list was incomplete.

---

[108] Underlined in the original. Gallop's minute, dated 15/3/1934, attached to FO 371/18369, R1543.

[109] FO 371/18370, R (Southern Department) 3527, Bentinck to FO, 30/5/1934; ibid. R3417, Waterlow to FO, 6/6/1934.

[110] FO 371/18370, R5051, 12/9/1934, and minute by Gallop dated 14/9/1934. Gallop was a good prophet: when Tito, in 1944, set out to create a South Slav federation, the Yugoslavs had forgotten all about it. The British proved to have had a stronger memory. As shall be seen, in 1944 Sir Orme Sargent argued against a Balkan federation by citing Henderson's remarks of 1934.

[111] FO 371/20434, R3104, Balfour's memorandum, dated 16/5/1936.

During the interwar period, Britain considered the Macedonian Question a 'sleeping dog' which should be allowed to lie at all costs. The pet itself, the Foreign Office thought, was incapable of producing serious problems. The Macedonians had no nationality to defend, despite IMRO's efforts to awake the 'sleeping beauty' of Bulgarian nationalism with bombs and assassinations, as they had done in the late nineteenth century. From such a view, which was both a deeply entrenched belief and a convenient hope, it followed that the Serbs did not have an impossible job to do, provided they granted the population a decent administration. Although fully aware of their shortcomings in doing so, the British tended to believe that, by the early 1930s, the assimilation of the Macedonians was making steady headway. Wartime developments, however, proved them wrong. It should be stressed, nevertheless, that they realized that the pet had to be accommodated somehow. A 'limited' autonomy, a 'local' one, or even a 'federal Yugoslav state' were some solutions the Foreign Office had thought of, but were incapable of enforcing. In a paradoxical way, it was Tito who would undertake this task.

There were, of course, more radical views, expressed mainly by British ministers in Sofia: border rectification, minority rights, and a Balkan federation with Macedonia as a unit. Such views were never approved by the Foreign Office; nor did they allow others to entertain them. The Balkan Slavs should learn to live together; but not in the same state. The creation of a Balkan federation could give the Macedonian 'dogs' enough room for manoeuvring. If this was allowed to occur, Salonica, no less than Adrianople, would feel their teeth. In 1934, the British were presented with an opportunity to reckon with such a danger; and they fully appreciated its profound ramifications. At that time, however, the question was 'hypothetical', and the Yugoslavs rushed to confirm this. In fact, the British had no reason to hurry matters. In 1934, the leader of the Yugoslav communists was one Gorkić.[112]

---

[112] Milan Gorkić was the leader of the CPY from 1932 to 1937, when he was accused of being an 'agent' and was succeeded by Tito. See Charles Zalar, *Yugoslav Communism: A Critical Study* (Washington DC 1961), 44–5.

PART II

WARTIME, 1939–1945

3

Chronicle of Failures Foretold: Britain and Bulgar–Yugoslav Relations, 1939–1943

THE IMPROBABLE RAPPROCHEMENT, 1939–1941

As the clouds of war started to gather over Europe at the end of the 1930s, the main British concern regarding the Balkans was to keep the area out of the German orbit by establishing a neutral bloc which would consist of Greece, Turkey, Bulgaria, and Yugoslavia. It was hoped that such a solution would not only relieve them of the military burden of sending an expeditionary force to the area, which they could not afford, but also minimize Italy's irritation.[1] If this plan were to succeed, however, an understanding had to be reached between Bulgaria and her neighbours. In this context, relations between Sofia and Belgrade were of paramount importance. As has already been seen, the interwar years had erected a thick veil of mutual suspicion and mistrust. It was to the frustration of the British that they found this veil impossible to lift.

The last years of the 1930s had been sending conflicting messages in this respect. In 1937, a laconic but ambitious 'Pact of Perpetual Friendship' was concluded between Yugoslavia and Bulgaria, which was followed in 1938 by the 'Salonica Agreement', signed by Bulgaria and the states of the Balkan Entente.[2] Despite the official rhetoric of the Balkan governments, however, this agreement did very little to bring about a substantial improvement in Bulgar–Yugoslav relations. True, the British Embassy in Sofia observed a significant 'Yugoslav influence'

---

[1] Elisabeth Barker, *British Policy in South-East Europe in the Second World War* (London, 1976), 11.

[2] For the pact see Chapter 1. In the Salonica Agreement the use of force was renounced, while Bulgaria was allowed to increase the size of her army. J. B. Hoptner, *Yugoslavia in Crisis, 1934–1941* (New York and London, 1962), 162.

in Bulgaria after the signature of the Pact, but they were reluctant to go any further. Bulgarian nervousness could hardly be concealed; they had suppressed IMRO in 1934, and they felt they deserved more concrete gestures from the Yugoslav side than just the removal of some miles of barbed wire along the frontier. King Boris appeared to be particularly disturbed about the situation, and in January 1938 remarked to the British minister in Sofia that the pact had failed 'to fulfill the purpose, which [he] attributed to it'.[3]

The Salonica Agreement seemed to have made no greater an impact. Although minor manifestations of solidarity did occur that year, which included a settlement of trade accounts, a direct air service from Sofia to Belgrade, and various visits by students and theatrical groups, a sense of disappointment was evident in Sofia. As was only to be expected, the Macedonian Question lay at the heart of the Bulgarian complaints. It was felt that, although they appeared to have—temporarily—shelved their irredentist claims against Belgrade, the Yugoslavs did not respond accordingly, for almost nothing had been done to ease the policy of 'Serbianization', so much resented in Sofia. Bulgarian papers were still banned in large areas of Yugoslav Macedonia, and even mail from Bulgaria was not delivered in the area, on the grounds of a technicality.[4] As far as Greece was concerned, the situation appeared to be no less disappointing. Athens had never been convinced that Bulgarian territorial aspirations had been put in cold storage, and the recent rapprochement between Sofia and Belgrade, no matter how fragile it was, raised new fears. As a result, any genuine understanding was impaired by a firmly rooted suspicion of Bulgaria's true intentions. Thus, after the pattern of Bulgar–Yugoslav relations, a number of minor signs of cooperation, concerning mainly economic matters, failed to cut much ice with Sofia.[5]

To make matters worse, the Munich settlement in 1938 caused a major sensation in Bulgaria. This substantial exercise in revisionism pointed to the Bulgarians the road they had to travel if their demands

[3] FO 371/22129, Annual Report for Bulgaria, 1937.

[4] The Yugoslavs insisted that no mail could be delivered in Macedonia, unless it bore the name of the addressee in Serbian. See ibid. For the limited repercussions of the Salonica Agreement see FO 371/23733, Annual Report for Bulgaria, 1938.

[5] For British assessments of Bulgar–Greek relations see: FO 371/23733, Annual Report for Bulgaria for 1938, and 22129, Annual Report for Bulgaria for 1937. In fact, Greek fears were so intense that the British felt obliged to reassure the Greek government that they did not encourage Bulgarian claims against Greece.

were ever to be met. Naturally, Bulgarian irredentism received a major boost after Munich, further complicating Sofia's delicate external relations. King Boris, however, assured the British minister, George Rendel, that he was making every effort to 'canalize' all irredentist agitation towards Southern Dobrudja, rather than Macedonia.[6] According to the British, the king's effort was somewhat facilitated by the fact that most Bulgarians had been feeling 'heartily sick' of the Macedonian terrorist activities.[7]

But the flow of the Vardar river could not be easily stopped, despite the efforts of Boris and his premier, Georgi Kioseivanov. As the 1930s faded away, Bulgaria's enthusiasm for the 1937 pact, if there had been any, was growing very thin indeed. In February 1939, the British Legation in Sofia reported that, although Bulgar–Yugoslav relations appeared to be 'satisfactory', only two Bulgarian papers, one being the official *Mir*, took the trouble to spare the pact a few lines, in contrast to the Yugoslav press which gave it more publicity. The prohibition of the Bulgarian press in Yugoslav Macedonia and the general Yugoslav policy on this question, were again cited as the causes of the Bulgarian's chilling attitude.[8] Apart from fuelling Bulgarian complaints, the Macedonian Question presented the British with another potentially dangerous development, namely the exploitation of this issue by either Rome or Berlin, in order to deepen the gulf between the two Slav states.

Kioseivanov, who appeared to be particularly anxious to improve bilateral relations, alarmed Rendel, in April 1939, about the possibility of renewed Italian 'intrigues' in Yugoslav Macedonia. The Bulgarian premier, 'extremely nervous' about this possibility, was certain that the Italians would not hesitate to rekindle the Macedonian flames 'if Yugoslavia behaved badly'.[9] British reports about the whereabouts of the notorious IMRO leader Ivan ('Vancho') Mihailov suggested that Kioseivanov's fears were not unfounded. All available information confirmed that Mihailov was in close contact with the Italians, and might have been hiding in Albania or Italy. In April, it was reported that he had been seen in Poland where he stayed at the expense of the

---

[6] Sir George Rendel, *The Sword and the Olive* (London, 1957), 171. Southern Dobrudja, where Bulgarians formed the largest ethnic group, was lost to Romania under the provisions of the Treaty of Bucharest, in 1913. For a brief period during the Great War Bulgaria regained the region, but they were forced to give it back to Romania in 1919.

[7] FO 371/23733, Annual Report for Bulgaria.

[8] FO 371/23727, R789, 28/2/1939.   [9] FO 371/23724, R2566, 11/4/1939.

German government. Even more worrying were reports to the effect that Mihailov had urged his followers in Yugoslav Macedonia to fight against Belgrade, apparently with the backing of Germany. Such a possibility was corroborated by a statement of the German minister in Belgrade, von Heesen, who said that, if Yugoslavia were to take any measure against the Macedonian separatists, it would be interpreted by his government as an 'unfriendly' move towards Sofia.[10]

It was renewed Italian concern with Macedonia that again focused British interest on this area. During 1939 and 1940, the British had been receiving reports indicating a surge in Italian interest in the area. In January 1941 Ronald Campbell, the British minister in Belgrade, sent the Foreign Secretary Lord Halifax a detailed report by the British vice-consul at Skopje, Thomas. According to this report, during the last months of 1939, the Italians had been trying to awake the Albanian factor. They had been very active in Kosovo and in the western, Albanian-speaking, part of Yugoslav Macedonia, where they were trying to stir up Albanian national sentiment by spreading rumours about a 'Greater Albania', and circulating irredentist literature and maps. The British vice-consul, however, remarked that not much headway had been made among the 'politically passive' Albanian peasants. Only their religious teachers, the Hodzas, were to a certain extent responsive to the Italian propaganda. The rest remained rather suspicious, due to their belief that the Italians were maltreating their kin 'over the frontier'. As far as the Slav-Macedonians were concerned, Thomas reached the conclusion that, although 90 per cent of the population certainly wanted some sort of autonomy from Belgrade, the demise of IMRO after 1934 had reduced support for a union with Bulgaria, and that most Macedonians would favour a federal restructuring of the Yugoslav state, with Macedonia being a unit within this state.[11]

The apparent ability of Italy, Germany, or the Soviet Union to capitalize on the national question in order to embarrass Yugoslavia or to lure Bulgaria, was a major cause of concern for the British. Britain had been, rightly, perceived by Bulgaria as a rigid supporter of the peace settlements, and this constituted a major liability in British approaches to Sofia. Yet, the necessity of keeping Bulgaria away of the German

[10] Information about Mihailov's activities in FO 371/23728, R3625 (FO minute), and R3099, 21/4/1939.
[11] FO 371/29785, R145, 6/1/1941. For further reports on Italian propaganda among the Albanians see FO 371/25030, R7684, 4/7/1940.

orbit, had persuaded some British officials that their dogmatism had to be tempered.

On 15 April 1939, Leo Amery, the wartime Secretary of State for India, reverted to the need to 'keep Bulgaria straight' and suggested to Halifax that he draw a lesson from the 1915 experience. Then, Amery argued, Germany had offered not only territories, but also '350,000 soldiers on the Danube'. In his view, the British should follow the same line. Thus, he proposed that Britain should give Bulgaria direct military help, consisting of five divisions. Regarding territorial transfers, Amery was cautious enough not to argue for the cessation of Macedonia to Bulgaria. Instead, 'we might persuade Rumania to give up Dobrudja'.[12] Amery was not alone in suggesting that at least a part of Bulgarian irredentism had to be accommodated by London. Rendel considered the Dobrudja question 'the easiest to deal with', and, indeed, he seemed to pin many hopes on the cessation of this province to Bulgaria. Such a move, coupled with a more sensible administration in Yugoslav Macedonia, would compensate Sofia for abandoning her Macedonian claims, and, therefore, would drive her closer to Britain.[13]

Military necessities, however, and the British fear of opening the Pandora's box of revisionism, militated against the suggestions put forward by Amery and Rendel. For a start, the dispatch of a British force in the Balkans had to be ruled out. 'Easier said than done,' commented a Foreign Office official on Amery's proposals. 'The Chief-of-Staff as well as the French will have something to say on the point.'[14] The card of cautious revisionism received a somewhat higher consideration, and in October Halifax seemed to favour it.[15] Yet again, nothing came out of this consideration, for fear of unravelling an uncontrollable wave of revisionist claims from Hungary or Russia, eventually carried the day. Besides, the Romanians were not prepared to cede Dobrudja in 1939, and flatly rejected any suggestion that they should; nor were the British prepared to press them strongly to do so. As shall be seen, the British were forced to change their attitude on the Dobrudja question, but only when other, more stout advocates of revisionism, had already stolen the wind from the British sails.

Thus, at the outbreak of war in Europe, the situation in the Balkans left much to be desired for the British. But the need to drive Bulgaria

---

[12] FO 371/23727, R3499, 15/4/1939.   [13] Rendel, *Sword*, 158.
[14] FO 371/23727, minutes attached to R3499.
[15] Barker, *British Policy*, 11, quoting Halifax to War Cabinet, 26/10/1939.

closer to Yugoslavia acquired particular importance. Halifax understood this perfectly well when he told the War Cabinet that Bulgaria was 'the key to the Balkans'.[16] But if the key was to be turned on the British side, then they had to act sooner rather than later, for the Germans might bring about a Bulgar–Yugoslav rapprochement first. Fears about a rapprochement under German auspices were given some circulation in the Foreign Office, shortly before the outbreak of war. In July 1939, Rendel raised the issue, informing London that, according to American sources, Kioseivanov was trying to negotiate a close Bulgar–Yugoslav understanding, guaranteed by Germany.[17] Rendel himself was rather reluctant to accept such a view, and despite his close observation of recent manifestations of Bulgar–Yugoslav solidarity, including a visit to Sofia by Yugoslav youth groups (Sokols), he failed to detect any Nazi 'taints'.[18] However, Kioseivanov's activity in mid-July, when on his way back to Sofia from Berlin he had talks with Prince Paul, caused some concern, and begged an unequivocal Yugoslav statement. This was duly delivered by the Yugoslav Minister for Foreign Affairs, Aleksandar Cincar-Marković, shortly afterwards. The minister decisively allayed the British fear by saying that there was 'no foundation for it of any kind'. The British were relieved to confirm where the sympathy of Prince Paul actually lay. As a minute put it: 'some good may have been done by this exchange of views'.[19]

Still, if the Germans had not managed to establish a Bulgar–Yugoslav bloc, the British could not register much more progress either. But, as was usually the case in the past, British opinions diverged significantly, both in assessing the causes of this unfortunate situation and on recommending the appropriate remedies. From Sofia, Sir George Rendel, being closer to Bulgarian anxieties, remarked that a serious problem in Bulgar–Yugoslav relations was the personal hostility felt by Prince Paul towards King Boris. This, along with the Bulgarian resentment of the prohibition of Bulgarian papers from Macedonia, was a permanent feature of his talks with Kioseivanov. The latter, however, admitted that the Yugoslav task was not an easy one. The Macedonians were not 'wholly Bulgarian', but 'obstinate and intractable people'. In any

---

[16] Barker, *British Policy*, 11, quoting Halifax to War Cabinet, 26/10/1939.
[17] FO 371/23727, R5463, 4/7/1939, R5896, 14/7/1939.
[18] FO 371/23727, R5687, 13/7/1939.
[19] FO 371/23727, R5703, 11/7/1939 (on Kioseivanov's meeting with Prince Paul), R5741, 13/7/1939 (for the Yugoslav assurances).

case, he thought that the Yugoslavs should treat them 'in a more liberal spirit'.[20]

That Prince Paul held strong views regarding the Bulgarian king was no secret to the British. Nor had he made any effort to conceal it. In December, Lord Lloyd of the Balkan Committee, during an audience with Prince Paul, assured him that Boris had given him 'his word of honour' as to his peaceful intentions. But Paul's mistrust was too deep to allow him to take royal promises at their face value. He laughed, and told Lord Lloyd he did not believe 'a single word'. He concluded by saying that Lloyd was just another 'victim of Boris' well known tactics'.[21] Reporting from Yugoslavia, Ronald Campbell, the British minister, was no less a captive of the view on the ground there. Although he did not share Paul's outspoken statements, he, nevertheless, held not entirely dissimilar views. He told the Foreign Office that Paul's suspicion of Boris's intentions was nothing personal, for this feeling was 'deeply rooted in Serbia'. Moreover, he felt that Yugoslavia had done enough for a rapprochement, and seemed to reject, politely but firmly, Rendel's charge that Yugoslavia's conduct had intensified Bulgaria's isolation and bitterness.[22]

In 1940, Bulgar–Yugoslav relations provoked an exchange of more heated arguments between Campbell and Rendel. In January 1940, the British legation at Belgrade furnished the Foreign Office with more Yugoslav views. The basic problem remained the same, namely the question of King Boris's true allegiances. Recent deliveries of German war material to Bulgaria had further fanned Yugoslav fears. Moreover, the Yugoslavs were questioning the gravity of Kioseivanov's influence in the shaping of Bulgaria's foreign policy. No doubt, he was a genuine supporter of friendship with Yugoslavia, but he was a diplomat, not a politician. So the Yugoslavs wondered 'whom did he really represent?'[23] Campbell appeared to throw his weight behind this reasoning. He was convinced that Sofia had no will to resist either Soviet or German pressure, and, therefore, no direct Yugoslav move to improve bilateral relations could be made. After having depicted Bulgaria as an almost hopeless case for Britain, his conclusion was by no means surprising: Britain should refrain from pressing Belgrade to make a move of

[20] FO 371/23727, R10545, 17/11/1939.
[21] FO 371/23727, R11729, 18/12/1939.
[22] FO 371/23727, R11744, 11/12/1939.
[23] FO 371/24881, R1969, 29/1/1940.

goodwill to Sofia. Any efforts towards this direction, he warned, would prove 'detrimental to our interests'.[24]

Such a profound sense of suspicion and mistrust on the part of the Yugoslavs certainly disappointed the Foreign Office. In January 1940, the prospects of establishing even a modicum of understanding between Bulgaria and Yugoslavia, not to mention a Balkan neutral bloc, looked as remote as ever. Having lost sight of any hope, since the Yugoslavs would not respond favourably to any British advice to make a conciliatory gesture towards Sofia, it was felt that perhaps things should be allowed to take their course. The prevailing trend was that nothing could be done to improve this particularly awkward situation, and therefore no specific instructions could be sent to the British ministers in the Balkans.[25]

At that time, only a slim chance of improvement shed some light onto this frustrating scenery, and it came from Turkey, rather than Sofia or Belgrade. The Turks had always been nervous about the German influence in Bulgaria, and shared Greek fears about the destabilizing role she could play. In late 1939, Turkish suspicions were further heightened by Bulgarian military concentrations along the Turco-Bulgarian frontier.[26] They were eager, nevertheless, to achieve a détente with Sofia. Both the British ambassador in Ankara, Sir Hugh Knatchbull-Hugessen, and Rendel worked tirelessly towards this end and in January 1940 an apparently successful visit was paid to Sofia by a special Turkish emissary, the distinguished diplomat Numan Menemencioğlu.[27] This was followed in February by a more formal visit by the Turkish foreign minister, Şükrü Saracoğlu. The Foreign Office could derive some comfort from Menemencioğlu's visit, especially because Cincar-Marković had intimated to Campbell that he hoped that some good could come out of these negotiations, which might have a positive impact on Bulgar–Yugoslav relations. In fact, it seemed for a brief moment that a Turco-Bulgarian understanding might have had wider repercussions in getting Bulgaria closer to her neighbours.

---

[24] FO 371/24881, R624, 8/1/1940.
[25] FO 371, minutes attached to R624 quoted above.
[26] FO 371/33128, R1650, memorandum produced by the FO R(esearch) D(epartment), at Balliol College, Oxford, entitled 'Notes on Bulgaria's position since the outbreak of war', dated 15/12/1941.
[27] For Rendel's efforts to achieve a Turco-Bulgarian détente see Rendel, *Sword*, 167. Menemencioğlu was an old friend of Rendel and his moderate views and hard-working manner greatly facilitated these deliberations.

As might be expected, Rendel was inclined to attach more importance to these deliberations than Campbell or the Foreign Office, for that matter. He felt, however, that his position was greatly strengthened, and in late January he reverted to the subject; this time with concrete proposals. After reiterating his views on the necessity of a rapprochement, if a barrier was to be erected against German and Russian influence, Rendel suggested that the Yugoslavs should take a number of initiatives. First, a top-level visit to Sofia, preferably by the Yugoslav premier or the Minister for Foreign Affairs, would settle the main issues at stake, and pave the way for a joint declaration of neutrality. Then, an ideal sequel would be a meeting between the two rulers. Anticipating Prince Paul's negative reaction, Rendel did not omit to suggest that a British royal letter could persuade the prince to put aside his personal feelings.[28]

Yet again, the view from Belgrade served as an antidote to Rendel's optimism. Campbell urged the Foreign Office not to send the proposed letter to Prince Paul, for its only outcome would be to 'leave us in an embarrassing and perhaps even a false position'. If there was to occur any improvement in Bulgar–Yugoslav relations, this could come only from within Yugoslavia, and not as a result of external pressure.[29]

Despite Rendel's strenuous efforts, the Foreign Office was left unmoved. It was agreed that any move on the part of the British would be unwelcome to Yugoslavia, and, therefore, 'serve no useful purpose'. It was with a sense of frustration, and perhaps with some hidden exasperation, that the Foreign Office took the trouble to refute Rendel's argumentation in late February. Apart from the fall of the Kioseivanov's government, who was succeeded in February by the pro-German Bogdan Filov, the officials of the Southern Department reminded Rendel of the crux of the matter: Germany and Russia, simply, 'can invade the Balkans more easily than we can'. Moreover, the Turco-Bulgarian agreement was rather a bad analogy, for, in this case, at least one power was willing to move, whereas neither Belgrade nor Sofia could be persuaded to act likewise. As a result 'no further action' was deemed necessary.[30]

Despite British pessimism, it was hoped that the convention of the Council of the Balkan Entente, scheduled for February in Belgrade,

---

[28] FO 371/24881, R1300, 21/1/1940.   [29] FO 371/24881, R1850, 1/2/1940.
[30] FO 371/24881, FO minutes, dated 22 and 23 Feb., attached to R2186, 10/2/1940, and minutes attached to R1300, 9/2/1040.

would alleviate the situation. In Belgrade, where the council held its last meeting, the Bulgarians were offered membership, and even a hint of some possible territorial concessions. But they declined the offer.[31] For the Yugoslavs, this refusal merely confirmed the pro-German orientation of the new Bulgarian government under Bogdan Filov. The Bulgarian foreign minister, Ivan Popov, explained later to Rendel the reasons behind this refusal: in his view, any kind of Balkan bloc with Bulgaria as a member would arouse the suspicion of Germany, which, in turn, would mean the coming of the war to the Balkans. It would be better for the Balkan states, Popov stressed, if Bulgaria remained neutral, and 'outside'.[32] Rendel shared this view. In January, he had suggested to Philip Nichols, of the Foreign Office, that the Yugoslav demand from Bulgaria to join the entente was like 'a sole convict in a prison joining the corps of Wardens'.[33]

From February 1940 onwards, it was becoming increasingly apparent that Britain had very little room for manoeuvre. Thus, in order to investigate any remaining options, the British diplomatic representatives in the Balkans were summoned to London in April for consultations. There, Rendel maintained again that there were still chances for a Bulgar–Yugoslav rapprochement, and again put forward his recommendation for a royal letter to Prince Paul. He also suggested that the Turks might be willing to offer their good offices for an improvement of the stalemate. As far as Bulgarian irredentism was concerned, Rendel stressed that an assurance of sorts had to be sent to King Boris, to the effect that the Bulgarian claims 'would not be overlooked'.[34] For a brief moment, Rendel could congratulate himself, for all his recommendations were endorsed by the Foreign Office. Consequently, Knatchbull-Hugessen was instructed to investigate the intentions of the Turks, and the dispatch of a royal letter, for which Rendel had fought so hard, was to be examined further.

Rendel returned to Sofia in a rather optimistic mood. But he was soon to realize that his victory in the London meeting was short-lived. Thus, the Turks found themselves unable to make any headway in bringing about any improvement in Bulgar–Yugoslav relations. On 27 May, Knatchhbull-Hugessen asked the Minister for Foreign Affairs whether any progress had been made. Saracoğlu 'replied in the negative'.

---

[31] For this meeting see J. B. Hoptner, *Yugoslavia*, 165.
[32] FO 371/24870, R6196, 15/5/1940.   [33] FO 371/24881, R1416, 23/1/1940.
[34] FO 371/24902, R4832, 11/4/1940.

Turkish pessimism was registered again in August.[35] The fate of the letter to Prince Paul was equally unfortunate. Rendel rushed to draft one in mid-May, urging the prince to take 'a timely personal initiative'. Although he was careful enough to acknowledge the prince's doubts regarding the Bulgarians' intentions, the matter was allowed to drop, for Campbell told the Foreign Office that the Yugoslav ruler was at the time 'very hot' on the Bulgarian question.[36]

Thus, in the summer of 1940, only the revisionist card was left to the British. Unfortunately for them, not only were they timid and rather clumsy practitioners of this art, but their timing was also wrong. For the initiative was in the hands of other actors less concerned with the effects of revisionism on their strategic interests. On 26 June, the Soviets presented Romania with an ultimatum asking for the cession of Bessarabia and Northern Bukovina. The Bulgarians seized the opportunity to press for their own claims on Dobrudja, and the press warmly supported the Russian moves. Shortly afterwards, in mid-July, the Bulgarian government tried unsuccessfully to negotiate the cession of Dobrudja with the Romanians. The failure of this move caused great misgivings in Sofia, and rumours about Romanian conduct in the province, where many Bulgarians were reported to have been arrested, were given wide circulation in the Bulgarian capital. At this juncture the Germans exploited the situation to the full and presented the Bulgarians with Dobrudja. After a series of meetings, which took place between 26 July and 9 August, between Filov, Popov, and high-ranking German officials, which included the German minister to Ankara Franz Von Papen and even Hitler, a final agreement was reached in Craiova on 7 September.[37]

The British, caught up in this almost erratic course of revisionism, made their first, and last, attempt to rid themselves of the image of a strict supporter of the status quo, in order to maintain at least a hint of influence in Sofia. In July, they intimated to King Boris that they would view with sympathy Bulgaria's claim to Dobrudja. This intimation caused a good impression in Bulgaria. Rendel reported that Filov, speaking at Tŭrnovo, the capital of the second medieval Bulgarian empire, on 21 July, said that Bulgaria's policy to 'abolish the injustices

---

[35] FO 371/24881, R6063, 27/5/1940, and R7100, 16/8/1940.

[36] FO 371/24902, R5729, 14/5/1940 (for Rendel's draft), and Barker, *British Policy*, 56 (for Campbell's observations).

[37] FO 371/33128, R1650, memorandum entitled 'Notes on Bulgaria's position since the outbreak of the war', dated: 15/12/1941.

of Neuilly . . . by peaceful means . . . has already produced results'.[38] In September a more public gesture was made, when Halifax told the House of Lords that Britain 'would be favourable to a modification of the status quo' provided that it was 'reached by means of free and peaceful negotiation'. HMG, therefore, regarded the settlement of the Dobrudja question 'with satisfaction'.[39] 'An excellent impression', however, was made in Sofia by Churchill's unequivocal statement in the Commons, that he had always felt that Southern Dobrudja should be returned to Bulgaria, and that the British 'should welcome any direct solution of this question between the parties concerned'.[40]

The British press was also instructed to publicize these declarations, and to depict Britain as being 'not anti-revisionist in principle'. These instructions, however, neatly epitomized the obvious limitations of British revisionism, for they stressed that Dobrudja was not Macedonia. The claim on the former was endorsed by the British, because it was justified on historical and ethnological grounds. But the outlet to the Aegean satisfied neither provisions. Not only was there no Bulgarian population left in eastern Greek Macedonia, but also repeated Greek offers for an economic corridor, provided for by the Treaty of Neuilly, were turned down by the Bulgarians.[41]

This cautious approach to revisionism did little to improve the British image in Bulgaria; a fact perfectly understood by the Foreign Office. In fact, while the British were expressing their 'satisfaction' at the settlement of the Dobrudja question, the pro-German mayor of Sofia was busy renaming two streets after Mussolini and Hitler. At any rate, not only was it too little, but it came too late as well. From the summer of 1940 onwards, Bulgaria had to navigate against much more difficult weather than a few months earlier. The fall of France had destroyed the fragile equilibrium between Germany and Russia, on which some Bulgarians had pinned much hope.

A thin ray of hope flickered in July, when Campbell reported that the Bulgarian minister in Belgrade remarked to the American military attaché that his government was 'most anxious to get on to close terms with Yugoslavia'. Fear of Russia, and unwillingness to throw in their lot completely with the Germans, were given as the reasons behind this Bulgarian move. George Clutton, of the Southern Department,

[38] FO 371/24870, R7341, 21/7/1940.   [39] Barker, *British Policy*, 57.
[40] FO 371/24870, 6/9/1940.
[41] Instructions to the press in FO 371/24880, R728, and 24877, R7394, 27/9/1940.

admitted that this was the first indication that perhaps Bulgaria wanted a rapprochement with Yugoslavia. He was quick, however, to conclude that 'there is nothing we can do to foster [a rapprochement] since for the moment the Balkan countries are unlikely to pay much attention to what we advise. Our role can only be that of a benevolent onlooker.'[42] His pessimism was echoed in Rendel's views. In August, he told the Foreign Office that fear of Italian and German aggression towards Yugoslavia had made the Bulgarians 'extremely reluctant' to enter into any sort of commitment towards Prince Paul.[43]

Clearly, the British plan for a Bulgar–Yugoslav understanding was dead beyond any doubt; and nothing could be done to revive it. Further blows followed soon: by the end of November Romania and Hungary had acceded to the Axis. Moreover, Italy's war against Greece, and Hitler's plans to come to the rescue, rendered Bulgaria's adherence to the Tripartite Pact a matter of most urgent consideration for Germany. The time of Bulgaria's final reckoning with the Axis looked imminent. In Sofia, Rendel still entertained a 'ray of hope', to the effect that Bulgaria was not finally lost.[44]

It was a very faint ray indeed, for the process of German infiltration, which had started in July, gathered an irreversible momentum. According to British reports, in late 1940 about 10,000 German 'tourists', all of them young males, accompanied by many technicians, could be found in Bulgaria; submarines had arrived, and German anti-aircraft pieces had been located at various sites. At the same time, a powerful pro-German campaign was launched. A German institute was opened in Sofia, and, by October, a strictly pro-German line was adopted by the Bulgarian censorship. Simultaneously, a wave of alarmist rumours against the British and the Turks was set in motion by Goebbels's disciples.[45]

This excessive preponderance of German influence in Bulgaria provoked the activation of the Russian factor. In late 1940, the British realized that the Kremlin was becoming increasingly nervous about German military infiltration in that country, and that it would be prepared to take some measures to restore a balance of influence, short of war. In September 1940, the Russian minister in Sofia had told Rendel that,

---

[42] Campbell's report in FO 371/24881, R6879, 31/7/1940, and minutes attached. Clutton's minute dated 3/8/1940.

[43] FO 371/24881, R6879, 4/8/1940.   [44] Rendel, *Sword*, 171.

[45] FO 371/33128, R1650, memorandum 'Notes on Bulgaria's position since the outbreak of the war', dated 15/12/1941.

if Germany occupied Bulgaria, which he then felt was 'unlikely', the Soviet government 'would not go to war for the sake of the Balkans'.[46] At the same time, the Foreign Office learned from the Yugoslav Ministry for Foreign Affairs that the German minister in Bucharest had admitted that Russo-German relations 'were not what they had been'. More important was a telegram from Knatchbull-Hugessen, sent on 1 October. Based on information given by the Greek minister in Ankara, Knatchbull-Hugessen reported that the Soviets had advised both Sofia and Belgrade of the need to get more closely together, in order to avoid an excessive dependence on Germany. Clutton, who attempted to summarize all available evidence, concluded that, although the Greek minister was 'a not too reliable source', Kremlin's uneasiness about Axis activities in Bulgaria was certain.[47] At this juncture, it seemed that British interests coincided with the Kremlin's anxieties.

Indications that Russo-German relations had deteriorated had multiplied since the negotiations over Dobrudja in July. Significantly, when the Bulgarians entered the province in September, the German, Hungarian, and Italian military attachés were invited, but not their Russian counterpart. Russian concerns were boldly underlined in November, when the secretary general of the Russian foreign ministry, Arkady Sobolev, paid a visit to Sofia. This visit gave rise to a wide variety of rumours, which the British were unable to confirm from either Moscow or Sofia. Nevertheless, Sobolev was reported to have offered the Bulgarians a pact of mutual assistance, or a guarantee against aggression. It was also alleged that he had threatened a Soviet occupation of the Black Sea's ports, if Bulgaria allowed the passage of German troops through her territory. Although Filov rejected the Russian offer, this manifestation of Russian interest in Bulgaria strengthened Boris's resistance to the Germans.[48] At the same time, an apparently nervous Russia made approaches also to Yugoslavia. In November, the Yugoslav

---

[46] FO 371/24870, R7763, 28/9/1940.

[47] FO 371/24881, R7783, 1/10/1940, and minutes attached. Clutton's minute, dated 4/10/1940.

[48] For the Sobolev visit see Barker, *British Policy*, 59–60; See also Nissan Oren, *Bulgarian Communism: The Road to Power, 1934–1944* (New York and London, 1971), 156–8. The Soviet proposal revealed their anxiety about threats 'directed against southern Russia through the Straits' and sought to secure Bulgarian assistance 'in case of a real threat to the interests of the Soviet Union in the Black Sea or in the Straits'. In return, the Kremlin declared its 'full understanding for the interests of Bulgaria in western Thrace . . . and is prepared to cooperate in their realization'. Oren, *Bulgarian Communism*, 157.

military attaché in Moscow was informed that the Soviets were prepared to supply lavishly the Yugoslavs with war material. But, as in the Sobolev case, the Russians did nothing to back up their offer with deeds.[49]

As had usually been the case, the intervention of the Great Powers in the Balkans was also reflected in the Macedonian scene, since every Power tried to mobilize its own Macedonian faction either for pressure or embarrassment, as the opportunity presented itself. In 1940, the communist faction—i.e. members of IMRO (United) and some elements of the Protogerovists[50]—was the weaker, but this did not deter the Kremlin from pulling this lever. In August, Rendel reported on a communist manifesto, issued in Sofia, which warned the Macedonians not to seek the support of the Axis Powers.[51] This warning was apparently an element of the Soviet strategy to counterbalance German influence in Bulgaria, and was combined with a resurgence of communist activity in the country, which reached its peak during the Sobolev mission.[52] Rendel also reported that the Protogerov faction, who had now become pro-communist, was in favour of a Russo-Yugoslav rapprochement.[53]

The British were well aware of the Great Powers' rivalry for the ill-defined loyalties of the Macedonians. As has been already mentioned, they knew about Mihailov's contacts with the Italians and the Germans. Against this background a most peculiar incident occurred in January 1940, when the British military attaché in Sofia was approached by a physician, by the name of Radan Sarafov, who claimed to have contacts with Mihailov, and said that he could enlist the support of the Macedonians against the Russians. Rendel, who kept a close eye on the activities of Mihailov, cautiously accepted him, and learned that the IMRO leader was anxious to cooperate with the Allies in order to 'save Bulgaria' from Germany and Russia. The response of the Southern Department was, of course, a plain refusal to consider this possibility. Brown minuted characteristically that 'we have nothing to do with the Macedonians', for the only result would be to 'burn our fingers'.[54] From mid-1940 onwards, further British reports confirmed the close links between the Germans and the Macedonians: in May Mihailov

[49] Barker, *British Policy*, 81–2.
[50] For IMRO (United) and the communist connection of the Macedonian movement see Chapter 1.
[51] FO 371/24880, R7075, 15/8/1940.   [52] Cf. Barker, *British Policy*, 59.
[53] FO 371/24887, R7275.
[54] FO 371/24880, R613, 5/1/1940, and minute by F. Brown, dated 17/1/1940.

emerged in Switzerland, where he was reported to have had contacts with the Gestapo, while in August the head of the National Macedonian Committee of Sofia, a Bulgar–Macedonian group, accepted a German invitation to visit Berlin.[55]

At the same time, more information reached the Foreign Office about the divisions within the Macedonian movement. According to Yugoslav sources, some Macedonian groups, which had broken with Mihailov, were working for the establishment of an Albanian–Macedonian state. The Bulgarian minister in London, however, observed that IMRO had to rely on funds coming mainly from American–Macedonian organizations, whose aim was an independent Macedonian state and not union with Bulgaria. As a result, he felt that they would not be able to provoke much harm to Bulgar–Yugoslav relations.[56] Naturally, the obscure intrigues of these groups, their conflicting aims, and their almost invincible loyalties puzzled the British, and provoked exasperated comments from the officials, who had to keep abreast with their activities. Thus, Rendel remarked that 'the Macedonians are notoriously difficult, and have many characteristics of the Irish, and my impression is that they are happiest in opposition to any existing regime', while Clutton minuted that they were 'anti-Yugoslav, anti-Greek, anti-Bulgarian, anti-German, and anti everything except possibly anti-Russian'.[57]

If the British were at pains to decipher the intentions of the Macedonians, those of the Bulgarians presented them with an easier task, for Bulgarian irredentism, this time in the direction of Macedonia, came again to the forefront. In July, the Bulgarian foreign minister, Popov, told Rendel that an outlet to the Aegean was a 'vital necessity' for his country. The British minister did not fail to observe that these remarks were caused by 'German and Italian instigation'.[58] A more serious incident occurred in November, in the *Sŭbranie,* where Petŭr Dumanov, a government deputy, stated that Bulgar–Yugoslav relations would never become normal until the Macedonian Question had been settled. 'Two million Bulgars', he said, had been left outside Bulgaria. The Yugoslav press reacted strongly to these comments, but Rendel downplayed the whole story: 'the man has a bad reputation and no influence'.[59] He,

---

[55] FO 371/24880, R5608, 23/4/1940, and FO 371/24880, R7325, 21/8/1940.

[56] FO 371/24880, R8104, 19/10/1940, and R7325, 21/8/1940.

[57] As quoted in Andrew Rossos, 'The British Foreign Office and the Macedonian National Identity, 1918–1941', *Slavic Review*, 53/2 (1974), 393.

[58] FO 371/24870, R7147, 17/7/1940.

[59] FO 371/24870, R8566, 24/11/1940.

nevertheless, took the matter up with Popov in December. The foreign minister was now more conciliatory, and replied in a manner already known from the interwar years. He repeated that, due to the presence of the Macedonian refugees in Sofia, it was impossible for the government to suppress all Macedonian activity altogether, and reminded Rendel that the Macedonians were 'difficult people'. Anyway, he concluded, 'words are less dangerous than bombs'.[60]

Despite these assurances, Rendel had reached the conclusion that Bulgarian irredentism was too powerful a factor in shaping Bulgaria's foreign policy, and, since this factor was pushing the country into the German 'new order', he felt that the British should perhaps start to consider the unthinkable: in late November he suggested, very timidly and hesitantly indeed, that Britain should inform the Bulgarians that 'we shall be prepared to discuss all international questions on their merits after the war', in order 'to remove their belief, that we are simply a status quo nation'.[61] Such a view clearly demonstrated Rendel's despair about the loss of Bulgaria to the Germans, for his suggestion was hardly practical politics. First, as Rendel himself admitted, it was too late for any British promise to have any serious effect in Bulgaria's orientation, given Germany's established influence. Moreover, even if Britain 'promised' to consider all Bulgarian claims after the war, it was highly unlikely that Bulgaria would be particularly moved, for the Germans were prepared to deliver the goods instantly. Consequently, it was almost certain that the Bulgarians would interpret the British move as nothing more than an empty gesture of temporizing.

It should be noted in this connection that the Foreign Office had already been confronted with suggestions of that sort. In July Lord Dickinson of the Balkan Committee had proposed to Halifax an outlet to the Aegean for Bulgaria. To support his argument, he remarked that 'the national character of the Bulgarians [was] far superior to that of any of their neighbours'. Dickinson's suggestion gave Clutton the opportunity to present an eloquent epitome of British views on the subject. After dismissing the ethnographic factor, by observing that national characteristics were 'a matter of taste, not of politics', he denied the value of any territorial concessions to Bulgaria, for these would be mere 'promises', whereas the Germans were offering 'immediate revision'. As far as the Greeks were concerned, Clutton echoed a widely

[60] FO 371/29729, R89, 31/12/1940.   [61] FO 371/24877, R7919, 27/11/1940.

shared view by saying that Britain should not give them 'cold comfort'.[62]
The validity of these arguments had been increased in November, and,
therefore, the Foreign Office declined to give Rendel's suggestion any
further consideration.

By January 1941, it seemed that the road to the Tripartite Pact was
a short cut for Bulgaria. In the beginning of this month, Filov paid
a visit to Vienna, ostensibly for medical reasons. During this visit, he
had talks with Joachim von Ribbentrop and Hitler, in which he was
unable to go further than stating that Bulgaria was 'in principle' ready
to adhere to the Tripartite Pact. The reasons behind his reservations
were obvious: fear of Russia and Turkey. He, nevertheless, agreed on
staff conversations, and left Hitler with the impression that Bulgaria was
'willing, but afraid'.[63] The irritation of the Germans was manifested
by press attacks on the Filov government, but it had become clear to
them that both dangers mentioned by the Bulgarian premier had to be
removed if he were to sign. As shall be seen, it was the removal of the
threat of Turkish aggression that greatly facilitated Bulgaria's adherence
to the pact.

On 5 January, Campbell furnished the Southern Department with
the latest update on Bulgar–Yugoslav relations, as seen from Belgrade.
Senior Yugoslav officials were convinced that Bulgaria was plotting with
Germany against Yugoslavia, and stressed that there was absolutely no
chance for a rapprochement, unless the Bulgarians made the first move.
Their pessimism was shared by the British. It was commented that
Bulgaria was so weak that she could do nothing without the approval
of Germany. Orme Sargent was ready to let the matter drop: 'it is not
any use devoting any more thought for the present to this intractable
question'. The kernel was that Bulgaria was not ready to shelve her
aspirations.[64] Rendel understood this, but refused to give up his efforts,
even at the eleventh hour. He argued that Bulgaria could not be asked
to abandon her claims formally, for this could only 'stiffen' her attitude.
In any case, the fact that she was particularly anxious to keep out of
the war, coupled with Yugoslavia's extremely delicate position, offered
in his view some room for a bilateral understanding on neutrality.

---

[62] FO 371/24891, R6896, 31/7/1940, and Clutton's minute attached.

[63] Martin Van Creveld, *Hitler's Strategy, 1940–1941: The Balkan Clue* (Cambridge
1973), 110–11. Cf. Filov's diary, entries for 4 and 7 January, 1941, trans. and ed.
Frederick B. Chary, in *Southeastern Europe*, 1 (1974), 59–60.

[64] FO 371/29729, R195, 5/1/1941, and minutes attached. Sargent's minute, dated
15/1/1941.

His insistence, however, that the Yugoslavs should take the initiative, provoked a minute from Reginald Bowker, who recalled that similar proposals had been turned down earlier.[65] The last twist to this question occurred in February, and again involved the Turks. Turco-Bulgarian relations had seen some improvement at the very end of 1940 after a difficult autumn, and in December 1940 negotiations were under way for the conclusion of a non-aggression pact. Campbell had suggested that a Turco-Bulgarian understanding could be possibly extended to include Yugoslavia.[66] Thus, the Turks were seen again as a possible bridge between Yugoslavia and Bulgaria. Clutton considered this 'in general OK', but the signature of the pact, in February 1941, was a disappointment for the British. In reality, the pact meant that Turkey washed her hands of Bulgaria. Thus, this agreement removed the Turkish danger from Bulgaria, and left her with no practical reason for not accepting the passage of German troops through her territory. In fact, as soon as the Bulgar–Turkish negotiations showed, in mid-January, that the Turks were willing to meet Bulgarian demands, Filov notified the Germans that they were willing to sign, asking, at the same time, for adequate German military protection against the British, and a written confirmation of Bulgaria's territorial gains.[67] The German press welcomed the pact, which, could be seen, retrospectively, as the last German move to clear the ground for the adherence of Bulgaria to the Axis camp, although Saracoğlu tried hard to convince the British that the policy of his government had not changed. As soon as Rendel obtained a copy of the pact, he was in no doubt about its true significance. The Turks had 'disinterested themselves from what Bulgaria might do'. The conclusion to be drawn was inescapable: such a move 'let us down badly'.[68] Twelve days later, Bogdan Filov signed the Tripartite Pact in Vienna, and Rendel, who had worked so hard to bring Bulgaria closer to Britain, had to leave the country. As a farewell gift, the Bulgarians planted a bomb in his luggage, which exploded in Istanbul, killing two of his staff.[69] A very ironic epilogue for a man who had tried to understand the Bulgarian point of view, and fought a lonely battle to accommodate it.

If seen as a whole, the British failure to achieve a rapprochement between Bulgaria and Yugoslavia, can be attributed more to intractable

[65] FO 371/29729, R294, 12/1/1941. Minute by Reginald Bouker, dated 12/1/1941.
[66] FO 371/29729, R617, 25/1/1941.   [67] Van Creveld, *Hitler's Strategy*, 113.
[68] Rendel, *Sword*, 172.   [69] For this incident see Barker, *British Policy*, 61.

Balkan problems, and the geopolitics of the region, than to serious British political errors. Thus, they were caught, not for the first time, in the vortex of Balkan squabbles, which they found impossible to solve. First and foremost, the deeply rooted mistrust of Prince Paul towards the Bulgarian king, significantly impeded any sort of understanding. For the Yugoslav prince, Boris was simply an untrustworthy and cunning enemy. This was not the impression of those British diplomats who knew him personally. Both Rendel, who knew him well, and Knatchbull-Hugessen, who had a long conversation with him in 1939, agreed that he lacked the qualities of leadership; he only followed events, he did not shape them. They stressed, however, that his principal aim was to keep Bulgaria out of the war, saving thus his country, and with it his throne and, ultimately, himself.

It can be said that the main feature of Bulgaria's foreign policy between 1939 and 1941, was an almost paralysing fear of Germany and Russia, a point Rendel understood all too well, but Prince Paul did not. History and geography had placed Bulgaria at the crossroads of two Great Powers, whose menacing threat Boris tried hopelessly, although sincerely, to avoid. Subsequent events showed that he was right: Bulgaria could not avoid the covetous eye of Germany and Russia. Thus, in March 1941 Germany won the first round. In September 1944, it was the turn of the Kremlin to win a more lasting victory. It cannot be doubted that this fear could have provided a basis, albeit a thin one, for an understanding between Sofia and Belgrade. The fact that it did not serve this purpose, was due not only to Prince Paul's mistrust, but also to Bulgarian irredentism. Centred mainly around Dobrudja, in 1940, but with an eye always on Macedonia, Bulgarian nationalism was quite a formidable force, which drove a wedge between Bulgaria and her neighbours, and, in a vicious circle, reinforced Belgrade's suspicions.

The British found this vicious circle impossible to break. Rendel, in an overcritical mood after he saw his hopes dashed, put the blame on the British, for they failed to give Dobrudja to Boris first. It may safely be said that such a view reflected the disappointment of the man, rather than the realities of the time. True, the British were half-hearted, to say the least, on revisionism; but even if they had persuaded the intransigent Romanians to surrender the province, the outcome could not have been different. First, it was obvious that Dobrudja would not compensate Bulgaria for the permanent loss of Macedonia, which the British could not, and did not, consider surrendering. Moreover, the experience of the Great War demonstrated that concessions without military backing were little more than empty gestures. Boris understood very well that Britain was 'too far away', and they could do nothing to prove him wrong. As a result, having to choose between Hitler and Stalin, it was not surprising that he chose the former. 'The choice', Boris told a leader of the Bulgarian opposition, 'is Germany or Russia. These are the two powers who will seal the future of Europe. Your feelings tell you Russia. But if you listen to your reason, you'll answer Germany.'[70]

Within this framework, all British efforts to win Bulgaria, short of military action, were doomed to fail. They tried to impress upon Belgrade and Greece the need to get Bulgaria closer; made some effort, very timid indeed, to persuade the Romanians to yield Dobrudja; used the Turkish factor; and tried to come to grips with Bulgarian revisionism. But, deprived of the most important asset as they were, i.e. the military one, their hopes were crushed by Germany's might, assisted by Romanian intransigence and Belgrade's suspicions. Rendel failed fully to appreciate the gravity of the military factor, and accused the Foreign Office of almost abandoning Bulgaria and unduly favouring Yugoslavia.

It was not the first time that British ministers in the Balkans allowed a local angle to colour their judgement. In the interwar years, it will be remembered, the British minister in Belgrade, Sir Nevile Henderson, frequently attacked London for supporting 'our enemies', the Bulgarians, instead of rewarding 'our allies', the Serbs, whereas after 1944 William Houstoun-Boswell, the British political representative in Sofia, also crossed swords with Sir Orme Sargent about the 'abandonment' of Bulgaria to the Kremlin. Interestingly, even the cultural outlooks of the Balkan sovereigns were given some consideration in this respect, with Henderson claiming that the Foreign Office favoured Boris, because he spoke some English, whereas King Alexander could not. In 1939–40, similar contrasts could be drawn: the Oxford-educated, cultured, and thoroughly Anglophile Prince Paul was opposed to the simple, more Balkan, and unpretentious Bulgarian king, who had famously declared that he was the 'only Bulgarian' in his country, for his 'wife was Italian, his army pro-German, and his country pro-Russian'. But cultural tastes do not normally shape foreign policy. Boris's case, however, proved that, unfortunately for the British, fear, self-preservation, and a generous dose of nationalism often do.

[70] Stephane Groueff, *Crown of Thorns* (New York, 1987), 274.

'ACRES OF PAPER': BULGAR–YUGOSLAV
RELATIONS IN BRITISH WARTIME PLANNING,
1941–1943

In early 1941 history appeared to repeat itself in the Balkans: for
the second time in a quarter of a century, Britain had failed to
turn 'the Bulgarian key' to her side. This distressing development
reinforced British fears about the difficulties of managing the Bulgarian
problem, so long as Bulgaria constituted an independent state ruled
by Boris's dynasty. The question which arose from this resonance was
not unexpected: if an independent Bulgaria were prone to choose the
wrong direction, then things could develop differently if the country
were somehow 'moulded' to mingle its identity with the more loyal
Yugoslavia or, preferably, with Greece and Yugoslavia, in a Balkan
federation of sorts. Although the obstacles in the way of such a proposal
were many and serious, the main argument which militated in favour of
the federation scheme was even stronger: the Bulgarian horse had to be
harnessed to a loyal chariot, if it was not to kick the British. Moreover,
as shall be seen, the inclusion of Bulgaria in a federation was part of a
larger and much more grandiose scheme for the erection of federations
stretching from the Baltic states to Crete, in order to provide a barrier
to future German or Russian penetration of east-central Europe.[71]

Suggestions that Bulgaria should give up her independent status
reached the Foreign Office as early as January 1941, in a rather
academic way. At that time, Rendel, who could still find time to reflect
on the future of Bulgar–Yugoslav relations, observed that a South Slav
Confederation would be very advantageous for the Yugoslavs. Not only
would it alter Yugoslavia's geographical orientation, and mitigate her
economic dependence on Italy, but it would also help the more Balkan
and Orthodox Serbs to redress the balance of religion and culture, for
the inclusion of millions of Orthodox and Balkan Bulgarians would
counteract the 'Central European' and Catholic Croats and Slovenes.
Moreover, Rendel argued that this scenario would eventually solve the
Macedonian Question. Macedonia would become a federal unit, and,
therefore, would cease to be the bone of contention.[72]

---

[71] For a general survey of the British federation plans see Barker, *British Policy*, 130–7;
Victor Rothwell, *Britain and the Cold War, 1941–1947* (London, 1982), 193–8.
[72] FO 371/29729, R4460, 15/1/1941.

Although Rendel himself felt that such a project would be difficult to achieve, due to the strong national consciousness which he attributed to Bulgarians, the importance of the solution of the Macedonian Question that a federation could achieve was not overlooked. Yet, from the British point of view, there were many problems in such a scheme, some of them intrinsic, others conditioned by the prevailing political situation. Thus, when the Southern Department was informed through the Polish minister in Sofia, in February 1941, that 'serious Bulgarian politicians' wanted Britain to register her support of a Bulgar–Yugoslav Confederation, the response was cautious, although it allowed for some flexibility. According to Clutton a 'South Slav Bloc' was rather 'inopportune' at present for neither Prince Paul nor royalist Bulgarians would support it; besides it could create nervousness in Athens. Nevertheless, he was quick to add that 'At a later stage we might consider such a plan'. Certainly, the political situation in the Balkans at the time did not encourage such largely theoretical discussions about the future of the area.[73]

The following months, however, provided the British with more than enough time to reflect on the Bulgarian problem. In March 1941, Bulgaria formally acceded to the Axis, and shortly afterwards Yugoslavia and Greece were overrun by the Germans. Yet again, a Bulgarian sovereign had chosen Britain's enemies, although King Boris, unlike his father, would not live to regret his decision.[74] This fact removed British reservations about federation plans, which in effect meant the doing away of the Bulgarian dynasty. On 23 May, Leo Amery sent Eden a paper on the future of Bulgaria, written by Dr Malcolm Burr, which advocated the incorporation of Bulgaria into a Greater Yugoslavia. Amery, and his son Julian, agreed with this solution, aware of the fact that it was premised on the disappearance of the Bulgarian dynasty.

[73] FO 371/29729, minute by Clutton, dated 20/2/1941.
[74] According to the official Bulgarian communiqué, Boris died on 28 Aug. 1943 of thrombosis of the left coronary artery. The fact that his death occurred after his visit to Hitler, when the Führer had pressed him to send troops to the Eastern Front, cast some doubt as to the real cause of Boris's death. Rendel, for instance, wrote that the Germans, irritated by Boris's refusal, substituted the drug which the king had been taking to help him on the journey, with some other substance, while the plane 'flew unusually high', in order to make him take it. Rendel, *Sword*, 180–1. Crampton argues that poison theory 'was almost certainly not the case', for the Germans would have derived little benefit from instability in Bulgaria, and they had no reason to believe that the succeeding regime would bow to them. Richard Crampton, *A Short History of Modern Bulgaria* (Cambridge, 1989), 127–8. Although most accounts support the latter view, Boris's death remains a fertile ground for speculation. Cf. Oren, *Bulgarian Communism*, 230–2.

Clutton considered the plan 'one of the more attractive solutions', but advised Eden to reply cautiously: 'it is one solution but it is as yet premature'.[75]

It was indeed early for the British to sponsor such ambitious plans, not least because the views of the other Balkan governments were still unknown to them. Soon, however, hints of their intentions begun reaching London. On 6 June 1941, Philip Nichols informed Reginald Leeper, Assistant Under-Secretary of State, that the Yugoslavs seemed to entertain designs for a Greater Yugoslavia, and the suppression of Bulgaria as an independent state. Such a prospect was viewed favourably in the Foreign Office, as it would remove the Bulgarian troublemaker once and for all. Philip Nichols noted that 'this might be the best solution and we may eventually find it necessary and desirable to give it our support'.[76]

This was not quite what Momčilo Ninčić, the Yugoslav foreign minister, had in mind. Thus, shortly after his arrival in London on 21 June, the British were presented with a clearer picture. Ninčić was against a Greater Yugoslavia. He knew all too well that a South Slav bloc would alarm the Greeks, no less than the Turks or the Romanians, and, therefore, it would cause more harm than good.[77] Within the Yugoslav government-in-exile, the South Slav Federation was advocated by Milan Gavrilović, minister to Moscow and later minister without portfolio. Gavrilović, who was considered by Rendel[78] to be an able observer of Russian affairs because of his excellent command of Russian, his contacts, and his experience of the country, predicted that the Bulgarian dynasty would not outlast the war, thus leaving the way open for the communists to hold sway, and turn the country into the Kremlin's province. The only way to prevent this, Gavrilović maintained, was to fuse Bulgaria into a Greater Yugoslavia.[79]

In late 1941, both Yugoslav politicians explained to the British their views in talks with Sargent and Rendel, and Ninčić's argument appeared to win the day. British suspicions, which traditionally surrounded the construction of a South Slav bloc, convinced the Foreign Office that Gavrilović's ideas did not suit their book. It was this deeply rooted

[75] FO 371/29729, R5425, 16/5/1941, minute by Clutton, dated 23/5/1941.

[76] FO 371/29721, R5868, 6/6/1941.

[77] Stevan Pavlowitch, *Unconventional Perceptions of Yugoslavia* (New York and Boulder, Colo., 1985), 37.

[78] After his service in Sofia, Rendel was appointed minister to the Royal Yugoslav Government-in-exile.

[79] Pavlowitch, *Perceptions*, 38.

suspicion and not Gavrilović's sound predictions about Bulgaria that urged Pierson Dixon, of the Southern Department, to minute that the Yugoslav minister 'is full of tiresome ideas about the future of the Balkans'.[80]

Another idea, however, less remote, and less tiresome to the British, was the Yugoslav initiative for the establishment of a Greek–Yugoslav federation.[81] Negotiations between the two allied governments-in-exile had been under way from October 1941 onwards, but their pace had been very slow. Ninčić's federal ideas, according to which the proposed federation would provide the nucleus around which an all-Balkan (and not exclusively Slav) federation would emerge after the war, left much to be desired for the Greeks, who not only entertained hopes for the rectification of Greece's Macedonian frontier at the expense of Bulgaria, despite the firm British refusal to consider this option, but also feared that a Balkan federation was bound to arise Russian suspicions. Moreover, the Greeks could not forget that Salonica's inclusion into Yugoslavia was one of the gifts with which the Germans had offered the Yugoslavs some months earlier.[82] As a result, different objectives, coupled with some suspicion, made the government of Emmanuel Tsouderos quite reluctant to enter into negotiations. The Greek cold shoulder irritated Ninčić, who complained to Sir Alexander Cadogan on 28 October 28 that, although he had communicated his proposals to the Greeks 'two or three weeks ago', he had not received a reply as yet. Ninčić then asked Cadogan to act as a go-between.[83] Rendel became the recipient of similar complaints a few days later. Ninčić wondered why the Greeks did not look at his proposal 'at once', and confided to the British minister that he was 'very much disturbed' by their attitude.[84]

For the British, Ninčić's plan was a timely and welcome move. In November 1940, the Polish and Czechoslovak governments had reached an agreement for close cooperation, which could serve as a nucleus for

---

[80] FO 371/33133, R57, and minute by Dixon, dated 6/1/1942, attached. Orme Sargeant was no less irritated by Gavrilović's insistence on a Bulgar–Yugoslav bloc: such a unit 'would be playing straight into the Russian hands', he told Rendel in August 1942, and emphasized that Gavrilović 'must be made to realize' that his plan meant nothing less than 'the absorption of Bulgaria into a Greater Serbia'. Stoyan Rachev, *Anglo-Bulgarian Relations during the Second World War, 1939–1944* (Sofia, 1981), 79.

[81] For this issue see Stephen Xydis, *Greece and the Great Powers, 1944–1947: Prelude to the Truman Doctrine* (Salonica, 1963), 19–22; Pavlowitch, *Perceptions*, 37–49.

[82] For Greek reservations see Xydis, *Greece*, 19–20; Pavlowitch, *Perceptions*, 39.

[83] FO 371/29838, R9497, 28/10/1941.

[84] FO 371/29838, R9736, 1/11/1941.

a northern European federation. So, the British and the Yugoslavs, but by no means the Greeks, envisaged the same role for the proposed Greek–Yugoslav agreement. 'We are interested', minuted Dixon, 'in this attempt to explore the possibilities of a Balkan Federation.'[85] Thus, it was after British pressure, through Eden and Michael Palairet, the British minister to the Greek government, that the unwilling Greeks decided to sign on 15 January 1942 the agreement for the 'Constitution de l'Union balkanique'.[86] At Tsouderos's suggestion, the agreement was signed at the Foreign Office.[87]

That day, however, demonstrated again that the two governments were looking in different directions. King Peter was markedly outspoken, in contrast to the Greek sovereign. He said that 'we have reason to hope that besides the Balkan Union a Central European one will be created on the basis of the Czech-Polish Agreement . . . these two Unions would create together a single common Supreme Organ . . . a great Organisation'.[88] The grandiose plans unveiled by the Yugoslav king alarmed the Greeks. Tsouderos felt that the Yugoslavs had gone too far by elaborating on so far-reaching a plan. His apprehension, so he told Dixon, was also due to the fact that, although he had given to the Yugoslavs the text of King George's speech, Ninčić did not reciprocate. Moreover, Tsouderos was against the participation of Turkey in the federation, for such a possibility meant in effect that Greece would be obliged to defend Turkey's Asiatic borders.[89] For him, that was surely too distant and dangerous a commitment. Further Yugoslav statements about the necessity for close cooperation between the two unions, fuelled Greek fears that these grand designs were certain to upset the Soviets,[90] and would not be appealing to the Turks. Besides, Tsouderos remarked to Dixon rather sensibly, decisions about the future of Europe were beyond the reach of small states.[91]

[85] FO 371/29838, R9497, 28/10/1941, minute by Dixon.

[86] For this agreement, which provided for political, military, and economic coopera-tion see Pavlowitch, *Perceptions*, 40; Xydis, *Greece*, 20. The text is given in FO 371/33133, R472. It has been published in Leften Stavrianos, *Balkan Federation: A History of the Movement toward Balkan Unity in Modern Times* (Northampton, Mass., 1944), 311–13.

[87] FO 371/33133, R142, 31/12/1941. Tsouderos told Dixon he wanted to stress that the agreement was to be concluded 'under the aegis' of the British.

[88] FO 371/33133, R472, 15/1/1942.   [89] FO 371/33133, R735, 20/1/1942.

[90] The critical point of Soviet attitude towards the proposed federations, which led eventually to their abandonment, will be discussed below.

[91] FO 371/33133, R735, 20/1/1941. Cf. Pavlowitch, *Perceptions*, 41; Xydis, *Greece*, 21.

What Tsouderos had failed to understand at the time, was that a state considerably bigger than Yugoslavia or Greece appeared to be ready to support Ninčić's ambitious plans.[92] In early 1942 the Southern Department debated the issue of federations, and most of its officials agreed that the Yugoslav idea could best serve Britain's strategic objectives. Although Dixon and Sargent admitted that the Yugoslavs had been 'tactless' in airing their views without prior consultation with the Greeks, it was agreed that close cooperation between the two 'poles' (that is between the two union schemes) offered 'the best hope of some really satisfactory and lasting post-war settlement'. The reasons behind the conflicting views of the two governments were also discussed. It was understood that the Yugoslavs, fearful of Russian domination, and knowing that the days of a centralized and Serbian-dominated Yugoslavia were gone, had no alternative other than the creation of a federation; not so the Greeks, who, furthermore, would have been extremely reluctant to welcome their arch-enemy, Bulgaria, into the Balkan federal fold, and to be caught into distant commitments.

But Greek susceptibilities had to bow to British interests. Despite Dixon's reservations, Sargent argued that in publicizing the Greek–Yugoslav Agreement, it should be stressed that the ultimate aim was a Balkan federation, including Romania and Bulgaria. The latter became again a central point: she could not be trusted if independent, so she had to be 'subjected to definite control'. Only the Northern Department, responsible for Russia, which raised 'strong objections' to the inclusion of Romania and Bulgaria in British propaganda, out of fear of Soviet reaction, somehow cooled Sargent's ardour. Thus, in the 'notes for the Press and the Political Warfare Executive' it was agreed that not much prominence should be given to a federal plan regarding these countries; nevertheless, the BBC was instructed to use the slogan 'the Balkans for the Balkan peoples', and warmly to praise the Greek–Yugoslav Agreement.[93]

So, by the beginning of 1942, the British had set the framework for their Balkan policy: 'the only instrument at our disposal to prevent Soviet domination in the Balkans', minuted Sargent, 'is the policy

---

[92] The following paragraphs are based on FO 371/33133, R934, minutes by E. M. Rose, 12/2/1942, and Dixon, 15/2/1942; FO 371/33133, R735, 20/1/1941, minutes by Rose, 21/1/1942, Frank Roberts, 16/2/1942, and Dixon, 23/1/1942; FO 371/33133, R490, minute by Sargent, 13/1/1942; FO 371/33133, R817, Sargent to Palairet, 12/2/1942.

[93] FO 371/33135(A), R427, 19/1/1942.

of a Balkan Confederation including Bulgaria and Romania'.[94] The inclusion of Bulgaria was again of paramount importance to the British, although they would not publicly admit it, owing to possible Russian objections. Bulgaria, however, was considered by the Foreign Office as a 'natural ally' of Russia, and would be shown after Germany's defeat to be a spearhead of Russian penetration. This, in turn, would drag Serbia and Macedonia into the Kremlin's fold, isolating Greece and throwing, ultimately, the Croats and the Slovenes into the hands of the Germans. After such a gloomy scenario, Sargent concluded in June that it was imperative for the security of both Greece and Yugoslavia to 'sterilize' Bulgaria, by means of an all-Balkan federation, which would, however, exclude Turkey. The need for sterilization was so vital for the survival of the Balkans, that Sargent did not hesitate to advocate 'force to compel Bulgaria to enter the Confederation and to prevent her from leaving it'.[95]

Although neither the perception of Bulgaria as a ripe plum for the Kremlin, nor the necessity of a Balkan federation was contested at the Foreign Office, the debate on the process of its construction did not achieve the same amount of consent. In early 1943, Rendel, who had been having frequent and long talks with Milan Gavrilović, appeared to have modified his earlier opinion about the difficulties of a Bulgar–Yugoslav bloc, and repeatedly questioned Sargent's proposal to use the Greek–Yugoslav federation as the nucleus for future arrangements.[96] According to his views, a reversal of the process initially envisaged was needed, for it was highly unlikely that Greece would have been prepared to accept Bulgaria's entry into the federation; therefore a Bulgar–Yugoslav union should be established first. In an effort to allay the fear of Russian domination of such a concrete Slav bloc, Rendel did not fail to note that it would be placed under the control of a 'Yugoslav Federal Monarchy'.[97]

Even the mention, however, of a South Slav bloc, caused almost allergic reactions in the Foreign Office. So, Sargent flatly rejected Rendel's argument, repeating that such a unit would be a spearhead for Russian penetration, and would overshadow the whole Balkan

[94] FO 371/33133, R216, 11/1/1942.
[95] FO 371/33134, R3793, 1/6/1942, Annex 'Pan-Slavism in the Balkans', and minutes in FO 371/37153, R2129, 9/3/1943. Sargent himself described the Confederation policy as 'perfectly sound', FO 371/33123, minute, dated 16/7/1942, attached to R4725.
[96] For Rendel's and Gavrilović's views see above.
[97] FO 536/3148(7), 21/4/1943, fo. 300.

Federation. Thus, not only the Greeks, but also the Croats and the Slovenes would refuse to join in.[98] Rendel replied by stressing the advantages of his proposal, namely the abandonment by the Bulgarians of an outlet to the Aegean, and the solution of the Macedonian Question, with the establishment of an autonomous Macedonian unit. But to no avail. Sargent insisted that a Slav bloc would be too powerful to be trusted, and the Greek–Yugoslav Union continued to be the only instrument for the realization of British plans in south-eastern Europe.[99]

At about the same time, the Foreign Research and Press Service of the Foreign Office produced lengthy and laboriously researched memoranda on possible future confederations, covering almost the whole of Eastern Europe.[100] This impressive amount of paperwork, which could be regarded as indicating how the world would look like if seen from Balliol College, Oxford, envisaged two large confederations: a northern one, including Poland, Czechoslovakia, and Hungary, and a southern one, consisting of Bulgaria, Yugoslavia, Greece, and Albania. Such an arrangement, it was argued, was essential if the main British interest regarding this area, the prevention of future German domination of Eastern Europe, was to be safeguarded.[101]

According to this plan Bulgaria and Yugoslavia should form confederal units. Macedonia was again presented as the most difficult issue regarding such a settlement. Although it was argued that within a federal state Macedonia could form a unit, she was considered too backward and 'primitive' to qualify for membership of the confederal structure that Balliol had constructed. Moreover, given the endless disputes about the nationality of its inhabitants, boundaries along 'ethnic' lines could not be drawn; nor was a plebiscite advisable in an area so 'disturbed and unruly'.

---

[98] Sargent was not alone in anticipating that panicking Slovenes and Croats would flatly deny participation in a South Slav bloc. Dr J. Krnjević, the Croat deputy premier, held the same views. FO 536/3150(4), 8/1/1942.

[99] FO 371/37173, R3674, 30/4/1943 (Rendel's proposal), and R4144, 7/5/1943 (Sargent's views). The debate is also recorded in the File FO 536 cited above.

[100] FO 371/35261, U1292, entitled 'Memoranda on Confederations in Eastern Europe', and dated 26/2/1943. This is a massive, 79-page-long document, which examines in minute detail the political, strategic, and economic dimensions of the confederal theme. This was not the first time that Britain entertained 'confederal' plans for the future of the Balkans: similar plans had been discussed during the Great War, when a 'confederal union between Serbia and Bulgaria' was suggested in 1917. But then, it was proposed that Bulgaria should acquire a considerable piece of Macedonia at the expense of both Serbia and Greece. See George Leontaritis, *Greece and the First World War: From Neutrality to Intervention, 1917–1918* (Boulder, Colo., 1990), 265.

[101] FO 371/35261, U1292, 5.

As a result, it was concluded that the pre-1941 boundaries should be respected. Bulgaria, however, was well catered for: as compensation for the loss of the Vardar Valley she could regain Tsaribrod and Bosilegrad, and even territorial concessions from Greece. It was realized, however, that despite these gifts, it would have been very difficult for Bulgaria willingly to join the federation. Thus, it was argued, as Sargent had suggested in 1942, that the use of some sort of force to convince her to join was more likely to be necessary.[102]

So, by mid-1943, the Foreign Office's experts had created a new architecture for the Balkan states, and indeed for the whole of Eastern Europe. In fact, the sheer amount of this paperwork confused even those, who supposedly, should have shed light on the issue. On 9 August 1943, Douglas Howard, head of the Southern Department, observed that 'acres of paper exist on alternative confederations . . . but we have no idea where our preferences lie'. He then went on to raise two fundamental questions: the extent of British-American cooperation and counselling over these plans, and the Russian attitude.[103] Before touching upon the latter point, however, it is important to stress that, while the British were elaborating grand schemes about the future of the Balkans, they did not seem to bother themselves with the actual state of the Greek–Yugoslav federation, on which they had pinned so much hope. Had they been more interested in this aspect, they would have realized how detached from the realm of practical politics their federal plans were.

As has already been seen, the Greeks had never been enthusiastic about the federation, and frequently clashed with the Yugoslavs over the objectives and the depth of it. Beneath the sound of the official rhetoric, these differences continued to simmer, a fact of which the British were aware, but to which they declined to give due consideration. Thus, when the two parties met on 25 September 1942, and agreed on further meetings to coordinate their policy, euphoria was in abundance. Dixon was very quick to consider this meeting a 'satisfactory development', which indicated that the two governments were 'determined to maintain close relations and to extend them', while Sargent, praising the 'good accord and good points', rushed to give the credit to Nincic.[104]

[102] FO 371/35261, U1292, 18, 20. It was proposed that Greece might give up Dedeagatch, (Alexandroupolis) or, alternatively, economic access to Salonica, Kavala, or Alexandroupolis.

[103] FO 371/37173, R6753, minute by Howard, dated 9/8/1943.

[104] FO 371/33134, R6626, 3/10/42; minute by Sargent, dated 10/10/1942. FO 371/33134, R6755, minute by Dixon, dated 9/10/1942.

Subsequent developments showed that British euphoria was completely groundless. The Greeks were not prepared to abandon their claims on southern Albania, and, as this question emerged at the end of 1942, many clouds gathered around bilateral relations. Moreover, developments in Yugoslavia in 1943 persuaded the Greeks that the Yugoslav government not only was not master in its own house, but the prospects of its becoming so in the future were extremely thin. On the other hand, the Yugoslav government's preoccupation with more pressing needs inevitably overshadowed the Union balkanique. The result was that the Greek–Yugoslav accord died a quiet death in 1943, and in January 1944 the Yugoslav prime minister, Dr Božidar Purić, forgot its second anniversary.[105]

It has to be said, however, that the Yugoslav premier had very good reasons to let the whole story slip into oblivion, for, two months earlier, even the British had been forced to do the same. It was no surprise that the reason was Russian objections. Initially, Soviet attitudes to confederations ranged from a somewhat diffident acceptance to a chilling 'wait-and-see' view. Stalin had told Eden that he would not object to the wish of 'some European states' to federate.[106] But Soviet reactions to the Greek–Yugoslav accord were much more reserved. Ninčić had assured Sargent on 31 December 1941 that the Russian minister to the Yugoslav government, Alexander Bogomolov, 'had shown a friendly interest' in the proposed accord. However, Andrei Vyshinsky, the Soviet deputy foreign minister, adopted a neutral attitude when presented with the draft of it in early January 1942.[107] During 1942 and 1943 it was becoming increasingly apparent that the Russians viewed British plans with intense suspicion. Both Vyacheslav Molotov and Ivan Maisky, the Soviet ambassador to Britain, had communicated to Eden their serious doubts as to whether the federations were directed only against Germany, but they did not go as far as to reject them.[108]

These hints of Russian disapproval did not deter the Foreign Office from continuing to work on their plans. True, some officials—Dixon and Howard, for instance, but, significantly, not Sargent—realized the need for the British to keep quiet about confederations in order not to offend the uncooperative Russians; and, as has been already seen, it

---

[105] See Xydis, *Greece*, 22; Pavlowitch, *Perceptions*, 42.
[106] See Barker, *British Policy*, 130.
[107] FO 371/33133, R57, 31/12/1941; FO 371/33133, R267, 9/1/1942.
[108] For Russian suspicions see Barker, *British Policy*, 132.

was agreed that British propaganda should downplay the inclusion of Bulgaria and Romania in the Balkan Federation.[109] Nevertheless, it can be argued that the Foreign Office, until late 1943, had not fully realized the extent of the Soviet suspicion. Thus it was repeatedly stressed that Russian goodwill would be essential for the construction of federations. Curiously enough, it was even suggested that the Kremlin's consent could be extracted, if the capitalist economy of these confederations were to be somewhat 'mild', excluding, thus, some unspecified characteristics which would be 'obnoxious' to Russian economic taste.[110]

It is, in fact, quite extraordinary that the British had hoped that the Russians would acquiesce in a bloc which was directed as much against Germany as against the spill-over of their own influence in Eastern Europe. Be that as it may, Molotov gave those plans a definitive *coup de grâce* at the Moscow conference in October 1943, when he termed them premature and artificial groupings, reminders of the 'cordon sanitaire'.[111] To the frustration of the British, the Americans seemed to be equally hostile to federations. It should be noted in this connection, that they knew of the British plans, and, at an earlier stage, they seemed to favour an Eastern European confederation. After Molotov's remarks, however, it was with a hidden sense of relief, that they rushed to kill the idea. Speaking to the Congress in November 1943, Cordell Hull stated that after Moscow there was no need for spheres of influence, alliances, balance of power, or 'other special arrangements'. The message was quite clear. 'Mr Hull', a Foreign Office minute read, 'had killed the Federation scheme stone-dead'.[112] Thus, by the end of 1943, Purić could be readily excused for having such a short memory.

British wartime planning regarding the future of the Balkans, apart from the customary Great Power arrogance which enabled Balliol to make and unmake frontiers, and to transfer regions from one federal unit to the other at a stroke of a pen, suffered from two fundamental weaknesses. First, the assumption, never stated, but implicitly accepted, that dispassionate reason, as understood in London, would be the only force which would dictate the foreign conduct of the countries

---

[109] Rothwell, *Britain*, 195. Cf. FO 371/33134, R4182, minute by Dixon, dated 9/7/1942.

[110] FO 371/35261, U1292, 'Memoranda on Confederations in Eastern Europe', dated 26/2/1943.

[111] Barker, *British Policy*, 137.

[112] For Mr Hull's speech see FO 371/37173, R13912, report by the London *Times*, 20/11/1943, and FO minute of the same day.

concerned. Secondly, the hidden hope that Russia would possibly be prepared to extend her support to a scheme that was ultimately directed against her. The latter point dealt British plans a deadly blow; but it is beyond doubt, that, in the long run, the former would have done the same.

The first assumption merits some analysis at this point. According to the British plans, the Balkan states should form a federation, for this solution was in their ultimate interest. Indeed it was a panacea for all evils: a bulwark against Russia and Germany, the road to economic prosperity, and a sound policy for 'sterilizing' Bulgaria. Yet, it does not follow from this that the view from London coincided with that of the Greek government. The Greeks fervently desired to sterilize Bulgaria, and Albania for that matter, but they had devised their own way of achieving this, namely the rectification of borders. Moreover, they had been quite reluctant to sign the union with Yugoslavia, and, significantly, to consolidate and expand it, but the British constantly overlooked this. So, despite the fact that the last meeting of the union took place in December 1942, the British had to read *The Times* and the *Izvestiya* in November 1943 to learn that the federations were 'stone-dead'.

Typical of this attitude were some extraordinary remarks made in the 1943 Memoranda on Confederations. There, with monumental paternalism, it was stated that 'it is in the general interest of security that the exiled governments should not return to their territories with the aim of treating them [their enemies] as ex-enemies, but should be prepared to consider their legitimate interests'. This meant that Greece might perhaps be advised not only to welcome Bulgaria into a federation, but also to cede a port to her. No provision, however, was made as regards the way to persuade the Greeks, even within a federation, to surrender territory to a country which, at that time, was subjecting Greece's northern provinces to a harsh occupation regime. In all, the British plans were far removed from the realm of practical politics, due to conflicting interests of the countries involved, nationalist aspirations, and Russian suspicions. What is interesting, nevertheless, is that although the British had ample evidence for all these factors, they hoped that they could bypass them.

As far as Bulgar–Yugoslav relations and the question of Macedonia were concerned, a more 'real' aspect of British wartime planning was that it served as a guide for their views of this problem. Thus, it was again emphasized that a Bulgar–Yugoslav union was an intrinsically destabilizing factor that should not be allowed to materialize. An exclusively Slav bloc could only be a spearhead for Russian domination of the whole of the Balkan peninsula. Bulgaria, of course, needed some sort of surgical operation to render her unable to give birth to trouble. Consequently, she should be fused into a federation; or coerced in doing so. But a Balkan federation should either include Greece, or should not exist at all.

Macedonia was granted less attention by the British, but no less mistrust. Throughout the wartime, she was considered an obscure pest, capable only of spelling misfortune. The Macedonian movement had a track record of standing on the wrong side of the fence, for it had connections with the Italians, the Germans, and the Russians; while the Macedonians as a whole were just 'difficult people', they had, according to the British, no clear-cut national loyalties, and it was more likely than not that they would have had serious difficulties in choosing one, if asked to do so. In general, this issue could be touched only at one's own peril. Such a poor view of the Macedonians made the British extremely suspicious of Macedonian unification. Perhaps Yugoslav Macedonia could form a federal unit within a strong and federal Yugoslavia—or within a South Slav bloc, as Rendel had suggested—for the British knew very well that the inhabitants of that province had no stomach for Belgrade. Yet again, the Macedonians were at their best in defining what they despised, rather than what they stood for. Therefore, it was better that their volatile loyalties should remain confined within the pre-war boundaries.

Although the British failed to construct a Balkan confederation they had devoted some time and energy in defining their views regarding this area, and, significantly, they knew what they did not want to see happening. This was not without importance, for, as shall be seen, in 1944 the Macedonian Question and the form of Bulgar–Yugoslav relations suddenly became a major issue in the British agenda. At that time, the British saw others trying to do what they dreaded. But if their wartime planning was nothing more than 'acres of paper', the conclusions they drew from these papers were real enough.

4

The Difficult Withdrawal: Britain and the Bulgarian Army in Yugoslav and Greek Macedonia, September–December 1944

At the end of the summer of 1944, Macedonia unexpectedly acquired a political and strategic significance, long absent from these Yugoslav and Greek provinces. At that time the Kremlin made its presence felt in the Balkans, by effectively occupying Romania and Bulgaria. For Britain, this development was pregnant with danger, for, although the British were prepared to tolerate a considerable amount of Soviet influence in these countries, they were, nevertheless, determined to resist fully fledged Russian domination. Moreover, the assertion of Moscow's power in the Balkans could endanger its position in Greece, at a time (September 1944) when the British had neither soldiers in the country nor a friendly—and anti-communist—government established on the ground to guarantee Greece's pro-Western orientation.

At this particular juncture, the question of the withdrawal of the Bulgarian occupation forces from Greek and Yugoslav Macedonia after the events of the Ninth of September in Bulgaria appeared to carry substantial political weight. The British were very anxious to see the Bulgarian army leave both parts of Macedonia, but the Bulgarians—and their Soviet patrons—had other designs. Thus, the active involvement of the three local actors in this question, coupled with the conflicting interests of Britain and the Soviet Union, further complicated the situation.

THE SETTING, 1944

The Balkan summer of 1944 proved to be very hot for the British. By the end of August, the Bulgarian government of Ivan Bagryanov was at pains to withdraw Bulgaria from the war, and had been trying to secure Western support in their efforts to conclude an armistice. On 26 August, Bagryanov declared Bulgaria's neutrality, while a few days earlier a Bulgarian emissary had contacted the British ambassador to Turkey, Sir Hugh Knatchbull-Hugessen, to enquire about armistice conditions. The British told him to go to Cairo, where he would be presented with the Anglo-American terms.[1]

The British Foreign Secretary, Anthony Eden, seemed not to be particularly anxious regarding Russia's attitude towards these deliberations. He had not asked for the Kremlin's views, but he felt that an agreement with the Soviets could be reached 'almost immediately'.[2] It is not clear from what source Eden derived his optimism. As early as May 1944, Stalin had made clear that he was not prepared to leave Bulgaria outside his sphere of influence. At that time, a propaganda campaign launched by the Soviet press forced Dobri Bozhilov to resign.[3] The Soviets, however, continued their 'verbal war' against the new government of Ivan Bagryanov, and by the beginning of August Eden was increasingly 'perturbed' about their objectives with regard to Bulgaria. He was at pains to decipher what their ultimate aim was, for the Bulgarians had changed their government, and had arranged for the withdrawal of the Germans from the Black Sea coast. On 10 August, Eden told Churchill that Stalin might have wanted to 'have a deal between Bulgaria and Yugoslavia' in order to consolidate his influence in the Balkans, and suggested that Churchill should raise the matter in his talks with Tito. Churchill agreed and two days later, in his meeting with Tito in Naples, he 'sounded a warning to Tito'.[4]

Against this background, it was no surprise that Moscow was quick to demonstrate how unfounded Eden's optimism was about the Bulgarian armistice. On 29 August, the official Soviet news agency, *Tass*, announced that Bulgarian neutrality was 'insufficient', and at the very end of the month, accused the Bagryanov government of continuing to help the Germans: German ships, it was said, were using the Black Sea ports, their forces in Bulgaria were not being disarmed, and the Bulgarians had been receiving German war material.

[1] For this mission see Elisabeth Barker, *British Policy in South-East Europe in the Second World War* (London, 1976), 220–1.

[2] Eden to the War Cabinet, as quoted by Barker, *British Policy*, 220.

[3] This propaganda war is recorded in FO 371/43583, R7269, R7333, 8-9/5/1944.

[4] Eden's suggestion in FO 371/43589, R44585, 10/8/1944, and Churchill's reply dated 12/8/1944.

At the same time, the Fatherland Front's radio-station, *Hristo Botev*, broadcasting from Soviet territory, stepped up its criticism of the government.[5]

Amid growing signs of Russian hostility, including the unexpected departure of the Soviet chargé d'affaires from Sofia, the Bagryanov government collapsed, and a new one, under the right-wing Agrarian Konstantin Muraviev, was formed on 2 September. But the Soviets were determined not to lose the initiative. *Hristo Botev* repeatedly rejected any government in which the Fatherland Front was not represented. The pro-Western Muraviev cabinet included neither communists nor leftist Agrarians, and consequently provoked a decisive Soviet move. On 5 September, despite the fact that Muraviev had declared war on Germany a few hours earlier, Moscow announced that, as from that day, 'not only was Bulgaria in a state of war with the USSR, but the USSR was also in a state of war with Bulgaria'.[6]

Clearly, Moscow was not prepared to let another power take the lead in Bulgaria; and for good reasons. From a military viewpoint, Bulgaria's neutrality could afford the Germans an orderly retreat from the Balkans, thus posing a serious threat to Red Army's advances. Political reasons were no less important. As British Balkan analysts put it on 6 September 1944: 'by declaring war on Bulgaria Russia is now in a position to lend direct support to the extreme political elements in Bulgaria and enforce either the formation of a Fatherland Front government, or the entry into Muraviev government of FF representatives'.[7] The Foreign Office, however, appeared to be particularly confused about these developments: on 5 September, a cable to the British ambassador in Moscow, Sir Archibald Clark Kerr, communicated their anxiety about the Russian declaration of war.[8] It did not take long for the Russian intentions to become clear. On 9 September, after a typically Balkan coup, the opposition disposed of Muraviev, and a Fatherland Front government was formed, in which four portfolios were held by communists, including the important Ministry of the Interior, which controlled the

---

[5] WO 201/1617, Balkan Political Review, issue no. 1, ending 6/9/1944, App. 'B'.

[6] For the text of the Soviet Declaration of war on Bulgaria see FO 371/14012, dated 5/9/1944.

[7] WO 201/1617, Balkan Political Review. The Fatherland Front (*Otechestven Front*) was the political organization of the Bulgarian resistance, and included Communists, left-wing Agrarians, Social Democrats, and *Zvenari*. For the FF see Nissan Oren, *Bulgarian Communism: The Road to Power, 1934–1944* (New York and London, 1971), 223–32.

[8] WO 201/1600, From FO to Moscow, No. 3126, dated 5/9/1944.

police.[9] From that day on, Bulgaria was theoretically an Allied state, but was rapidly becoming—in effect—a Soviet protectorate.

THE BULGARIAN ARMY IN YUGOSLAV MACEDONIA, 1941–1944

The change in the international position of Bulgaria in September 1944 obviously had profound ramifications, affecting her overall orientation, and, inevitably, the position of the Bulgarian army; an enemy of Yugoslavia and Greece, so unexpectedly turned into an unwelcome ally. In Yugoslav Macedonia, few were able to foresee such a transformation, and—as will be apparent—even fewer were inclined to accept it.

The Bulgarians had been occupying the largest part of Yugoslav Macedonia, which coincided with the Slav-speaking areas of the province, since April 1941. The western, predominantly Albanian, zone was given over to the Italian-sponsored 'Greater Albania', much to the irritation of the Bulgarians. Sofia deeply resented Italy's gains and armed border incidents between the two 'allies' were not rare.[10] Another irritating question regarding the newly acquired territory was its legal status: the Germans acquiesced in the occupation of Macedonia by Bulgaria, but they refused to concede to its formal annexation in order to keep the fate of the province as a useful bargain for the extraction of more concessions from Bulgaria in the future.

In Bulgaria, however, few bothered themselves with such a 'technicality', and the Filov government swiftly proceeded to the formal incorporation of the 'liberated territories' into the 'Motherland'. The province was divided into two *oblasti* (administrative districts), with Skopje and Bitolj as their respective centres, while the Sofia *oblast*

---

[9] On the revolution of the Ninth of September, see Oren, *Bulgarian Communism*, 254–8.

[10] For German–Bulgarian negotiations regarding Macedonia see Rastislav Terzioski, 'IMRO-Mihajlovist Collaborators and the German Occupation: Macedonia, 1941–1944', in Pero Morača (ed.), *The Third Reich and Yugoslavia, 1933–1945* (Belgrade, 1977), 388–9. For Italy's insistence on the Albanian zone see Galeazzo Ciano, *Diplomatic Papers*, ed. Malcolm Muggeridge (London 1948), 437–8. Despite Bulgarian pressure, the Germans refused to allow Bulgaria to annex the Albanian part after the capitulation of Italy in September 1943, and German units rushed to occupy Gostivar and Tetovo. The Bulgarians retaliated by expelling a good number of Albanians from Skopje. See WO 204/9677, 'Memoranda on Axis-controlled territories: Macedonia under the Bulgarians', dated 29/8/1943.

was expanded to include the area along the pre-war Bulgar–Yugoslav border; the border, however, was not officially abolished and some formalities continued to be observed. Between March and July 1941, all the administrative details were settled, and the Bulgarian press was in exuberant mood: *Tselokupna Bŭlgariya* (Undivided, Complete Bulgaria), it was declared, was at last a reality.[11] As was to be expected, symbolic rituals took place to celebrate the occasion: a flame was ignited in Preslav, the medieval Bulgarian capital, and was carried across the 'unified' country.[12]

The Bulgarian army made every effort to ensure that the 'Undivided Bulgaria' remained so, although Macedonian enthusiasm for the Bulgarian presence gradually wore thin.[13] At the later stages of the occupation the Bulgarian army, assisted by IMRO bands, resorted to severe punitive expeditions, which further alienated the population. In mid-1944, British liaison officers in Macedonia reported, there were few villages that had not had some houses burned down, while in many cases during anti-guerrilla operations the Bulgarians seized the peasants' modest food and drove off their livestock.[14] As might be expected, the Macedonian Serbs were dealt with by even more repressive measures. The Serbian community of Veles, for example, faced massive deportations, and out of the 25,000-strong Serbian population in Skopje, only 2,000 remained in the city by the beginning of 1942. It should be noted that IMRO bands were again quite active in the deportation of, and the punitive expeditions against, the Serbs.[15]

[11] On the administrative structure of Yugoslav Macedonia under the Bulgarians see FO 371/43649, Political Intelligence Centre Middle East, App. 'C', 3/1/1944. For the term 'Undivided Bulgaria', which was used to denote the 'Greater Bulgaria' first materialized in the San Stefano era, see Krŭstiu Manchev, 'Natsionalniyat Vŭpros na Balkanite do Vtorata Svetovna Voyna' [The National Question in the Balkans until the Second World War], in Institut po Balkanistika pri B.A.N., *Natsionalni Problemi na Balkanite: Istoriya I Sŭvremenost* [National Questions in the Balkans: History and Current Situation] (Sofia, 1992), 15.

[12] Stephane Groueff, *Crown of Thorns* (New York, 1987), 302.

[13] Cf. Chapter 6.

[14] Information on the Bulgarian occupation by British Liaison Officers in Macedonia, in FO 371/43592, R19998, dated 30/11/1944.

[15] Information included in a publication by the British Royal Institute of International Affairs, entitled 'Bulletin of International News', dated 11/12/1943, in WO 208/2028. Needless to say, the Bulgarian bibliography is pointing only to the brighter aspects of the occupation. See Lilia Filipova, introd., in Institut za Voena Istoriya, *Vardarska Makedoniya, 1941–1944 v Iugoslavskata Istoricheska Literatura* [Vardar Macedonia, 1941–1944, in Yugoslav Historical Literature] (Sofia, 1992), 8–12, and Dobrin Michev, 'Bŭlgarskata Komunisticheska Partiya I Makedonskiyat Vŭpros do 9 Septemvri 1944

For most of the wartime period the Bulgarian army carried out their duties almost unchallenged, for their opponents had to settle their internal problems first. These were not in short supply. Between 1941 and the beginning of 1943, the Macedonian regional committee of the Communist Party of Yugoslavia (CPY) was dominated by pro-Bulgarian elements, who had decided in 1941 to abandon the CPY and to join the Bulgarian Communist Party (BCP).[16] They, therefore, refused to wage a guerrilla war against the Bulgarians. Under the leadership of Metodi Šatorov (alias Šarlo), the Macedonian committee followed the BCP line closely, and argued that guerrilla operations could not be sustained in Macedonia, as conditions there were 'different', and 'not ripe' for revolutionary war as advocated by Tito. In fact, Šatorov went as far as to accuse Tito of being 'Anglophile', because he dared to proclaim that Yugoslavia (and Macedonia) was 'enslaved by the occupiers'.[17] Obviously, for Šatorov the 'occupiers' were the Serbs, not the Bulgarians.

Tito, furious with the 'Old Bulgar' (i.e. Šatorov), appealed to the Comintern to solve the dispute. The Russians, desperate to keep as many Germans as possible away from the Eastern Front, supported Tito's line for armed struggle. Moreover, they appeared reluctant to concede the enlargement of Bulgaria suggested by the official fusion of the Skopje Committee with the BCP. Thus, in September 1941, the Comintern, in a reserved resolution, ruled that 'for technical reasons', and 'for the time being', the Skopje Committee should remain within the CPY. The Bulgarians swiftly backed down, and Šatorov sought solace in Bulgaria.[18]

godina', [The Communist Party of Bulgaria and the Macedonian Question until 9 September 1944], *Voenoistoricheski Sbornik*, 6 (1986), 18.

[16] The BCP was then called *Bŭlgarska Rabotnicheska Partiya* (Bulgarian Workers' Party) but became 'Communist' again in 1948.

[17] Ivo Banac, *With Stalin, Against Tito: Cominformist Splits in Yugoslav Communism* (Ithaca, NY and London, 1988), 5. For the situation in the regional committee of the CPY between 1941 and 1943 and the role of Šatorov see also Stephen Palmer and Robert King, *Yugoslav Communism and the Macedonian Question*, (Hamden, Conn., 1971), 65–7; Paul Shoup, *Communism and the Yugoslav National Question* (London and New York, 1968), 52–4; Elisabeth Barker, *Macedonia: Its Place in Balkan Power Politics* (London, 1950), 84–8. The Yugoslav (and Macedonian) case is presented in Svetozar Vukmanović (General Tempo), *Struggle for the Balkans* (London, 1991), 1–10. For the Bulgarian view see Kostadin Paleshutski, *Iugoslavskata Komunisticheska Partiya I Makedonskiyat Vŭpros, 1919–1944* [The Yugoslav Communist Party and the Macedonian Question, 1919–1944] (Sofia, 1984), 284–91.

[18] For the text of the Comintern's resolution see Stephen Clissold, *Yugoslavia and the Soviet Union: A Documentary Survey* (London, 1973), 153. For the reasons behind the Russian decision, see Palmer and King, *Yugoslav Communism*, 678.

Despite the Comintern's decision the situation in Yugoslav Macedonia still left much to be desired for Tito, for the pro-Bulgarian attitude of the Macedonian communists remained a formidable obstacle. Between 1941 and 1943, Tito sent no less than five emissaries to Macedonia, to persuade his ill-disciplined comrades to follow the official line and launch guerrilla war. Their efforts met with only limited success, and the Skopje Committee was effectively controlled by the Bulgarian 'representatives' Petŭr Bogdanov and Boyan Bŭlgaranov. The fifth of Tito's delegates, the Montenegrin Svetozar Vukmanović, who came to Macedonia in February 1943, proved to be the most effective. Vukmanović, nicknamed Tempo after his favourite phrase—'we must accelerate our tempo'[19]—was a forceful speaker with strong organizational skills, and, significantly, had demonstrated unfailing loyalty to Tito.[20] Moreover, he had a considerable amount of local knowledge, and, being Montenegrin, did not share the anti-Serbian syndromes of the Macedonian communists.[21]

Tempo's descent into the internal squabbles of the Macedonian communists marked the decline of Bulgarian influence, and the corresponding rise of Tito's authority. Perhaps his most important initiative was the creation of the Communist Party of Macedonia (CPM). Aware that even the mention of the word 'Yugoslav' provoked almost allergic reactions among the Slav-Macedonians, Tempo worked out a compromise that could satisfy both sides. The word 'Macedonian' in the title of the new party played on the sensitivity of the Macedonians, affording them some sort of 'political individuality'. At the same time, however, Tempo stressed that the newly formed party was—and would always be—an integral part of the CPY under the leadership of Tito.[22] In all, by the

[19] The source for Vukmanović's *nom de guerre* is Milovan Djilas, *Memoir of a Revolutionary* (New York, 1973), 354.

[20] Vukmanović, together with the Serbian Aleksandar Ranković, the Slovene Edvard Kardelj, and the Jewish Pijade formed the upper echelon of the CPY. They all belonged to a rather compact layer of communist cadres, which was 'crystallized' at the time of Tito's chairmanship of the CPY after extensive purges. See Ivan Avakumović, *History of the Communist Party of Yugoslavia* (Aberdeen, 1964), 137.

[21] Tempo had been engaged in propaganda work before the war in Skopje along with Djilas, another Montenegrin. Both tried hard to persuade the Macedonians to stick with the CPY. Strangely enough, it seemed that Montenegrins were among the key players in the Macedonian Question. For Tempo's pre-war activity in Macedonia see Stephen Clissold, *Whirlwind: An Account of Marshal Tito's Rise to Power* (London, 1949), 135, and Barker, *Macedonia*, 92.

[22] Palmer and King, *Yugoslav Communism*, 76–8. Naturally, the exact amount of the 'political individuality' of the Macedonians, as opposed to the political centralism

summer of 1943 Tempo had managed to reinforce Tito's authority in Macedonia. Naturally, he had many doubts about the durability of his success. But his main achievement was that the wartime pro-Bulgarian trend receded into the background of Yugoslav–Macedonian politics.[23]

Naturally, these internal problems greatly impaired the development of guerrilla warfare in the area. The first few *Partizanski Odredi* (Partisan Detachments) in Macedonia, formed by Lazar Koliševski, in 1941—poorly trained and ill-organized—proved no match for the Bulgarian army, and were easily destroyed. Their leader's fate was equally unfortunate: he was arrested under suspicious circumstances.[24] The guerrilla movement had to wait for more propitious times. It started to develop only after Tempo's 'restructuring' of the Skopje organization. Tempo decided to shift the focus of Partisan action from the Bulgarian to the Italian zone, where the terrain was more favourable and the occupation regime less efficient.[25]

Despite Yugoslav propaganda, however, especially after 1944, the Macedonian armed units never became the formidable military force their leader, Mihailo Apostolski, claimed they were.[26] Their performance

sponsored by Tito, remained a permanent source of friction between Belgrade and Skopje, and is an issue of paramount importance for a more balanced assessment of the development of the Macedonian Question within the 'New Yugoslavia'. For more details and analysis see Chapter 6.

[23] Tempo's mission is given in his own account: Vukmanović, *Struggle for the Balkans*, which bears the burden of the author's role, and therefore should be used with caution. A much more balanced approach is given in Palmer and King, *Yugoslav Communism*, 76–83, which draws extensively on Yugoslav archival sources, including Tempo's worrying telegrams to Tito. These telegrams and letters clearly demonstrate the discrepancy between the realities in the field and Tempo's depiction of the struggle of 'the Macedonian nation'.

[24] Tempo alludes to the suspicion that Koliševski was arrested as a result of betrayal by the pro-Bulgarian elements of the Skopje Committee. Vukmanović, *Struggle*, 29. Koliševski—initially sentenced to death but subsequently to life imprisonment—spent the war in the prisons of Skopje and Pleven, in Bulgaria. He was set free in Sept. 1944, when he came back to Skopje and became the first premier of the 'People's Republic of Macedonia'. His time in Pleven had not been without some benefit, for his inmates were prominent members of the BCP.

[25] Palmer and King, *Yugoslav Communism*, 83.

[26] Lt. Gen. Mihailo Apostolski was one of the very few Macedonian officers of the Royal Yugoslav Army, and since 1941 became one of Tito's close aides. After a brief period—under a false name—in Sofia university, where he conducted underground work, he came back to Tito's HQ in 1942. In 1943 he was sent to Macedonia with Tempo. It should be noted that most of the Slav-Macedonian bibliography on the Partisan warfare in Yugoslav Macedonia has been written by Apostolski himself. See e.g. Mihailo Apostolski, 'La Guerre de la libération en Macédoine', *Revue d'histoire de la Deuxième Guerre mondiale*, 87 (1972), 15–32. Information about Apostolski combined

in the field, despite their bravery, hardly deserved the official praise lavished on them. British liaison officers, attached to Macedonian Detachments in 1944 and very keen to assess their actual military strength, drew a rather gloomy picture. The Partisans, despite their immense suffering and hardships, remained little more than a nuisance to Bulgarian and German forces, at least until the summer of 1944. Despite the Italian capitulation in September 1943, which afforded them some room to manoeuvre in the western part of the region, the Partisans suffered from an almost total lack of training, and displayed a striking ignorance of military tactics. Unable to carry out serious military operations, they tried to preserve their forces, something that Apostolski did not hide from his BLOs. It should be stressed that they were so ill-equipped to cope with the hardships of guerrilla warfare that in desperation they asked the British to supply them with boots, for only one-third of them possessed adequate footwear. As a result many Partisans died of exposure in the winter of 1944.[27] Their need for material of all kinds prompted them to steal equipment from the British 'Brasenose' mission. Even Cvetko Uzunovski, veteran of the Spanish Civil War and a prominent Macedonian military leader, indulged in appropriating British war material.[28]

As might be expected, Apostolski used inflated language to describe both the number and strength of his Partisans. By the end of 1944, he maintained, the National Army of Macedonia amounted to 23 infantry brigades—1 motorized—4 artillery brigades, and cavalry, organized in 7 divisions and 3 army corps, a total of 66,000 men.[29] This estimate, however, conveys a rather deceptive picture. For a start, the Partisans remained extremely poorly armed throughout the war, with no artillery, and had to content themselves with mules rather than motorized transport. Apart from that, many Partisans did not even have weapons, and only after the British dropped significant quantities in the summer did the guerrillas become sufficiently armed and clothed.

from British sources. See FO 371/48184, notes on Macedonian personalities compiled by Sqd. Ldr. Hill, BLO with the Macedonian HQ, attached to R13695, from Ralph Skrine Stevenson to Ernest Bevin, 6/8/1945.

[27] See the detailed report of Capt. Macdonald, attached to Apostolski's HQ in FO 371/43739, entitled: 'Report of Mission Brasenose by Capt. Macdonald, BLO', dated 11/10/1944. Macdonald asked Bari for some sorties, but it was decided that all available war material should be send to Tito. Although some material was sent to the Macedonians in April–May, a 'crying need' of boots was not met until July.

[28] WO 202/1209, report by 'Brasenose' mission, dated 11/10/1944.

[29] Apostolski, *La Guerre*, 27, 32.

They received more after the events of the Ninth of September, when large quantities of Bulgarian war material fell into their hands. After that, they enjoyed the luxury of motor transport, and the equipment of a Bulgarian cavalry regiment.[30]

Further, it is difficult to trace a hint of the 'four artillery Brigades' mentioned by Apostolski, for, as shall be seen, during the operations leading to the liberation of Macedonia in the autumn of 1944, all the artillery support for the infantry was provided by the Bulgarian army. The size of the Partisan forces also appeared to be a gross exaggeration. Although the strength of the Macedonian brigades varied greatly, as late as October 1944 BLOs reported that there were fifteen brigades operating in Yugoslav Macedonia.[31] Even allowing for the fact that Apostolski was markedly uncooperative and tried to prevent the British from obtaining military information, it may safely be said that the number of 60,000 men was wishful thinking rather than reality.

As far as their fighting qualities were concerned, it seems that they did not depart from the typically Balkan 'brigand' tradition: 'hit-and-run' attacks, mainly ambushes, poor discipline, a dependence more on personal bravery than on military planning, and a 'cyclical' concept of military action, which required a prudent apathy during the winter and attacks during the spring.[32] According to this pattern, their offensive spirit grew stronger from spring 1944 onwards. At that time they managed to inflict heavy losses on the Bulgarians, who unsuccessfully tried to encircle them, while by the end of summer, armed with British supplies, they created some 'liberated zones' mainly in the Albanian part of Yugoslav Macedonia, and always in close collaboration with the Kosovar Brigades. In general, during Partisan operations the BLOs did not fail to observe frequent desertions and a considerable amount of naiveté concerning military planning.[33]

---

[30] Information about the Partisans' military strength and equipment derived from the report of Capt. Macdonald in FO 371/43739, cited above.

[31] Macdonald Report. It should be added that there were also two Kosovo Brigades, the second operating around Skopje. According to the British their fighting abilities thwarted the Macedonians. Apostolski himself intimated to Capt. Macdonald, in Jan. 1944, that the Kosovars did most of the fighting, while the latter looked constantly down on the Macedonians, saying that a Kosovar Brigade could do better than a Macedonian Division.

[32] Such a pattern of warfare had been well known in Macedonia since the early 20th cent., when Greek and Bulgarian bands clashed in a 'Struggle for Macedonia'.

[33] Macdonald Report.

As is usually the case in a guerrilla war, however, the most important aspect of Partisan ventures in Macedonia was its political rather than its military dimension. It is well known that, regular armies cannot be defeated by guerrillas;[34] so it would have been too much to expect this to happen in wartime Yugoslav Macedonia. In fact, it was in the political sphere that the true significance of the Partisan detachments was actually revealed.

These detachments primarily served as a political instrument for the indoctrination of the Macedonians along the lines set by the CPY. From this perspective, they must be seen as the military wing of a wider network set up and politically backed by the CPY. This network consisted of the CPM, the National Liberation Committees, and various youth and women's organizations, and aimed at integrating the 'ethnically' and politically diverse Macedonian society, and promoting the idea of 'brotherhood and unity' with the other peoples of Yugoslavia. The Macedonian army, therefore, was an instrument for the 'Macedonianization' of the Macedonians. It practised the politics of integration by including in its rank and file men of all inclinations. Even ardent pro-Bulgarians joined in, when they thought it wise not to clash with the new rulers of the region. Moreover, Apostolski tried hard to suppress the traditional enmity between the Serbs and the Macedonians, by intensifying political agitation, and forming mixed—i.e. Serbo-Macedonian—bands.[35] Although the Serbs felt little 'brotherhood' and the Macedonians wanted no 'unity', the fact remained that Apostolski's effort to foster 'comradeship in arms' was among the first attempts to overcome this enmity in the history of the Yugoslav state.

Apart from these aspects, the Macedonian army, being the only centre of political activity in the area, furnished the newly founded People's Republic of Macedonia with its first cadres and officials. Thus it was not surprising that Apostolski was among the key figures during the First Session of *Antifašističko Sobranie na Narodnoto Osloboduvanje na Makedonija* (Anti-Fascist Assembly of the National Liberation of Macedonia, ASNOM), in the St Prohor Pčinjski monastery on 2 August 1944. It is perhaps of interest to note that the guerrilla leader attended the session in a magnificent uniform sent by Tito especially

---

[34] On the significance of guerrilla warfare and its limitations see Walter Laqueur, *Guerrillas: A Historical and Critical Study* (London, 1976).

[35] WO 201/1122, Balkan Political Intelligence, Copy No. 95, 31/7/1944.

for the occasion.[36] Given that many Partisans had died of exposure for lack of boots in the previous winter, it can be said that such a uniform must have created a deep impression indeed.

As the Partisan movement was struggling to establish a foothold in Macedonia, it seemed that the Bulgarian occupation forces also faced problems; but of a different kind. As early as January 1944, the Foreign Office had become the recipient of reports pointing to the low morale of the Bulgarian troops.[37] More detailed information, received by the Southern Department during the summer and the eventful September of 1944, conveyed the impression that, although a wholesale collapse had to be ruled out, the prevailing mood among the Bulgarian troops was for a return to their own country rather than for war. Fitzroy Maclean, head of the British Military Mission to Tito, reported on 2 September that the Bulgarians were affording the Germans valuable time by pushing back the Partisans, who were attacking the withdrawal of the German E Army from Greece.[38] It became evident, however, that their main objective was to keep their own lines of retreat to Bulgaria open.[39]

Desertions to the Partisans were not a rare phenomenon, although a significant number of anti-German Bulgarians were reserved about joining them, especially in early and mid-1944. Evidence from Eastern Serbia, for example, showed that many soldiers did not want to assist the Germans, but remained unconvinced about Allied victory. Moreover, many regarded the Partisans as undisciplined bands, and held them in low regard.[40] There were also desertions in Macedonia, and, in May, the Partisans formed the *Hristo Botev* battalion, which was formed from Bulgarian deserters. Naturally, this battalion has been constantly praised by Bulgarian and Macedonian authors alike, but according to British reports it included only 150 soldiers and some non-commissioned officers. According to the same source, Tito and Vlahov were not popular among these officers.[41]

[36] FO 371/43592, R19998, 30/11/1944. For the ASNOM and the making of the People's Republic of Macedonia see Chapter 6.

[37] Information given to John Balfour, British chargé d'affaires in Moscow, by the Soviet vice-commissar for foreign affairs, Dekanosov, on 14/1/1944. FO 371/43587, R2601.

[38] WO 201/1600, No. 41526, 2/9/1944.

[39] FO 371/43608, R13746, 1/9/1944.

[40] FO 371/43589, R8665, 12/5/1944, for information on the low morale of the Bulgarian army. Cf. FO 371/43589, R8943, 25/5/1944, report by a BLO who interrogated Bulgarian deserters. See also FO 536/11, 12/5/1944.

[41] See report by BLOs in FO 371/43579, R6168, 12/4/1944.

In short, by the beginning of September, all the information available to the British suggested that the Bulgarian army in Macedonia, although capable of offering stubborn resistance to the Partisans, had its morale badly shaken. But the role of this army, after the events of the Ninth of September in Bulgaria, was to disturb more interested actors than just the British.

SINISTER DESIGNS: SEPTEMBER–DECEMBER 1944

As has already been seen, the situation in the Balkans was dramatically altered with the Soviet declaration of war on Bulgaria, and the fall of the Bulgarian government. After the Ninth of September, Bulgaria was, on a theoretical level, an Allied state and the prospect of the recognition of her army as co-belligerent haunted the British. Such a prospect would not only entitle Bulgaria to the status of an Allied state, but it would also enable the Bulgarian army to postpone their withdrawal from the Yugoslav and Greek portions of Macedonia. This the British were not prepared to accept.

As early as February 1944, the Foreign Office had clear ideas about this sensitive question: 'we support anyone who is fighting against the Germans . . . but there is a difference in assisting Bulgarian Partisans to fight the Germans *in Bulgaria*, and giving assistance to fight Germans *in Yugoslavia*'. It is apparent from this that it was feared that military cooperation between the two Slavic states might help the creation of a Balkan federation. Moreover, 'complications with the Greeks' were bound to occur.[42] Needless to say, British policy in the Balkans frequently revolved around the clash of long-term political objectives with short-term military necessities.[43] In any case, whenever the issue at stake was the fate of Greece or the dramatic rise of communist power in the Balkans, the British always preferred to sacrifice military efficiency rather than prejudice their fundamental political aims. Undoubtedly, the preservation of the status quo ante bellum was of paramount importance for the British; and so it was for Stalin, when in 1941 he

[42] FO 371/43587, R1650, FO minute dated 1/2/1944.
[43] This point is well documented. See Barker, 'Decision Making over Yugoslavia, 1941–1944', in Phylis Auty and Richard Clogg (eds.), *British Policy towards Wartime Resistance in Yugoslavia and Greece* (London, 1974), 22–58. Naturally, the FO tended to favour the former, and the SOE the latter option.

ruled that the Yugoslav part of Macedonia should remain within the
Yugoslav state.[44]

Before October 1944, however, this aspect of Soviet policy was not
entirely clear to the British. Consequently they made every effort to
drive the Bulgarians out of Yugoslavia. In August, the Foreign Office
sent instructions to the BLOs in Yugoslav Macedonia to persuade the
Bulgarians either to return to Bulgaria—even with their arms—or
to surrender to Tito's Partisans.[45] It appeared, however, that the
Partisans were no less keen to see the Bulgarians leave their country.
On 6 September, a day after the Soviet declaration of war, the Serbian
Partisan commander General Koča Popović—in agreement with the
BLOs—demanded the immediate withdrawal of the Bulgarians; only
those who wished to join them could be allowed to stay in Yugoslavia.
According to British reports, very few chose to do so, for the general
desire was just to 'return home'.[46] The Foreign Office had reasons to
believe that this feeling was particular strong. In a memorandum of the
Northern Department, responsible for Russia, it was asserted that after
the Ninth of September the Soviets forced the Bulgarians to operate
in Yugoslavia 'against their own will'. It was even suggested that this
question might 'draw the Russo-Bulgarian relations to a low ebb'.[47]
In fact, it would be too much to expect the Bulgarians to shed their
blood and clear Macedonia of the Germans, only to hand it over to
the Serbs.

At the same time, the British were at pains to ensure the Bulgarians
would leave soon. In late September they communicated their views
to Molotov: the Allies should issue a joint démarche to the Bulgarian
government, asking for an immediate pull-out of their forces from
both Yugoslavia and Greece, as a prerequisite to the conclusion of
the armistice; the British ambassador to Moscow, Sir Archibald Clark
Kerr, made clear to Molotov that the matter was considered by his
government 'most urgent'. To this demand, they received an 'oral
statement' from the Soviet commissar, stating that the Kremlin accepted
the British suggestion: the Bulgarians should withdraw from both
countries 'within 15 days'; a joint military mission would supervise their
withdrawal.[48]

[44] Stalin's decision has been discussed earlier in this chapter.
[45] WO 202/404. Instructions to 'Brasenose' mission, dated 29/8/1944.
[46] WO 201/1122, Balkan Political Review, dated 6/9/1944.
[47] FO 371/43335, N (Northern Department) 8065, 18/12/1944.
[48] FO 371/43610, R16109, 18/9/1944; FO 371/43610, R14721, 20/9/1944.

But the situation at the time remained fluid and a number of worrying signs soon emerged. The Bulgarians were not in a hurry to evacuate Greek and Yugoslav territories, nor did the Soviets seem to press them in this direction. It was evident that the Bulgarians had reverted to temporizing, and even entertained hopes that their presence in Greece could be prolonged. On 16 September, British anxiety was justified when the Bulgarians—instead of pulling out—issued a standstill order for their forces in Greece. The pretext they used was that an immediate evacuation would bring about all-out civil war between the communist-led National Liberation Front (EAM) and its military arm, the Greek People's Liberation Army (ELAS) on the one hand, and the Greek nationalist guerrilla bands of Antonios Fosteridis (Tsaous Anton), on the other.[49] The British insisted that their duty was to withdraw as soon as possible, and not the maintenance of public order, but in vain.[50]

At about that time, the British received another indication that things had been taking a most dangerous turn. On the night of 18 September, after having enjoyed British protection at the island of Vis, Tito secretly 'levanted'—to use Churchill's telling word—to Moscow, where he had talks with Stalin on the future of the Yugoslav government.[51] What is of interest here, however, is that Tito also discussed with Stalin and Dimitrov the question of military cooperation between the Bulgarian army and the Partisans. Concrete results of this visit followed very soon. On 6 October 1944, the Foreign Office learned from Maclean that a day earlier Tito had concluded at the Romanian city of Craiova an agreement with a high-ranking Bulgarian delegation, which included the Communist minister without portfolio, Dobri Terpechev, regarding military cooperation.[52] The Craiova Agreement was trumpeted by the Bulgarian media shortly afterwards. The statements issued over the following days were full of typical communist rhetoric, but, as shall be seen, they reflected wishful thinking rather than realities. According to these euphoric communiqués, Tito was reported as saying that 'the Bulgarian nation is as near to me as the peoples of Yugoslavia', while the Bulgarian delegation noted that the negotiations were conducted 'in a

[49] WO 201/1618, Balkan Political Review, 8/11/1944. For a more detailed account of the developments in Greek Macedonia see below.
[50] See instructions to Clark Kerr, FO 371/43610, R14721, 20/9/1944.
[51] Tito had gone to the Dalmatian island after he escaped the German seventh offensive.
[52] FO 371/43608, R14643, 6/10/1944.

very friendly way', which paved the way for the discussion of all mutual questions 'in a spirit of fraternity and common interest'.[53]

Unfortunately, nice words are almost always misleading, and the Craiova Agreement can also be counted among the most hotly contested issues regarding wartime Bulgar–Yugoslav relations. Thus Slav–Macedonian authors maintain that the agreement was a statesmanlike gesture on the part of Marshal Tito, aimed at helping the isolated Bulgarians to clear their honour, by allowing them to fight their former allies. According to Bulgarian accounts, a different picture emerges: Tito did not want the Bulgarians in Macedonia but, during the talks with Tito in September, it was Stalin himself who had asked the Yugoslav Marshal to allow Bulgarian soldiers to fight the Germans in Macedonia.[54]

So, it can be said that the prime mover behind the agreement was the Kremlin. For a start, it should be noticed that Stalin did not value the Partisans highly. He even went so far as to humiliate Tito over this particular issue.[55] Moreover, the Soviet interest in incorporating the Bulgarian army in the final operations against the Germans was manifested before 5 October, to the irritation of Tito: on 17 September the Marshal was informed that the Bulgarian army had already been placed under the jurisdiction of Marshal Fyodor Tolbukhin, commander of the Third Ukrainian Front. Shortly afterwards he was informed that the Russians had already decided that the Bulgarian army should participate in the operations against the Germans.[56] Thus, Tito was presented with a fait accompli. He had no other option but to accept it; and so he did.

The British did not fail to draw the necessary conclusions. For Fitzroy Maclean there were no doubts: 'it is a Russian not a Partisan matter', he suggested; 'Tito was forced into it.'[57] There were also other

---

[53] FO 371/43608, R16211, 9/10/1944 (statement in the Bulgarian radio); FO 371/43608, R16618, 13/10/1944 (statement in the Bulgarian press).

[54] For the Macedonian view see Slobodan Nesovic, *Yugoslav–Bulgarian Relations, 1941–1945* (Skopje, 1979), 22–42. The Bulgarian version is given in Georgi Daskalov, *Bŭlgaro-Iugoslavskata Politicheski Otnosheniya, 1944–1945* [Bulgar–Yugoslav Political Relations] (Sofia, 1989), 80–102. For Stalin's demand see ibid. 94–5. Cf. also Paleshutski, *Iugoslavskata*, 321.

[55] In a meeting with Tito, recorded in Milovan Djilas, *Conversations with Stalin* (London, 1962), 89, Stalin 'teased' Tito by saying: 'The Bulgarian Army is very good—drilled and disciplined. And yours, the Yugoslav—they are still Partisans, unfit for serious front-line fighting. Last winter one German regiment broke up a whole division of yours. A regiment beat a division!'

[56] Nesovic, *Yugoslav*, 22.

[57] Maclean's cable to the FO in FO 371/43608, R14643, 6/9/1944.

interpretations. The British section of the Allied Control Commission for Bulgaria asserted that perhaps Tito needed the Bulgarian army 'to put down the Serbs', and to provide military backup for a joint Bulgar–Yugoslav démarche for Salonica. The Foreign Office, however, declined to accept this gloomy scenario, and endorsed Maclean's view.[58]

Be that as it may, this development was most unfortunate. The retention of Bulgarian troops on Yugoslav territory was clearly an ominous sign. The British therefore tried hard during the tortuous negotiations for the Bulgarian armistice to ensure that the occupiers-turned-liberators would leave their former possessions. The task was not an easy one, for General Ivan Marinov, the Bulgarian commander-in-chief, told the Allied Control Commission on 6 October that the Bulgarians had no intention of evacuating Yugoslavia.[59] For a brief moment, however, the British could congratulate themselves. On 11 October, they managed to present the Bulgarian government with a prerequisite clause, postulating that the three Allied states demanded the withdrawal 'from Yugoslav and Greek territory of all Bulgarian officials and troops' within fifteen days. The conclusion of the armistice could proceed only after the evacuation.[60]

It was too little too late. The Bulgarian government, having secured Soviet support, announced the same day that their forces would evacuate Greece, but those in Yugoslavia were 'excluded' from the clause. They were fighting the Germans under Soviet—i.e. Allied—command, and with the consent of Tito, after all.[61] This declaration caused considerable nervousness at the Foreign Office: 'This no doubt suits the Soviet book . . . but it does not suit ours'.[62] In fact, the Soviets followed a two-track policy on this issue, which frustrated the British. Although in public they seemed to endorse the prerequisite clause, in order to present a facade of Allied cooperation, in effect they afforded the Bulgarians all the support they needed for their engagement in the final stages of the war.

The British, however, did not give in. On 13 October, while Churchill and Eden were in Moscow for the Percentages Agreement, the Foreign Office cabled the Foreign Secretary, informing him that the Bulgarians were leaving Greece but not Yugoslavia. He was urged to 'insist that

Bulgarian forces should evacuate Yugoslav territory as well'.[63] But Eden had done so two days earlier. On 11 October, the day the Bulgarians announced that their soldiers would stay in Yugoslavia, Eden informed Molotov of his disapproval of Tito's secret visit to Moscow. If only he had kept the British informed, Eden maintained, they would have wished him 'bon voyage'. The Soviet commissar responded with a long tirade about the 'peasant Tito' who could not understand the subtleties of international politics, and denied any Soviet connection with his 'voyages'. Moreover, anxious not to rock the boat of the Percentages Agreement, he promised to drive the Bulgarians out of Yugoslavia and Greece 'tonight'.[64] Certainly, in his deliberations with Eden, Molotov was less urbane than his Yugoslav comrade. Thus, he did not reveal that Tito had left Vis together with General N. V. Korneev, head of the Soviet mission to Tito.[65] Nor did he inform Eden that, against all British objections, the Kremlin was determined to use the Bulgarian army in Yugoslavia. As a result, the 'night' of 11 October proved to be very long indeed, for the Bulgarian army only left Yugoslavia in May 1945, eight months later.

The Foreign Office seemed to prefer to take Molotov at face value, and continued to press for the implementation of the prerequisite clause. On 23 October, the British section of the Allied Control Commission for Bulgaria received a note from London, instructing them to pay particular attention 'to the strict observance of the undertaking to withdraw [Bulgarian] troops from Greek and Yugoslav territory'. At the same time, fully aware of plans for a Bulgar–Yugoslav federation, the Foreign Office urged them to afford no encouragement 'in any form to the Macedonian movement, nor to any idea of Bulgar–Yugoslav federation'.[66] The British objections were formally accepted by the Soviets, who had decided to give London a false sense of Allied consensus over this issue, while at the same time they pursued their own policy.

So, the Second Article of the official Bulgarian Armistice Terms, concluded in Moscow and accepted by the Bulgarian government on 28 October, provided for the withdrawal of all Bulgarian troops and administrative personnel from Greece and Yugoslavia.[67] Unfortunately for the British, developments in both parts of Macedonia prior to the

[63] FO 371/43611, R16534, FO to 'Tolstoy', 13/10/1944.

[64] Anthony Eden, *Memoirs: The Reckoning* (London, 1965), 482–3. Cable from 'Tolstoy' to the FO, FO 371/44279, R16330, dated 16/10/1944.

[65] Nesovic, *Yugoslav*, 22.   [66] FO 371/43616, R17076, 23/10/1944.

[67] The full text of the Armistice as quoted by the Bulgarian Radio is in WO 201/1617, App. 'A', of Balkan Political Review, dated 1/11/1944.

signature of the terms, rendered this article obsolete. By 25 October, the Bulgarians had completed their evacuation of Greek Macedonia and Thrace,[68] while in Yugoslav Macedonia, as shall be seen, they were playing an active part in polishing the area off the retreating Germans. Within this particular context, the Armistice Terms reflected a reality which offered the British little comfort: irrespective of the 'percentages' agreed on Yugoslavia, the Kremlin intended to regard this country as falling within its sphere of influence. The Foreign Office was soon to realize that the Yugoslav example would not be the only one.

The British were not alone in resenting the presence of the Bulgarian army in Yugoslavia. Although the official Yugoslav rhetoric monotonously referred to the 'brotherhood and unity' of the two Slav states, it is certain that the Macedonian and Serbian Partisans could hardly feel any brotherhood with their former occupiers. For a start, it would be too much to expect the Partisans to embrace the same forces they had been fighting a little earlier. It should be stressed in this connection, that the Macedonian guerrillas had developed a particularly virulent anti-Bulgarian attitude during wartime, which affected their strategy. According to the Italian consul at Bitolj, the Partisans attacked only Bulgarian targets, showing little interest in the Germans.[69] Knowing the peculiarities surrounding the national loyalties of the Macedonian peasants, the Partisans were extremely anxious to ensure that the Bulgarians would leave and never come back, for their primary concern was to educate the peasants in nationalist Macedonian ideology. They went as far as to openly admit that it was convenient that villages were burned to the ground by the Bulgarians during the occupation, so they could start the education of the peasants from scratch.[70] In Serbia, there were similar concerns. The concentration of Bulgarian forces there provoked the intense suspicion of the Serbian Partisans. Their initial reaction was to consider the Bulgarians as a leopard who had changed its spots. The moral to be drawn was not unexpected: the unwanted liberators were not to be trusted.[71]

---

[68] FO 371/43611, R17977, 7/11/1944.

[69] WO 202/256, report by the Italian consul at Bitolj, to BLOs, dated 30/2/1945. The consul insisted that this was absolutely true for Bitolj, but he was inclined to believe that it generally holds true for other parts of Macedonia as well.

[70] WO 202/1209, report by the 'Brasenose' mission, dated 1/10/1944. According to this source, such comments were frequently heard.

[71] For the situation in Eastern Serbia see the interesting and detailed reports in FO 371/43609, report on the Bulgarian Army in Serbia by John Henniker-Major, dated

Apart from political reasons, there were also more personal motives. As has already been seen, the Partisans had to content themselves with only rudimentary clothing and light weapons. Consequently, they resented seeing their Bulgarian 'liberators' wearing smart and warm uniforms, and bearing modern weapons, supplied to them by the Germans during wartime.[72] Perhaps a typical expression of the prevailing mood was the incident that occurred in Skopje in November, when the Partisans refused to allow Damyan Velchev, Bulgarian minister of war, to enter the city, for, as they said, four years of Bulgarian occupation had done more harm to Macedonia than twenty years of Serbian yoke.[73]

Military realities, however, made this incident look very ironic indeed, for Skopje was liberated by Bulgarian forces, while the Macedonian Partisans remained in the surrounding hills, and came down only to celebrate their entrance to the city. Similar scenes occurred in many other towns of Macedonia and Serbia, pointing to the fact that, from a military perspective, the Russians were right: the Bulgarian army was the only force capable of driving the Germans quickly out of Yugoslavia.[74] Needless to say, the official Slav-Macedonian historiography, written mainly by Apostolski himself, understandably played down the crucial role of the Bulgarians. The glorification of the Partisan movement—an essential component of the post-war Yugoslav political culture—and the more personal Partisan considerations left little room for such 'technicalities'.[75]

The successes of the Bulgarian army certainly did not come as music to British ears either. Thus, it was with a sense of disappointment that the Foreign Office received reports stressing that the Bulgarians 'have been doing very well against the Germans'. George Clutton minuted on this development in unequivocal language, which clearly reflected the British determination to prevent Bulgaria from becoming an officially

4/12/1944, and FO 371/43611, R20624, 12/12/1944, 'Notes on Serb-Partisan–Bulgar Relations during the Period August–November 1944'.

[72] For complaints of that kind see WO 201/1122, Balkan Political Review, 18/10/1944. Maclean also reported about this feeling. Cf. FO 371/43608, R14643, 6/10/1944.

[73] For this incident, and its background, see Ch. 6.

[74] For information on the military situation in Macedonia and Serbia and the role of the Bulgarian army see FO 371/43608, R17271, 24/11/1944; FO 371/44279, R16642, 14/10/1944; FO 371/43630, R19495, 24/11/1944; WO 208, 113B, 12/9/1944. These sources, which contain intelligence reports from BLOs, confirm the decisive role of the Bulgarian army in the liberation of Skopje, Niš, Prilep, and the Morava Valley.

[75] Cf. Apostolski, 'La Guerre', and Nesovic, *Yugoslav*.

recognized co-belligerent state. 'We do not recognize the Bulgarians as co-belligerents, so we soft-pedal references on these successes'. Nevertheless, he felt obliged to justify his views on moral grounds: 'There is a tendency in Great Britain to regard Bulgaria as having been hardly treated, but she has black and treacherous record.'[76] The BBC was accordingly instructed not to boost the Bulgarian contribution to the war. Thus, although the American and Soviet radio correctly attributed the liberation of Skopje to the Bulgarians, the BBC ignored their vital role, infuriating Sofia.[77]

Tito seemed equally disconcerted about the protracted Bulgarian presence in Yugoslavia. From late October onwards, he had tried to persuade the Soviets to order the withdrawal of his comrades, but without success. As the Bulgarian army completed its duties in Macedonia and Serbia in December and started moving north, Tito's patience ran out. Amidst numerous reports on the conduct of the Bulgarians, which resembled the complaints about the Red Army after 1948, the Marshal stepped up his pressure.[78] In May 1945, when the whole of Yugoslavia had been liberated, he undertook a more definitive move to pay off his political scores with his 'allies'. Tempo and the commander of the Yugoslav National Army, Arso Jovanović, were sent to Vienna to demand from Marshal Tolbukhin an immediate withdrawal. Tolbukhin agreed, and the Third Yugoslav Army was quick to issue the order of the day, which describes best not only the Yugoslav relief, but the semantics of the communist rhetoric at the time as well: 'Say good-bye

---

[76] FO 371/43630, R18509, minute by Clutton, 14/11/1944.

[77] FO 371/43630, R19488, 18/11/1944. It is perhaps of interest to note here that the British historiography on Yugoslavia also downplayed the critical role of the Soviet and Bulgarian armies in the liberation of this country, and appears to support the view that Yugoslavia was liberated by the Partisans alone. The fact that Belgrade was liberated with the help of the Red Army, and Skopje by the Bulgarians, is rarely mentioned. It can be said that the political situation in the 1960s and early 1970s, when in Western Europe Tito commanded a fair amount of admiration, as an example of non-Stalinist communism, was a not negligible factor for such an overrated assessment. This has also coloured assessments of Tito. A typical example is Auty's biography of Tito. See Phyllis Auty, *Tito: A Biography* (London, 1970). A more balanced view, although unfriendly to the Marshal, is offered in Stevan Pavlowitch, *Tito: Yugoslavia's Great Dictator* (London, 1992). On Tito's mediocre calibre as a guerrilla leader see also Djila's account, in Milovan Djilas, *Tito: The Story from Inside* (New York and London, 1980), 11.

[78] Cf. e.g. complaints from Partisans in Eastern Serbia, according to which the Bulgarians were stripping the houses of all removable property. FO 371/43609, R17688, 22/11/1944. For a longer list of complaints see Nesovic, *Yugoslav*, 55–6.

to your Bulgarian comrades,' read the order, 'emphasizing the unity of our peoples.'[79]

PERCENTAGES OBSERVED: GREEK MACEDONIA, SEPTEMBER–OCTOBER 1944

The dramatic events of September 1944 in Bulgaria and the prospect of an Allied Bulgarian army were bound to have profound ramifications in Greece. In fact, the prospect of seeing the Bulgarian army 'liberating' an area it had previously ravaged, instantly provoked strong reactions. Unlike the Yugoslav case, the Bulgarian occupation in eastern Greek Macedonia was from the very beginning excessively harsh. Bulgaria sought to annex the Greek lands she occupied, and embarked on a 'denationalization' policy, aiming at altering the demographic composition in northern Greece, which, following the influx of hundreds of thousands refugees after 1922, had become overwhelmingly Greek. As a result of this policy, thousands of Greeks were driven out of Greek Macedonia, to escape the wrath of the new rulers. Those who decided to stay were obliged to declare themselves Bulgarians if they wanted to get access to various provisions, including food coupons provided by the 'Bulgarian Club' of Salonica.[80]

The possibility of a continued Bulgarian presence in Greece horrified the political world of the country, across ideological boundaries. Immediately after the events of the Ninth of September in Bulgaria, the prime minister, Georgios Papandreou, accompanied by the EAM minister Alexandros Svolos, visited General Henry Maitland Wilson, the Supreme Allied Commander in the Mediterranean theatre, in Italy to express their grave concerns about the situation. They were particularly worried about possible operations of the Bulgarians as co-belligerents against the Germans in Greek soil. This, they intimated to Wilson,

---

[79] Nesovic, *Yugoslav*, 119.

[80] For the Bulgarian occupation in Macedonia see Athanasios Chrysohoou, *I Katochi en Makedonia* [The Occupation of Macedonia], vols. ii and iv (Salonica, 1950–2); Hagen Fleischer, *Stemma kai Svastika: I Ellada tis Katochis kai tis Antistasis* (Crown and Swastika: Greece in Occupation and Resistance) (Athens, n.d), 90–102; Hans-Joachim Hoppe, 'Bulgarian Nationalities Policy in Occupied Thrace and Aegean Macedonia', *Nationalities Papers*, 14/1–2 (1986), 89–100; Xanthippi Kotzageorgi, 'Population Exchanges in Eastern Macedonia and in Thrace: The Legislative "Initiatives" of the Bulgarian Authorities, 1941–1944', *Balkan Studies*, 37/1 (1996), 133–64.

'was an insult to Greek sovereignty, which could not be tolerated'.[81] At the same time, the Greek ambassador to London furnished the Foreign Office with an alarmist memorandum on the same issue. The British reply was reassuring: in the armistice terms there would be an 'explicit demand' for the immediate and complete withdrawal of the Bulgarians from Greece.[82]

It became clear very soon, however, that the Bulgarians had no such intention. Extremely polarized local conditions further complicated the situation. In eastern Macedonia, unlike the rest of Greece, the communist-led EAM had never been very strong. The vacuum was thus filled by extreme nationalist guerrilla bands, led by Antonios Fostiridis, a Turkish-speaking refugee widely known as Tsaous Anton.[83] The fact that a bloody civil war between the EAM and the nationalists looked imminent, offered the Bulgarians a unique opportunity to justify their presence in Greek Macedonia by posing as the guarantors of public order. This prospect fanned Turkish fears as well. On 30 September, the Foreign Office was informed from the British embassy in Ankara that the Turkish press had circulated rumours to the effect that the Red Army would occupy Greek Thrace in order to help the Bulgarians to maintain law and order.[84] The British declined to attach importance to these rumours. Nevertheless, they stressed in their representations to Molotov, mentioned previously, that Bulgaria's duty was immediately to evacuate Greece and not to protect public order. But the Bulgarians issued a standstill order on 13 September, trying, apparently, to buy time.

At the same time, both Greek political camps, nationalists and communists, tried to make the most out of the unstable situation prevailing in the area, and they did not hesitate to drag the Bulgarians into their fratricidal feuds. Two BLOs, Major Miller and Captain Reddle, who had arrived in Drama on 14 September, approached General Sirakov, the commander of the Bulgarian Second Corps, asking him to prevent ELAS forces from capturing Drama and to hand the cities the Bulgarians were still occupying to the nationalists. Sirakov

---

[81] FO 371/43610, R14377; WO/201, 16000, 9/9/1944.

[82] FO 371/43610, R14463, Greek aide-memoire (12/9/1944) and the British reply (12/11/1944). See also George Kazamias, ' "The Usual Bulgarian Stratagems": The Big Three and the End of the Bulgarian Occupation in Greek Eastern Macedonia and Thrace, September–October, 1944', *European History Quarterly*, 29/3 (1999), 323–47.

[83] Fostiridis's activities during the war are related in his own self-inflated account. See Antonios Fosteridis, *Ethniki Antistasi kata tis Voulgarikis Katochis* [National Resistance Against the Bulgarian Occupation] (Salonica, 1952).

[84] FO 371/43610, R15644, 30/9/1944.

refused to offer an answer without instructions from Sofia, and at that stage Miller decided to proceed to Sofia to clear the matter up with the Bulgarian government. Thus, two days later, accompanied by a nationalist delegation he visited Sofia, asking the Bulgarians to hand them Seres, Drama, and Kavala, threatening attacks if their demands were not met.[85] News of the BLOs' involvement reached the Foreign Office through Ankara, and infuriated Sir Orme Sargent. 'I did not know', minuted Sir Orme, 'that BLOs have got entangled in this mess.' Their action, he insisted, ought clearly to be condemned.[86] The Foreign Office demanded that the Bulgarians should not be party to any agreement with Greeks, nor should they hand over the administration of Greek Macedonia to any authorities other than the official representatives of the Greek government. Both local Greek sides, however, were anxious to consolidate their position in the region, and seemed not to be concerned by the dangers that might be caused by the involvement of the Bulgarians.

Miller and the nationalists were anxious, however, to enlist the support of Sirakov. For a brief moment on 17 September, they even managed to persuade him to evict ELAS forces from their strongholds in eastern Macedonia, but the Bulgarian general, probably fearing the reaction of his own government, withdrew his support two days later.[87] At about the same time, the CPB was also engaged in deliberations with the local EAM forces in Greek Macedonia. Dobri Terpechev, second secretary of the Central Committee, visited the area on 11 September and had talks with Giorgos Erythriadis, secretary of the Greek Communist Party for eastern Macedonia. The result of these talks was the transfer of the administration of the big cities to the EAM. It should be stressed, however, that when news of Erythriadis's negotiations reached the Central Committee of the KKE in October, the party was quick to announce that no agreements should be reached with the Bulgarians and repeated that the 'line' was for an immediate withdrawal.[88]

---

[85] Stoyan Rachev, *Anglo-Bulgarian Relations during the Second World War, 1939–1944* (Sofia, 1981), 189–93.

[86] FO 371/43610, R14721, 16/9/1944. Minute by Sargent, dated 20/9/1944.

[87] Rachev, *Anglo-Bulgarian*, 194–5.

[88] Evangelos Kofos, *I Valkaniki Diastasi tou Makedonikou Zitematos sta Chronia tis Katochis kai tis Antistasi* [The Balkan Dimension of the Macedonian Question during the Occupation and the Resistance] (Athens, 1989), 30–5. For Terpechev's mission see also Rachev, *Anglo-Bulgarian*, 184–5.

Meanwhile, tension was mounting, and as EAM started to transfer troops from western Macedonia to the eastern part, fighting broke out between the communists and the nationalists, around Drama, in late September. The Bulgarians actively participated in the fighting by helping EAM to destroy Anton's bands. A Bulgarian guerrilla leader turned colonel in the Fatherland Front's army, Ivan Radev, known locally also as Rhodopoulos, played an active part in supporting EAM. Eloquently described by Woodhouse as 'Greek by birth, a Bulgar by naturalisation and an international communist by persuasion', Radev tried to prevent the BLOs from arranging a truce between the warring factions, and placed one of them under house arrest.[89] According to British reports, the Bulgarians also assisted the communists in attacking nationalist bands in Thrace in early October.[90]

Clearly, the main Bulgarian objective in their negotiations with both the nationalists and the communists, was to postpone the evacuation of Greece, presenting themselves either as guarantor of public order or as a co-belligerent army. Technically they were co-belligerents, for Sirakov's forces in Greece had already been placed under the command of Marshall Tolbukhin's forces on 16 September.[91] But, unfortunately for them, Greece was not Yugoslavia, and the Soviets were not prepared to back them up. Soviet intentions had already been made clear in September, when they refused to accept the demands of the Communist Party of Greece for entrance of the Red Army in Greece.[92] Thus, in the Percentages Agreement the Bulgarians saw their hopes dashed. On 11 October, they started withdrawing from Greece, and five days later two representatives of the Greek government, Lambrianidis and the communist Porphyrogenis, arrived at Drama. An uneasy truce was concluded between the communists and the nationalists, and by 25 October the Bulgarians had completed the evacuation of Greek Macedonia. The Percentages Agreement for Greece was observed; and strictly so.

As far as the British were concerned, in late 1944 the Macedonian Question became actual for the first time in the 1940s. It also had the dubious privilege of being interconnected with much wider issues, regarding the spheres of influence of the Great Powers in the Balkans,

[89] WO 201/1618, Balkan Political Review, app. 'E', dated 8/11/1944. For Radev see C. M.Woodhouse, *Apple of Discord: A Survey of Recent Greek Politics in their International Setting* (London, 1948), 91.

[90] FO 371/43611, R17515, 6/10/1944.

[91] Rachev, *Anglo-Bulgarian Relations*, 195.   [92] Kofos, *Valkaniki Diastasi*, 34.

and the 'New' Yugoslavia then emerging under Tito. Thus developments in the Macedonian parts of Yugoslavia and Greece not only acquired a sudden and unexpected significance, but also became a testing ground for the intentions of both Britain and Russia, concerning this part of the world.

It has been said of the Macedonian Question that every move which pleases two sides inevitably embitters three. The role of the Bulgarian army clearly supports this gloomy view. Those who stood to benefit were Bulgaria and, to a lesser extent, the USSR. The former tried to capitalize on the performance of her army, in an effort to exorcize the stigma of her wartime record. In this, she failed, for her army was never recognized as a co-belligerent. Nevertheless, the successes of the Bulgarian army were used for the enrichment of the Fatherland Front's propaganda, and served as a face-saving clause. At least, these operations enabled the Bulgarians to announce that their troops had decisively contributed to 'the liberation of our brother nations, the Serbs and the Macedonians'.[93] The Kremlin achieved more concrete results. As a well-equipped and disciplined force under the high command of Marshal Tolbukhin, the Bulgarians afforded the Red Army valuable time to continue its advances through Yugoslavia. Subsequent developments, however, showed that Stalin did not make the most out of Bulgaria's participation in the final operations against the Germans. It can be said that Stalin wanted to use Bulgaria's record in Yugoslavia in an attempt to give her Allied status, which, in turn, would enable Bulgaria to enter in a formal federation with Yugoslavia. As shall be seen, however, the Russians tried to use this argument in February 1945, but the British thought otherwise.

The opposite side had a surprising composition, for it included not only the British and the Greeks, but Tito and his Partisans as well. The Greeks could derive comfort from the fact that they had been placed under the indisputable tutelage of the British; something that Stalin thought it wise to observe. Consequently, Bulgarian efforts to fish in the troubled waters of Greek Macedonia, helped by overtures from both the communists and the nationalists, achieved nothing. Unfortunately for Tito, this was not the case for Yugoslavia. Certainly, the Marshal and his almost barefoot Macedonian Partisans resented the presence of their warmly clothed allies. The fact that they contributed heavily to the liberation of southern Yugoslavia, mattered little. Besides, after 1948, very few Westerners would care to remember this detail.

---

[93] See the communiqué issued on 10/12/1944, in FO 371/48149, R615.

Naturally, the British had good reason for preferring to forget it. Bulgaria had to remain an enemy state for the sake of Greece, and the British lines of communication the latter commanded. Moreover, the pre-war territorial settlement should be preserved, and any sign of Bulgar–Yugoslav cooperation or federation had to be effectively challenged. So, the Bulgarians should evacuate Yugoslavia as well. The problem was that in Yugoslavia the Percentages Agreement signed in Moscow was moulded by Stalin to fit his plans. The British could do little more than draft prerequisite clauses and armistice terms. In fact, the question of the Bulgarian army in Yugoslavia was the first indication that no sooner had the ink dried than the Percentages Agreement regarding Yugoslavia had become obsolete.

5

Ghost Resurrected: Bulgar–Yugoslav Negotiations for Federation, and the British Response, 1944–1945

Since the complexities of the national question never ceased to generate friction and conflicts among the Balkan states and to threaten their internal stability, alternatives to the nation state began to be discussed quite soon. Among them, the idea of a Balkan federation figured prominently. Advocated mainly by socialists and communists from the late nineteenth century onwards, the federal concept reflected not only their firmly rooted belief in the capability of Marxism to untangle national problems, but also demonstrated a rather over-optimistic assumption, shared by all European socialists, that worker solidarity could triumph over 'bourgeois' nationalism. The European socialists learned very soon, after the experience of the Great War, that 'proletarian internationalism' should wait for a more propitious time; the Balkan Wars taught their local comrades the same lesson.[1] Nevertheless, the slogan of a Balkan federation continued to dominate communist rhetoric for years to come.

At the same time, plans and schemes for federations also attracted the interest of the Great Powers. In fact, grouping the states of south-eastern Europe under their tutelage became an increasingly promising option for the consolidation of their influence in an area where the conflicting interests of the Great Powers, coupled with permanent social and national unrest, offered little prospects for stability. In the interwar years, the Soviet Union was quite energetic in that direction. By sponsoring a federation of communist Balkan states the Kremlin aimed at killing two birds with one stone: first, to break the 'imperialist encirclement' by detaching Yugoslavia

---

[1] For these issues see Ch. 1.

and Romania from the French-inspired Little Entente, and secondly to replace it by a buffer zone consisting of loyal communist satellites.

By the 1940s, however, the Western Powers also began to entertain federal ideas for the future of south and east-central Europe. This was a major shift in their policy towards the region. In the interwar years, their efforts had been confined mostly to the creation of anti-revisionist alliances (France and the Little Entente), or to the support of fragile systems of collective security in the Balkans (Britain and the Balkan Pact). But shortly afterwards, in an effort to neutralize both Germany and the USSR, Britain worked out a rather grandiose and ambitious plan for the post-war reconstruction of the whole of south and east-central Europe on a (con)federal basis. As we have already pointed out these plans, overtaken by wartime developments, ended in utter failure.[2]

Given this perspective, the Yugoslav–Bulgar negotiations for federation (conducted from late 1944 to early 1945) were hardly a surprising development. They nevertheless constituted a major turning point in the relations between the two countries and, had they been fruitful, they would have profoundly affected the post-war architecture not only of the Balkans but of Eastern Europe as well. These negotiations, however, were met with strong and determined resistance from the British, who saw in those plans a Soviet attempt to control the troubled peninsula. As vital British interests in the area seemed to be at stake, they stepped in, forcing the Balkan communists and their allies in Moscow to abandon their grandiose plans. The aim of this chapter is twofold: first, to explore and analyse the deliberations between Bulgaria and Yugoslavia within their context, and secondly to investigate the role of the British connection at a time when the British felt that they had both the willingness and the power to make their presence felt in the Balkans. The first section charts the background: it traces the evolution of Tito's wartime Balkan policy until 1944, and examines the conflicting views of the Balkan communists on the future of their states. The second section deals with the British reaction and analyses its objectives and repercussions. Furthermore, as the focus of analysis shifts from local to international politics, due importance will be paid to Soviet policy, as perceived by the British, as well as to the Anglo-American 'special relationship' concerning the Balkans.

---

[2] For the British plan on the federal future of the region see Ch. 3.

AMBITIONS AND REALITIES: TITO'S BALKAN POLICY, 1942–1944

The rulers of the 'First Yugoslavia', that is, the court and the upper echelons of the Serbian political elite, had been shaping their foreign policy upon two fundamental principles: (*a*) a determination to defend the peace settlement and to keep the status quo in the Balkans intact, and (*b*) to eliminate the menace represented by the perpetuation of the Macedonian Question. In both respects they failed, partly due to international developments in the 1930s, and partly because of their own shortcomings and short-sighted policies. The destruction of the state by the Axis Powers, however, and the turmoil that followed, prepared the ground for the emergence of a 'Second [i.e. Tito's] Yugoslavia'.

During the first stages of the war, nevertheless, the situation appeared to be—as it was in Greece—confusing: the legal government, increasingly estranged from the country, exercised only limited control over it,[3] while at the same time the Communist Party of Yugoslavia (CPY), became gradually the sole source of authority in the field, enjoying a considerable amount of legitimacy and power emanating from the armed resistance against the invaders. As was to be expected, the foreign policy objectives of the two contenders were anything but identical. The royal government, largely under British influence, was willing to cooperate with the Greek government-in-exile for the formation of a Balkan federation,[4] but Tito had other ends to meet.

Despite the hardships of the guerilla war in Yugoslavia, Tito never ignored the sensitive domain of foreign policy. As far as his Balkan policy was concerned, the idea of a Balkan federation was its cornerstone. It appears that Tito had formulated his views quite early. In the summer of 1942 the radio station of the CPY, 'Free Yugoslavia', stated that 'when Bulgaria rids herself of her oppressors she will be welcomed into our fraternal federation', a clear indication that Bulgaria was considered

---

[3] The only organized force in Yugoslavia, loyal to the pre-war regime, had been the *Četnik* bands of General Mihailović. A nationalist Serb and colonel of the General Staff in the Yugoslav Army, Mihailović was promoted in 1942, by the royal government, to general and minister of war. For the Četniks see Joso Tomasevich, *War and Revolution in Yugoslavia, 1941–1945: The Chetniks* (Stanford, 1975).

[4] Cf. Ch. 3.

as the first state to join in.[5] The fact that 'Free Yugoslavia' operated from Soviet soil, suggests that the proposed federation had at least the tacit approval of Moscow; besides, Tito had been behaving at the time as a completely loyal communist and, despite the assertions of the post-1948 Yugoslav literature, there were no visible signs of dissension.

In general, during the early phases of the war the issue of federation was somewhat toned down, apparently in order not to offend Western susceptibilities. The CPY, however, was kept busy, undertaking major political initiatives which aimed at establishing a commanding position among the Balkan communist movements. Although it was never admitted that these initiatives were part of a wider plan leading to a Balkan federation, it is reasonable to assume that they were little less than preparations for that, for if they had been successful, they would have rendered the formation of a federation a mere formality.

Perhaps the least-known Yugoslav initiative is the one undertaken first. From 1939 onwards, the CPY had tried to place the weak and divided Albanian communist movement under its absolute control. Initially they did remarkably well. A Serb, Miladin Popović, Tito's first emissary to Albania, was instrumental in bringing the various communist groups of the country together and laid the foundations for the formation of the Communist Party of Albania (CPA). Another Yugoslav emissary, the Montenegrin Dušan Mugoša, who succeeded Popović after the latter's arrest in 1941, completed the job: in September 1941, a conference for the unification of the Albanian communist movement was held in Tirana, organized by Mugoša, and ended in the formation of the CPA, with Enver Hoxha, a French-educated intellectual, as its first secretary general. Thus almost from its earliest steps, the CPA had became a Yugoslav pawn.[6]

Patronizing the CPA could have proved more fruitful for the Yugoslavs than might have been expected at first sight. First, it should be noted that both Popović and Mugoša tried to ensure that the new

---

[5] WO 201/1622, Balkan Political Intelligence Notes, no. 70, 9/5/1944.

[6] Unfortunately, Yugoslavia's Albanian venture has not attracted much interest, despite its significance. Most accounts are still based on Vladimir Dedijer's book, *Jugoslovensko–Albanski Odnosi, 1939–1948* [Yugoslav–Albanian Relations] (Belgrade, 1949), which is the official Yugoslav view. See e.g. Robert Lee Wolff, *The Balkans in Our Time* (Harvard, Mass., 1956), 216–22 and Charles Zalar, *Yugoslav Communism: A Critical Study* (Washington, DC, 1961), 150–2. For critical appraisals on the early history and formation of the CPA see Nicholas Pano, *The People's Republic of Albania* (Baltimore, 1968), 45–58. See also Reginald Hibbert, *Albania's Liberation Struggle: The Bitter Victory* (London, 1989), 11–28.

party was modelled on the CPY and adopted similar views on the necessity of large-scale armed resistance against the Italians, aiming not only at national liberation but also at the conquest of power. No matter how premature it was in 1941 for the Yugoslavs to foresee the eventual victory of the CPA in 1944, it was certain that—unlike the Greek Communist Party (KKE)—the militant attitude of the Albanians towards the question of the political power allowed a considerable amount of optimism about their victory; there was no doubt, the Yugoslavs thought, that victory would automatically place the country under Yugoslav control.

On the other hand, the political consequences of Yugoslav domination over Albania were far more obvious. In the interwar years Italy's prominent position in Albania was a permanent cause of friction between the two countries.[7] A communist takeover would have offered the most firm assurance that this would never happen again. Strategic objectives were no less important, since Albania—'the doorman of the Adriatic'—is located in a sensitive area, commanding Yugoslavia's access to the Mediterranean. Although the reasons mentioned above would have been sufficient in justifying Tito's policy towards Albania, perhaps his most important motivation emanated from within Yugoslavia.

During the war the Italians had tried and to a considerable extent had succeeded in stirring irredentist aspirations among the predominantly Albanian population of the Kosovo and Metohija area. According to Tempo, 'conditions for armed struggle were more unfavourable in Kosovo than in any other area', due, among other reasons, to 'the hostility towards the Partisans on the part of the Albanian population'.[8] Thus, Albanian intransigence represented a serious threat to Tito's plans for a unitary, albeit federal, state. A friendly Albanian government, willing to join in a Balkan federation under Yugoslav tutelage after the war was over, was, therefore, rightly regarded as the only way for the Yugoslavs to accommodate minority demands for closer relations with Tirana, without facing unpleasant separatist questions.[9]

[7] For the interwar background see Ch. 1.
[8] For Kosovar-Yugoslav relations see Ivo Banac, *The National Question in Yugoslavia: Origins, History, Politics* (Ithaca, NY and London, 1988), 291–306. Cf. Tempo's report to the CC of the CPY, of 8 August 1943, in Stephen Palmer and Robert King, *Yugoslav Communism and the Macedonian Question* (Hamden, Conn., 1971), 95–6.
[9] Djilas alluded to that when he argued that a Yugoslav–Albanian union 'would have solved the question of the Albanian minority in Yugoslavia'. See Milovan Djilas, *Conversations with Stalin* (London, 1962), 104.

During 1943, Yugoslav intentions became much clearer and their plans even more ambitious. The issue which dominated their Balkan policy was the question of the formation of a Balkan Headquarters (BHQ) to coordinate the resistance movements of Albania, Yugoslavia, Greece, and Bulgaria. Svetozar Vukmanović conceded, in his own detailed account, that the idea of the formation of the BHQ was his own.[10] It could hardly have been. It is unreasonable to suggest that Tempo could have tried to implement such an ambitious design with far-reaching repercussions, without prior consultation with Tito.[11] During mid-1943 Tempo set out to put his plan into action. He started with the responsive part, and in early June he established contact with the Albanian communists.

In a meeting held at the village of Kutsaka, near Korçë, Tempo met the Central Committee of the CPA, which immediately accepted his idea 'without objection'.[12] The Albanians agreed to send partisan units to the north of the country and to the Kosovo-Metohija area in order to neutralize the influence of the nationalist organization *Balli Kombëtar*, and to help the Yugoslav partisans to put the region under their control, 'for it is one thing for Serbian partisans to tell the Albanian masses that, after the expulsion of the invader, they will decide their future for themselves, but it is quite another thing if Albanian partisans tell them this'.[13] It was also agreed that Albanian and Macedonian bands should cooperate in the Korçë–Prespa–Ochrid area.

Having secured Albanian support, Tempo sought to bring in the Greeks as well. He had already sent a letter, while in Skopje, to the Communist Party of Greece asking them to send a delegate to Albania 'to talk about cooperation'. So, he was pleased to learn in Kutsaka that a Greek representative, Tilemachos Ververis, nicknamed Grigorije,[14] had arrived to meet him. Much to his resentment, however, Grigorije knew nothing of the letter and he had come to Albania to contact the Soviets through the Albanian and Yugoslav partisans. Moreover

---

[10] Svetozar Vukmanović (General Tempo), *Struggle for the Balkans* (London, 1990), 67.

[11] German sources, quoting from intercepted Yugoslav radiograms, also support this interpretation. According to German counter-intelligence services, Tempo was reported as saying that his plans had been based upon Tito's 'verbal instructions'. Hagen Fleischer, *Stemma kai Svastika: I Eellada tis katochis kai tis Antistasis, 1941–1944* [Crown and Swastika: Greece in Occupation and Resistance] (Athens, n.d.), 418.

[12] Vukmanović, *Struggle*, 104.   [13] Ibid. 103.

[14] Grigorije is the Serbianized form of the Greek name Grigoris, the *nom de guerre* of the Greek representative.

he was not authorized to take part in any deliberations affecting the KKE.

Tempo remained undeterred, and tried to impose on the Greek delegate not only his views on wartime cooperation, but also the Yugoslav solution on the Macedonian question. Thus a part of the conclusions reached in Kutsaka read as follows: '. . . Macedonia has been divided and has served only as a bargaining chip in imperialist wars. It is essential that the Supreme Command of interested Balkan countries issue a joint declaration recognizing the right of the Macedonian people to decide their future for themselves.'[15] The Greek representative refused to agree with such a wording. Although he admitted that 'in the regions of Edessa, Florina and Kastoria . . . 60% of the population are Macedonians', he immediately sensed the danger emanating from the raising of this sensitive issue, which could 'alienate Greeks from the KKE'. Thus he did not sign the agreement, despite the combined efforts of his Albanian and Yugoslav comrades, and said he would refer the issue to the Central Committee of his party.[16] In the end, nothing concrete came out of these negotiations.

More important negotiations with the Greeks, however, were about to start. Tempo, accompanied by the Albanian representative Koci Hoxe, entered Greece late in June and had talks with Andreas Tzimas (Samariniotis), political instructor of ELAS, on 25 June, and with the leadership of ELAS, consisting of Andreas Tzimas, Stefanos Sarafes, and Ares Velouhiotes, on 6 July. In these meetings Tempo tried to impress upon his Greek comrades the necessity of forming a BHQ and also to 'correct' their attitudes over the question of political power. The Greek view, put forward by Tzimas, that this question would be solved by elections and as a consequence would be decided in the largest towns, seemed totally unacceptable to Tempo, who argued for the adoption of the Yugoslav model, that is the preponderance of the uncompromising 'revolutionary war'. Moreover, Tempo strongly criticized the 'legalistic' attitude of the KKE, which was in his view completely subordinated to the Middle East Allied Command and to the British, a fact which could eventually reduce their hopes for post-war supremacy.[17]

Although the Greeks refused to break off their relations with the Allies and along with Napoleon Zervas, a right-wing guerilla leader, signed the British-sponsored plan for the formation of a Joint General Headquarters

[15] Vukmanović, *Struggle*, 76.   [16] Ibid. 77.   [17] Ibid. 110–11.

(JGHQ) they made some concessions to Tempo's demands.[18] In particular, they allowed Slav-Macedonian bands to enter Greek territory and to cooperate with ELAS units in the area around Florina, Kastoria, Gevgeli, Monastir, and Almopeia. Moreover, the Yugoslavs were allowed to carry out various irredentist activities among the local Slav population and to spread the use of the Macedonian language, but their demand to declare 'the right of the Macedonian people to self-determination' was not met.[19] Thus, it seemed that Tempo had eventually succeeded in persuading the Greek communists to 'cooperate' with the Macedonian Liberation Army. In fact, it appeared that Tzimas, a Vlach fluent in Bulgarian,[20] had gone too far. The leadership of KKE was quick to realize that the situation was potentially dangerous: the creation of the communist-sponsored GBS after the dissolution of the Comintern by Stalin, at a time when the British were anxious to materialize their plan for the unification of the Greek guerilla forces in the JGHQ, was indeed a serious cause for concern. On the other hand it was fairly clear that Tempo's arrogant and fierce criticism of the KKE's wartime tactics left little room for true cooperation.

A meeting in central Greece, held in August, between Tempo and the leadership of the KKE, consisting of Giorgos Siantos—acting general secretary—K. Gyftodimos, and P. Karagitsis, gave an opportunity for these issues to be finally settled. The temperamental Yugoslav once more pushed his arguments regarding KKE tactics: he strongly criticized the participation of the KKE in the JGHQ, interpreting it as 'a policy of reliance on the British'.[21] Siantos, on the other hand, argued for a 'low profile' policy on the part of the KKE; the party should try to strengthen EAM, the communist identity of which should be carefully concealed, and secure the ministries of interior and defence in the national government which would be formed after the war was over. As far as military questions were concerned, EAM opted for the preservation of its forces rather than for 'constant offensive operations' against the enemy. Tempo

---

[18] For the agreement on the JGHQ see Fleischer, *Stemma*, 387–424.

[19] Evangelos Kofos, *I Valkaniki Diastasi tou Makedonikou Zitematos sta Chronia tis Katochis kai tis Antistases* [The Balkan Dimension of the Macedonian Question in the Years of the Occupation and Resistance] (Athens, 1989), 16.

[20] Tzimas's fluency in Bulgarian has created the wrong impression that he was a Slav. See e.g. Palmer and King, *Yugoslav Communism*, 98.

[21] 'The agreement reached between them and the British HQ in the Near East is tantamount to interference in the internal affairs of Greece.' Vukmanovic, *Struggle*, 121. For this meeting see also Elisabeth Barker, *British Policy in South-East Europe in the Second World War* (London, 1976), 189–90.

voiced strong reservations for the efficiency of such a policy and warned Siantos that his 'opportunist retreat' had few prospects for success.[22]

In this meeting conflicting views on the BHQ were also expressed. The *Geros* (Old Man) of the KKE, Siantos, pointed out that 'it is too early to set up such an HQ, especially today, after the demise of the Comintern'. Had the KKE agreed to that, it would have been accused of 'organizing a new Balkan International'. Some sort of agreement, however, was reached over cooperation between ELAS and the Macedonian National Liberation Army on the border of northern Greece. Another result of these talks was the formation of the *Slavomakedonski Naroden Osvobotiditelen Front* (SNOF) in Greek Macedonia, and the emergence of Slav-Macedonian military units in late 1943. Ostensibly under KKE control, SNOF preached the gospel of Macedonian self-determination in Greece, to the irritation of many members of EAM/ELAS. The KKE tolerated the presence of SNOF, partly because it did not have much room for manoeuvring in west Macedonia, as the Slavs were deeply suspicious of any Greek organization, and partly because the Greek communists could not afford to severe their relations with Tito. There were also some who thought that the existence of SNOF was one way to approach Slavs who, in its absence, might have continued to favour Bulgaria. In any case, relations between the KKE and the increasingly irredentist SNOF deteriorated rapidly, and in late 1944, the Slav-Macedonian units were forced by the Greeks to seek refuge in Skopje.[23]

On the other hand, Tempo's agonizing efforts to secure the right of the self-determination for the 'Macedonian people' met with only limited response from the cautious Greeks, who conceded only a rather vague statement, emphasizing that all these issues should be solved after the war.[24] By the end of 1943, however, Tito abandoned the idea of a BHQ,

---

[22] Vukmanović, *Struggle*, 119–21.

[23] For the SNOF and its relations with the KKE see Kofos, *Valkaniki Diastasi*, 18–30. See also Ioannis Koliopoulos, *Plundered Loyalties: World War II and Civil War in Greek West Macedonia* (London, 1999), 114–68. Spyridon Sfetas, 'Autonomist Movements of the Slavophones in 1944: The Attitude of the Communist Party of Greece and the Protection of the Greek-Yugoslav Border', *Balkan Studies*, 36/2 (1995), 297–317; for the mutual mistrust between the SNOF and the Greek communists see also Andrew Rossos, 'Incompatible Allies: Greek Communism and Macedonian Nationalism in the Civil war in Greece, 1943–1949', *Journal of Modern History*, 69/1 (1997), 42–76.

[24] Vukmanović, *Struggle*, 122–3; Palmer and King, *Yugoslav Communism*, 98.

which, in a letter to Tempo, he attributed to 'our allies'.[25] Although concrete evidence about Tito's decision is lacking, it is reasonable to assume that he feared Western, and especially British, reaction, which would inevitably follow if Greece was included in any Yugoslav plan. It should also be noticed that by that time Britain had started revising its attitude towards the various Yugoslav resistance movements, a process which culminated in the abandonment of Draža Mihailović; a British military mission under William Deakin was parachuted to Tito in May, followed by Fitzroy Maclean in July. Moreover, the Partisans had been for some time receiving war material from the British. As a result, the Yugoslav Marshal might well have sensed that it would have been unwise to break with the British at that particular time.[26]

On the other hand, it seems unlikely that a Soviet diktat played any role, for the Yugoslavs had not been keeping Stalin thoroughly informed about their political initiatives. In fact, Stalin had not been informed about the Bihać and Jajce conferences which proclaimed the New Yugoslavia, and it was highly unlikely that he knew about the BHQ. As a result, in 1943 Tito appeared to have adopted a legalistic attitude towards Greece by respecting the existing boundaries. In a letter sent to Tempo in December he emphasized that 'we must . . . be on our guard *not to overstep formally the legal boundary* in our speeches'.[27] Despite the use of the word 'formally', which leaves much room for speculation about second thoughts, it was certain that Tito had decided to soft-pedal his ambitious plans. He could afford himself, however, the luxury of admitting that 'in our opinion, and also in the opinion of the *Djeda* [the Communist International] we must be the centre for the Balkan countries, militarily as well as politically'.[28] In 1943 this fact was an asset for the Yugoslavs; a year later it was thought that it should start to pay off.

---

[25] 'I do not know', wrote Tito, 'who originated this idea, but I fear that it might have been planted indirectly by one of our allies.' Vukmanović, *Struggle*, 142.

[26] For British policy toward Yugoslavia at the end of 1943 see Barker, *British Policy*, 164–8, Sir Llewellyn Woodward, *British Policy in the Second World War* (London, 1971), iii. 296–307. The British missions to Tito are described by their heads. See F. W. D. Deakin, *The Embattled Mountain* (Oxford, 1971); Fitzroy Maclean, *Eastern Approaches* (London, 1949), 275–532.

[27] Lazar Mojsov, article in the Yugoslav journal *Komunist*, see n. 30.

[28] Palmer and King, *Yugoslav Communism*, 104.

SLAV UNITY AT WORK, SEPTEMBER
1944–FEBRUARY 1945

By the end of 1944 many things had changed in Yugoslav Macedonia. Tempo's efforts to keep the CPM in line with CPY policy seemed to have succeeded; Italy's capitulation in September 1943 gave the opportunity to Macedonian Partisan detachments to 'liberate' much territory and to establish some 'free zones', while the politically compromised and militarily weak IMRO had failed to establish an 'independent' Macedonia under the aegis of the Germans on September 1944.[29] In addition to domestic developments, external conditions had also worked in Tito's favour. The Germans were in full retreat and unable to exercise any influence in the region; Tito emerged as a triumphant and legitimate ally of the Great Powers, in sharp contrast with a defeated and discredited Bulgaria. Further, by that time Stalin had ruled out any possibility of Yugoslav Macedonia being included into Bulgaria. The situation became even more favourable for Tito after the political change of *Deveti Septemvri* (Ninth of September) in Bulgaria. That day, the Fatherland Front, backed by the Red Army, seized power, thus removing many political obstacles which might well have impaired the Bulgar–Yugoslav rapprochement.

The Yugoslavs were quick to take full advantage of the situation and displayed considerable energy and determination in imposing on the Bulgarians their views on the definitive solution of the Macedonian Question.[30] Their grandiose plan, however, for the establishment of a

---

[29] In Sept. 1944 the Germans had tried to establish an independent Macedonia under the IMRO leader Ivan Mihailov. See Ch. 6.

[30] As usual in Bulgar–Yugoslav relations, the existing voluminous bibliography on the question of federation is, to say the least, extremely polarized. Therefore, a note on the sources of this chapter is essential here. From the Yugoslav viewpoint the most important accounts include those by Moša Pijade and Lazar Mojsov, published after the outbreak of the Tito–Cominform dispute. Mojsov's account is a 45-page-long article, published in the official organ of the CPY, *Komunist*, in 1950, 'About the South-Slav Federation', which can be found in FO 371/87469, R1077/1, from Chancery, Belgrade to Southern Department, dated 4/10/1950 (hereafter Mojsov 1950). Pijade delivered a lengthy speech to the Yugoslav National Assembly in 1949, 'On the Balkan Federation', which was published in the Belgrade newspaper *Borba*. See FO 371/87560, from Chancery, Belgrade, to Southern Department, dated 30/12/1949, (hereafter Pijade 1949). Slobodan Nesovic's book, *Yugoslav–Bulgarian Relations 1941–1945* (Skopje, 1979), draws on unpublished Yugoslav archival sources and gives useful details. From the Bulgarian angle, Tsola Dragoytseva's book, with the clumsy and misleading title *Macedonia: Not*

South Slav federation under Yugoslav tutelage, did not conceal their primary consideration, which was the immediate annexation of the Bulgarian part of Macedonia. That this was the case became apparent quite soon. During the first days after the Ninth of September Tempo and Koliševski went to Sofia for consultations with the Central Committee of the BCP.[31] At those talks Tempo, according to his own account, 'really put the pressure on them'.[32] After severely reprimanding his Bulgarian comrades for their attitude during the occupation, the temperamental Yugoslav asked them to grant the Pirin region 'cultural autonomy', so that 'the people in the two parts [of Macedonia] would be able to make political preparations for unification'.[33] The Bulgarians, so Tempo claimed, 'admitted all their mistakes. . . and agreed to everything'.[34]

That picture of an easy Yugoslav victory proved very deceptive indeed. Vera Aceva and Ljupčo Arsov, Yugoslav delegates in Pirin, began to send reports about the delaying tactics of the Bulgarians, prompting Tempo and Lazar Koliševski to step up their pressure. In two letters, sent in October to the Central Committee of the BCP, they reminded them of the Sofia deliberations asking the Bulgarians 'to implement sincerely our joint agreement'. Although they were tactful enough in pointing out that immediate unification was not actual, their demand for the formation of 'Macedonian' Partisan units and 'national liberation committees' in the Pirin area could do little to allay Bulgarian suspicions.[35] Shortly afterwards more alarming reports followed as the Bulgarians reverted to temporizing: in early November a BCP regional conference was held in Blagoevgrad, in which Vladimir Poptomov, the old Macedonian

a Cause of Discord but a Factor of Good Neighbourliness and Cooperation (Sofia, 1979), is the official Bulgarian review. Kostadin Paleshutski's *Iugoslavskata Komunisticheska Partiya i Makedonskiyat Vŭpros 1919–1945* (Sofia, 1984), is highly informative. Georgi Daskalov's work, *Bŭlgaro-Iugoslavski Politicheski Otnosheniya 1944–1945* (Sofia, 1989), 270–312, is an even more detailed account. See also Dobrin Michev, *Makedonskiyat Vŭpros I Bŭlgaro-Iugoslavskite Otnosheniya, 9 Septemvri 1944–1949* [The Macedonian Question and Bulgar–Yugoslav Relations, 9 September 1944–1949] (Sofia, 1994), 191–223, and Milcho Lalkov, *Ot Nadezhda kum Razocharovanie: Ideata za Federatsiyata v Balkanskiya Iugoistok, 1944–1949* (From Hope to Disappointment: The Idea of Federation in South-East Balkans) (Sofia, 1994), 143–220.

[31] The Bulgarians attending the meeting were Traicho Kostov, Tsola Dragoycheva, Todor Pavlov, and Georgi Tsankov.
[32] From a letter to CPM see Vukmanović, *Struggle*, 266.   [33] Ibid. 265.
[34] Ibid. 266. Cf. Paleshutski, *Iugoslavskata*, 320–1.
[35] For the letters sent to BCP, see Vukmanović, *Struggle*, 269–70, 279–80. For Kostov's evasive reply see ibid., 270.

revolutionary and Bulgarian foreign minister after 1949, clearly stated that 'the question of the unification . . . should not be raised at the present time', for 'it is not one being raised by the population itself', and therefore 'it is not a real issue'.[36] Much later, other high-ranking Bulgarian functionaries accused the 'arrogant Skopje delegates' of trying to fish in the troubled waters of 1944 and to prematurely detach the Pirin region.[37] Thus, to their surprise, the Yugoslavs realized that their main asset, the unenviable international position of Bulgaria, was failing to make the BCP more responsive.

The Bulgarians were not the only ones who found themselves held captives of their international position in late 1944. At the end of September, as has already been seen, Tito secretly fled from the island of Vis, to the annoyance of the British.[38] His destination was Moscow, where he stayed from 21 to 28 September. While there, Tito had meetings with Stalin and Georgi Dimitrov, and discussed the issue of a South Slav federation. According to Dimitrov, there was 'perfect mutual understanding' concerning 'the formation of a union between Bulgaria and Yugoslavia', but he admitted 'difficulties especially on the part of the English and their Great Greek and Great Serbian agents'.[39] After Moscow, Tito proceeded to the Romanian city of Craiova. There, at the headquarters of Marshal Tolbukhin he received a Bulgarian delegation headed by Dobri Terpechev, asking for an armistice. Further, it was agreed that the Bulgarian army should participate in the final operations against the Germans in Yugoslavia. Yugoslav accounts have interpreted the Craiova Agreement, signed on 5 October, as 'a friendly, courageous and statesmanlike act of Marshal Tito' aiming at helping the Bulgarians to save their honour at a time of almost complete isolation.[40] But it could hardly have been so. It can be suggested that it was Russia's

[36] The Yugoslavs were kept constantly informed about the developments in Pirin by Vera Aceva and Arsov. The latter, who attended the conference, sent a detailed report on Poptomov's speech. Vukmanović, *Struggle*, 271–2. See also Elisabeth Barker, *Macedonia: Its Place in Balkan Power Politics* (London, 1950), 99.

[37] e.g. this is the view taken by Dragoycheva, throughout her account *Macedonia.*

[38] In late May 1944 the Germans launched their Seventh Offensive against Tito's headquarters in Drvar. Having escaped capture, Tito and the AVNOJ moved to the island of Vis, where they stayed for almost three months. Vladimir Dedijer, *Tito Speaks* (London, 1953), 215–20. While in Vis, Tito had talks with Churchill and Ivan Šubašić (in Italy) on the question of the future Yugoslav government. See Woodward, *British Policy*, 339–48.

[39] Ivo Banac, *The Diary of Georgi Dimitrov, 1933–1949* (New Haven and London, 2003), 337.

[40] See e.g. Slobodan Nesovic, *Yugoslav*, 22–43, esp., 26.

proposal to use the well-equipped Bulgarian army against the Germans rather than the elevated intentions of the Yugoslavs, which prompted them to accept the Bulgarians as liberators of their own territory.[41] In Craiova nothing was said or agreed on the question of the future shape of Bulgar–Yugoslav relations, apart from a vague declaration that all these questions 'should be settled in the spirit of fraternal and common interests' of the two peoples.[42]

So, by the end of October, considerable amount of nervousness was evident on both sides of the fence. Despite heavy pressure the Yugoslavs appeared to have been failing to extract Bulgarian approval of the immediate cession of Pirin, while the BCP was trying to gain time. Reflecting this conflict, Dimitrov sent a letter to Tito on 27 October, asking him 'not to raise the question of annexing Bulg[arian] Macedonia', and insisting that no pronouncement on the matter should occur 'without preliminary clearance from the CC of the CP Bulgaria'.[43] The Yugoslavs nevertheless remained undeterred, and from the beginning of November they renewed their efforts for the creation of a federation. To that effect, from November 1944 till the end of January 1945, a series of six draft proposals were exchanged between the two sides. The amount of paperwork notwithstanding, conflicting views emerged from the very beginning. The first Yugoslav draft, sent to Sofia in early November, provided for a federal South Slav state, which would be comprised of the six Yugoslav republics and Bulgaria, reducing her to the status of a mere federative unit.[44] The Bulgarian reply, a few days later, tried to redress the balance: they proposed a 'union' between the Yugoslav federation as a whole and Bulgaria on the principle of parity. As far as the future of Pirin was concerned, the Bulgarian draft mentioned unification with Yugoslav Macedonia only after the creation of the federation, by contrast to the Yugoslav draft, which demanded immediate annexation.[45]

The Soviet attitude towards those deliberations seemed to favour the Yugoslav plans. On 22 November a delegation, including Ivan Šubašić and Edvard Kardelj, visited Moscow for consultations over the Tito–Šubašić agreement, reached a month earlier.[46] There, at a meeting

---

[41] This issue is examined in detail in Ch. 4.   [42] Mojsov 1950, 22.

[43] Ivo Banac (ed.), *Diary*, 341.

[44] The Yugoslav draft also asked for a joint command of Bulgar–Yugoslav army, with Tito as its head. Daskalov, *Bŭlgaro-Iugoslavski*, 275–6. Cf. Lalkov, *Nadezhda*, 159–61.

[45] Daskalov, *Bŭlgaro-Iugoslavski*, 277.   [46] Woodward, *British Policy*, 351–3.

with Stalin the Soviet leader urged the Yugoslavs to speed up the process of federation 'for if the people wants it nobody could prevent it'.[47] They did so without delay.

In late December, Kardelj went to Sofia for talks with the Bulgarians on the question of federation. He was confronted with another Bulgarian draft, worked out on instructions by Dimitrov sent from Moscow a day before. Dimitrov, it should be noted, was a firm supporter of a South Slav federation and in a letter to Stalin (and Molotov) in April 1944 he had spoken in favour of a federation 'of Bulgars, Serbs, Croats, Slovenes, Montenegrins, and Macedonians' but 'all on an equal footing'.[48] He seemed to doubt, however, that 'Macedonia' was a homogenous land: after a meeting with Vlahov on 22 April, he noted in his diary: ' "The Macedonian nation" or the *Macedonian populace*! (Bulgars, Mac[edonians], Slavs, Greeks, Serbs).' And although he acknowledged the existence of Macedonians he still had some questions for Vlahov: ' "Macedonian *national* consciousness"? (*Where* and *how* does it exist?)'[49] Be that as it may, the new draft was not different in essence from the previous one; it considered the two countries as 'allies against Germany', allowed for the incorporation of Pirin to the Macedonian republic after the formation of the federation, and in short provided for little more than a pact of mutual assistance.[50] It became apparent that the two sides were trying to pull their 'common' future in opposite directions. In particular, the Bulgarians were anxious to obtain 'Allied' status as a co-belligerent in the struggle against Germany, in an effort to clear their wartime record and to escape paying the price for their conduct up to the Ninth of September. At the same time, they persistently sought to retain the Pirin region within their borders, by formally allowing the Yugoslavs to swallow it up only after the creation of a federation. In effect, the Bulgarians had been asking for too many things, giving almost nothing concrete in return.

Kardelj took all these matters up with his Bulgarian comrades on 22 and 23 December, when he had talks with Traicho Kostov and a certain 'Vladimirov', whose true name was kept secret, only to be revealed by the Yugoslavs after the 1948 split. In December 1949 Moša Pijade was pleased to announce that 'Vladimirov' was none other than Vŭlko Chervenkov, then ruler of Bulgaria, the

---

[47] Pijade 1949, 19.   [48] Ivo Banac (ed.), *Diary*, 315.
[49] Ibid. Emphasis in the original.   [50] Daskalov, *Bŭlgaro-Iugoslavski*, 282–3.

same man who brought Kostov to trial for his allegedly 'treacherous' talks with Kardelj in 1944. Pijade did not miss the opportunity to comment on that: 'Such moral monstrosities were borne by the Cominform'.[51]

In 1944, however, Kostov was in a position to negotiate the future of his country together with Chervenkov. He did so to the irritation of Kardelj. The Yugoslav delegate found the Bulgarian draft totally unacceptable. In a letter sent to Tito from Sofia on 23 December, a day before his departure, he informed him about the negotiations and voiced strong criticism. Kardelj considered such a pact 'valueless', asking instead for 'an alliance which our masses will accept as first step towards union'. Moreover he strongly opposed the parity principle adopted by the Bulgarians in the proposed 'Yugoslav–Bulgarian Unity Commission'. In line with the Yugoslav proposals, Kardelj wanted the commission to be 'mixed', i.e. to have in it representatives of Bulgaria and 'of our federal units as representatives of Yugoslavia'. As expected, the future of Pirin was no less of a problem. Kardelj was not prepared to accept the temporizing tactics of the Bulgarians, aiming at postponing the cession of that area to Yugoslavia, and argued that the 'Macedonians [in Pirin] have such rights [to secession] regardless of whether the federation with Bulgaria should take place or not'.[52] Despite his reservations, Kardelj clearly understood that he could not press for more concessions and after some modifications of the Bulgarian proposal a draft agreement was reached in Sofia. It was also agreed that the final form of the treaty should be discussed in Belgrade. Although the Sofia Agreement fell short of Yugoslav expectations for a settlement tailored to their needs, the willingness of the Bulgarians to continue the deliberations and to say their final word after consultations with Tito in Belgrade remained a promising sign. This point acquires particular significance for subsequent developments showed that in Moscow Dimitrov and Stalin thought otherwise.

---

[51] Pijade 1949, 21. In Dec. 1949, Kostov was accused of conspiring with Tito and Kardelj for the inclusion of Bulgaria into a South Slav federation, and of spying for the Western Powers. For the trial, which prepared the ground for Chervenkov's rise to power see J. F. Brown, *Bulgaria under Communist Rule* (London, 1970), 20–2, and Richard Crampton, *A Short History of Modern Bulgaria* (Cambridge, 1989), 170–2. The official Bulgarian account for Kostov's trial is given in *The Trial of Traicho Kostov and his Group* (Sofia, 1950), published by the Press Department [of the Ministry of Information and Arts].

[52] For these negotiations see Pijade 1949, 19–23; Mojsov 1950, 33; Michev, *Makedonskiyat Vŭpros*, 197–8.

In early January 1945, both sides continued their paperwork and worked out new drafts, this time openly speaking of federation. But the divergence of views remained, with the Bulgarians insisting upon the parity principle and the Yugoslavs continuing to consider Bulgaria the 'seventh' republic. At the same time the Yugoslavs sent to Sofia Vladimir Popović and shortly afterwards Pijade and Veljko Vlahović to ensure that the Bulgarians would come to Belgrade to discuss the draft agreement reached in December with Kardelj. They did not seem to be very keen on going. Initially the Bulgarians said they would go to Belgrade on 19 January; their departure was then postponed for a week, only to be cancelled again on the twenty-first. According to Bulgarian accounts the cause for the latest cancellation was a telegram from Georgi Dimitrov instructing the BCP 'to not hurry up'.[53] A day later Vyacheslav Molotov asked both sides to send delegates to Moscow. Premier Kimon Georgiev and Anton Iugov, Minister of the Interior, headed the Bulgarian delegation; the Yugoslav delegation was led by Pijade. For yet another time in Bulgar–Yugoslav relations the final word would be said in Moscow.

As soon as the two delegations arrived in the Soviet capital it became evident that the Russians did not consider the creation of a federation opportune. Instead, they urged the two sides to prepare a treaty of economic and political cooperation, which obviously delighted the Bulgarians but left the Yugoslavs deeply disappointed. The latter had to swallow their ambitions and to follow the Soviet diktat. On 27 January, Andrei Vyshinski drafted a treaty for close cooperation between the two countries, which was accepted by both delegations.[54] By that time, however, the settling of the Macedonian Question, as well as the future shape of Bulgar–Yugoslav relations, had entered the delicate domain of international politics. So, even the signing of a supposedly harmless treaty of mutual cooperation was abandoned at the request of the Soviets on February 1945. Any assessment, therefore, of the Soviet attitude begs the question of British—and to a lesser extent American—policy towards that part of the world. This point leads to the examination of the British connection, for, as will be seen, it was of crucial importance.

---

[53] For the developments in early Jan. see Paleshutski, *Iugoslavskata*, 325–6, see also Mojsov 1950, 25–8.
[54] Pijade 1949, 28.

BRITISH ATTITUDES TOWARDS
BULGAR–YUGOSLAV UNION, APRIL–DECEMBER
1944

'Peace ends where Serb, or rather Yugoslav-Bulgar, union begins... With the Balkan States as at present constituted, the balance of power is fairly well distributed. But this is at once altered if Bulgaria unites with Yugoslavia.'[55] Thus Sir Nevile Henderson, British minister to Yugoslavia, in 1934, at the time of conclusion of the Balkan pact, and of a Bulgar–Yugoslav rapprochement. As seen from the perspective of the political situation in 1944, there was little evidence to suggest that Sir Nevile's statement was considered by the Foreign Office particularly dated.[56] In fact, it appeared that the spectre of a Slav Balkan bloc, which haunted the British during much of the interwar and wartime period, had resurfaced in 1944 with all of its dangerous implications. All the more so, as the various British wartime plans for an east-central confederation had failed to materialize. Had those schemes been successful, the two Slav states would have been confederate republics, by and large under British tutelage.

Soviet fears, however, of a new cordon sanitaire obliged the British to abandon their grandiose plans. As a result, in 1944 the fate of Yugoslavia and Bulgaria remained a serious cause for concern. The first serious indication which gave rise to fears that a Balkan federation was entertained by the Yugoslavs came in April, after an interview given to the *New York Times* by Tito's foreign minister, Josip Smodlaka. During this interview, which was conducted in French, Smodlaka was extremely cautious. He admitted that the Partisans wished for a Balkan federation, with the union of Bulgaria and Yugoslavia being the first step, and 'full autonomy' for Macedonia, 'within the federal state'. However, he was quick to add that he was referring to 'Slav

---

[55] FO 371/18369, 'A memorandum on the Influence of the Yugoslav Idea on Balkan Politics', enclosure in Henderson to FO, written in Mar. 1934.

[56] For British views on a South Slav federation in the interwar period, including Henderson's memorandum, see Chapter 2. For Britain and Bulgar–Yugoslav federation in 1944–5 cf. also Todor Čepreganov, *Velika Britanija I Makedonskoto Nacionalno Prašanje, Avgust 1944–1948* [Great Britain and the Macedonian National Question] (Skopje, 1997), 131–5.

Macedonia . . . [for] Greek Macedonia naturally belongs to Greece'.[57] Smodlaka's carefully worded reference to Greece did little to allay British suspicions that Greece's territorial integrity was at stake. Bulgarian pretensions were considered no less of a potential threat. In late April the Foreign Office voiced strong concern about Soviet intentions to support Bulgarian claims to Greek Thrace and Yugoslav Macedonia in return for Bulgarian collaboration in the struggle against Germany. To the Foreign Office, Soviet intentions, coupled with Tito's ambitions and the position of EAM, which was perceived as accepting the cession of Greek Macedonia, 'meant that the question is non-academic'. Thus, the British ambassador to Moscow, Sir Archibald Clark Kerr, was instructed to take the matter up with Vyshinski, emphasizing that Britain stood for the territorial integrity of Greece and Yugoslavia. Regarding the slogan for an 'autonomous Macedonia' Clark Kerr was informed that 'H.M.G. do not wish to commit themselves on this matter until the peace settlement and then only in agreement with fully representative Yugoslav and Greek governments'. To this alarmist telegram, the British ambassador responded reassuringly by saying that it was unlikely that the Russians would support the Bulgarians at a time when they are preoccupied with giving their full backing to Tito.[58]

It seemed that by the middle of 1944 it was not clearly understood whether the major threat against Greece was represented by Bulgaria, Yugoslavia, or by a federation of the South Slavs. An answer, therefore, was clearly needed. In May, Churchill himself asked the Foreign Office to prepare a note on the subject. The Permanent Under-Secretary of State for Foreign Affairs, Sir Alexander Cadogan, while asking for it, commented that the idea of a Bulgar–Yugoslav bloc 'does not seem very pleasant at first sniff'.[59] Anthony Eden, who replied a week later, attempted a more comprehensive assessment. According to the foreign minister, from a purely British viewpoint such a bloc was 'a doubtful proposition', for it could constitute a serious danger for Greece, and would afford the Soviets a commanding position in the Balkans. In short, he stated, a Slav federation meant having them on the shores of the Aegean. What is particularly interesting, however, is that Eden's

---

[57] Smodlaka supported his statement with a reference to the ethnographic profile of the Greek province: 'Formerly it had a Slavic majority, but since 1922 it was colonized with Greek money by Asia Minor Greeks'. Interview by C. Sulzberger. FO 371/44270, R 6338, 21/4/1944.

[58] FO 371/43583, R 6485, 26/4/1944; FO 371/43583, R 7030, 30/4/1944.

[59] FO 371/43608, R 7785, 5/5/1944.

objections were confined only to the international aspects of a Slav bloc. As far as its local repercussions were concerned, he was much more inclined to consider it a sensible solution to some intractable Balkan problems. In his view, a Balkan federation would solve the Macedonian Question, with the creation of an autonomous Macedonian unit. Further, the inclusion of the Bulgarians in such a state was seen as an element of cohesion, in that they would help the Serbs to counterbalance the Croats.[60]

Given that Eden could not count a thorough knowledge of Balkan history and politics among his other attributes, it can be suggested that his views on the beneficial aspects of a Slav federation were little more than an echo of the wartime British planning on federations. As has already been shown, during the course of that planning it was argued by some British officials that the federal solution of the Macedonian Question was the only viable one; on the other hand it was suggested that the Serbian Slavs, who had acquired some sort of 'Ottoman' outlook, would have been greatly helped by the presence of the Bulgarians in the same state, for their weight combined would keep at bay the more 'Westernized' and European-oriented Croats and Slovenes.[61] So, from the British perspective the fundamental question to be dealt with was not whether a Slav federation was either feasible or beneficial (for it could be both), but rather who would exercise control over it. Eden's opinion that it would be the Russians was a solid reason for the whole question to be viewed with suspicion. At the same time it became evident that from the very beginning the British would view the Macedonian Question mainly from an international power-politics angle, aiming at preventing Moscow from establishing a commanding position in the Balkans and the eastern Mediterranean.

In late May, the deputy Under-Secretary of State Sir Orme Sargent, an experienced diplomat with considerable knowledge of the Balkans, produced a paper on Soviet intentions towards Bulgaria in which he touched upon the Macedonian Question and the prospect of a Slav federation, sketching out some basic considerations which were to shape

---

[60] Eden's reply in FO 371/43608, R 7785, dated 12/5/1944. In August, Eden confirmed again to Churchill that the 'prospect' of a communist-sponsored federation is 'anyway unattractive to us'. See Elisabeth Barker, 'Problems of the Alliance: Misconceptions and Misunderstandings', in William Deakin, ead. and Jonathan Chadwick (eds.), *British Political and Military Strategy in Central, Eastern and Southern Europe in 1944* (New York, 1988), 50.

[61] Cf. Ch. 3.

British policy in the near future. Sir Orme agreed with Eden that a federation of that kind might provide a solution to the Bulgar–Yugoslav friction over Macedonia, but it was against British interests, for it would isolate Greece, revive Bulgarian claims to Greek territory, and give the Russians a dominating role in the Balkans. He proposed, nevertheless, that an autonomous Macedonian federal unit could be compatible with British interests, provided that it was included in an all-Balkan confederation.[62]

The assumption underpinning those suggestions was that the future structure of the Slavic parts of Macedonia did not carry a weight of its own. If Britain was to enjoy some influence in the area, by the inclusion of Greece and even Turkey in the federation, then the unification of the Vardar Valley with the Pirin mountains could do no harm. What was potentially dangerous was an exclusively Slav bloc, which, under Soviet patronage, would advance claims against Greece. Thus, a united Slav Macedonia was undesirable only in so far as it constituted a (Soviet) arrow and not a unifying link in an all-Balkan chain.

Apart from the somewhat arrogant British assumption that Balkan alignments could be made and unmade at will, it was, to say the least, doubtful whether an all-Balkan confederation was within the realm of practical politics. The formidable obstacles to a Greek–Yugoslav federation, attempted in 1942, were known to the British, as was Greece's unwillingness to share the burden of the defence of Turkey's eastern border. Those propositions, however, focusing on the role that Greece and Turkey could play in the Balkans, at any rate had the merit of consistency. In June, in a memorandum on Soviet policy in the Balkans, the Foreign Office charted the policy most likely to be followed in that area suggesting that Britain should consolidate its position in Greece and Turkey and 'utilize Turco-Greek friendship as a fundamental factor in South-East Europe and the Eastern Mediterranean'.[63]

Be that as it may, Sir Orme Sargent had remarked in May that 'we certainly ought to keep our eyes open', regarding Bulgar–Yugoslav relations. It was wise advice, indeed, for realities and perceptions did not always coincide. Fitzroy Maclean, for instance, a man who had the ear of the prime minister and was afforded considerable influence in the formulation of British policy towards Yugoslavia, held the opinion

[62] FO 371/43583, R 8542, 31/5/1944.
[63] FO 371/43646, W.P.(44) 304, memorandum by Secretary of State for Foreign Affairs, dated 7/6/1944.

in May that Tito had no territorial pretensions apart from the Slav-populated Italian provinces. Maclean went so far as to say that Tito was even prepared to 'contemplate a readjustment of the frontiers of Macedonia in favour of the neighbouring states, should a plebiscite justify this'.[64] Undoubtedly, such a statement, made on the eve of Tito's drive for the annexation of the Pirin area, can only be attributed to lack of knowledge regarding the real intentions of the actors in the Macedonian theatre.

As expected, the Yugoslavs did nothing to clarify their own intentions. Instead, Tito always tried to allay British fears and to reassure them by emphasizing that he had no intention of engaging in a Macedonian adventure. He did so on every occasion. In September, only a few days after the political change in Bulgaria, Tito met the Yugoslav diplomat Milan Gavrilović on the island of Vis and confided to him that he viewed the Bulgarians with deep suspicion. Good relations with them, he added, 'could not be established until at least one or two generations had died out'.[65] Although that clumsy statement was not taken at its face value, lack of information rendered an all-round assessment of the situation quite difficult. Thus, when a report reached London in November mentioning a secret agreement between Yugoslavia and Bulgaria for the cession of Pirin to Yugoslavia, the officials of the Southern Department could not hide their confusion. 'I am thoroughly fogged', minuted George Clutton, 'as to what exactly is going on as regards Macedonia.'[66] In the same minute Clutton asked for more details, since the information from Belgrade was 'fragmentary' and Maclean's mission was not trained to send political reports.[67] At the same time the British political representative in Bulgaria, William Houstoun-Boswall, was instructed to take the matter up with the Fatherland Front government. A few days later on 24 November, Petko Stainov, the Zveno foreign minister, told Houstoun-Boswall that such an agreement had not been reached. On the question of Bulgar–Yugoslav federation Stainov was evasive, pointing out that the first issue to be tackled was 'who would federate with whom'; to Stainov, that point was 'not clear at present'.[68] Despite those equivocal statements, the British did not rest assured. Orme

---

[64] Maclean expressed those views in a paper on Soviet–Yugoslav relations. FO 371/44331, R7935, 20/5/1944. In the same paper Maclean did not consider the prospect of a Bulgar–Yugoslav federation to be 'likely at present'.

[65] FO 371/43608, R16200, 28/9/1944.

[66] FO 371/43649, R1863, 16/11/1944, minute by Clutton, dated 17/11/1944.

[67] Ibid.   [68] FO 371/43649, 11/11/1944.

Sargent's comment on Stainov's views—'not very convincing'—was quite telling.[69]

Although the Balkan communists afforded the Foreign Office only scanty information, a comprehensive assessment of the policy to be followed by Britain on the Macedonian Question was soon to appear. On 30 November 1944, Sir Orme Sargent wrote a long memorandum, which formed the centrepiece of British policy. Eden read it, and agreed with 'every word in it'.[70] It was a timely paper, for there were enough signs 'which showed that Tito's Yugoslavs were beginning to think about Yugoslav-Bulgarian federation, and that the Bulgarians were going once again to foster the so-called Macedonian claims'.[71] After a short outline of the turbulent Bulgar–Yugoslav relations, Sargent quoted approvingly the words of Henderson, who had written in 1934 that 'Peace ends where Serb, or rather Yugoslav-Bulgar, union begins'. In accordance with his previously expressed views, he remarked that Britain should oppose any exclusive Slav union 'because it would disturb the balance of power between the Balkan states, because it would isolate Greece and endanger her position as a Balkan state, and because it would enable Bulgaria, who has in both World Wars joined Germany against her Balkan neighbours and against the Western democratic Powers, to escape by this process from the consequences of her acts by merging her identity in that of one of the United Nations'. In the same memorandum Sargent made two interesting points: (*a*) that Britain should put forward an all-inclusive Balkan federation, including also Turkey, as an alternative to the Bulgar–Yugoslav union, and (*b*) that 'although we are prepared to acquiesce to the creation of a Macedonian state in the future Federal Yugoslavia, we must insist that this state shall not annex or lay claim to any territories whatsoever belonging to either Bulgaria or Greece, on the ground that these territories are "Macedonian"'.[72] The practical difficulties concerning the first point have already been discussed earlier in this chapter. However, it should be noted here that Sargent himself thought the whole idea to be useless, due to firm Soviet opposition to the Greek–Yugoslav attempt for federation, and to the presence of the Red

---

[69] FO 371/43649, minute by Sargent, dated 28/11/1944.

[70] FO 371/43649, R19712, 'The Macedonian Problem and the Idea of Union between Yugoslavia and Bulgaria', memorandum by Sargeant, dated 30/11/1944. Eden's view as cited in Andrew Rossos, 'Great Britain and Macedonian Statehood and Unification 1940–1949', *East European Politics and Societies*, 14/1 (2000), 140. Cf. Čepreganov, *Velika Britanija*, 104–8.

[71] 'Macedonian Problem', 1.   [72] Ibid. 2, 4.

Army in Bulgaria, Romania, and Yugoslavia.[73] So, the suggestion for an all-Balkan federation, although not a practical proposition, was advanced by the British for the sake of it rather than with the aim of achieving it.

The second suggestion also merits some analysis. It clearly points to the potentially destructive implications that the recognition of a Macedonian nationality could have for the security of both Greece and Bulgaria. Indeed, if the Slavs of Monastir were considered Macedonians, a case can be stated to the effect that so were those of Florina or Blagoevgrad. In the preceding decades the Balkan specialists of the Central Department were of the view that the 'Macedo-Slavs' had no national consciousness whatsoever. During the 1940s the Foreign Office continued to approach that question with extreme caution, mainly due to their anxiety to preserve the territorial integrity of Greece. Thus, when the Antifascist Assembly of National Liberation of Macedonia (ASNOM) sent a telegram to Churchill, expressing 'heartfelt greetings' from the 'Macedonian people', it was agreed that Maclean should send only a simple acknowledgement. Anything beyond that might encourage them to believe that their aims of creating an autonomous or Greater Macedonia enjoyed London's support.[74]

By November 1944, a Macedonian federal state had been created, and the definition of its national status was the last thing that preoccupied Sargent. He realized, nevertheless, that irredentist aspirations could pose a grave danger to Greece. As a result politics put ethnography aside and a middle way was taken: the southern Yugoslavs could call themselves as they wished, but they should accept state frontiers as being national ones too. That would be to the benefit of all sides. Greece would remain safe, and the federal unit of Macedonia could call its citizens as it pleased. What Sargent failed to see was that the solution he proposed would remain satisfactory only for as long as Britain was in a position to enforce it and the international political situation was favourable to it; but certainties of that sort do not lead (very) long lives.

In 1944 Britain not only thought that she exercised some influence in the Balkans but was also willing to use it. By the end of December the Foreign Office became convinced that a Bulgar–Yugoslav union was imminent. Many signs had been pointing in that direction: the press in both countries carried an increasing number of articles praising

---

[73] Ibid. 4.
[74] FO 371/43665, R12920, 16/8/1944. Cf. Čepreganov, *Velika Britanija,* 76–7. For ASNOM see Ch. 6.

South Slav unity and preparing public opinion;[75] the appointment on 2 December of Petŭr Todorov as the first Bulgarian representative to Tito confirmed the cordial relations between the two countries, especially after a statement he made renouncing Bulgarian claims on Macedonia.[76] In addition, the prominent Yugoslav politician Velimir Velebit, while talking to journalists in Moscow, was reported to have said that Bulgaria—and possibly Albania—would join a Balkan federation.[77] This statement alarmed the British, and Tito's remark that Velebit had no authority to make such a statement could hardly be considered satisfactory.[78] Although the British were informed by Tito, shortly afterwards, that Velebit had not actually made any such statement, it became apparent that some sort of action was needed. So far the British had been watching what appeared to be a threatening development. In late December it was thought that words should be replaced by deeds.

BRITISH INTERVENTION, DECEMBER 1944–MARCH 1945

In late December, the Foreign Office started its effort to prevent a Bulgar–Yugoslav union. It was decided that the views of the British government on that question, set out by Sargent in his paper of 30 November, should be made known to Bulgaria and Yugoslavia. Before that communication, however, the British ambassadors to Moscow and Washington were instructed, on 28 December, to inform their respective governments about the British position.[79] What was particularly revealing about British intentions was that at that stage they did not want consultation with the Soviets or the Americans, nor did they request their views. Moreover, according to the instructions, the ambassadors should keep the decision 'to convey an intimation' to Tito and to the Bulgarians secret and should use it 'for [their] information only'.[80]

As regards the Soviets, the British decision not to let them know of their move is easily explainable. The Foreign Office was determined to prevent the Yugoslav plan for federation, and consultations with

---

[75] FO 371/43608, R16960, 16/10/1944, for articles on the Bulgarian press. For the (similar) view from Belgrade see FO 371/43609, R21344, 18/12/1944.

[76] WO 201/1617, Balkan Political Review, 6/12/1944.

[77] FO 371/44395, R21094, 27/11/1944.

[78] Tito's response was given on 16/12/1944.

[79] FO 371/48184, R11861, Annex A, 28/12/1944.   [80] Ibid.

Stalin—who seemed to approve of it—could provoke tension and perhaps lead the Soviets to take a harder line on other delicate questions; on Greece, to name but one. The sidestepping of Washington is more surprising. It can be suggested that the British, having faced considerable difficulties with the uncooperative attitude of the Americans on the 'spheres of influence' question only a few months earlier, might have considered that any notification about their prospective move could not only cause loss of valuable time, but also reveal tactical—or political—differences.[81] Be that as it may, John Balfour (now at the British Embassy in Moscow) wrote to Molotov on 1 January, and a day later Halifax spoke to Edward Stettinius.[82]

At the same time Churchill, anxious to take whatever measure was needed to stabilize the situation in Greece, wondered whether the British views on Macedonia should be made known to Archbishop Damaskinos, who was appointed regent on 30 December, in order to create 'a feeling of unity to which even the bulk of ELAS might respond'; he asked Eden to consider the 'pros and cons'. Denis Laskey, of the Southern Department, minuted that if that happened, the whole story would become 'public property'. This could cause Britain considerable embarrassment, for it was not known what the attitude of Stalin and Roosevelt would be. Eden endorsed Laskey's reservations, and added that Tito and the Bulgarians had not yet been informed of the British views, and therefore any communication to the Greeks was premature; Churchill agreed and the Greeks were left uninformed.[83]

It should be noted, however, that the *Dekemvriana* civil strife, in which ELAS forces clashed with the British in Athens in December

[81] Between May and June 1944 Churchill had been struggling to persuade President Roosevelt to acquiesce in a 'temporary' division of influence in the Balkans, according to which the Western Powers would have a free hand in Greece and the Soviets in Romania. The State Department firmly opposed the plan, on the grounds that it could lead to the establishment of concrete spheres of influence. Finally, after a series of telegrams and notes, Roosevelt reluctantly accepted the British idea, but only for a period of three months. Woodward, *British Policy*, 115–18. It is perhaps of interest to note here that the above question had not been the only point of divergence between Britain and USA as regards the Balkans. In late 1943, Roosevelt's unexpected decision to support the intransigent Greek king against British advice that the king should return to Greece only after a plebiscite, infuriated the FO. Robert Frazier, *Anglo-American Relations with Greece: The Coming of the Cold War, 1942–1947* (London, 1991), 37–45. Cf. Prokopis Papastratis, *British Policy towards Greece During the Second World War, 1941–1944* (Cambridge, 1984), 151.

[82] FO 371/48181, R224, 2/1/1945; FO 371/48181, R566, 8/1/1945.

[83] FO 371/48181, prime minister's note dated 31/12/1944; Laskey's minute, 2/1/1945; Eden's reply to the prime minister, 10/1/1945.

1944, had made Churchill lose his temper. On 19 December, a few days before his dramatic visit to Athens, he sent Eden a note asking whether it would not be better 'to let the Greeks feel this North wind. Why should we be defending them when they are shooting us?' The reply, written by Eden's private secretary, Pierson Dixon, was short and abrupt: 'the Foreign Secretary is not proposing to send a reply to the P.M.'s minute of December 19'.[84] Churchill did not pursue the matter further; nor did Eden.

The course of events in Yugoslavia, however, prompted the British to postpone their action in Belgrade and Sofia. In January 1945 the young King Peter of Yugoslavia voiced serious objections to the Tito–Šubašić agreement of the previous October, with the possible encouragement of the Americans.[85] Those objections could jeopardize the agreement and make Tito lose his fragile patience. A British démarche on Macedonia at that particular moment would certainly 'indispose' Tito. On the other hand a possible American move to support the king, especially after he gave a copy of a strongly worded declaration to American journalists, urged the Foreign Office to reconsider its policy regarding consultation with Washington. On 18 January it was decided that no communiqué should be made in Belgrade or Sofia before American and Soviet views were received.[86]

But situations and perceptions were changing swiftly. On 15 January, the Yugoslav commissar for public works stated that an official Bulgarian representative to the second session of ASNOM had acknowledged that Bulgaria would definitely cede Pirin to Yugoslavia.[87] Houstoun-Boswall, the British political representative in Bulgaria, immediately raised the issue, only to receive an evasive reply. Stoinov remarked that, although it is difficult to stop the 'Pirin people' from uniting with their 'brethren . . . the time is not yet ripe'.[88] Shortly afterwards, another declaration, this time from the Yugoslav side, completed the picture: Metodi Antonov, president of ASNOM, said in an interview to

---

[84] Churchill's minute (19/12/1944) and Dixon's letter to 10 Downing Street in FO 371/43649, R20809.

[85] The king's main constitutional objection was that according to the agreement he was not allowed to choose the regents. Further he was against the AVNOJ's role as the supreme legislative body in the country, pending the election of the Constituent Assembly. Woodward, *British Policy*, 357–62. On the American connection with his refusal see Barker, *British Policy*, 171.

[86] FO 371/48181, FO minute on R566, dated 18/1/1945.

[87] Article in *Politika*, on 15/1/1945. FO 371/48181, R1161, 15/1/1945.

[88] FO 371/48181, R1636, 19/1/1945.

the Bulgarian newspaper *Rabotnichesko Delo* that 'soon, the unity of all Southern Slavs will become a fact'.[89] Those reports caused considerable nervousness to the British. Indeed, it was felt that the recent Bulgarian and Yugoslav indiscretions rendered their action all the more necessary. Only the question of timing was left open. On 22 January, Sir Orme Sargent minuted that 'it is for consideration' whether they should wait 'another few days'.[90]

In fact they did not wait for long. On 24 January an extremely important telegram reached the Foreign Office from Sofia: according to what was described as a 'most reliable source' it was reported that the Bulgarian premier Kimon Georgiev had left Sofia to discuss with Tito the establishment of a South Slav federation, and the cessation of Pirin to Yugoslavia.[91] The British 'source' was partially right. Georgiev had left Sofia two days earlier for Moscow to discuss inter alia the future of Bulgar–Yugoslav relations; but he was to talk to Stalin not to Tito.[92] In any case, it was immediately agreed that the time for action had come. All the more so, as the Conference of Yalta—due to take place at February—was only a few days away. The British were quick to realize that it would have been much more difficult to tackle the problem there, when they should have to consult so many parties, than before. That aside, it had always been more effective to stop a process in the making than to dismiss a fait accompli. As far as the Russians were concerned, Sargent commented that 'we have given [them] ample warning'.[93] However, as has already been pointed out, the Soviets knew only of the British views and not of their intentions to act unilaterally; but technicalities hardly matter at a moment of a crisis.

Instructions to Maclean and Houstoun-Boswall were produced swiftly; the two representatives should let the Balkan communists know that HM Government (*a*) disapproved of an exclusive Slav federation, (*b*) would welcome an all-Balkan one and (*c*) although they would agree to the creation of a Macedonian state within the Yugoslav framework, 'they are strongly opposed to the creation of a Greater Macedonian state involving claims on Greek territory'. Moreover the British stressed that they 'do not recognize the right of the Bulgarian government to transfer without the consent of the United

---

89 FO 371/48181, R1315, 17/1/1945.   90 FO 371/48181, R1586, 22/1/1945.
91 FO 371/48181, R1848, 24/1/1945.   92 Pijade 1949, 27.
93 FO 371/48181, R1848, FO minutes dated 25/1/1945.

Nations any part of Bulgarian territory to the Yugoslav Federal State of Macedonia'.[94]

On 28 January, Maclean conveyed to Tito the British position on Macedonia. The Marshal was 'cool and laughed'. He reiterated his stale theme, that the time was not ripe for a federation and that he had no predatory intentions. All those issues, he said, could be raised only at the Peace Conference. Needless to say, Maclean was not deceived by Tito's harmless rhetoric. His impression was that everything 'has already been settled with Moscow', and that Tito was simply buying time.[95] The Bulgarians seemed to be much more concerned and philosophical; Altvinov of the Bulgarian Ministry for Foreign Affairs, when informed by Houstoun-Boswall, stated only that 'a man who has been warned is worth of two'.[96]

But if the Balkan actors in the play had been notified, others had been not; and they were to learn of the démarche in a way that was rather embarrassing for the British. On the last day of January Houstoun-Boswall thought it well to inform on his own initiative the American and Soviet representatives to the Allied Control Commission of the action taken four days earlier by him and Maclean. The Foreign Office was disturbed: 'it was not intended that this should be done', since their governments had not been officially informed. Anyway, it was felt that Boswall's indiscretion could do little harm; 'both know our views' after all. The Soviets revealed their own on 1 February. They included a fair amount of surprise. Dekanosov, vice-commissar for foreign affairs, professed ignorance of deliberations on federation. Instead, he conceded that negotiations were under way for a pact of alliance and mutual assistance between Yugoslavia and Bulgaria, and the Soviet government's attitude to that was favourable. As far as federations were concerned, the question was not 'at present actual and is of no practical importance'.[97]

Thus, the Foreign Office had found another catchword—'pact'—to deal with. Maclean cabled them, somewhat puzzled, asking for instructions in case Tito touched upon it. He was told to refrain from expressing any views, but he was informed that the objections were the same as

---

[94] FO 371/48181, R11861, Annex E (instructions to Houstoun-Boswall), and Annex D (instructions to Maclean), both are dated 26/1/1945.
[95] FO 371/48181, R2183, 29/1/1945.
[96] PRO FO 371/48181, R2054, 27/1/1945.
[97] FO 371/48184, R11861, from Moscow to FO Annex B, 1/2/1945.

for the federation.[98] Indeed, a Bulgar–Yugoslav pact was from the very beginning perceived as a step towards federation, and therefore it should be written off as soon as possible.[99]

The question of Bulgar–Yugoslav relations was raised at the Yalta Conference on 10 February. There, at a meeting of the three Foreign Secretaries, Eden, after expressing his satisfaction with the Soviet attitude towards the South Slav federation, voiced his concern about the proposed pact. Regarding the technicalities of the matter, Eden stated that a country still under an armistice regime should not be allowed to conclude treaties. Molotov argued that Bulgaria was an ex-enemy country, and was fighting the Germans; his government's view on the proposed pact was 'favourable'. But Eden, determined to settle the issue, remained firm: Bulgaria 'was not free to do what it wished'. Stettinius supported Eden, but decided that the final word could wait. He proposed that the pact should be discussed later in Moscow between the American and British ambassadors and Molotov, the last of whom, of course, agreed.[100]

If the postponement agreed in Crimea suited the Soviet Foreign Secretary, it offered to Eden little comfort. He did nothing to conceal this, nor did he hide his determination to bring the question to a quick end. A week later he cabled the Foreign Office from Cairo, 'anxious' to untie that Balkan knot. He proposed that Ralph Skrine Stevenson, the new British ambassador to Yugoslavia, should inform Tito 'as soon as [an opportunity] presents itself' of the British disapproval of the pact. Moreover, Halifax should invite the State Department to take similar action and press the Soviets. Adding some muscle to his cable, Eden asked the British ambassador to Moscow to warn Molotov that if the Russians made any move in support of the pact, the British 'would be obliged to make [their] position publicly clear'.[101] So, Britain was still determined to act unilaterally and to prevent a Slav bloc from materializing. What is more important, however, is that the British were even prepared to take the risk of a head-on collision with Stalin over that particular issue. Whether they actually were in a position to issue such a challenge to the Soviets, given the realities of 1945 in the area, can only be a matter of speculation; but it seems plausible to suggest

---

[98] FO 371/48181, R2457, 2/2/1945.   [99] FO 371/48181, R2361, 7/2/1945.
[100] For this meeting, on 10/2/1945, see Foreign Relations of the United States. Diplomatic papers, *The Conferences of Malta and Yalta* (Washington, 1955), 876–7.
[101] FO 371/48184, R11861, Annex F, 18/2/1945.

that such a tough line revealed their decisiveness rather than their power to back it up with deeds.

At the same time the Foreign Office received the long-awaited American reply on federation. Although federative plans were considered at the time obsolete by all parties concerned, Eden could derive some comfort from the fact that the State Department concurred in his views; the pre-war frontiers were considered the legal ones, a Slav bloc was viewed as a 'disturbing rather then a stabilizing factor', and any arrangement in the Balkans should be liable to 'international sanction'.[102] Only a somewhat puzzling detail needs to be briefly examined here. In the reply it was stressed that 'there is no legitimate basis for any claim made on behalf of "Macedonia" whether as an independent State or as a part of Yugoslavia . . . to territory within the boundaries of Greece on the ground that such territory is "Macedonian" '. The wording of this statement closely follows that of the British note handed to them two months earlier. However, the allusion that Macedonia could be *either* Yugoslav *or* independent—which is absent from the British text—certainly allows some room for guesswork, for no one officially questioned the territorial integrity of the Yugoslav state.

Be that as it may, the British continued to press Soviets and Americans alike to give the matter urgent consideration, and to proceed with a three-power representation to Bulgaria and Yugoslavia. On 1 March, Molotov told Sir Archibald Clark Kerr that the Russian views remained favourable to the proposed pact. He also expressed his 'desire' for further talks in Moscow, as agreed in Crimea.[103] The Americans appeared to refrain from committing themselves. Halifax informed the Foreign Office that although they agreed on the destructive implications of the pact they 'had not made up their mind as to what action they would take'.[104] A few days later on 7 March, British pressure persuaded them to follow suit: the American ambassador in Moscow, Averell Harriman, was instructed to convey to Molotov that a Pact 'would not be desirable'.[105] Thus after the British and American notifications of their disapproval

[102] FO 371/48184, R11861, Annex C, from Earl of Halifax to FO, dated 28/2/1945, just two months after the first British enquiry!

[103] FO 371/48184, R11861, from Clark Kerr (Moscow) to FO, Annex I, dated 1/3/1945.

[104] FO 371/48183, R4088, 1/3/1945.

[105] The text of the American views on the Pact is in FO 371/48184, R11861, Annex J, from Washington to the FO, dated 7/3/1945. The same day Molotov was accordingly informed by Harriman. FO 371/48183, R4504, 7/3/1945.

the ground had been prepared for the issue to be definitively settled in Moscow.

The consultations due to take place 'soon' in Moscow, however, never materialized. Stalin downplayed the issue; the Balkan communists did not conclude any sort of agreement, and Harriman was briefed for the talks by the State Department in July 1945, only a few days before the Potsdam Conference.[106] As no one seemed particularly interested in the matter—for little had happened officially since March—the Macedonian Question was not raised at the Hohenzollern palaces. By the autumn of 1945 it was clear that all interested parties had agreed to let it drop.

The basic strategic objective of British policy with regard to Macedonia during the critical years of 1944–5 was to safeguard the territorial integrity of Greece against the menace represented by a unified—and Greater—Macedonia within a communist-controlled Balkan federation. Convinced at an early stage that Greater Macedonia would inevitably lead to a lesser Greece, the British spared neither pains nor determination in the pursuit of their end. Difficulties did not fail to present themselves. Information concerning deliberations between the Balkan communist parties was scanty and fragmentary, leaving the impression that Balkan communism should be treated as a monolithic world with no internal strife and conflict. Such a view led to another received wisdom: that every Balkan initiative was instigated by Stalin, who, in turn, seemed to entertain predatory aspirations regarding an outlet to 'warm waters'. As a result a bleak prospect haunted the Foreign Office: Slavdom, with its headquarters in Moscow, had been concocting the destruction of Greece, posing a grave danger to British communications in the eastern Mediterranean basin.

Although an all-round evaluation of those perceptions is beset by the lack of Soviet sources, it seems plausible to suggest that Stalin did not consider Greece to fall within his sphere of influence, a fact clearly shown in the—cynical but effective—Percentages Agreement. In contrast to his Greek policy, Stalin's Balkan objectives appeared to be much more obscure. Initially, in November 1944, he seemed to approve of a Balkan federation. He had his reasons. At that time, Marshal Tito, who hastily initiated the federation process, was a loyal communist and despite some signs of friction during the wartime, he remained faithful

---

[106] FO 371/48137, R11767, 11/7/1945.

to Stalin.[107] In view of the above, the readiness of the Soviets to abandon the plan when the British aired their concerns can be attributed more to Stalin's decision to avoid an escalation of tension between Russia and its wartime allies, than to Stalin's attitude towards Tito.

In 1945 Soviet influence in the Balkans, an area traditionally coveted by Moscow, was already established—a fact that the British could not contest; nor did they want to. In this framework, the Balkan federation could come only as a formality, which would confirm an already established situation. By abandoning the plan, Stalin had very little to lose. The pact could only bring an unnecessary confrontation with Britain and the Americans, and that was too high a price for him to pay.

For the British the prevention of the federation was a victory of sorts. As the Red Army barracks designated the area which belonged to the Soviet side of the fence, it was felt that they had contributed to keeping Greece out of it. The fact that the Soviet soldiers seemed not to have the intention to move southwards in the first place, should not make their moves appear less daring. Policies should be evaluated within their proper historical context, and against the views prevailing at the time. In 1945, it was thought that a Slav federation, with Stalin's support, would eventually move against Greece, and—as usually happens in politics—perceptions matter.

---

[107] Needless to say, after the 1948 split the Yugoslav historiography had tried, rather unconvincingly, to give undue importance to early signs of friction between Yugoslavia and Russia by projecting back to the wartime period the bitterness caused by 1948. This notwithstanding, tension between the two 'comrades' before 1948 was not absent. Stalin had objected to the publicizing of the communist character of the Partisan army, while the arrival of a Soviet military mission in Tito's HQ only after that of a British one deeply irritated the Marshal. Moreover, the conduct of the Soviet army in Yugoslavia during 1945 left much to be desired. Last but not least, Yugoslavia's economic exploitation by Moscow was no less of a problem.

PART III

FROM WAR TO COLD WAR, 1945–1949

6

Between Centralism and Separatism: The Emergence of the Yugoslav Republic of Macedonia, 1944–1948

'BULGARIANS', 'MACEDONIANS', AND OTHERS

If war is the continuation of politics by other means, then Macedonian politics in 1944 was the continuation of war by peaceful means. As the Partisan movement gained momentum in late 1944 and established a commanding stronghold in the area, an equally important political process was at the same time under way; namely the establishment of the Communist Party of Yugoslavia through its local organization—the Communist Party of Macedonia as the only legal political authority in Yugoslav Macedonia. Thus, while the Partisans tried to fill the military vacuum created by the withdrawal of the German and Bulgarian occupation forces, the CPM struggled to create those political bodies and institutions which would eventually enable the Yugoslav communists to exercise firm political control in Macedonia at a time when fluidity and uncertainty prevailed. In fact they had more than one reason to hurry matters, for they needed not only to prevent the Germans and the Bulgarians from 'fishing in troubled waters', but also to present as soon as possible the new 'architecture' of Macedonia as one of the federal states of Yugoslavia, in order to deter any aspiring contender.

It is necessary, therefore, to attempt at this stage an analysis of the various political, 'national', and social forces in Yugoslav Macedonia, which could help in providing a more sober appraisal of the formative years of the new state and a balanced appreciation of CPY policy. Needless to say, it should be borne in mind that any 'mapping' of that kind is liable not only to some sort of simplification but also to the Ovidian metamorphoses of men, ideas, and attitudes, which traditionally characterizes this 'most Balkan piece of the Balkans'.

Perhaps the most striking feature of the Macedonian political setting was the rapidity with which the *ancien régime* collapsed, dragging down its supporters in the region. Some thirty years of Serbian rule were enough to create an anti-Serbian sentiment of which many Bulgarian propagandists would be jealous. Under such conditions it was not surprising that the *Četnik* organization of General Dragoljub-Draža Mihailović could claim but a very limited following in Macedonia, confined to the towns. Nevertheless they had set foot in the area and formed quite a few bands.

They were not very keen on resistance, and it seemed that some chiefs had opted for the preservation of their forces rather than for armed struggle against the invader. Thus when a group of them was arrested in 1942, they were promptly released by the Bulgarians, who realized that they would do more good than harm. However, the personal representative of Mihailović in Macedonia, Vojo Trbić, did offer some resistance to the Bulgarians in east Macedonia.[1] If we make the assumption that he acted on instructions given by Mihailović, we may have some deviation from the wartime pattern followed by the general himself in Serbia, according to which the ultimate aim was the preservation of *Četnik* forces until the 'Great Day' of the Allied invasion in the Balkans.[2] It seems plausible to suggest that Mihailović may have viewed the situation in Macedonia differently, not least because a wide range of solutions could be found for the future of that area other than its incorporation into a 'Greater Serbia', which seemed to be Mihailovic's 'solution'.[3] Be that as it may, the *Četnik* movement in Macedonia, hindered by a strongly anti-Serbian population, made little headway and it was easily liquidated by the Partisans in late 1944.

---

[1] Information for *Četnik* activity in Macedonia from FO 371/48183, R8570, memorandum on 'The Partisan Movement in Macedonia and its Opponents', written by Stephen Clissold, press secretary, dated 4/5/1945, enclosure from Ralph Skrine Stevenson (Belgrade) to Eden.

[2] As the controversy on the *Četnik* wartime tactics still continues it is of little surprise that the bibliography on that question is legion. Approaches to this question are offered by Mark Wheeler, *Britain and the War for Yugoslavia, 1941–1943* (New York and Boulder, Colo., 1980); Jozo Tomasevich, *War and Revolution in Yugoslavia: The Chetniks* (Stanford, 1975); Elisabeth Barker, *British Policy in South East Europe in the Second World War* (London, 1976); and W. R. Roberts, *Tito, Mihailović and the Allies, 1941–1945* (New Brunswick, 1973).

[3] According to Zivko Topalović, Mihailovic's political adviser, the general had even adhered to the idea of a Yugoslav federation. But such a declaration was to remain purely theoretical. See WO 210/1621A, memorandum on 'The Question of a Yugoslav Federation', by the American Research and Analysis Department of the OSS dated 8/7/1944.

Another prop of the *ancien régime* in Macedonia, which shared the latter's fate, was the local party system. In broad terms, political parties had never been strong enough among the population, for these were little more than mere offshoots of the main Serbian political groups. The following of such parties could be found mainly among the Serbian element of the region although some politicians claimed adherence to the idea of a confederation and, consequently, to a wider following.[4] Since the great majority of the Serbs were expelled by the Bulgarians, including most of the colonists, any possibility of organizing political life again along pre-war party lines had definitely to be ruled out. Thus from a party politics angle in late 1944 there was in Macedonia a complete vacuum.

While the strength of the military and political pillars of the old Yugoslavia was undermined, it was high time for its foes to weigh up their own position. Considering that anti-Serbian sentiment was rampant, it is beyond doubt that into this category fell the great majority of the population. Nevertheless, opposition to Serbian centralism was the only unifying element among the inhabitants of Macedonia, who, aside from that point of agreement, expressed a wide variety of views about their future, ranging from incorporation into a Greater Bulgaria to autonomy within a loose Yugoslav confederation. Although a pro-Bulgarian inclination, fed by the Serbian assimilationist policy, has been always strong among the Macedonians, it reached its peak in 1941, at a time when the Bulgarian troops were welcomed as 'liberators'. In many places celebrations—organized mainly by the *Bŭlgarski Aktsioni Komiteti* (Bulgarian Action Committees)—were taking place, during which the villagers scattered flowers on the Bulgarian soldiers.[5]

That picture, however, proved more deceptive than one might have expected. The Macedonians began to understand very soon that what

[4] FO 371/ 29785, R145, 'Report on the General Situation in Southern Serbia', by the British vice-consul at Skopje, Thomas, dated 6/1/1941, enclosure from Campbell (Belgrade) to Halifax.

[5] The Action Committees had been formed and made their mark during the period of the interregnum, the short period which elapsed between the disintegration of Yugoslavia and the advance of the occupation forces. The Filov government dissolved them as soon as the new Bulgarian administration took responsibility over the 'Liberated Lands' in May 1941. For a Macedonian account of these committees, see Rastislav Terzioski, 'I.M.R.O.-Mihajlovist Collaborators and the German Occupation: Macedonia, 1941–1944', in Pero Morača (ed.), *The Third Reich and Yugoslavia, 1933–1945* (Belgrade, 1977), 541–2. For a Bulgarian (and more detailed) study see Dimitŭr Minchev, 'Formirane I Deynost na Bŭlgarskite Aktsioni Komiteti v Makedoniya prez 1941 godina', [Formation and Action of the Bulgarian Action Committees in Macedonia in the year 1941], *Izvestiya na I.V.I.*, 50 (1990), 39–93.

actually had happened was the replacement of one kind of centralism with another, and the fact that this time centralism was coming from Sofia instead of Belgrade hardly mattered. The Bulgarians, in an effort to ease the tensions, intended to hand over the local administration to their Macedonian brethren, but they realized that few had the qualifications or the willingness for such a job. As a consequence in 1944 the majority of the officials came from Bulgaria.[6] The quality, both moral and administrative, of these officials represented an even more serious threat. Most of them were incompetent, short-sighted, and arrogant towards the indigenous element, forcing Bogdan Filov to admit that 'it is not surprising if because of the bureaucracy, the population begins not to regret the Serbian regime'.[7] At about the same time, the Bulgarian Minister of the Interior, Docho Kristov, in a speech at Skopje in October 1943, had to remind Bulgarian officials serving in Macedonia that they should behave like liberators and not as though they were invaders.[8] Certainly, the facts that they were underpaid and compulsorily driven to Macedonia from Bulgaria, offer a partial explanation, but the result was that many Macedonians came to resent the presence of their 'brothers'.[9] When the minister of war of the Fatherland Front government, Damyan Velchev, visited the liberated Macedonia in late 1944, he was not allowed to enter Skopje, for—as the Partisans told him—'4 years of Bulgarian occupation had done more harm than 20 years of Serbian oppression'.[10]

On the other hand, the agonizing effort made by Yugoslav–Macedonian historians to prove that Bulgaria's appeal was completely eliminated, appears to be quite misleading.[11] The 'Bulgarian idea' continued to command the loyalty of many Macedonians, mainly among the local intellectuals, but the prestige of the Bulgarian state suffered badly and its claim to provide a better option than the Yugoslav

[6] WO 204/9677, memorandum on 'Yugoslav Macedonia under the Bulgarians' in a series of Memoranda on 'Axis-controlled Europe', prepared by the FO Research Department, dated 29/8/1944.

[7] Filov's Diary, entries for 9 and 10 July 1943, ed. and trans. by F. B. Chary, in *Southeastern Europe*, 3/1 (1976), 64.

[8] As quoted in the Bulgarian paper *Dnes*. PRO WO/204, 9677, memorandum on 'Yugoslav Macedonia under the Bulgarians'.

[9] Marshal Lee Miller, *Bulgaria during the Second World War* (Stanford, 1975), 123–5.

[10] FO 371/48137, R498, dated 5/12/1944.

[11] Alexander Hristov, *The Creation of Macedonian Statehood, 1893–1945* (Skopje, 1972); Rastislav Terzioski, 'The Bulgarian Institutions in Occupied Macedonia, 1941–1944', *Macedonian Review*, 1 (1976), 72–8.

misery of the interwar period was dealt a severe blow. As early as 1942, German intelligence reports noted that 'the Macedonians, who during the period of Yugoslav rule had regarded everything Bulgarian with admiration, now are exceedingly disillusioned after becoming acquainted with a completely corrupt as well as incompetent Bulgarian administration'.[12] The repercussions emerged quite soon. In 1944 more Macedonians could be found willing to accept a different solution from the incorporation of their homeland into a Yugoslavia dominated by a corrupt Belgrade, or by an unwise and insensitive Sofia. More than twenty years of Serbian rule rendered the former option unthinkable; less than four years were enough for the latter to be written off.

If the general feeling was that of a society which in essence was adrift, there were other forces in Macedonia with more concrete views and aims. The Internal Macedonian Revolutionary Organization ranked high among them, although its role has been disproportionately underestimated.[13] First, it should be borne in mind that under that name there could be distinguished two separate factions, which had been engaged in a bloody fratricidal feud since the late 1920s: the Mihailovist IMRO and the Federalists, a faction that, apart from the communists of the IMRO (United), also included some followers of General Protogerov.[14]

As was to be expected, the two factions conducted a completely different policy during the Bulgarian occupation. It seemed that the Federalists—by stressing their autonomist profile—had understood better the signs of the times and enjoyed a considerable following, especially among the Macedonian refugees in Bulgaria. Moreover they tried to infiltrate through the Macedonian partisan movement, reinforcing its already strong sense of independence from Belgrade. Although evidence is scanty, it seemed that many high-ranking partisan officials had a connection with the Federalists, while a military unit, the Eleventh Macedonian Brigade composed of Macedonian refugees in Bulgaria, was largely the work of the Protogerovists.[15]

[12] As quoted in Marshal Lee Miller, *Bulgaria*, 123.

[13] See e.g. Elisabeth Barker, *Macedonia: Its Place in Balkan Power Politics* (London, 1950), 36–45. For this criticism cf. Stephen Palmer and Robert King, *Yugoslav Communism and the Macedonian Question* (Connecticut, 1971), 220.

[14] On IMRO's internal strife see Ch. 1.

[15] FO 371/48184, R13695, 'Memorandum on the Present Situation in Macedonia', by Henniker-Major, dated 24/7/1945. Enclosure from R. Skrine Stevenson (Belgrade) to Bevin, 14/8/1945.

The Mihailovist IMRO was confronted with more formidable difficulties. Its leader, Mihailov, had thrown in his lot with the Germans and had been living since 1941 in Zagreb under the protection of Ante Pavelić, with whom he had established close ties since the 1920s, while his representatives in Macedonia were (to a great extent) mere tools of the Bulgarians. As a consequence the Supremists, as Mihailov's followers were also called, lost much of their prestige, for they had identified themselves with a regime that most Macedonians wanted to get rid of.[16] Discredited and compromised in the eyes of many Macedonians, the Mihailovists, apart from assisting the Bulgarian army during their mopping-up expeditions, kept a rather low profile during the occupation, partly due to the fact that their main aim had been accomplished. In 1944, as the occupation in Macedonia was coming to an end, they had been preparing themselves for underground activity; a fact that would seriously impede the future rulers of the region.

Despite their diversity, the collective attitudes mentioned above reveal the common concern of the Slav element in Macedonia over their relations with Sofia and Belgrade. But Macedonia also included a fairly numerous minority with totally different aspirations, who tended to seek political support from the West and the South, rather than from the North or the East. According to the 1931 census the Albanians formed 25 per cent of the population. Inhabiting the western part of Yugoslav Macedonia and being mostly illiterate peasants, they suffered harsh discrimination, extreme poverty, and the adverse effects of Serbian colonization. Apart from some small-scale armed activity, however, the politically passive Macedonian Albanians had not posed a serious threat to Belgrade.[17] The war upset that balance. From 1940 onwards Italy sought to spread her influence and tried persistently to awaken Albanian nationalism, promising incorporation into a 'Greater Albania'. The realization of Italian plans, a year later, was generally welcomed; Albanian bands actively assisted the Italian army during operations against the Partisans, while the CPY had made no headway among them. Their stubborn anti-Serbian sentiment created serious problems for Tito and Tempo who tried to organize the resistance movement in 1943. The extent of the Albanian threat to Tito's Yugoslavia was

---

made clear in 1944, when a rebellion of Albanian bands in Kosovo was brutally suppressed.[18]

The position of the Turks, approximately 128,000 in 1931, was quite different. According to British assessments, the Turkish minority, more educated and socially stratified than the Albanian, was the only group in Macedonian society which was not overtly anti-Serb and conceivably had some interest in the continuation of the pre-war status quo.[19] During the occupation they remained passive but their strong anti-communist feelings would render their subjugation to a communist regime quite a difficult task. It can be argued that only the lack of an effective leadership and an organized movement among the Turks, spared the Partisans a serious threat.

Apart from the above aspects, centred more or less around the national question, the Yugoslav communists had also to cope with another range of issues, emanating from the social structure of the region. Being an overwhelmingly peasant area with a very small industrial proletariat, Macedonia certainly did not possess the social audience the communists were looking for. In fact the peasants, politically inarticulate and sharing conservative social values, felt much closer to their priests than to the communist agitators. In the interwar years the CPY was particularly strong—the party won Skopje in the municipal elections of 1923—but that success was due to the fact that the party was the most anti-Serbian group that existed in Macedonia. Thus although the CPY had exploited to the full that situation, the question of the relation between the peasantry and the communists remained open.[20]

The examination of the actual strength of communism among the Macedonian peasantry shifts focus to the political force, that is the CPY, which would undertake the thankless task of uniting—and reorganizing—the dismembered Yugoslavia. The formidable obstacles which impaired the CPY during the period 1941–3, in its effort to keep the Skopje Committee under control, have already been discussed.[21] Suffice it here to highlight some other dimensions of the Macedonian communist movement with far-reaching repercussions for the years to

---

[18] For wartime developments and the failure of the CPY to enlist Albanian supporters, see Banac, *With Stalin*, 206–11. For Vukmanović's difficulties with the Albanians see Palmer and King, *Yugoslav Communism*, 94–6.

[19] FO 371/29785, R145, report on Southern Serbia, dated 6/1/1941.

[20] On the interwar policy of the CPY in Yugoslav Macedonia see Palmer and King, *Yugoslav Communism*, 19–57.

[21] See Ch. 4.

come. First, their activities during the occupation suggested that they were among the least Yugoslav-minded communists in the country. In the streets of Skopje the slogans painted in red on the walls read not the typical Partisan 'Death to the Invader', but 'Down with the Filov Government', while their revolutionary committees had not been labelled 'National Liberation Committees' but simply 'National Committees'.[22] In other words the reality was that no matter how loyal the leadership was to the CPY, the rank and file of the CPM remained much less so. Secondly, the communists were the only organized political group in Macedonia in 1944 which had been indoctrinated for some years to uphold the view that the Macedonian Slavs were neither Serbs nor Bulgarians, but a separate nationality.[23] Although the wartime period proved that few did believe they were Macedonians, it is reasonable to assume that most of them would find it expedient to be called Macedonians shortly afterwards, since the only alternative—for which they certainly had no stomach—would be to be called Serbs.

In the light of the above it became apparent that the Partisans' drive for power in Macedonia could not be an easy one. However, if the internal conditions left much to be desired, the international situation worked in their favour: in late 1944 it was certain that Yugoslavia would retain her pre-war territories and as a consequence Yugoslav Macedonia would continue to be so labelled. This fact gave a free hand to the communists, for no foreign intervention would prevent them from consolidating their power.

THE MAKING OF THE PEOPLE'S REPUBLIC OF MACEDONIA, 1944–1948

The Partisans wasted no time. On 2 August 1944, the first *Antifašističko Sobranie na Narodnoto Osloboduvanje na Makedonija* (Antifascist Assembly of the National Liberation of Macedonia: ASNOM) was held at the St Prohor Pčinjski monastery. During its sessions ASNOM, being the supreme legislative and executive body in Macedonia, proclaimed the People's Republic of Macedonia (PRM) to be an equal

---

[22] FO 371/48183, R8570, memorandum on 'The Partisan Movement in Macedonia and its Opponents', written by Stephen Clissold, press secretary, dated 4/5/1945, enclosure from Ralph Skrine Stevenson (Belgrade) to Eden.

[23] For communist approaches to the issue of the nationality of the Macedonians see also Chapter 1.

federal state within the new Yugoslavia. Metodi Antonov (alias Čento), a pre-war Agrarian and elected president of ASNOM, hailed its convention as 'the result of a rather long period of blood, battles and superhuman efforts of the Macedonian people, beginning with 1903'. At the same time he pointed out that only the CPY had recognized the existence of the Macedonian nation.[24] The Macedonian language was decreed the official language of the new state, 2 August—the anniversary of the Ilinden Revolt (new calendar)—was proclaimed an official holiday, and the 'equality of the minorities' was guaranteed.[25]

The euphoria radiated by the official statements on the 'achievements of the Macedonian nation' could not conceal some brutal facts which offered the Partisans little comfort. In the first instance it should be noticed that the communists had tried to set up ASNOM much earlier but the obvious lack of 'suitable' delegates prevented them from doing so.[26] This fact was reflected also in the numbers of participants in the first session: of the 125 elected representatives no more than 95 actually attended.[27]

Moreover even the word *Sobranie* gave rise to speculations as to where the true affiliations of the Macedonians actually lay. The word is clearly Bulgarian (*Săbranie*, meaning assembly), while most of the other Yugoslav equivalents of ASNOM used the Serbo-Croat word *Vijeće* (Croat version) or *Veće* (Serbian version), which is rendered as 'council'. If this linguistic aspect can be attributed to the fact that the 'purification' process of the Macedonian language from its Bulgarian connections had not yet started, there were even more worrying signs. Most of the other Yugoslav regional Liberation Committees had used the word *Zemaljsko* (provincial), which meant that these organizations were *part* of a wider structure. In the case of ASNOM this word was omitted, perhaps an

[24] *Nova Jugoslavija*, 11/8/1944 in FO 371/43649, R16175, 26/9/1944.
[25] See the Resolution adopted in the first session of ASNOM and the 'Declaration of the Fundamental Rights of the Citizens of Democratic Macedonia' in University of Kiril and Metodj, *Documents from the Struggle of the Macedonian People for Independence and a Nation State* (Skopje, 1985), ii. 617–21.
[26] BLOs in Macedonia reported in July that 'no regional [Macedonian Liberation] council is established due to the lack of nationally concious Macedonian leaders'. WO 201/1122, Balkan Political Intelligence, Copy No. 95, dated 31/7/1944.
[27] WO 204/9677, memorandum on 'Yugoslav Macedonia under the Bulgarians' in a series of memoranda on 'Axis-controlled Europe', prepared by the FO Research Department, dated 29/8/1944. According to Bulgarian accounts the number of the participants was even lower: only 60 delegates attended the session. Kostadin Paleshutski, *Iugoslavskata Komunisticheska Partiya I Makedonskiyat Văpros, 1919–1945* [The CPY and the Macedonian Question] (Sofia, 1985), 319.

indication that the Macedonian communists wanted to emphasize their individuality against the other Yugoslav peoples.[28] Before discussing the various problems revolving around this 'individuality', it should be stressed that no matter how late the ASNOM was convened, it came early enough to show to many quarters who was to govern the region. Timing mattered in Macedonia. In early September 1944 the retreating Germans persuaded Ivan Mihailov to go to Skopje in a desperate attempt to establish an independent Macedonia under their auspices. But it was too late. Germany's strength was no more, the Partisan movement was gaining momentum, and, last but not least, Mihailov and his men had been badly compromised as foreign agents. It was no surprise Mihailov's attempts ended in complete failure.[29]

Turning again to ASNOM, it became quite clear that the Macedonian communists continued not only to demonstrate anti-Serbian tendencies but also to try to secure a semi-independent status within the emerging Yugoslav federation. Macedonian officials emphasized that they were determined to enjoy the maximum autonomy they could get and not to tolerate attempts from Belgrade to restore any sort of 'Greater Serbian' hegemonism. Manifestations of that kind increased after the liberation of Skopje in November 1944: thus, the return of Serb colonists in Macedonia was banned by an ASNOM decree, published on 3 December 1944, amidst growing signs of anti-Serbian sentiment.[30] An important factor accounting for these 'separatist' inclinations of the Macedonian communists was the fact that many members of ASNOM interpreted Yugoslav federalism—and Macedonia's role in it—in a far broader sense than did the CPY. As the Partisans gained momentum and became the undisputed rulers of Macedonia, opportunism, fear, and later on a quest for various privileges prompted many Macedonians to side with the CPM. Party membership sky-rocketed, rising from a mere 400 in 1941 to more than 27,000 seven years later.[31] Apart from

---

[28] WO 204/9677, memorandum on 'Yugoslav Macedonia under the Bulgarians'. Concerning the term 'Sobranie', see also the observation of Elisabeth Barker, *Macedonia: Its Place in Balkan Power Politics* (London, 1950), 97. Cf. the names of the following provincial Liberation Committees: *Zemaljsko* Antifašističko *Vijeće* Narodnog Oslobodjenja Hrvatske [Provincial Anti-Fascist Council of National Liberation of Croatia], *Zemaljsko* Antifašističko *Vijeće* Narodnog Oslobodjenja Bosne i Hercegovine [Provincial Anti-fascist Council of National Liberation of Bosnia and Hercegovina].

[29] Cf. Palmer and King, *Yugoslav Communism*, 112–13.

[30] WO 204/9677, information provided by the American OSS, dated 9/3/1945.

[31] Palmer and King, *Yugoslav Communism*, 135. Cf. the figures on CPM membership quoted by Stefan Troebst: 1945: 6,077 members, 1946: 11,570 members, 1947: 14,405

their material expectations, many of these new members brought with them much more radical alternatives for the future of the area, among which an independent and Greater Macedonia figured prominently.[32]

Even more revealing was the composition of the presidium of ASNOM: communists loyal to the CPY line, such as Vera Aceva, Apostolski, and Uzunovski, political commissar of the Macedonian partisans, 'cohabited' with ex-IMRO members, like Mane Chuskov, who had worked for the Bulgarians during the occupation, and with the 'Skopje intellectuals' Kiril Petrušev and Lazar Sokolov, who just a year before had criticized the Partisans for not adopting the slogan of an 'Autonomous Macedonia within a Balkan [i.e. not Yugoslav] Federation'.[33] Moreover, a pre-war politician, Antonov, was elected president of the ASNOM. As shall be seen, two years later he was charged with subversive activities and was sentenced to eleven years' hard labour.[34]

Needless to say, if the Macedonians' faith in the new Yugoslavia was less solid than was expected, that of the main 'architect' of PRM, Tempo, was exactly the opposite: in November 1944 he delivered a speech to the congress of the Antifascist Assembly of National Liberation of Serbia (*Antifašistička Skupština Narodnog Oslobođenja Srbije*) in which he maintained that the 'Macedonian people desired to join themselves to the Motherland', i.e. Yugoslavia.[35] But, as we shall see, this statement represented Vukmanović's wishful thinking rather than the real situation.

At the same time the Macedonian government started to seek support from other quarters. In order to strengthen their independence from Belgrade they called on their 'brethren' from Bulgaria to return and help the new state to create its almost non-existent infrastructure.

members, 1948: 27,029 members. Stefan Troebst, 'Yugoslav Macedonia, 1943–1953: Building the Party, the State, and the Nation', in Melissa Bokovoy, Jill Irvine, Carol Lilly (eds.), *State–Society Relations in Yugoslavia, 1945–1992* (New York, 1997), 251. On party-building in Macedonia see ibid. 248–50.

[32] Report by Henniker-Major, FO 371/48184.

[33] Biographical notes of the most prominent Macedonian leaders in FO 371/48184, prepared by Sqd-Ldr. Hill, BLO with the Macedonian HQ, in enclosure from R. Skrine Stevenson (Belgrade) to Bevin, R13695, dated 6/8/1945. For the 'Skopje intellectuals', see Palmer and King, *Yugoslav Communism*, 84. In this account Petrušev is not referred to as 'Kiril', which has Bulgarian connotations, but as 'Kiro', which sounds more 'Macedonian'. For the loyalty of Aceva to Tito see Banac, *With Stalin*, 194, and for the 'Bulgarophile autonomism' of Sokolov see ibid. 198.

[34] FO 371/66985, R1296, dated 11/1/1947.

[35] WO 204/9677, information provided by OSS, dated 19/11/1944.

There is some evidence to suggest that the Federalists, who were particularly strong in the *Blagoevgradski okrŭg* (the Blagoevgrad region, in Bulgaria) were instrumental in these deliberations. In September 1944, Macedonian émigrés in Bulgaria held a meeting and asked for material and moral support for the PRM while in December the Macedonian commissioner for justice visited Sofia and said that 'we shall not stop anyone who wishes to return to Macedonia'.[36]

This news alarmed the leadership of the CPY. It was understood that strong measures were needed to redress the balance. The opportunity came in late December, when the second session of ASNOM was held in Skopje. Edvard Kardelj, Tito's right-hand man, attended the session as official representative of the *Antifašističko Veće Narodnog Oslobodenja Jugoslavije* (Antifascist Council of National Liberation of Yugoslavia, AVNOJ) and did not mince his words: 'Macedonia', he declared, 'will remain an integral part of Yugoslavia'. He prompted the Macedonians to 'know [who are] their friends and enemies', and concluded by saying that 'all separatist tendencies must be eliminated'.[37] Vukmanović's speech was also carefully worded: 'We have won the fight on the battlefield. We must also win it in the political field.'[38] At the end of the session a new ASNOM presidium was elected with Antonov as president and Lazar Koliševski as first vice-president.

Although both Kardelj and Tempo struggled to make ASNOM policy conform with that of the CPY, the new presidium included some members who thought otherwise. We have already noted the case of the ill-fated Antonov. Perhaps of equal importance was the appointment of Pavel Šatev. Šatev, a lawyer from Kratovo, was an old friend of Vlahov and member of IMRO (United).[39] According to British sources, he tried to negotiate directly with the Bulgarian government—and independently from Belgrade—the frontiers of PRM[40] It is also worth

---

[36] FO 371/48181, R605, dated 5/1/1945.

[37] His speech in FO 371/48181, R316, 4/1/1945.

[38] FO 371/48181, R310, 3/1/1945.

[39] In 1903 Šatev, then a young (born in 1882) and fearless member of the 'Sailors' group (*Gemidžii*), distinguished himself in the blowing-up of the French steamship *Quadalquivir*, in the port of Salonica. See his own recollection of this incident in Stoyan Cristowe, *Heroes and Assassins* (London 1935), 97–9. In 1925, Šatev, along with Vlahov, became a founding father of IMRO (United). Joseph Swire, *Bulgarian Conspiracy* (London, 1935), 217. See also Banac, *With Stalin*, 198.

[40] FO 371/48184, report by Henniker-Major.

mentioning that the new presidium of ASNOM signalled the beginning of the political career of Kiro Gligorov, a young lawyer from Štip, who was appointed commissioner for finance.[41] Needless to say, the wide variety of views among the ASNOM members, regarding relations with Sofia and Belgrade, was nothing more than a reflection of the Macedonian political scene, which was equally divided. In the Bitolj area, for instance, according to American OSS reports, there were three distinct political groups: (*a*) a pro-Bulgarian section that wanted federation with Bulgaria, (*b*) a pro-Serbian faction under the influence of Mihailović, and (*c*) a 'Federalist' group favouring a 'Greater Macedonia' including Salonica.[42]

As it became increasingly clear that the view from Belgrade was not identical with that from Skopje, the sensitive domain of foreign policy emerged as a serious cause of friction and mutual mistrust. Since November 1944 a fierce press campaign had been launched by the Macedonian communists against the 'monarcho-fascist terror' that Papandreou's government had imposed in Greek Macedonia. In general, anti-Greek statements had not been in short supply in 1944, nor had major Yugoslav politicians refrained from engaging in them; Milovan Djilas, during a speech on the anniversary of the October revolution, accused Papandreou of following a 'chauvinistic policy' aiming at 'terrorising the Macedonians' in Greece.[43]

As was to be expected, Macedonian officials were more eloquent. During its first session ASNOM had emphasized the Piedmont-like role of the new state for the 'unification of the entire Macedonian people'.[44] During the second session, the campaign was intensified, and the 'Greek connection' of the Yugoslavs became more visible. On 31 December, a delegate spoke in no uncertain terms: 'I am speaking to you as a Greek Macedonian', he said, and 'as a delegate from Greek Macedonia. The three Macedonias must unite within the framework of the new Yugoslavia.'[45]

---

[41] After the dissolution of Yugoslavia Gligorov was elected president of the 'Republic of Macedonia' in 1991. According to a noted scholar he was 'the most moderate, able, and statesmanlike leader in the Yugoslav successor states'. J. F. Brown, *Hopes and Shadows: Eastern Europe After Communism* (Durham, NC, 1994), 183.

[42] WO 204/9677, information provided by OSS, dated 27/1/1945.

[43] WO 201/1122, British report of the speech, dated 15/11/1944.

[44] Paleshutski, *Iugoslavskata*, 319.

[45] For this campaign see FO 371/48184, 'The Yugoslav Press Campaign Concerning Greek Macedonia', prepared by Stephen Clissold, Press Attaché to the Belgrade Embassy, App. A in R13695, from Stevenson to Bevin, dated 6/8/1945.

These incidents came at a time when Greece was trapped in the vortex of the civil strife of the 'December Events' (*Dekemvriana*) civil strife[46] and acquired special significance for it seemed that the Yugoslavs were matching their action with words. A brigade—the First Macedonian Brigade—had been formed in Bitolj, recruited from Partisans from Greek Macedonia; negotiations between Tito and EAM were under way and there was evidence of troops moving towards the Greek–Yugoslav border. As alarming reports reached the British, Brigadier Maclean was instructed to take the matter up with Tito himself in mid-December. Tito gave firm assurances that none of his troops had or intended to move southwards, and that any misunderstanding that occurred was due to his local commander, Mihailo Apostolski.[47] Whatever Tito's intentions during the critical December might have been, the fact was that he made no move to help the Greek communists in their struggle against the 'monarcho-fascists', of which he and his subordinates were so fiercely critical.

From the point of view of Belgrade–Skopje relations, however, the 'Greek question' acquired another important dimension. Many prominent Macedonian leaders wanted a more aggressive policy towards Greece and found it extremely difficult to conform to the 'non-interventionist' line that Tito seemed to adopt. It was fairly clear that support for the 'Macedonian cause' in Greece had acquired significant proportions in Yugoslav Macedonia. In two cases the token Macedonian Army openly defied Tito's orders. On January 1945 the fifteenth Macedonian Corps was given instructions to advance towards Serbia, but an artillery Brigade refused to do so, demanding instead to move against Greece, while the First Macedonian Brigade, which had been sent to Gostivar, mutinied in April when it was realized that they were

---

[46] For the *Dekemvriana* see John Iatrides, *Revolt in Athens: The Greek Communist 'Second Round'* (Princeton, 1972); Lars Baerentzen, 'The Demonstration in Syntagma Square on Sunday the 3rd of December, 1944', in *Scandinavian Studies in Modern Greek*, 2 (1978), 3–52.

[47] A detailed examination of Tito's relations with the Greek National Liberation Front (EAM) and of his intentions against Greece during and after the *Dekemvriana* fall beyond the scope of this chapter. For a sober account see Evangelos Kofos, *The Impact of the Macedonian Question on Civil Conflict in Greece, 1943–1949* (Athens, 1989), 16–17, 31–2. That study was also published in John Iatrides and Linda Wrigley (eds.), *Greece at the Crossroads: The Civil War and its Legacy* (University Park, Pa., 1995), 319–30. See also Elisabeth Barker, *British Policy in South-East Europe in the Second World War* (London, 1976), 200.

to fight Albanians and not Greek 'monarcho-fascists'.[48] There were also rumours that the Macedonian government was even considering the possibility of setting up a ministry for foreign affairs of their own.

During the second session of ASNOM in December 1944, Tempo, echoing Kardelj and Apostolski, used strong language in condemning irredentist aspirations against Greece, the only result of which would be the creation of 'difficulties' between Yugoslavia and the Allies, and the undermining of Partisan authority in Macedonia.[49] It should also be noted that the British made no effort to conceal their grave concerns about aggressive public pronouncements regarding Greece, nor did they let the Yugoslavs believe that they could get away with it. In an incident typical of the situation, in early January 1945, Maclean, on his way to his HQ saw Kardelj, who had just returned from Skopje and was about to have talks with Tito. The text of his (moderate) speech to ASNOM was 'sticking out of his pocket', noted a vigilant Maclean, who seized the opportunity to warn him that 'he had read every word of it'. At this Kardelj looked 'sheepish'.[50]

Although the actual effect of Maclean's tactics on Kardelj is difficult to gauge, there was no doubt that he fully appreciated the need to restrain the Macedonian hotheads. American sources quoted Kardelj admitting that 'the Macedonians, like all young people, are rash and zealous', and described his aim as being 'to cool their ardour'.[51] At about the same time, Tito did all he could to pour cold water on the Macedonian demands for immediate action against Greece. In late February 1945, the entire Macedonian leadership urgently left Skopje. Antonov, Apostolski, Vlahov, and Šatev were all summoned to Belgrade for consultations with Tito, and, apparently, for a catechism

[48] FO 371/48184, R13695, dated 6/8/1945, from Skrine Stevenson to Bevin, 'Appendix B2, Greek Macedonia', compiled by Sqd. Ldr. Hill, BLO.

[49] WO 201/1622, dated 27/2/1945. Maclean reported in Jan. that all the main speakers at the second ASNOM, including Tempo, Apostolski, and others, unequivocally attacked 'irresponsible elements, who agitated for immediate occupation of Greek Macedonia'. Report on these speeches in FO 371/48181, R1956, 25/1/1945.

[50] For Maclean's psychological warfare against Kardelj, see FO 371/48181, R310, 3/1/1945.

[51] WO 202/256, report by the American OSS, dated 23/1/1945. In fact, Kardelj's speeches on Macedonia at the time were moderate and emphasized the need for Macedonia to remain within the framework of Yugoslavia. Cf. his speech, entitled 'A strong free Macedonia: a necessity for Yugoslavia', broadcasted by the radio Free Yugoslavia, in 4 Jan. 1945, and translated by the BBC, in FO 371/48181, R555, 8/1/1945.

on the subtleties of international politics.[52] Belgrade's concerted and determined intervention appeared soon to be quite effective and the press campaign against Greece ceased.

The Greek question, nevertheless, continued to be a delicate one for years to come. Belgrade tried, as it did on other issues, to strike a balance: Tito would occasionally allow the Macedonians to raise their anti-Greek tones, in order to satisfy their newly found nationalism and to secure their consensus for more important matters; the limits of Skopje independence from Belgrade, for instance. On the other hand Tito would find it particularly easy to 'orchestrate' a campaign against Greece whenever this suited him. This peculiar political acrobatics, however, could be tolerated only so far as it would not jeopardize Yugoslavia's international position. The following years were to confirm that whenever that point was reached Tito found both the determination and the means to reduce the Macedonian irredentist chorus to silence.

The first year of the new state, 1945, was to see almost the same struggle between Belgrade and Skopje, with the former trying to keep the Macedonians in order and the latter continuing to interpret the 'federal' status of Macedonia in a far broader sense than CPY was willing to accept. Striking a balance between centralism and the peculiar kind of separatism that the Macedonians attempted to establish was not an easy task, nor was it achieved without grievances from both sides. Any analysis, therefore, of the issues that emerged in Macedonia in the following years should always take into consideration this important context.

The problem of the resettlement of the Serb colonists, for instance, is particularly illuminating. As has already been pointed out, after the liberation of Macedonia some of them had tried to regain their lands—given in the interwar period mostly at the expense of Albanian peasants—but an ASNOM decree prevented them from doing so. In March, the Macedonian Ministry of the Interior ordered them simply to 'wait instructions' from the federal government. A month later the federal minister for Macedonia said that the question was a matter for the Macedonian government to decide, and although, in addressing the Macedonian Assembly in March, he denounced the tendency of 'some extremists' to forbid Serb's access to Macedonia, and confirmed that all Yugoslavs were entitled to freedom of travelling, few Macedonians

<hr>

[52] WO 202/264A, report dated 23/2/1945.

bothered to pay attention. As a consequence, many Serbs who entered Macedonia were jailed by the Macedonian police.[53]

The treatment of the colonists was not an isolated incident. The Macedonian government made every effort to keep the Serbs out of the administration. Even the loyal Lazar Koliševski, first prime minister of Macedonia, stated that the republic had no need of the Serbs since there were enough Macedonians to staff the civil services. Koliševski added that Serbian officials were completely corrupt and incompetent, and they would have been incapable of running the administration since transactions had to be conducted in the Macedonian language, of which they had no command.[54] As should be expected, the strong anti-Serbian sentiment prevailing in Macedonia at the time was also reflected in the education system that the new rulers were hurriedly setting up. In September 1945, the Macedonian education minister felt confident enough to claim that half of the villages had elementary schools, with 92,000 students. However, although there were thirty-five Turkish and ninety Albanian schools, no provision whatsoever was made for Serbian schools.[55]

As far as the recruitment for the administration was concerned, if the Serbs were unable to communicate in the Macedonian language, this apparently was not a problem for the Bulgarians. Many officials who had worked for the Bulgarian occupation regime continued to hold their posts and to offer their services to the new administration, but on condition that they denounced the Greater Bulgarian ideology of their former employers; most of them thought it wise to do so quickly. The shortage of educated persons remained a formidable obstacle and local newspapers carried frequent advertisements calling on educated Macedonians to apply for administrative posts. But they were in short supply. The first lawyer who set up an office in Skopje came in August 1945, almost a year after the liberation of the city.[56] It was evident

[53] British reports on the fate of the colonists in FO 371/48183, R7478, 13/4/1945, R6937, 17/4/1945; WO 201/1622, 13/3/1945. It should be added that the Macedonian police was composed entirely of Macedonians to the irritation of Belgrade.

[54] The first Macedonian federal government was elected on 16/4/1945. Koliševski was appointed prime minister with Ljupčo Arsov (also loyal to Tito) as first vice-president. FO 371/48183, R7400, 17/4/1945. For Koliševski's statement see Henniker-Major's report in FO 371/48184, R 13695, quoted above.

[55] Reported by the British vice-consul at Skopje ('Diary' for Sept. 1945). FO 371, 48873, R18700.

[56] FO 371/48185, R16833, 'Skopje Diary, August 1945', by the British consul at Skopje, A. L. Scopes, enclosure in R. Skrine Stevenson to Bevin, 12/9/1945.

that the Macedonian leadership was prepared to accept all sorts of civil servants, provided they were not Serbs. If the applicants could satisfy this provision, few other questions would be asked.

The Church was another important issue. As early as in 1943 the Macedonian Partisans had expressed their wish for the establishment of a Macedonian Church[57] and a year later Metropolitan Joseph, acting head of the Serbian Church, had expressed his fears that such a possibility might come true. These fears were justified: on March 1945 a church congress was held in Skopje to set up a Macedonian Church.[58] From that time onwards, the Macedonian Church, although nominally a part of the Serbian Church, enjoyed a considerable degree of autonomy. Finally in 1967, a synod of Macedonian clerics declared its independence, despite strong Serbian opposition.[59]

The pro-Yugoslav forces, however, did not sit back. During the summer of 1945 an intense campaign for the 'brotherhood and unity' of the Yugoslav peoples was under way. The local press emphasized this much-praised slogan, the Skopje radio was placed under the strict control of Belgrade, while on 17 June the official *Borba* attacked 'Macedonian chauvinists', who continued to stir up troubles with the Serbs.[60] The Macedonian army was used again as an instrument of integration. Divisions consisting of Serbs and Croats were placed alongside the Macedonian units in order to create a semblance of 'comradeship in arms'. Prominent Yugoslav politicians visited Skopje to impress upon the Macedonians the necessity to accept the situation as it was. The eminent and respected Dr Ivo Ribar, president of the AVNOJ, in a speech in Skopje during the commemoration of Ilinden on 2 August 1945, stated that Macedonia 'was and will remain Yugoslav'.[61] Few months earlier Lazar Koliševski, in an interview in *Politika*, had warned that some elements—namely an assortment of

---

[57] Palmer and King, *Yugoslav Communism*, 166–73.

[58] WO 201/1622, report dated 13/4/1945.

[59] The title of the new church was 'Archbishopric of Ochrid and Macedonia'. It has not been recognized, however, by the other autocephalous churches, or by the Ecumenical Patriarchate of Constantinople. For the Church question in Macedonia see also Stella Alexander, *Church and State in Yugoslavia since 1945* (Cambridge, 1979), 254–68.

[60] The article followed an armed attack by Macedonians against two houses belonging to Serbs, in a village near Skopje. Such incidents, the Belgrade paper warned, only played into the hands of 'Great Serb' elements. FO 371/48184, R10559, 19/6/1945.

[61] FO 371/48185, R16833, 12/9/1945, report by the British consul at Skopje. Dr Ribar, a Croat, was president of the AVNOJ from 1942 to 1945; then he became president of the Presidium of the Federal People's Assembly of Yugoslavia (1942–53).

'agents of foreign reaction, fascists, Mihailovists, Supremists and Great-Bulgars'—wanted to 'exploit Macedonian nationalism for separatist and chauvinistic claims'.[62]

Overall, as has already been noted, Belgrade tried to strike a balance: while determined to show to the Macedonians who was really in charge, the federal government was careful not to make them regret this too much. Thus, vital sectors of the region's economy, like mines and railways, were placed directly under federal control, Serbs were appointed as technical advisers despite Macedonian opposition, and UNRRA supplies to Macedonia were cut off.[63] At the same time, however, the Macedonians were granted full cultural autonomy and freedom to develop their Macedonian nationalism, an arguably small compensation for not being granted the autonomy they sought.

If the relations between Belgrade and Skopje dominated political developments in Macedonia, opposition to the regime was no less of a danger for both of them. The Supremist wing of Mihailov's IMRO, although a spent force, was perceived, nevertheless, as a potentially serious threat. Mihailov had continued to advocate an independent Macedonia under the protection of a great power, and he still had some men on the spot. Some of them appeared to be willing to revive the tactics used against the Serbs in the interwar years. In April 1945 the Yugoslav press agency, *Tanjug*, reported a trial in Bitolj, always a politically active area, where a group of IMROists had been discovered. A number of Mihailović's supporters had also been brought to trial, and their leader was sentenced to death.[64] Underground activities, however, which sometimes took the form of attacks by armed bands, did not cease.

The beginning of 1946 saw a recrudescence of armed struggle against the regime. The most serious incident occurred in February, when well-equipped and trained bands attacked garrisons at Štip and Veles and slit the throats of government officials. A confusion about the perpetrators of this attack led the British to hold responsible the wartime Macedonian hero Lt. Gen. Mihailo Apostolski, who at that time appeared to have broken with the Macedonian government.[65] Shortly afterwards, however, it was discovered that it was the work of

[62] FO 371/48184, R9317, 28/5/1945.
[63] FO 371/48184, R13695, report by Henniker-Major.
[64] FO 371/48183, R7479, 14/4/1945.   [65] FO 371/59461, R4281, 19/3/1946.

IMRO. Later that year another IMRO group was discovered, again in Štip. Among the accused was Dimitйr Madarov. According to the British report of the incident, Madarov was a close aide of Mihailov, whom he had met in Zagreb in August 1944, in order to prepare the latter's Macedonian venture in September. He was sentenced to death.[66]

The IMROists were not the only element which resented the state of Macedonian affairs. It can be said that many high-ranking officials were becoming increasingly impatient. In their view an independent Macedonia would be a far more desirable option than the restoration of Serbian domination, even under communist cover. Perhaps the Antonov affair represented these wishes in the most dramatic way. In late November 1946, Antonov, being twice president of the ASNOM Presidium and a member of the AVNOJ, was charged with subversive activities. According to the prosecution, he had tried to go to Paris and ask the Peace Conference to declare Yugoslav and Greek Macedonia mandated territory under the protection of the Western Powers. It appeared that Antonov had agreed to act with IMRO on this matter. Banko Zagoranliev, a senior IMROist, was also arrested in connection with that affair. The CPY tried to suppress the embarrassing incident, and acknowledged it only after the split with Stalin in 1948.[67]

Although the record of unrest in Macedonia was substantial, it should be emphasized that communist (and Tito's) authority in the region was not as vulnerable as it appeared to be. In the first instance the pro-Yugoslav members of the Macedonian government, under the leadership of Koliševski and Arsov, kept it in order. One of Koliševski's constant themes in his speeches and conversations was that 'extreme national tendencies' represented the major danger to the present regime.[68] At the same time the communists tried to eliminate their internal foes and to neutralize potential ones. The task was entrusted to the *Odeljenje za Zaštitu Naroda* (Department for the Defence of the People, OZNA),

---

[66] FO 371/66985, R1935, 4/2/1947.

[67] Antonov was sentenced to eleven years' hard labour and Zagoranliev to five. Two other members of that 'conspiracy', Mitre Mitrevski and Nedelko Makrevski, received minor sentences. For British reports on the Andonov case see FO 371/66985, R1296, 11/1/1947. See also Paul Shoup, *Communism and the Yugoslav National Question* (New York, 1968), 167.

[68] FO 371/48183, R7573, 26/4/1945.

the infamous Yugoslav secret police. Being under firm communist control, OZNA guarded the sensitive frontier with Serbia, and managed to arrest more than 600 members of armed bands, mostly IMRO members, between 1945 and 1947.[69] More often than not, its men used their 'big stick', and guns, against the (real or perceived) foes of the regime, after the finest tradition of the Serbian gendarmes of the interwar years. In February 1945, for instance, thirty-three civilians were shot dead by OZNA, in Veles, only to provoke an outcry from the local population. In an effort to calm the situation, OZNA was obliged to sentence to death three of its officers.[70] Nevertheless, persecution against some, was skilfully accompanied by some appeasement towards others. Thus, Albanians and Turks were given seats in both ASNOM and the government, and some minority schools were opened at an early stage. It is interesting to note that minority delegates were, or were considered to be, 'loyal' to the regime although not necessarily communists.[71]

What is even more important, however, is that the Macedonian government was preoccupied from the very beginning of its rule with the reconstruction of the devastated country. In an effort to persuade a suspicious population that a government linked (albeit halfheartedly) to Belgrade was not automatically corrupt and incompetent, the communists were engaged in reconstructing Macedonia with both enthusiasm and determination. The agrarian reform, and especially the distribution of land to the peasants, was a particularly successful step towards the welfare of the majority of the population. Although the situation in 1946 left much to be desired, there were grounds which allowed a modest sense of optimism for the future.[72] Yet again, the Macedonian government declined to accept the participation of Serb technical advisers in the reconstruction planning. Notwithstanding the lack of experienced and well-trained personnel, the Macedonians thought it better to work alone rather than to compromise their autonomy.

[69] Evangelos Kofos, *Nationalism and Communism in Macedonia* (Salonica, 1964), 159.

[70] WO 202/256, information about OZNA activities provided by the American OSS, report dated 5/2/1945.

[71] FO 371/48184, R8571, 3/5/1945, for minority delegates to the Macedonian government.

[72] FO 371/58615, R6927, 2/5/1946.

AN IDEOLOGY THAT FITS THE TIME:
THE FUNCTION OF MACEDONIAN NATIONAL
IDEOLOGY IN YUGOSLAV MACEDONIA,
1944–1948

Apart from the oscillation between the centralism sponsored by Belgrade and the 'separatism' promoted by Skopje, the one single issue that dominated the Macedonian Question as far as Yugoslav Macedonia was concerned was the emergence of a Macedonian national ideology. The examination of the uses of that ideology appears to be a demanding task, for it not only had far-reaching repercussions within the framework of Yugoslavia, but also shaped the Macedonian controversy by putting it in a new context and perspective.[73]

For the period under consideration (1944–7), apart from the local newspapers, and especially the official *Nova Makedonija*, one of the most official and authoritative works which forged the new ideology was a book written by the ageing Dimitar Vlahov, *Govori i Statii 1945–1947* (Speeches and Articles), and published by the State Publishing House of Skopje in 1947.[74] Vlahov, the founder of IMRO (United) in the interwar years, was the most senior Macedonian figure to side with Tito. Given the shortage of pro-Titoist Macedonians Vlahov's symbolic significance was not lost on Tito, and in 1943 he appointed him to the Presidium of the Antifascist Council of National Liberation of Yugoslavia (AVNOJ), to the irritation of the Bulgarian communists and Georgi Dimitrov.[75] He also became president of the People's Front of Macedonia, and vice-president of the Yugoslav Federal National Assembly.

[73] For a discussion of that issue see also Palmer and King, *Yugoslav Communism*, 153–74.

[74] Quotations from this book are from a Greek translation, deposited at the Institute for Balkan Studies, Salonica, Greece.

[75] Tito had also appointed to the AVNOJ presidium the Bulgarian communist Vladimir Poptomov, an old associate of Vlahov, but interestingly, this occurred without the prior knowledge, or approval, of Moscow. In fact, Georgi Dimitrov was against that move, for Vlahov was 'an émigré lacking any connections with Yugoslav Macedonia', whereas Poptomov was 'a former Bulgarian Communist deputy and currently a Bulgarian commentator for Soviet foreign radio'. Both were 'known in Bulgaria as Bulgarian Communists'. He asked Tito to rectify this unfortunate decision, but Tito refused to comply. Ivo Banac (ed.), *The Diary of Georgi Dimitrov, 1933–1949* (New Haven and London, 2003), 291, 313–14.

Vlahov's book had all the limitations which burdened the author at that time. Thus throughout his work Vlahov praised the CPY for recognizing the existence of the Macedonian nation. He also lavished much praise on the 'political genius of Marshal Tito' who managed to create a country based on the 'principle of equality' of its peoples, and on their 'brotherhood and unity'.[76] But the CPY was not the only communist party to acknowledge the Macedonian national individuality, nor did the concept of 'brotherhood and unity' inspire all the Yugoslavs, let alone the Macedonians.[77] Be that as it may, since the purpose of this polemical work was to indoctrinate and educate the population in the spirit of 'Macedonianism', its historical inaccuracies are hardly relevant. The point at issue was to present a textbook of Macedonian nationalism, and as a consequence the interpretation of facts counted more than the facts themselves. If nationalism is 'imagined' it would be too much to expect that an official publication would do anything less than that.[78]

Vlahov's book covers a wide range of issues. He provides an outline of Macedonian history where he stresses the national individuality of the Macedonians, despite the 'cultural yoke' imposed by Greeks, Serbs, and Bulgarians. Naturally, the history of the IMRO and the development of the Macedonian Question from the late nineteenth century onwards is examined in considerable detail. According to Vlahov, the Macedonians constitute a separate nationality for they: (*a*) live in a common territory, 'in Macedonia within our *geographical* borders', (*b*) live under common economic conditions, (*c*) possess a 'comon culture', and (*d*) have a common language.[79]

The complexities of the language question urged him to spill much ink. He realized, of course, that the standardization of the Macedonian language was still an unfinished process, for 'we do not have yet a definitive grammar'. But this defect would soon be rectified, and 'our language will soon become one of the most beautiful languages'. At a time when the majority of the Macedonians spoke dialects with a close affinity to Bulgarian and the communist leaders were busy changing

---

[76] Vlahov, *Govori*, 77.

[77] The BCP, for instance, had admitted the existence of a Macedonian nation in 1923. See Dimitŭr Minchev, 'Bŭlgarskata Komunisticheska partiya I Makedonskiyat Vŭpros do 9 Septemvri 1944 godina' [The Bulgarian Communist party and the Macedonian Question until 9 September 1944], *Voenoistoricheski Sbornik*, 6 (1986), 12.

[78] The *locus classicus* is of course Benedict Anderson, *Imagined Communities: Reflections on the Origin and Spread of Nationalism* (London, 1983), 6.

[79] Vlahov, *Govori*, 31.

their names by putting the Macedonian ending 'ski' where a Bulgarian 'ov' or 'ev' figured prominently, Vlahov's agonizing effort was quite understandable. In order to eradicate any Serbian or Bulgarian linguistic influence, Vlahov pointed out that neither the Skopje dialect nor the one spoken in the eastern part of Macedonia should be taken as the basis for the new Macedonian literary language; the former had been exposed to Serbian and the latter to Bulgarian cultural hegemony. Struggling to find an area free from any 'foreign' linguistic presence, he opted for the dialect spoken in the Prilep-Bitolj (Monastir) region, which is also close to the dialect spoken in Ochrid. These dialects, he did not fail to add, had 'a long literary tradition'.[80] The creativity of the Macedonian officials in promoting the new national ideology was also reflected in the variety of outlets they employed to popularize it: on 9 May 1945, the Macedonians enjoyed the first performance of the newly minted Macedonian opera (although in Italian) while the first film with Macedonian subtitles (a Soviet production) was screened on 29 May 1946. They had to wait, however, for some ten years to hear the first Macedonian libretto: predictably the title of the first Macedonian opera was 'Gotse', a reference to Gotse Delchev, the legendary IMROist chieftain.[81]

The main points made by Vlahov formed the nucleus around which the Macedonian national historiography continued to revolve for years to come: (*a*) Macedonia, within its geographical and not state boundaries, was a geographical, national, and an economic entity, (*b*) the Macedonian nation had an age-old history and some manifestations of its national individuality had been expressed since the late nineteenth century (with the 'autonomist' wing of the IMRO, its leaders—especially Gotse Delchev and Jane Sandanski—and the short-lived 'Kruševo Republic' (1903), as the most important historical landmarks), and (*c*) the Macedonian language was neither Serbian nor Bulgarian but a separate South Slav language, whose historical credentials were not inferior to those of the other Slavic languages.

It is not the purpose of this study to discuss the historical validity of Vlahov's arguments, nor to examine the course and transformations of the Macedonian historiography. On the other hand, since 'nations do not make states and nationalisms but the other way round',[82] the task of

---

[80] Vlahov, 31–3, 261–8. Cf. also Troebst, 'Yugoslav Macedonia, 1943–1953', 250–5.

[81] Troebst, 'Yugoslav Macedonia', 253.

[82] Eric Hobsbawm, *Nations and Nationalism since 1780* (Cambridge, 1990), 10.

refuting Vlahov's arguments on historical grounds does not appear to be very profitable. From this point of view, whether the Byzantine emperor Basil II, nicknamed *Voulgaroktonos* (the Bulgar-Slayer), had actually destroyed the 'Macedonian state' of Samuel, as Vlahov pointed out,[83] is quite irrelevant. What is of interest here is to examine the social and political context of Macedonian nationalism, its functions, and its wider repercussions in the development of the Macedonian state during its formative years. Within this framework, Vlahov's book, briefly discussed above, is presented only as a sample indicative of the content that the official version of Macedonian nationalism had assumed during these early years.

At first, it should be emphasized that Macedonia arguably enjoyed a greater degree of cultural autonomy than any other federal unit, a fact the Macedonians were very keen to demonstrate even on inappropriate occasions; in August 1945, for instance, a Serbian Partisan concert group gave a concert in Skopje to propagate the 'brotherhood and unity' of the Yugoslav peoples. However, the degree to which the Macedonian government understood that slogan became evident the day after the concert, when the young Serbian musicians were arrested and shut in a disused school, for they had sung a song referring to the Serbian Šumadija region, and another written by a Serb.[84] The official reason for their detention was that their songs were 'reactionary'. There is no doubt, however, that the real reason was that Serbian songs were no music to Macedonian ears.

In their effort to purify the cultural domain of their republic from the Serbian remnants of the past, the Macedonians demonstrated that their speed was not inferior to their imagination. In 1945, after a visit in Macedonia, the Soviet writer Ilya Ehrenburg wrote for the *Izvestiya* a 'letter from Macedonia'. He remarked that Skopje's roads were similar to those in America, for the street signs bore no names, but just numbers: '86th Street or 247th Street'. The careful writer swiftly proceeded to explain that such a sign was not due to 'imitation of America'; rather, the old names of the roads were considered expressions of the Serbian heritage of Macedonia, and since the Macedonians have

[83] Vlahov, *Govori*, 249.

[84] FO 371/48185, R16833, report of the British vice-consul at Skopje, A. L. Scopes, enclosure: from Skrine Stevenson to Bevin, dated 12/9/1945. Šumadija was a centre of Serb guerilla activity during the Serbian uprisings against the Ottomans in the 19th century.

not yet decided on new names, they used numbers.[85] Moreover, apart from the effort to enhance the Macedonian national identity through education, which for the first four years provided for instruction only in Macedonian, and a determined opposition to Serbian cultural influences, the Macedonian leadership devoted no less attention to the sharpening of the anti-Bulgarian edge of their sword. Having realized that the Balkan collective memory had already branded as Bulgarians many heroes of the Macedonian movement, they spared no effort in reclaiming names (and places), as if they had been kidnapped from their Macedonian nursery by the Bulgarian midwife of history. Within this framework, the remains of Delchev, who was now considered a Macedonian national hero, were brought to Skopje from Bulgaria in 1946.[86]

To make the population understand better that the Vardar river was now flowing against Bulgaria, show trials were also used: courts were established in early 1945, to try offences against 'Macedonian national honour'. During these highly publicized trials, with Lazar Mojsov acting as the public prosecutor, many real (or imaginary) collaborators and pro-Bulgarians were sentenced to death for having betrayed their motherland. These parodies of justice, however, caused very soon a considerable amount of dissatisfaction in Macedonia. In August 1945, Pavel Šatev, then minister of justice, confided to a British official that the courts had to be dissolved; he also felt obliged to acknowledge that the main problem was the lack of 'properly trained jurists'.[87] It was, nevertheless, in this atmosphere of (almost unrestricted) cultural autonomy and (much more disputed) internal freedom that Macedonian nationalism flourished.

The driving force behind this movement is a far more complex issue. The argument put out by the Yugoslav–Macedonian historians and publicists, that post-1944 developments were simply the manifestations of the national sentiment of an age-old nation which had suffered

[85] Ehrenburgh's picturesque and romantic account of Macedonia was part of a series of 'letters' he wrote for the republics of Tito's Yugoslavia, which were published in *Izvestiya* in late 1945. See trans. of his Macedonian 'letter', in FO 371/48876, R20563, 27/11/1945.

[86] Paul Shoup, *Communism and the Yugoslav National Question* (New York, 1968), 151. It should also be added that the Macedonian Institute of National History, founded in Skopje in 1946, ensured that the Macedonians would catch up with their neighbours sooner rather than later on all matters historical.

[87] FO 371/48183, R5285, 19/3/1945 (for the announcement concerning the courts); FO 371/48184, R13005, 2/8/1945 (for Šatev's decision to dissolve them).

from oppression and 'denationalization', does not leave much room for scholarly debate. On the other hand, Greek and Bulgarian accounts, being obviously neither disinterested nor unprejudiced, seem to converge in their assessments. Both sides argue, the latter more blatantly than the former, that the inhabitants of Yugoslav Macedonia had always been pure Bulgarians and that it was Tito, with the help of his local communist allies, who transformed the population into Macedonians.[88] Besides the fact that the Macedonian peasants had not been as ethnically conscious as some of these accounts would like them to be,[89] both approaches tend to overlook some aspects of the internal dynamics of Yugoslav Macedonia and do not always see that the views of Belgrade and Skopje on the national question had been anything but identical.

True, a concerted effort was undertaken to make the Macedonians feel 'Macedonian', and a considerable amount of propaganda was needed to persuade them to speak 'their' own language, avoiding conscious or unconscious slips into either Bulgarian or Serbian.[90] There is sufficient evidence, nevertheless, to suggest that the prime mover in this operation was the *local* ruling communist party and not the leadership of the CPY. Undoubtedly Tito, who tried hard to keep Macedonia within the pre-war Yugoslav frontiers, badly needed a cultural barrier between Macedonians and Bulgarians. Consequently, he facilitated the 'Macedonianization' process and granted the new state full cultural autonomy. But it was the local Communist Party of Macedonia, not the CPY, which tried desperately to forge the new identity, to standardize the Macedonian 'literary' language, and to find the appropriate textbooks to educate both the teachers and the students.

The fact that Macedonian national ideology proceeded mostly from Skopje rather than from Belgrade is illustrated by the difficulties that

---

[88] For Bulgarian accounts see Dobrin Michev, 'Makedonskiyat Vŭpros v Bŭlgaro-Iugoslavskite Otnosheniya na Sŭvremenniya Etap' [The Macedonian Question in Bulgar–Yugoslav Relations in the Contemporary Stage], in L. Panayotov, K.Paleshutski, and D. Michev, *Makedonskiyat Vŭpros I Bŭlgaro-Iugoslavskite Otnosheniya* [The Macedonian Question and Bulgar–Yugoslav Relations] (Sofia, 1991), 97–124, esp. 102–3. Cf. also Michev, *Makedonskiyat Vŭpros I Bŭlgaro-Iugoslavskite Otnosheniya, 9 Septemvri 1944–1949* [The Macedonian Question and Bulgar–Yugoslav Relations, September 1944–1949] (Sofia, 1994), 76–100. For nuanced Greek approaches see two articles by Evangelos Kofos: 'The Making of Yugoslavia's People's Republic of Macedonia', *Balkan Studies*, 3 (1962), 375–96, and 'The Macedonian Question: The Politics of Mutation', *Balkan Studies*, 28 (1987), 157–72.

[89] See Ch. 1.

[90] For this process see Evangelos Kofos, 'The Macedonian Question', as well as Palmer and King, *Yugoslav Communism*, 153–74.

Tito himself had faced in his efforts to keep his Macedonian comrades in order. The strong 'nationalist tendencies' that Kardelj, Tempo, and Koliševski repeatedly condemned, along with a general atmosphere of tension between Skopje and Belgrade—already examined in this chapter—emerged too early and were too strong to be considered as Tito's work, which got out of his control. In other words, it is not convincing to suggest that Tito communicated the Macedonian virus to the Macedonians in 1944, for shortly afterwards he was confronted with an epidemic. Moreover, Macedonian nationalism—as it was expressed in 1944–7—had too strong an anti-Yugoslav dimension to be to his liking.

It can be argued, that it was precisely this anti-Yugoslav sentiment that nourished the Macedonian movement after 1944. In the inter-war years rampant anti-Serbianism in Yugoslav Macedonia fed mostly Bulgarophil tendencies. Some discontent was also channelled through communism, but this current remained rather weak. At that time, however, the Bulgarian option had its appeal almost intact. Although the Mihailovist IMRO had not managed to establish a commanding stronghold in the area, whenever a Serbian policeman was assassinated by an IMRO gunman, the population—irrespective of national or political inclinations—felt little or no sympathy for the victim. Thus the result of the interwar oppression was that the Macedonians had been lost to the Yugoslav state and continued to gravitate towards Sofia for a better future.

Tito and the CPY championed the idea of federation, a rather sensible solution to the national question. But the brutal fact was that the Macedonians had no stomach for any kind of Yugoslavia. Although Tito had very wisely denounced the 'Great Serb hegemonists' who had created 'a regime of gendarmes, of social and national injustice', his assurances did not carry much conviction.[91] Initially, it will be remembered, the Macedonian communists followed the beaten track, and from 1941 up to 1943 placed themselves under the control of the Communist Party of Bulgaria (CPB). But the course of international politics dictated otherwise: Yugoslavia was to regain her pre-war territories. At the same time, as has already been seen, the Bulgarian heavy-handed attitude towards the so-called 'liberated territories' had left bitter (and recent) memories.

---

[91] Article by Tito published in *Proleter*, official organ of the CC of the CPY, in Dec. 1942. Trans. in WO 201/1622, App. B, to Political Intelligence Centre Middle East.

Thus at the end of the wartime period a peculiar kind of 'national vacuum' was evident in the former Southern Serbia. At this juncture, the Macedonian national ideology was the only alternative which would fill that vacuum. It met the needs of most Macedonians. First and foremost the mounting anti-Serbianism found a convenient shelter. It is here that the significance of the new ideology actually lay. It provided the only available option (and one that was sanctioned by Tito) for anti-Serbianism to be expressed openly and in a legitimate way. In the interwar years this sentiment took the form of Bulgarophilia. In the post-war era it was transformed into Macedonianism. This particular dimension of Macedonianism is clearly illustrated by the fact that anti-Serbianism was the only sentiment shared by the various Macedonian personalities and groups which became the champions of the Macedonian idea: from the loyal communists (Koliševski) to the 'separatists' (Antonov), and from the old members of the communist wing of IMRO (Vlahov, Šatev) to the 'Skopje intellectuals' (Lazar Sokolov), the entire Macedonian political spectrum saw in a possible restoration of Serbian hegemony the bleakest prospect of all.

The ideological prerequisites of Macedonianism had made their appearance in a diffident manner during the pre-war period. The idea of a Macedonian nation was not a wartime novelty. Some of the organizations and personalities listed above are an indication of this. Thus the Balkan communist movement had been indoctrinated in that direction during the interwar period. The fact that the rulers of Macedonia after 1944 were communists made acceptance of Macedonianism much easier, not least because an authoritarian regime leaves pretty little room for individual choice. On the other hand the concept of Macedonian 'autonomy' had a long history. There is hardly a single faction of the Macedonian movement, which had not advocated, with varying degrees of sincerity, a Macedonian autonomous unit, occasionally within a *Balkan* (Communist or not) federation. The communists did so from the early 1920s. Even the Supremist Mihailovist IMRO—albeit nominally—made some noises to that effect, not to mention IMRO (United). Consequently Macedonian politicians, of whatever persuasion, had been familiar with that slogan. In fact they had fought for it. As a result, the offer of the CPY in 1944—i.e. a relatively autonomous Macedonia within a *Yugoslav* federation—was the only alternative which resembled to some degree the old slogan that most of the Macedonians would have opted for. Certainly it was the lesser of two evils. True, many would have liked to see the back of Yugoslavia altogether, but then at the end of the war that option was not feasible. In this context, Macedonianism served the Macedonians well, in a way that neither Bulgarophilia nor total autonomy could.

No doubt, the vast majority of the Macedonian peasants, being neither communists nor members of IMRO (United), had not been previously affected by Macedonian national ideology. The British officials who attempted to tackle this issue in the 1940s noted the pro-Bulgarian sentiment of many peasants (emphasizing at the same time their disillusionment with Bulgaria) and pointed out that Macedonian nationhood rested 'on rather shaky historical and philological foundations' and, therefore, had to be constructed by the Macedonian leadership.[92] Given that the Macedonian peasants were not noted for their stubbornness on the national question, the Macedonian nation-building did not appear to be a particularly difficult process. According to the British Consulate at Skopje, 'the average Macedonian is not interested in the subject [of nationalism]', and is rather 'passive'.[93] Moreover, since the alternatives were the restoration of Belgrade's unrestricted authority on one hand and incorporation into the Bulgarian state, which treated them so unwisely, on the other, being a Macedonian was definitely not the worst option. Equally certain was the fact that the national loyalties of stout pro-Bulgarians, mainly along the Yugoslav–Bulgarian frontier and around Ochrid, continued to be commanded by Sofia. Their conversion to the new ideology took much longer. Opportunism and access to privileges and jobs, which could be materialized only through communist membership, lured quite a few, as the exponential rise of CPM membership clearly illustrates. For those who still resisted the new disposition, grim alternatives were in store: they were left to OZNA. Such an analysis of the Macedonian national ideology suggests that 'Macedonianism' emanated from the internal dynamics of the Yugoslav–Macedonian area. Tito and the CPY had been instrumental in the consolidation of that ideology, but it quickly acquired its own dynamics, set its own dimensions, and, at the local level, served local needs, not always compatible with those of Tito and Yugoslavia. The years to come were to demonstrate that, however 'fictitious' this ideology

---

[92] FO 371/72192, R13517, report by the British consul at Skopje, Hilary King, dated 14/11/1948.

[93] FO 536/5384(19), S.2/2/51, 'Skoplje Hotch-Potch for February', from the British Consulate, Skopje to the British Embassy, Belgrade, dated 23/2/1951.

was (as its Bulgarian and Greek critics asserted), the needs it served and its ramifications were quite real.

Armed with an ideology that had both anti-Serbian and anti-Bulgarian edges, firmly controlled by a communist party which was (with varying degrees of sincerity) 'loyal' to Tito, and guarded by an omnipresent secret police, the Republic of Macedonia would be well prepared to meet the challenges that lay ahead. One of the most serious of these challenges was not far away: the Tito–Stalin split in 1948. Given the tension that this rift provoked (which also allowed the Bulgarians to regain for the first time since the war the offensive on the Macedonian Question) one would expect serious turbulence in the newly established Macedonian republic, and a resurgence of pro-Bulgarian feeling. And yet, not only was there not much evidence of popular apprehension, let alone mobilization, in the region, but importantly the CPM stood firm in support of Tito. According to one estimate, the percentage of CPM cadres who were purged as 'Cominformist agents' was the smallest in the country, and very few noted Macedonians sided with the Cominform: Bane Andreev, Lasar Sokolov, Pavel Šatev, and the poet Venko Markovski. Sokolov, however, was subsequently rehabilitated.[94] Two government reshuffles (in October 1948 and in March 1949) allowed the pro-Titoist leadership to excise swiftly from the fabric of the CPM its less reliable members, although, according to British assessments from Skopje, their expulsion had probably more to do with their inability to carry out their duties properly than with their presumed Cominformist inclinations.[95] In fact, the only serious problem that the communist leadership encountered during that crisis was confined to the trade unions, whose leadership was thoroughly purged in February, 1949. Yet again, Bulgaroplilia cannot be counted as the sole reason behind the unrest, as the main leader of the Cominformist fraction in the Macedonian trade unions, Remzi Ismail, was Turkish.[96] Firm leadership, however, was only one of the advantages that the pro-Yugoslav forces enjoyed in Macedonia in 1948; prices were another: Belgrade did not fail to note that the prices of basic goods in Skopje were

---

[94] The most senior Macedonian Cominformist, Andreev (alias 'Ronkata'), had developed pro-Bulgarian views during the wartime period, but the dearth of 'reliable' Macedonian communists forced the Macedonian leadership to overlook his chequered past. For Cominformist agitation in Macedonia see Shoup, *Yugoslav Communism,* 173, and Ivo Banac, *With Stalin, Against Tito: Cominformist Splits in Yugoslav Communism* (Ithaca, NY, and London, 1989), 189–205.

[95] FO 371/78333, R6531, 29/6/1949.   [96] Shoup, *Yugoslav Communism,* 173.

much lower than in Sofia; this, coupled with the fact that Macedonia paid much less to the state treasury than, say, Slovenia, sent a very loud message to the Macedonian peasant.[97] In a very real sense, being 'Macedonian' allowed the peasants literally to have their (very modest) cake and eat it relatively undisturbed. Given the history of the region, that was not an insignificant gain.

[97] FO 371/78333, R6531, Charles Peake to Bevin, 29/6/1949.

7

Britain and the Macedonian Question, 1945–1949

No sooner was the Second World War over in the Balkans than signs began to appear, signalling the beginning of a new war, which was to outlast the former and dominate the political affairs of the region for the decades to come. Between 1945 and 1948 the gradual erection by the communists of a cordon sanitaire in Eastern Europe had also been shadowing the Balkan Slavs, leaving the communists the indisputable masters in Bulgaria, and—as a by-product of the war—also in Yugoslavia. As a result of those profound changes Moscow established beyond any doubt its influence in the area, while the British embarked on a painful process of (re)assessing their own: its extent and, even more important, its worth. At the same time Bulgar–Yugoslav relations continued to produce friction between Sofia and Belgrade, and nervousness in Moscow and London, as Tito's Yugoslavia made a new bid for the creation of a South Slav federation, only to be forced into the defensive after the spectacular break with Stalin in the summer of 1948.

In what follows an attempt will be made to evaluate British reaction to a new Bulgar–Yugoslav rapprochement within its proper historical context. The chapter consists of two main sections. The first focuses on British views of Bulgaria and Yugoslavia, and aims to provide some background against which British policy towards Bulgar–Yugoslav relations should be evaluated. The second, and longer, section deals with Bulgar–Yugoslav relations and investigates British reactions. Some concluding remarks and observations are offered in the final section.

YEARS OF REASSESSMENT: BRITAIN AND THE BALKANS, 1944–1948

As the war was approaching its end, the situation in south-eastern Europe left much to be desired from the British point of view. In

Yugoslavia, the excessive preponderance of military considerations over long-term political objectives offered Tito much-needed Allied support and war material, but deprived the British of any real influence in the country, despite the hidden hope that wartime links might exert a pull again in the future. As was to be expected, Britain's position in Bulgaria looked even more uncertain. Britain has shown little practical interest before the war in a country where pro-Russian sentiment, although exaggerated by many observers, remained strong. It is perhaps illuminating to note that in 1940 the smoking habits of the British public ranked higher than political priorities towards that country, preventing Britain from purchasing Bulgarian tobacco and allowing the Germans to establish tight control of the Bulgarian economy.[1] Moreover, Britain had managed to establish only very modest contact with Bulgarian Partisans, equal to the one she had with the political world of the country.[2]

In 1944 all the assumptions upon which the British had placed their hopes in establishing a modicum of influence in the area had been proved futile. It had been hoped that at about the end of the war Turkey would have been co-belligerent, British soldiers would have set their foot in the Balkans and their plans for a confederation of east-central Europe—including the Balkan states—would have materialized unopposed.[3] None of this happened. Moreover, only to make matters worse, in early 1944 the Soviets appeared to announce—for the first time since the outbreak of the war—their interest in Greece by criticizing the British conduct over a mutiny of the Greek armed forces, and attacking (in April) the Greek premier Sophocles Venizelos.[4]

As it was realized that their leverage was a commodity in rather short supply in the Balkans, the British started to formulate their future policy, fully aware of their own share of responsibility for the 'disturbing' situation they had to cope with. 'If anyone is to blame for the present situation in which the Communist-led movements are the most powerful elements in Yugoslavia and Greece it is we ourselves. The Russians have merely sat back and watched us doing their work for

---

[1] Sir George Rendel, *The Sword and the Olive* (London, 1957), 142–3.

[2] On the wartime British contacts in Bulgaria see Elisabeth Barker, *British Policy in South-East Europe in the Second World War* (London, 1976), 214–15.

[3] These (optimistic) assumptions were formulated in a minute by Sir Orme Sargent, dated 11/1/1943. FO 371/33157, R8820.

[4] On 31 Mar. 1944 a mutiny erupted in the Greek units stationed in the Middle East. For the Russian accusations see George Alexander, *The Prelude to the Truman Doctrine: British Policy in Greece, 1944–1947* (Oxford, 1982), 16–17.

them.' The balance, in terms of the expected benefit, was disappointing, albeit even. 'In Yugoslavia at least we have obtained a military dividend, but EAM in Greece has given us nothing but trouble and annoyance.'[5] Apart from the burdens of the past, however, Soviet strategic desiderata in the Balkans constituted a more urgent problem to reckon with.

In mid-1944 the Foreign Office had eagerly conceded the predominant position that the USSR was bound to play in the Balkans, and, in an effort to avoid any unnecessary confrontations, it was prepared to meet what were considered as almost legitimate Soviet interests in the area. But by this they meant little more than the establishment of moderately pro-Soviet governments in Yugoslavia, Bulgaria, and Romania, the absence of undue influence of any other Great Power, and, perhaps, some military facilities, like air bases in Bulgaria. As a result, it was concluded that the British should concentrate on the protection of their vital interests in Greece and Turkey, while availing themselves 'of every opportunity to spread British influence' in the other states.[6] The British efforts, however, to accommodate the Russians while retaining a fair amount of influence, were very soon overtaken by the events that followed. As the Red Army was establishing itself in the Balkans in the summer and autumn of 1944, Churchill tried to regulate the influence of the Great Powers in the Balkans, concluding the Percentages Agreement with Stalin in October 1944. The numbers agreed upon, however—apart from the deal on Greece—reflected neither the Balkan realities nor Britain's ability to substantiate them with deeds. It can be argued that from the very moment of its conception the October Agreement had become obsolete.

From 1945 onwards the British embarked on a rather painful process trying to break the vicious circle of inability which haunted their Balkan policy. At about the same time, many voiced their doubts as to whether they should actually do so. Sir Orme Sargent, in March 1945, was led to ask 'how far and how long we are going to fight the losing battle' of enforcing the Western version of democracy in areas which

---

[5] FO 371/43646, WP (44), 304, 7/6/1944, memorandum on 'Soviet Policy in the Balkans', by Eden and Annex, dated 4/6/1944.

[6] Ibid. Cf. minute on this question by Christopher Warner, head of the Northern Department (responsible for the Soviet Union), who argued that 'we should hold our hand before assuming that there must be a dirrect and irreconcilable clash of interests [between Britain and the USSR] there [in the Balkans]'. See FO 371/43646, R9092, 31/5/1944. See also FO 371/43335, N (Northern Department) 1008/183/38, memorandum on 'Probable Post-War Tendencies in Soviet Foreign Policy as Affecting British Interests', dated 29/4/1944.

'at any rate are not vital to British interests' and where the Western interpretation of democracy 'has never flourished'. Sir Orme suggested that the British should cease to criticize the internal conduct of the emerging Communist states and reconcile themselves to the inevitability of totalitarian regimes in Eastern Europe.[7] Such a viewpoint echoed an increasing frustration about the inability of the British to do anything to alleviate the unsatisfactory state of affairs in the area.

The Foreign Office could follow Sir Orme's realistic line much more easily in Yugoslavia than in the other satellite countries, like Bulgaria. In Yugoslavia, the British, although fully aware of the ugly conduct of OZNA, admitted that Tito's regime did enjoy the support of the majority of the population. Moreover, Yugoslavia, as an Allied Power, was spared the Allied Control Commissions, which maintained—albeit superficially—some Western influence on Bulgaria. This aside, the West perceived Yugoslavia as the stoutest follower of Moscow. It was, to use the telling words of the French ambassador in Belgrade, the *fille aînée de l'église communiste*.[8] As a result, the British had little room for manoeuvre. Disarmed of any internal or external source for pressure, Bevin was led to remark in November 1945 that 'it would be futile to continue to cavil indefinitely at internal Yugoslav arrangements', and suggested that the time had come for Britain and the US to establish 'normal and friendly relations' with Tito.[9]

Bulgaria, however, was considered a very difficult mouthwash for the British to swallow. The opposition there was much stronger, it carried more moral weight than in Yugoslavia, and the regime was excessively ruthless. The general policy was to deny the Soviets absolute control in a country from where they could have been able to maintain a serious threat against Greece and to endanger British communications in the Mediterranean. Over the question of tactics, however, opinions diverged. The timing for the ratification of the peace treaty and the Yalta 'Declaration on Liberated Europe' created in some the feeling that Britain could reassert her right to have a share in the

[7] FO 371/48219, R5083, minute by Sir Orme Sargent [who was about to become Permanent Under-Secretary of State (1946–9)] dated 15/3/1945.
[8] For Western perceptions of Yugoslavia until the unexpected 1948 split see Beatrice Heuser, *Western 'Containment' Policies in the Cold War: The Yugoslav Case, 1948–1953* (London, 1989), 18–20.
[9] Foreign and Commonwealth Office, *Documents on British Foreign Policy Overseas*, ser I, vol. vi, ed. M. E. Pelly, H. J. Yasamee, and K. A. Hamilton assisted by G. B. Bennet (London, 1991), 225–7, from Bevin to the Earl of Halifax (Washington), dated 17/11/1945.

shaping of the future of the former Axis satellites. It was felt that the declaration could be a starting point for breaking British 'inactivity' in Bulgaria. In a memorandum addressed to the Earl of Halifax, written in November 1945 but *before* the Bulgarian elections, Bevin adopted a seemingly strong line, arguing that the declaration 'not only entitled but obliged' the British to 'interest themselves in the political affairs of all the countries to which the declaration applied'. They, therefore, should make clear to the Russians that 'unrepresentative and repressive governments' could not be recognized. Even more important was Bevin's remark that the Percentages Agreement, responsible for the British 'inactivity' in the Balkans, was found 'on reflection' to be unsatisfactory, and was superseded by Yalta.[10]

Taking Yalta too seriously, however, was a line the Southern Department found increasingly difficult to follow. The lengthy and argumentative minutes attached to Bevin's memorandum, drafted *after* the Bulgarian elections, revealed a more realistic, and somewhat dispirit-ed, attitude. The most important consideration should be the withdrawal of the Red Army from Bulgaria and Romania and the conclusion of the peace treaty with Italy; both could be achieved only with the conclusion of peace treaties with the former satellites, regardless of the dictatorial character of their governments. Protests and public pressure were not only of no avail, but could also lead to a further deterioration in Anglo-Soviet relations. As a result the question of the totalitarian regimes should be abandoned, and peace treaties had to be concluded, as the only policy that could offer 'the best prospects of securing satisfactory governments at a later date'.[11]

As should be expected, the view from London did not coincide with the one held in Sofia. William Houstoun-Boswall, attached to the British section of the Allied Control Commission as the British political representative to Bulgaria, frequently crossed swords with Sargent over this particular issue. In a letter to Sofia in November 1945, Sargent stressed that Britain should not 'indulge in gestures which are not either calculated to bring definitive advantage to ourselves or are essential for other reasons'. But, given the fact that the Bulgarian government was a Soviet puppet, Houstoun-Boswall replied, any friendly gesture would

---

[10] FO 371/48220, R18970, memorandum on 'The Balkans', enclosure: from Bevin to the Earl of Halifax, dated 9/11/1945.

[11] FO 371/48220, minutes by D. Stewart (26/11/1945) and M. S. Williams (27/11/1945).

'alienate Bulgarians, . . . [and] earn their contempt'. In addition to that, such a move would encourage Stalin to believe that Britain would bow to all his demands.[12] In 1946 Houstoun-Boswall continued to urge the Foreign Office to support the Bulgarian opposition—and especially the left-wing Agrarian Nikola Petkov—and to ask the awkward question of whether Britain deems it important to retain some influence in the country or just wants to 'get the tiresome Bulgarian problem out of the way'.[13] It was evident, however, that Houstoun-Boswall, as well as Major General Oxley, who suggested the withdrawal of the British section of the Allied Control Commission of which he was the head, was fighting his own losing battle. In 1946 the prevailing trend of thinking in the Foreign Office was drifting toward the conclusion of the peace treaties and the granting of recognition of the Bulgarian government 'at the first opportunity'; for the alternative could only be 'an indefinite continuation of the war of nerves'.[14] The opportunity came in 1947, and the Bulgarians used it to hang Petkov.

This tragic outcome, however, should not invoke undue criticism about the 'abandonment' of Bulgaria by the British. At that time, democracy—in both versions of the term—'Western' as well as 'Soviet'—was brought into the Balkans by the bayonet rather than by conviction. So it was brought by the British to Greece during the *Dekemvriana* civil strife in December 1944. The same could not have been done in Bulgaria, where the Red Army imposed its own interpretation of the word. With no soldiers in the area, the British had to devise other tactics to tackle the Bulgarian question. Such a task was inhibited by many factors. First, it was becoming increasingly difficult for the Foreign Office to see what sort of British vital interest was at stake in Bulgaria. They could see little, apart from the 'Macedonian' threat to Greece and the protection of a very modest volume of trade. They did something for the former, and the latter was too weak a factor to be taken seriously. Further, their hands were tied by the anxiety to conclude a peace treaty with Italy, and put that country into the Western orbit. It was known, however, that the Russians would trade off Italy with the former satellites. All parameters considered, the only option left open was the withdrawal of the Red Army, which might have enabled the West, or so the British

---

[12] *Documents on British Foreign Policy Overseas*, 245–7, letter from Sargent and reply by Houstoun-Boswall. The British Mission to Bulgaria, to which Houstoun-Boswall was attached, was led by Major General Walter Oxley.

[13] FO 371/58513, R1586, 30/1/1946.

[14] Cf. FO minutes in FO 371/58612, R12867, 26/8/1946.

thought, to deal with the Bulgarian themselves rather than with the Russians. This could have been done only by the conclusion of the peace treaties. Yet again, the fact that the views of both Bulgarians and Russians were identical rendered this policy an utter failure. It appeared to be, nevertheless, the only possible choice.

If in the domestic arena of the satellites the Yalta Declaration was left to die a natural death, in the domain of foreign policy the British played a more active role. Containment was always perceived as a more serious issue than the establishment of representative governments. Thus the British did not hesitate to prevent a Bulgar-Yugoslav federation and to demonstrate their resolve against a resolute Tito on Trieste and Carinthia, in an incident that irritated Moscow no less than it did London and Washington.[15] As the British could not discern the differences arising within the supposedly monolithic communist world, they made every possible effort to persuade Stalin that, if the percentages agreed in Moscow were somewhat fluid, the containment line was much more solid. Stalin apparently fully understood Western concerns, although this was not very evident at the time; but not so Tito. This particular dimension only added further problems to issues already surrounded by tension and suspicion.

In this framework, the re-emergence of the Macedonian Question—after the first abortive attempt at a Slav federation in 1944–5—was an ominous sign. All the more so, since it came at a time when the British were thinking of abandoning Greece, the bastion of Western influence in the Balkans, initiating a chain of events that led to the Truman Doctrine in 1947.[16]

BRITAIN AND THE MACEDONIAN QUESTION, 1945–1948

As has already been seen, after the intensive diplomacy of early 1945, the British had managed to prevent a Yugoslav-sponsored Balkan

---

[15] As Tito was more than reluctant to abandon Trieste, in June 1945, Stalin sent him an unequivocal ultimatum: 'Within 48 hours you must withdraw your troops from Trieste, because I do not wish to begin the Third World War over the Trieste question.' See Banac, *With Stalin, Against Tito*, 16–17.

[16] For a detailed discussion on the question of British decision to withdraw from Greece, see Robert Frazier, *Anglo-American Relations with Greece: The Coming of the Cold War, 1942–1947* (London, 1991), 120–56.

federation.[17] As subsequent developments were to show, Tito had not abandoned his Macedonian plans; nor did the British believe that he had. As the Macedonian Question seemed to recede in the wake of the sound and fury of the Yalta and Potsdam meetings, the Foreign Office continued to monitor the Yugoslav moves on this sensitive issue, and to decipher what they perceived as sinister designs. Since March 1945, some worrying signs about such designs had emerged, and the British were not prepared to allow them to pass unanswered. Some indiscretions, coming shortly after Yalta, from prominent Yugoslav politicians alarmed the British. In March, Dimitar Vlahov, president of the Macedonian National Liberation Front and, it will be remembered, the most eminent Macedonian persona to side with Tito, declared in Sofia, during a 'Slavonic Week', that 'the Macedonian problem will be finally settled and Macedonia will unite but in Titoist Yugoslavia'.[18] The British ambassador in Belgrade, Ralph Skrine Stevenson, took the matter up with Šubašić, who remarked that Vlahov was not a member of the Yugoslav government and, therefore, his views were not official statements. He added that he had asked the federal minister for Macedonia to 'explain' this to Vlahov.[19] If the ageing revolutionary had little respect for the subtleties of international politics, Tito seemed to be much more reserved, although far from being reassuring. In April, in an interview for the *New York Times* while in Moscow, he spoke only of the Yugoslav claims in Istria and Austrian Carinthia, reiterating, as was his habit, that the Greek portion of Macedonia was not 'of interest' at present. He did not fail, however, to allude to his designs by saying that his country could not oppose 'the wishes of the Macedonians to unite'.[20]

Tito's allusions were all the more ominous for coming on the eve of a major press campaign against Greece. During the summer of 1945 the Yugoslav press—including the official *Politika*—carried out a fierce polemic against the 'reign of terror' prevailing in Greek Macedonia. According to repeated accusations from *Politika, Borba,* and *Nova Makedonija* the Greek 'Monarchofascist' government had unleashed its might against 'innocent Macedonians', prompting thousands of them to seek refuge in Skopje. Assisted by 'nationalist gangs', the Yugoslavs asserted, Greek gendarmes had been torturing and killing Slavs on an unprecedented scale. Only to make matters worse, the Soviet press joined the campaign in August, criticizing the Greek government

---

[17] See Ch. 5.   [18] FO 371/48209, R5862, 13/3/1945.
[19] FO 371/48183, R6129, 3/4/1945.   [20] FO 371/48826, R77231, 19/4/1945.

and 'notorious bandits' for numerous atrocities.[21] The British were particularly disturbed by the Yugoslav campaign and followed it closely. There were good reasons for that. First, that campaign—unlike the previous one, staged in late 1944—was believed to be orchestrated by Belgrade rather than Skopje, acquiring thus an 'official' character. It is significant that it started in Yugoslav Macedonia only after the Belgrade press set the tune. If the British could dismiss the previous outburst against Greece on the grounds that it represented little more than an irritating expression of the relations between Skopje and Belgrade, this new campaign, emanating from Belgrade, had to be taken seriously.[22] Apart from that, reports from BLOs pointed to increasing collaboration between the ELAS forces and Slav–Macedonian units in both Greek and Yugoslav Macedonia. According to those reports, Partisan bands had been freely crossing the Greek border, while a number of uniformed ELAS *andartes* (guerrilla fighters) were seen in Skopje. It was also reported that the Bitolj area was a centre 'for Greek activities' and that ELAS functionaries—like Andreas Kendros (alias Sloboda)—were convening there with leading Macedonian officials, including Vlahov.[23]

In fact, 1945 witnessed the resurrection of Slav–Macedonian armed activity in Greece's northern provinces. The difficulties with which the SNOF experiment had met did not deter the Slav-Macedonian zealots, and small bands were operating in Greek soil as early as December 1944. In 1945, the *Naroden Osvobotitelen Front* (NOF)—SNOF's scion—was formed and started agitating for the 'self-determination of the Macedonians'. Initially, the Communist Party of Greece (KKE) officially denounced NOF as 'chauvinistic' and 'provocative', although some KKE's Slavophone cadres were having talks for cooperation in Skopje. A divergence of opinions haunted the party's policy from the occupation years, and it paid dearly for it. In 1946, however, the secretary general of the party, Nikos Zachariadis, after negotiations with NOF, endorsed it as a 'democratic' organization. But the relations between KKE and NOF remained tense throughout the Greek Civil War.[24]

---

[21] FO 371/48184, R10348, 15/6/1945. For the attitude of the Soviet press, see FO 371/48241, R14809, 1/9/1945.

[22] For the previous press campaign and its character see Ch. 6.

[23] FO 371/48184, notes on 'Greek Macedonia', prepared by Sqd. Ldr. Hill, BLO with the Macedonian HQ. 'Appendix B.2', attached to R13695, dated 6/8/1945, from Skrine Stevenson (Belgrade) to Bevin.

[24] See Evangelos Kofos, *The Impact of the Macedonian Question on Civil Conflict in Greece, 1943–1949* (Athens, 1989), 17–19. On NOF see also John S. Koliopoulos,

Disturbed by signs of collaboration across the border and the rising of tension, the Foreign Office considered the Yugoslav press campaign a 'serious matter'. They particularly feared that it might lead to claims on Greek territory, especially as it was felt that their failure in Carinthia could divert the Yugoslav appetite for land southwards. Stevenson was accordingly instructed to raise the issue with Šubašić 'if he thinks there are serious ground for disquiet'.[25] In July things came to a head when Tito himself fiercely attacked the Greek government for oppressing Slavs and Greeks alike and indulging in provocations along the Greek–Yugoslav frontier. Tito's speech alarmed the Southern Department, and it was decided that the Marshal's ardour should be cooled. Sargent asked Stevenson to arrange for an interview with Tito 'to stop his utterances'. If the Yugoslavs have complaints against the Greeks, Sargent minuted, they should start talks with the Greek government, using the British as mediators. But the press 'is not the place for such a discussion'.[26]

Needless to say, the Marshal was not interested in learning the fine art of the diplomatic conduct from the British, and was not prepared to enter into negotiations with the Greeks. The British reaction, however, intended to impress upon him the fact that London had fixed its eyes on Greece and would not tolerate any violation of her territorial integrity. The tough line adopted by the British in the Trieste and Carinthia at that time, meant that they were determined to contain Tito, and the presence of British soldiers in Greece was a similarly significant—and visible—deterrent. It should also be noted that Stalin's unequivocal disapproval of Yugoslav moves in Trieste and Carinthia, in May–June 1945, sent a clear message to the Marshal that Yugoslav irredentism had to be restrained.[27] In short, the international situation in the Balkans

Plundered Loyalties: World War II and Civil War in Greek West Macedonia (London, 1999), 221–55.

[25] Instructions to Skrine Stevenson in FO 371/48184, R10372, 21/6/1945.

[26] FO 371/48833, R11967, 8/7/1945, Sir Orme Sargent's minute, dated 16/7/1945. Representations were also made to the Yugoslav political representative in London, on 19/7.

[27] For Stalin's attitude see Banac, *With Stalin*, 16–17. In Jan. 1945, Stalin had confided to Dimitrov that the Yugoslavs wanted 'to take' Greek Macedonia, Albania, and parts of Hungary and Austria. He remarked to Dimitrov that 'this is unreasonable. I do not like the way they are acting'. The Belgrade leadership, he added 'are going too far'. As cited in Ivo Banac (ed.), *The Diary of Georgi Dimitrov, 1933–1949* (New Haven and London, 2003), 353. Cf. Kostadin Paleshutski, *Iugoslavskata Komunisticheska Partiya I Makedonskiyat Vŭpros, 1919–1945* [The Yugoslav Communist Party and the Macedonian Question] (Sofia, 1985), 326.

in 1945 was certainly unfavourable to Tito's plans, but it remained uncertain to the British whether he was responsive to the signs of the times.

Moreover, further Yugoslav statements—about Bulgarian Macedonia this time—fanned British fears. In August, Tempo, while in Kumanovo, attacked the Bulgarian press for airing the slogan of an 'autonomous Macedonia', adding that the 'Macedonian right to unity cannot be disputed'. His words were echoed, a few days later, by the president of the Macedonian government, Lazar Koliševski.[28] The concerns of the Macedonian officials were understandable. From the beginning of 1944 the Fatherland Front had been playing up the idea of a 'free and independent Macedonia' with a twofold aim: (*a*) to prevent Tito from treating the Macedonian Question as an internal problem, and (*b*) to deny Yugoslavia absolute control over the Vardar Valley, by stressing the fact that the whole issue was an all-Balkan one, in which Bulgaria should have a role.[29] As shall be seen below, after the Tito–Stalin split, the latter dimension of that slogan acquired particular weight.

What interested the British, however, was whether the noises about 'Macedonian unification' reflected official Yugoslav policy or whether they were mere 'utterances' by Macedonian zealots for internal consumption. This possibility could not be easily dismissed for the Foreign Office knew that, although the Macedonian government had 'fantastic' territorial claims against Greece, which extended 'as far south as Mount Olympus', they were much more outspoken than Tito.[30] Thus, Stevenson had two meetings with Tito in September and November. On both occasions, the Marshal assured him that 'he had no kinds of designs against Greece'. He also added—in November—that he had instructed the Yugoslav ambassador in Greece to convey this to the Greek government.[31]

As NOF continued to operate in Greek soil, Tito's assurances were not taken at their face value. It seemed, nevertheless, that his reserved

---

[28] FO 371/48185, R17759, 18/8/1945, R18037, 22/8/1945.

[29] In Dec. 1943 the Fatherland Front issued a declaration on the Macedonian Question. The declaration stressed that Macedonia, the 'cradle of the Bulgarian Renaissance', had always been 'the apple of discord', and suggested the slogan of a 'free and independent Macedonia' as the only solution for this intractable problem. Needless to say, Tito fiercely attacked this slogan as 'German policy'. See Paleshutski, *Iugoslavskata*, 312–13.

[30] FO 371/48184, enclosure in R 13695, 6/8/1945, from Skrine Stevenson (Belgrade) to Bevin, 'Memorandum on the present situation in Macedonia', by Henniker-Major.

[31] *Documents on British Policy Overseas*, 197, from Skrine Stevenson to Bevin, 9/11/1945.

attitude, in sharp contrast to the extreme views expressed by the Macedonians, meant that he was not prepared to extend official support to the 'Macedonian right for unification', which his subordinates so much preached. It can be said that British pressure played a major part in his decision to maintain an officially restraining policy on the Greek question. In doing so, he could enjoy some amount of manoeuvre in his relations with the British, while at the same time he could keep helping the Greek communists, offering them much-needed manpower—through NOF—and logistical support.

What appeared to be a two-track policy regarding Greece, and the obscurity of the Yugoslav plans towards Bulgaria, was bound to create confusion. Thus the view of each of the British representatives in the Balkans was coloured by the 'atmosphere' prevailing on the ground and the Foreign Office was receiving conflicting assessments. In January 1946, Houstoun-Boswall remarked from Sofia that after the proclamation of a republic in Bulgaria 'a South-Slav federation might be established in close relation with the USSR'. He followed up in April by pointing to a speech by the Bulgarian prime minister on 'Pan-Slav unity under Russian guidance'. In his opinion the federation theme was 'quite alive', for 'some strengthening of the bonds between the stooge Tito and our local stooges would probably suit Moscow some way'.[32]

If Houstoun-Boswall stressed the Soviet strategic objectives, however, George Clutton, now chargé d'affaires at the British Embassy at Belgrade, characteristically shifted the focus to Tito's considerations. Although he admitted that Tito might well have grandiose designs about Macedonia he emphasized that in mid-1946 the whole issue was not 'actuel'. To Clutton, Venezia Giulia and Carinthia formed the core of Yugoslav demands, and, therefore, Macedonia's time would only come after the settlements of these claims. He advanced two further arguments to explain Tito's low profile on Macedonia. First, any open endorsement of Macedonian unity would do irreparable damage to the Greek and Bulgarian communists, who had already suffered—especially the former—from accusations of harbouring autonomist ideas; and secondly, the swift fusion of the three Macedonias in Yugoslavia could undermine her centralism by unduly strengthening the position of Skopje. Thus, Tito's interest in the Slavs in Greece, argued Clutton, was 'platonic'. Having suggested that, Clutton advised the Foreign Office not to pay particular importance to the anti-Greek

[32] FO 371/58540, R519, 9/1/1946; FO 371/58629, R6391, 18/4/1946.

outbursts voiced mainly by Vlahov and other Macedonian officials. The old revolutionary, he argued, might be of some importance to Tito, due to his 'Macedonian' credentials, but his political weight was insignificant.[33]

As expected, the view from Greece was quite different. Clutton referred to British sources from Athens, according to which 'there is already on foot a Yugoslav plan for the incorporation of Greek Macedonia within the borders of Yugoslavia'.[34] On the other hand, the Greek government was very keen on alarming the British. During the first half of 1946 the Greeks furnished the Southern Department with successive memoranda which painted a gloomy picture: a federation project—directed personally by Stalin—was under way aiming at bringing Bulgaria, Yugoslavia, and Albania together in a communist bloc with a common army and foreign policy. Agreement, the Greeks retorted, was already reached, but it will be revealed after the ratification of the peace treaties. It was added that, after the establishment of the federation, 'great pressure will be exerted on Greece in order to maintain a continuous threat against the Mediterranean highways of the British Empire'.[35]

These messages were received by the Foreign Office with caution and scepticism. It was pointed out that there were no indications as yet that such a grand design was entertained either in Moscow or in Belgrade, while its value for Moscow was also doubtful. There was no need for Stalin to create a communist bloc, which could only arouse the suspicion of the West. According to the British predictions, the conclusion of a web of treaties between the communist satellites—'a new Balkan Entente'- appeared a more likely option. Such a web would serve Soviet objectives, for they would have 'the essence of federation without the form'.[36]

Indicative of the caution prevailing at the Foreign Office as regards Tito's plans in mid-1946, were also the comments on the manifesto

---

[33] See Clutton's despatches in FO 371/58869, R6239, 24/4/1946, R7631, 10/5/1946. See also his despatch of 6/6/1946, quoted in FO 371/78333, R6378, memorandum by the Research Department of the FO, entitled 'Note on the chief developments affecting Yugoslav Macedonia and Bulgarian Macedonia since 1945', dated 30/6/1949.

[34] Letter of the British Consulate General to the Chancery at Athens, quoted in Clutton's despatch of 6/6/1946, in FO 371/78333, R 678; FO memorandum, 'Note on the chief developments'.

[35] FO 371/58629, R3709, Greek aide-memoire, dated 16/7/1946, Cf. another Greek aide-memoire, 29/4/1946, in FO 371/58487, R6644.

[36] See FO minutes in FO 371/58466, R10748, 3/8/1946; FO 371/58629, 30/3/1946.

issued by the First Congress of the National Front of Macedonia, held at Skopje in August. The congress greeted the delegates from Greece and Bulgaria as 'representatives of their [Macedonian] brothers from Pirin and Aegean Macedonia', stressing that their presence has 'turned the Congress into a manifestation of the wish of the Macedonian people of all parts of Macedonia to be free and united in the Republic of Macedonia'. Clutton remarked that although 'it is quite clear what is in the air' he was not inclined to see anything more than 'platonic sympathy' in the attitude of the Yugoslavs towards Greek Macedonia: the cessation of Pirin was openly demanded by both the Bulgarian delegate and the manifesto, but references to the Greek part, he thought, were less concrete. His view was strengthened when, after repeated enquiries, he received evasive responses from the Yugoslav Ministry for Foreign Affairs. One official characteristically confided that he could not understand 'what the Macedonians were up to'. His overall impression, therefore, was that Tito's Macedonian policy was not yet 'fully crystallized'. The Southern Department seemed to agree that for Belgrade Macedonia was not 'of immediate importance', for the Yugoslavs were preoccupied with Trieste. As a result the Macedonian Question was kept alive in order to keep the Greeks in a state of alert, and to enable Tito to use to his advantage any change in the international situation. Michael Williams, acting head of the Southern Department in 1946, minuted that no significant developments would occur in the immediate future and remarked that the 'best thing' the British could do was 'to keep the Greeks calm'.[37] Bevin himself seemed to approve of Williams's views and in November regarded 'most of the trouble on [Greece's] northern frontier' as being merely 'propaganda moves'. In his judgement, Belgrade was making some noise in order to convince the Russians that Yugoslavia was in need of support: Belgrade was indeed 'blackmailing Moscow'.[38]

Calming the Greeks, however, was a task increasingly difficult for the British to undertake. At the time, Britain was losing its hold in Yugoslavia, while Russia was tightening its own. As a result, it was felt that there was not much room left for British intervention in the Balkans

---

[37] FO 371/58615, R12398, Clutton's despatch on the Proceedings of the first Congress of the National Front of Macedonia, held at Skopje, 2nd–4th Aug., dated 13/8/1946. Minute by Williams attached, dated 27/8.

[38] Alexander, *Prelude*, 224.

on behalf of the Greeks, as had happened in early 1945. In mid-1946 the British continued to oppose an exclusive union between the two Slavic states, but they doubted whether they were in a position to prevent it if the Balkan communists were determined to carry through a federation. The timing of the conclusion of the peace treaties helped Britain to retain a very small amount of influence over Bulgaria; but this leverage was of little practical value, and it would disappear after the conclusion of the treaties; the current situation could not last for long. The only way out seemed to be to refer the matter to the United Nations and to argue in this forum that a federation would be a destabilizing factor in the Balkans. Even this, however, was considered 'difficult to prove'. Thus the Foreign Office decided that assurances to the Greeks should be of a non-committal and 'general' manner.[39]

Scepticism concerning the possibility of blocking a Balkan federation through the UN was well justified. The newly established organization found itself from the very beginning trapped into the vortex of East–West rivalry, a deficiency that greatly reduced any chance for swift—and independent—action. The organization's record in 1946 clearly demonstrated that the UN could do little more than to host complaints, lodged mostly for propaganda reasons, and to produce acrimonious debates on them. The end of those discussions was always predictable: the British and the Americans would veto the Soviet proposal and vice versa.[40]

This was the reason behind Bevin's disapproval of Tsaldares's initiative to lodge a complaint with the UN over the Macedonian Question in November 1946. The Greek premier, Konstantinos Tsaldaris, wanted to publicize the support the communist insurgents enjoyed from the Eastern bloc and to 'prove' that the Soviets were the prime movers of that menace. But Bevin dismissed his fears, and—against the views of the Foreign Office—confided to one of Tsaldaris's aides that the Greek premier should concentrate on the domestic agenda and avoid another international adventure. Tsaldaris, however, decided not to

---

[39] FO 371/58629, FO minutes attached to R3709, Greek memorandum, dated 16/7/1946. Cf. minutes in FO 371/58566, R10748, 27/7/1946.

[40] The 1946 record on the Balkans was indicative of the prevailing trend: the USSR (in January) and the Ukraine (in August) lodged a complaint against Greece in order to embarrass the British by criticizing the internal conduct of the Tsaldares government. In August the Anglo-Americans rejected Albania's application for membership, to which Moscow responded by vetoing the applications of Siam, Transjordan, Portugal, and Ireland. See George Alexander, *The Prelude to the Truman Doctrine: British Policy in Greece, 1944–1947* (Oxford, 1982), 171, 211–12.

follow Bevin's advice and, having secured American support, lodged the Greek complaint in December 1946. The outcome of this initiative could have not been more predictable: the Greek accusations provoked a forceful response from the Yugoslav representative, who argued that Tsaldaris had been 'childish' in trying to shift international attention from his ugly internal policy to Greece's neighbours. After further, and loud, reaction from the Albanian, Bulgarian, and Soviet representatives, a compromise was reached: the American representative suggested that an inquiry was needed and proposed the setting up of a commission to deal with the issue. So nothing concrete came out of the complaint and the commission's lengthy report, which was submitted in the summer of 1947, achieved nothing apart from publicity for internal consumption and three Soviet vetoes.[41]

In 1946, however, while the British were trying to decipher the Yugoslav intentions, developments in both Greek and Bulgarian Macedonia in the second half of the year appeared to justify some of their perceptions. As far as Greek Macedonia was concerned, it became evident that Tito was proceeding with extreme caution. No doubt the KKE-led revolt in 1946 received a major boost from Yugoslavia. This time, however, the Yugoslav connection was much more discreet than it had previously been, although by no means less clear or decisive. To begin with, in late 1946, following high-ranking talks between the KKE and CPM, the Yugoslavs agreed to place NOF under the control of the KKE and to dissolve their units; neither separate Slav-Macedonian bands nor an exclusive 'Macedonian' political organization were allowed to operate on Greek soil. The KKE, in return—always in need of manpower—recruited the Slavs in its own units, and conceded—or at least claimed that it did—a proportional representation of the Slav-Macedonians in the party's *apparat*.[42] Moreover, the spread of 'Macedonianism' was tolerated, but open secessionist agitation was

[41] For the Greek complaint and the British reaction see Alexander, *The Prelude*, 230–2. The only step of some significance that was taken after the submission of the Report was the formation of a Special Committee on the Balkans (UNSCOB), which was dissolved in 1951.

[42] The percentage of the Slav-Macedonians in the communist DAG (which had 35,000–40,000 men in 1948) still remains a controversial topic. Although their number fluctuated, all available evidence suggests that it had been fairly high. Their numbers have been put between 30 per cent and 50 per cent of the Greek forces, but the latter number is certainly inflated. Kofos estimates that their number was 6,000 in 1947, but by the end of 1948 there were some 14,000 Slav-Macedonian fighters in the DAG. See Kofos, *Impact*, 21. Cf. Banac, *With Stalin*, 36.

not.[43] Despite the agreement, tension was rife and the temperamental Tempo, as well as many other Macedonian activists and historians, never ceased to criticize the KKE for its uncooperative and even 'anti-Macedonian' attitude.

In October 1946, Tito reacted with moderation to Koliševski's complaints that the Greeks were uncooperative with NOF. Tito urged him to not 'mix with . . . the direction of the armed struggle in Greece', and to limit his involvement in secondary issues like 'assistance with the press e.t.c.'.[44] His caution was also manifested in that he did not allow the Yugoslav-Macedonians to play any major part in his Greek policy. Thus, the delicate issue of the supplies to the Greeks—which included a substantial amount of war material, clothing, and food—was handled by a trusted and loyal Serbian, Aleksandar Ranković, the number three of the CPY, behind Tito and Edvard Kardelj. Moreover, the base of the DAG in Yugoslavia was conveniently located at Bulkes in Vojvodina, away from the 'flammable' atmosphere of Yugoslav Macedonia.[45]

At the same time, the signs of caution emanating from Greek Macedonia were accompanied by the stepping up of the Yugoslav efforts for the cessation of Pirin Macedonia. By the end of 1946, the renewed Yugoslav pressure on the BCP had brought about significant gains of a wide variety. A major indication of Sofia's new, pro-Yugoslav, orientation was an open attack launched against the remnants of IMRO, which vehemently opposed a Bulgar–Yugoslav rapprochement. Houstoun-Boswall reported in June that the police rounded up a number of prominent Macedonians and, in a typical interwar-like incident, a close aide of Mihailov was surrounded by militia men and shot dead in the streets of Sofia; at about the same time a 'little rumour' appeared in the Bulgarian capital suggesting that IMRO had placed death sentences on senior figures, including Dimitrov and Dragoycheva, causing some sensation in the Bulgarian capital. The police thought it prudent to change all the bodyguards at Dimitrov's house.[46] In August, things came to a head when, after a show trial in Sofia, ten IMRO members were convicted as 'terrorists' and received harsh sentences ranging from

---

[43] For the 1946 Agreement see Kofos, *Impact*, 19–20, Cf. Paul Shoup, *Communism and the Yugoslav National Question* (New York, 1968), 158–9.

[44] Kofos, *Impact*, 19–20, quoting from unpublished Yugoslav archival sources.

[45] For details about the Yugoslav supplies to the DAG see Banac, *With Stalin*, 35.

[46] FO 371/58519, R8643, 10/6/1946. For IMRO's threats against the Bulgarian politicians see FO 371/58519, R8210, 27/5/1946.

death to life imprisonment.[47] This heavily publicized trial, which lasted one week, was intended to demonstrate that the Bulgarian government paid at least lip-service to the idea of 'brotherhood and unity' of the Slav peoples, which implied the cessation of Pirin, by officially denouncing the organization that continued to preach the Bulgarian character of Yugoslav Macedonia.[48]

That month, however, the Bulgarians made even more important concessions. In a secret resolution adopted at its Tenth Plenum, the BCP agreed to the incorporation of Pirin into the Yugoslav Republic of Macedonia, stating that the cessation of the Bulgarian province should *precede* the South Slav Federation.[49] After the 1948 split, the Yugoslavs made excessive use of this document, in order to embarrass the Bulgarians. A few months later, in December, an officially sponsored census in Pirin marked out the population as 'Macedonian'.[50] Apart from these concessions, the Bulgarians permitted the 'Macedonianization' of Pirin by allowing Yugoslav 'cultural workers' to spread their irredentist propaganda in the area. Thus, the Macedonian language, still in the process of being standardized, was introduced in schools, the theatre in Blagoevgrad staged Macedonian plays, and a page written in Macedonian appeared in the local paper *Pirinsko Delo*. At the same time, however, the BCP was careful enough not to allow the Yugoslavs to penetrate the local communist mechanism, which remained under firm Bulgarian control.[51]

Those developments clearly pointed to the direction of an imminent unification of Macedonia within the 'new' Yugoslavia. But Tito, under continuing British monitoring, did all he could to conceal his plans. In October, he received—again!—Sulzberger, of the *New York Times*, causing the raising of some eyebrows in the Foreign Office for his weakness for publicity. In that interview the Marshal did not depart

[47] FO 371/78333, R6378, memorandum by the Research Department of the FO, dated 30/6/1949.

[48] Ibid.

[49] For this resolution and the controversy it provoked see Shoup, *Communism*, 151.

[50] For the Dec. census see ibid. 153.

[51] Stephen Palmer and Robert King, *Yugoslav Communism and the Macedonian Question* (Hamden, Conn., 1971), 124. It should be noted that the Bulgarian opposition was understandably much more outspoken in denouncing Yugoslav demands for immediate annexation. In 1946 the opposition papers have been repeatedly voicing their concerns and strongly accused the Yugoslavs of 'interference' in Bulgarian affairs. See e.g. a particularly forceful article on the left-wing Agrarian *Narodno Zemedelsko Zname* of 15/11/1946, reported in FO 371/58527, R16967, 15/11/1946. This article was a response to a demand by *Borba* which asked for the annexation of Pirin.

from his favourite tactics. He said nothing offensive against Greece and dismissed allegations that a Bulgar–Yugoslav Federation was under way. He admitted, however, that he wanted to 'strengthen' the economic, political, and cultural ties between the two countries. He also stated that there were no negotiations on a wider, Danubian, federation.[52]

Tito's restraint, however, was not matched by the Bulgarians. In February 1947, while in Washington, the Bulgarian vice-premier Alexandǔr Obbov spectacularly lifted the veil covering Bulgar–Yugoslav relations, only to justify the British 'worst case scenario'. He stated that a Balkan federation was 'essential' and 'inevitable', and revealed that the two governments had been already working on this direction. The only thing they had been waiting for was the conclusion of the peace treaties. The talkative Bulgarian proceeded to set the time-table: a customs union would follow the conclusion of the treaties; then Albania would conclude an 'alliance' with Yugoslavia, and after that the three countries would form a Balkan federation. As regards Greece, he remained strikingly moderate: the federation's only demand would be an economic corridor to the Greek port of Kavala.

The British did not fail to detect Obbov's 'striking moderation' regarding Greece.[53] But his allusions, coupled with the developments in the second half of 1946, persuaded the Foreign Office that a Balkan federation was the main objective of the Balkan communists. They were, thus, relatively informed in order to evaluate a number of alarmist reports, coming from various sources. In February 1947, for instance, the British legation in Stockholm reported that, according to Swedish sources, a plan for the creation of a 'united Macedonia', sponsored by Moscow, was under way. The Southern Department branded it 'credible as an interim plan', for the ultimate remained a Balkan federation.[54]

It should be noted, however, that the British were not alone in worrying about the new trend in Bulgar–Yugoslav relations, as the Bulgarian opposition did not hesitate to air publicly their concerns. In a speech during the budget debate, given in April by Nikola Petkov in the *Veliko Narodno Sǔbranie* (Grand National Assembly), the outspoken opposition leader spoke of 'friendship' with Moscow and Belgrade but strongly denounced plans to detach Pirin from

[52] FO 371/59389, R15854, 21/10/1046.

[53] FO 371/66905, R2368, 16/2/1947. Such proposal was indicative of the communist concern not to offer any possible pretext for Western intervention.

[54] FO 371/66985, R2179, 6/2/1947, and minutes attached.

Bulgaria. He also attacked Greece, which should have a 'democratic' government, and—echoing Stamboliiski's demands made twenty-five years earlier—asked for western Thrace to be given to Bulgaria.[55] But developments in 1947 appeared to make the prevailing trend look almost irreversible. In June, a Macedonian conference was held in Sofia, and decided to dissolve the Macedonian emigrant organizations, traditionally an IMROist stronghold. Instead, new 'Minority Societies' were formed with a clearly pro-Macedonian orientation. A 'Committee Initiative' was created to coordinate their activities, placed under the leadership of Yugoslav sympathizers.[56] In addition to that, Georgi Chankov, organization secretary of the BCP, in an article published in *Rabotnichesko Delo* in October, praised the 'Macedonian nation' and denounced the 'Great Bulgarian chauvinism', which could be found even within the Fatherland Front.[57]

Amid growing indications that some kind of a more formal rapprochement between the two Slavic states was imminent, the spectre of a 'United Macedonia' flickered again, and the Foreign Office became the recipient of the nervousness of many. This time it was not only the constantly worried Greeks, but also the Turks, who, in the summer of 1947, expressed their 'intense fear' of a unified Macedonia. Their concern was that a Balkan federation would exert pressure on Greece to surrender her own Macedonian part, to the detriment of the country. But if 'there is no Greece', the Turks argued, 'there is no Turkey' either.[58]

By the summer of 1947, Bevin had evidently become disturbed about such a gloomy prospect for Greece, and the resurrection of the Macedonian ghost in 1947 haunted him as much as it had his predecessor in 1944. Many things, however, had changed in the meantime. In 1944 the British alone shouldered the responsibility of keeping Greece in the Western orbit, by pouring into the ruined country soldiers, advisers, and money, and feeling confident enough to use each of these materials as the situation requested. But, as from the spring of 1947, they could no longer afford it, and, with the Truman Doctrine, Greek security rested with the United States. Further, as has already been seen, Britain's position in the Balkans as a whole was greatly diminished since the end of the war.

As a result Bevin could not step in and jeopardize the communist plans as Eden had done in early 1945. The only thing he could do was to

55 FO 371/66905, R4985, 12/4/1947.   56 FO 371/67140, R8074, 15/6/1947.
57 FO 371/66909, R14451, 29/10/1947.   58 See n. 59.

appeal to those responsible; and so he did. In a forceful memorandum in July, he communicated to the State Department his anxiety about 'the promotion of a new state of Macedonia including the Greek one, either in Yugoslav or in Bulgar–Yugoslav federation'. The Foreign Secretary directly linked this plan with Moscow, observing that 'although the Soviet attitude remains equivocal . . . nothing has happened to dispel the fear that communist policy still aims at detaching Macedonian territories from Greece'. His fears were so intense that he deemed it extremely important 'to prevent the Macedonian Question from becoming a practical issue or even a subject of international discussion'. After reminding them of the 1945 incident, Bevin urged the State Department strongly to declare their resolve to oppose—along with the British—a united Macedonia and to make their position 'publicly clear' if the opportunity arose.[59]

Bevin's move could not have been better timed, for at the end of July the Balkan Slavs appeared to make a very serious step towards what their rhetoric called 'a full mutual understanding and brotherly cooperation'. In July, the Bulgarian premier Dimitrov, accompanied by senior ministers and other high-ranking officials, visited Yugoslavia and had important talks with Tito at the Slovenian resort of Bled. There an agreement was reached, providing for close political, economic, and cultural cooperation between the two countries. According to the official communiqué, issued on 1 August, the two states agreed, among other things, to make preparations for a customs union, to fix a rate for their currencies, and to link more closely their railway system. Moreover, Yugoslavia renounced the reparations allotted to her. As far as the political level was concerned, the communiqué was less detailed, the only reference being to the need for a close cooperation 'with relation to the frequent border provocations of the Greek monarcho-fascists'.[60] The fate of Pirin, however, continued to cause much friction, as the Bulgarians steadily refused to offer it on a plate to the Yugoslavs: 'We should not work', wrote Dimitrov in his diary on 1 August, 'for a dir[ect] joining of the Pir[in] region to the Mac[edonian] republic.'[61] Two months later, Tito returned the visit,

[59] Bevin's memorandum to the State Department (which also contained the alarmist Turkish memorandum) in FO 371/66985, R10224, 21/7/1947.

[60] The Bled Agreement, as it was given by the official Yugoslav news Agency *Tanjug*, is provided in FO 371/66958, R11099. See also Royal Institute of International Affairs, *Documents in International Affairs, 1947–1948* (London, 1952), 290–2.

[61] Ivo Banac (ed.), *Diary,* 420.

and in Evksinograd, near Varna, a twenty-year pact of 'Friendship, cooperation and mutual assistance' was concluded. The two countries, the first article read, 'will collaborate closely intimately and in every sphere in the future in all questions which relate to the future of their people'.[62]

Although the Bled–Evksinograd agreements appeared to be, if not the realization of a full-fledged federation, at least a rather sinister design, the British representatives in the Balkans tended to downplay its importance. Sir Charles Peake, the British ambassador to Yugoslavia (1946–51), observed from Belgrade that the whole story 'fell far short of the "historic" character specifically claimed for them'. Apart from the customs union, none of the measures announced at Bled was either new or unexpected: consultation on the Greek issue was already a well-known practice as was economic cooperation. Even the grandiose Yugoslav gesture to renounce the reparations due to her was long anticipated in Sofia. Considering the possibility of a federation, Peake was not inclined to believe that the matter could be decided by the Balkan communists, for the domain of foreign policy remained an exclusively Soviet preserve. His overall impression was that the only purpose of Bled was to demonstrate a strong spirit of regional Slav solidarity in order to counterbalance the American intervention in Greece.[63] Peak reverted to the subject of Macedonia in December. He still remained unconvinced that a federation was genuinely wanted in Belgrade; nor that the population was prepared for it.[64] Moreover, Peak argued that the fate of Macedonia was still unsolved: a notable absentee from Tito's company in Sofia was the outspoken Vlahov, thus allowing the suggestion that 'for the time being the Macedonian Question was put into cold storage'.[65]

In assessing the Evksinograd talks from Sofia, John Sterndale-Bennett, British minister in Bulgaria since September 1947, drew similar conclusions. He went as far as to suggest that the 'original intention' of both sides might have been to announce something concrete about a federation, but at the end it was decided not to do so. The British minister did not fail to observe that references to federation were made only by

---

[62] For the full text of the treaty see FO 371/66958, R15818, 29/11/1947.

[63] The Yugoslav foreign minister, Stanoje Simić, characteristically remarked to one of Peake's staff: 'You see, we also have our own Marshal Plan'. FO 371/66958, R12039, 16/8/1947.

[64] FO 371/67363, R16434, 3/12/1947.

[65] FO 371/66985, R16758, 10/12/1947.

Tito, while Dimitrov spoke only of 'Brotherhood and Unity'. He also detected some other signs, indicating that such a slogan did not reflect the reality. The Yugoslav military attaché, who accompanied Tito, said that the reception 'had not been quite so warm as the Marshal had himself expected'. Moreover, it seemed that Tito somehow overshadowed Dimitrov, in their public appearances, forcing Sterndale-Bennett to remark that the Marshal appeared like 'a prospective purchaser coming to inspect the estate with a view to take it over'. In his judgement, a personality clash of sorts was a formidable obstacle to a Balkan federation.[66]

All in all, the assessments from the Balkan capitals converged in depicting the Bulgar–Yugoslav meetings more as frustrated efforts to foster cooperation than as an expression of objectives already agreed upon. More Bulgarian concessions to the Yugoslavs, however, ran contrary to these assessments; or so it seemed. A Draft Law was published, after Tito's visit, in the official Bulgarian paper *Otechestven Front* (Fatherland Front) authorizing the appointment of fifty-six Macedonian teachers from Yugoslavia to teach their language in Pirin for three years.[67] As a result, the Foreign Office remained suspicious about the recent developments, and thought that the Bled Agreement was more substantial than the British representatives in the area suggested. In December, a circular cable despatched from the Foreign Office to all British embassies in the Balkans predicted that, although communist confederations in Eastern Europe would not be formed, a Bulgar–Yugoslav federation and a 'United Macedonia' were considered a 'more likely development'.[68] Senior officials shared this view: Christopher Warner, head of Northern Department (1942–7) and assistant under-secretary, commenting on a memorandum on the military situation in Greece after Bled, minuted that 'some form of an independent Macedonia' might well be envisaged by Moscow.[69]

British eyes, apparently, were fixed on Greece, and on the 'Eastern connection' of the Greek civil war. The Yugoslav material support to the Greek communist insurgents, and the prospect of their recognition as a legitimate government by Belgrade, combined with the ever-present Soviet factor, created an explosive mixture. It was natural that the Foreign Office, constantly preoccupied with the Slav 'menace' to Greece, was

[66] FO 371/66958, R16486, 4/12/1947.
[67] FO 371/66985, R16948, 18/12/1947.
[68] FO 371/72162, R95, 23/12/1947.   [69] FO 371/67072, R10421, 1/8/1947.

inclined to give in to bleak scenarios for a united Macedonia, which distracted its attention from less alarmist voices.[70] From late January 1948 the Macedonian Question pursued an almost erratic course, which culminated in June with the Tito–Stalin split. On 28 January, Sterndale-Bennett cabled from Sofia that a Bulgar–Yugoslav federation was now 'imminent', for the 'Draft Program' of the Fatherland Front, prepared for its February congress, included the 'construction of a Federation of the Southern Slavs'.[71] For a brief moment the Foreign Office could have congratulated themselves, for their predictions had proved more accurate than Bennett's. That moment was very brief indeed: that very day *Pravda* administered a sharp rebuke to Georgi Dimitrov, who in December had spoken to journalists of a 'Danubian Federation'. What these countries need, the editorial read, was not 'a federation or a customs union but consolidation of their independence and sovereignty'.[72]

This incident somewhat puzzled the British, especially about the necessity to rebuke so senior a communist leader in public. Sir M. Peterson, of the British Embassy in Moscow, suggested that 'Dimitrov was getting too big for his boots', and pointed out that a federation was not practical politics for Kremlin, for it would be destroyed by internal friction; besides, Eastern Europe could be ruled more effectively through the communist parties. Hence Stalin's decision to use the organ of the Soviet party, *Pravda*, instead of the official governmental *Izvestiya*.[73] Most officials, however, agreed with a view put forward by Peake: Moscow's move was a direct response to a speech by Bevin in the House of Commons, in which he had said that a Western union was needed because there already was an Eastern one. Such a prospect prompted Stalin to reaffirm in a spectacular way his

---

[70] As late as Jan. 1948, Sterndale-Bennet continued to report that the Bulgar–Yugoslav Federation has 'receded into background' because of disagreement over Macedonia. PRO FO 371/72162, R730, 16/1/1948, and R484, 9/1/1948. For Greek–Yugoslav relations in 1947 see Barker, 'Yugoslav Policy towards Greece, 1947–1949', in L. Baerentzen, J. Iatrides, and O. Smith (eds.), *Studies in the History of the Greek Civil War, 1945–1949* (Copenhagen, 1987), 263–72.

[71] FO 371/72162, R1084, 28/1/1948.

[72] FO 371/72162, R1319, 29/1/1948. Stalin was indeed infuriated: 'It is hard to figure out', he wrote to Dimitrov, 'what could have made you make such rash and injudicious statements at the press conference'. Dimitrov's reply was totally capitulatory: 'I am grateful to you for your remarks. I shall draw the proper conclusions'. Banac (ed.), *Diary*, 435.

[73] Reference to Peterson's telegram in a minute by Watson, dated 4/2/1948. FO 371/72162, R1984.

commitment to 'sovereignty' of the communist states, in order to avoid an unnecessary increase in tension with the West.[74]

The new twist in Moscow's relations towards the Balkans was followed by the abandonment of federation plans by all parties concerned. Dimitrov swiftly backed down, stating that federative plans were 'premature', and was forced to accept a new aide, General Damianov, described by the British as 'a most Russianised Bulgarian communist'.[75] Moreover, the First Congress of the Fatherland Front, in February, made no reference to Macedonia.[76] As far as the Yugoslavs were concerned, the Foreign Office had speculated that the unequivocal Soviet editorial would send a warning to Tito not to continue his high-profile policy. Stalin did more than that, and in February he summoned the Yugoslavs and the Bulgarians in Moscow for consultations. Apart from Dimitrov's remarks and the question of Bulgar–Yugoslav relations (the Soviet press had ignored Bled and Evksinograd), Stalin was particularly irritated about Yugoslavia's powerful presence in Albania, especially in January 1948, at a time when the Yugoslavs had asked Enver Hoxha to allow two Yugoslav divisions to enter Albania.[77] Within this context, Tito decided that he 'was not feeling well', and declined the honour to visit Moscow. Djilas, Kardelj, and Vladimir Bakarić headed the Yugoslav delegation. The Bulgarian representatives were Dimitrov, Kolarov, and Kostov.

The Montenegrin's testimony reveals that Stalin was furious over Dimitrov's 'nonsense' of a Danubian federation. It also points to an interesting detail: the Bulgarians had been keeping the Kremlin fully informed on the treaty with Romania, but only Molotov knew about it, not Stalin. Moreover, Stalin and Molotov attacked both delegations about the Bulgar–Yugoslav treaty of 1947. That treaty, Molotov asserted, was reached 'not only without the knowledge of, but contrary to, the views of the Soviet government'. Kardelj muttered that the Soviet government was kept informed about Bled. But Stalin was not in a mood to listen. 'Nonsense,' he replied. At the same

[74] For FO comments on the incident see FO 371/72163, R2374, 20/2/1948 (Peake's view), and FO 371/72162, R1984, for further minutes.

[75] FO 371/72162, R1391, 30/1/1948, and minute on Damianov's appointment attached.

[76] Palmer and King, *Yugoslav Communism*, 126.

[77] Kardelj, while in Moscow for the meeting with Stalin, told Djilas that the 'direct cause of the dispute with Moscow' was Yugoslavia's request for the entry of two divisions in Albania. Milovan Djilas, *Conversations with Stalin* (London, 1962), 133. For the implications of Yugoslavia's presence in Albania cf. Banac, *With Stalin*, 38–40.

time, Stalin did not fail to attack Kardelj about the question of the Yugoslav army in Albania, which 'could lead to serious international complications'. After the rebuke came the diktat. Stalin ordered the Yugoslavs to proceed immediately with a Bulgar–Yugoslav federation, 'right away, if possible, tomorrow', apparently aiming at making them believe that normality has been restored, in order to prepare his next move.[78] The Yugoslavs sensed the danger and let the matter drop. In March, they sent a letter to the Bulgarians abandoning the idea of a federation, while in May, Koliševski openly attacked 'some Bulgarian chauvinists' who saw Macedonia as a compromise between Bulgaria and Yugoslavia, and continued to regard the Macedonian language as a Bulgarian dialect.[79] But the Yugoslav move to soft-pedal their plans came too late: from March onwards an exchange of letters occurred between the Kremlin and Belgrade, and on 28 June 1948 the Communist Information Bureau (Cominform) informed the world that 'the leadership of the CPY' — Tito, Kardelj, Djilas, and Ranković were mentioned by name— 'has broken with the international traditions of the CPY and has taken the road of nationalism'. The price for this sin was excommunication.[80]

FULL CIRCLE: THE 1948 SPLIT AND ITS AFTERMATH

Few dates in the history of the Macedonian Question have had both the intensity and the profound effect of the Tito–Stalin split; for it not only definitely halted the Yugoslav offensive against Pirin, but also made the developments of the last decade more obsolete than ever. Indeed, since 1941, and especially after 1944, the Bulgarians had suffered the arrogance of the Yugoslavs and their drive to impose their own 'architecture' on the Macedonian landscape. But after June 1948, this period looked as if it were a mere interlude. Seen with hindsight, that date marked the re-emergence of a pattern already known in the

---

[78] For this extraordinary meeting see Milovan Djilas, *Conversations*, 135–7.

[79] Kolisevski's speech, dated 23/5/1948, was reported to the FO in PRO FO 371/72192, R7730, 5/8/1948.

[80] The letters between the two parties are provided in Royal Institute for International Affairs, *Documents on International Affairs, 1947–1948* (London, 1952), 348–89, 389–97 (official Cominform communiqué), 397–404 (Yugoslav reply).

interwar years, with Yugoslavia on the defensive and Bulgaria on the offensive.[81]

Since that eventful June, all the brakes that applied to the conduct of the Balkan communists were abolished overnight, and the much-praised 'brotherhood and unity' descended into the abyss of various accusations and counter-accusations. Thus, the Yugoslavs denounced the 'chauvinism' of the BCP and their refusal to recognize the Pirin Macedonians as a separate national group. They also accused the Bulgarians of obstructing the spread of 'Macedonianism' in Pirin, in violation of the Bled Agreement. Some BCP local cadres, the Yugoslavs said, expressed their appreciation of the Macedonian language by using *Nova Makedonija* for lighting their stoves. Needless to say, they did not miss the opportunity to comment on 'pipe-smokers', who returned to their country—liberated by the Russians—by plane.[82] The Bulgarians did not sit back. The Sofia press did not mince its words when referring to the 'middle-class bourgeois nationalistic psychosis' evident—in their view—in Belgrade. Passions were so inflamed that it was also suggested that under the Turks the situation in Yugoslav Macedonia was better: Bulgarian schools and papers could be seen at that time, but not now.[83]

Apart from levelling accusations against each other, the split did not shed much light on the tortuous deliberations before and after Bled. A picture of sorts, however, emerged. Tito asserted that the Bulgarians in principle had agreed at Bled to a South Slav federation, and Dimitrov, on two occasions in 1948, alluded to that. The fate of Pirin remained a source of dispute. The BCP insisted that the area should be under Bulgarian sovereignty until the materialization of the federation. In return, they wanted to annex the areas given to Yugoslavia after the

---

[81] For the interwar developments see Introduction. For the 1948 split see Wayne Vucinich (ed.), *At the Brink of War and Peace: The Tito–Stalin Split in a Historical Perspective* (New York, 1982).

[82] FO 371/78333, R31, 29/12/1948 (on Yugoslav accusations). FO 371/72192, R9693, 10/8/1948 (on the uses of a newspaper). The reference to Georgi Dimitrov's smoking habits was made by Pijade, the most outspoken Yugoslav anti-Cominformist. The day of Dimitrov's arrival in Sofia, the Yugoslav press published a picture of him smoking a pipe on the staircase of the plane. FO 371/72192, R10222, 28/8/1948.

[83] FO 371/72586, R9407, reporting on an article in the *Otechestvent Front*, dated 6/8/1948. Indeed, the Ottomans suffered in the hands of the communists in 1948. The Turkish record as a yardstick for democracy was used also in the Cominform Communiqué, which accused the leadership of the CPY of imposing on the party 'a disgraceful, purely Turkish, terrorist regime'. Royal Institute for International Affairs, *Documents on International Affairs (1947–1948)* (London, 1952), 393.

First World War. The Yugoslavs—who obviously wanted the direct annexation of Pirin—were not prepared to accept such a condition, and kept accusing the Bulgarians of not facilitating the 'cultural autonomy' agreed at Bled. In short, it can be said that the only concrete result of those negotiations was the dissolution of the pro-IMROist Emigrant Fraternities, and the promotion of 'Macedonianism' in the Pirin; but even then they had different objectives: the Yugoslavs considered that compromise as being too little, while for the Bulgarians it was a mere smoke screen in order to buy time, and Yugoslav propaganda in the area was never wholeheartedly supported.[84]

In any case, the first priority of both countries after the initial confusion was to (re)assert their authority in their respective parts of Macedonia. In Yugoslav Macedonia, despite the almost accomplished elimination of IMRO bands, the task appeared to be quite challenging. The volatile expressions of the Macedonians' national sentiments, having been shaped by opportunism rather than concrete 'ethnic' affiliations, could not be taken for granted by the regime in Skopje. The Macedonian government, fully aware of this fact, launched in 1948 a forceful campaign with a twofold aim: (*a*) to sharpen the anti-Bulgarian feelings of the population, and (*b*) to foster the 'Macedonian identity' in an area where the reception of national ideas has had a rather poor record.

The first objective was carried through largely by the state-owned radio and the press. Both media became quite keen on emphasizing the most bleak aspects of the Bulgarian occupation, circulating sensational stories about Bulgarian atrocities. Heavily publicized trials of 'war criminals'—for 'crimes' committed four years earlier—were staged in late 1948 for propaganda reasons. In one of those trials ten collaborators were accused of appalling atrocities, including carving out the heart of one peasant and gouging out the eyes of another.[85] If such a depiction of Bulgarians targeted the emotions of the Macedonians, another initiative aimed at something more telling: the quality of their everyday life. Thus, it will be remembered that during the 1948 crisis with Stalin the press constantly reminded the Macedonians of the 'fact' that the cost of living in Bulgaria was much higher than it was in Skopje. Such

---

[84] Tito's account was published in *Borba* in 1949. Dimitrov made references to the question of federation at the 16th Plenum of the BCP (12/7/1948) and at the 5th Congress of the Party (19/12/1948). Cf. Shoup, *Communism*, 129; Palmer and King, *Yugoslav Communism*, 124–7.

[85] FO 371/72192, R13518, 26/11/1948; FO 371/72567, R13502, Weekly Summary of Events, ending 26/11/1948.

information, of course, was accompanied by references to the Yugoslav federal financial assistance to the Republic, which made that possible.[86] Although the word 'Yugoslav' might not have been to their liking, the 'financial assistance' definitely struck a chord.

An equally important development was the fostering of the Macedonian culture and language. As has already been seen, Macedonia enjoyed a considerable amount of 'cultural autonomy' within the New Yugoslavia.[87] After 1948, this privilege was exploited to the full. Writers and publicists were encouraged to write as much as they could in the Macedonian language, in order to make it a literary weapon against the Bulgarians. At the same time, much ink was spilt over the question of Macedonian history, Vlahov emerged as a prolific historian, and all the heroes of the Macedonian revolutionary movement, classified in the collective memory of the Balkan peoples as Bulgarians, were vehemently reclaimed by the Macedonians.[88]

In strengthening their Macedonian shield, the Yugoslavs could rely on a valuable asset: the loyalty of the Communist Party of Macedonia. This was a matter of paramount importance, for during the wartime period the pro-Bulgarian sentiment of the local communists caused Tito enormous difficulties.[89] In 1948, however, the situation was entirely different. The CPM—founded by Tempo in 1943—was at the time of the 1948 split a politically young and inexperienced party. So were its cadres, having been recruited during wartime, but mainly after 1944, when most Macedonians could easily realize who was the new master of the region. Given their age and the circumstances of their recruitment, most of these men consisted of fervent anti-Bulgarian and pro-Titoist elements, who guaranteed that the Cominform campaign against Yugoslavia would have found surprisingly few supporters among the communists in Macedonia. It is significant, in this respect, that most delegates in the First Congress of the CPM, held in December 1948, had been members for five, or less, years. The British Consul at Skopje, Hilary King, noted that of the 541 delegates only 31 were members of the communist movement before 1939, and 193 had joined it before

---

[86] FO 371/78333, R6531, from Sir Charles Peake (Belgrade) to Bevin, dated 29/6/1949.

[87] See Ch. 6.

[88] A detailed account of the intellectual aspect of the Macedonian nation-building in 1948 was provided to the FO by the British Consul at Skopje, Hilary King. FO 371/72192, R13517, 26/11/1948.

[89] Wartime developments in Macedonia are examined in Ch. 6.

1943. As far as the party membership was concerned, King estimated that 'nearly half have joined since December 1947'.[90]

The combination of the factors discussed above, coupled with the alienation of many Macedonians from Bulgaria due to the occupation, brought about a significant and unexpected result. By the time Sofia tried to turn Yugoslavia's expulsion to her advantage and to penetrate the Vardar Valley, the soil had ceased to be fertile ground for Bulgarian agitation. The Yugoslav vice foreign minister, Ales Bebler, was right when he confided to the French ambassador that he was never afraid of Cominformist pressure on Macedonia, a view shared by Sir Charles Peake. Indeed, as has already been seen, the CPM not only survived the Cominformist pressure, but proved to be less vulnerable than the Serbian or the Croatian parties.[91] Needless to say, Belgrade was quick to show the world that the CPM stood firmly in favour of Yugoslavia. In July, *Borba* published a resolution of the CPM condemning the Cominform, and in December, the First Congress of the party was a triumph for Tito. Loudspeakers were transmitting the proceedings in the streets of Skopje, but few bothered themselves.[92] Communism had never been Macedonia's forte.

If the Yugoslav Macedonian shield proved to be strong enough, the Bulgarians did not fail to polish their own; for it also had cracks. For propaganda purposes the Bulgarian press constantly accused Radio-Skopje of 'broadcasting lies' about the situation in Pirin Macedonia. The Pirin organization of the BCP, the statements asserted, was unanimously pro-Cominformist, and there were no 'delegations' from Bulgaria who wanted unification with Skopje.[93] In fact, the cracks were more serious an affair than the Bulgarians would have liked. The first Bulgarian move was to eradicate the most evident manifestations of 'Macedonianism' in the area. Thus the Macedonian bookshops were closed, plays in Macedonian were now outnumbered by those in Bulgarian, teachers from Skopje were banned from entering Bulgaria, and *Pirinsko Delo* lost its Macedonian page. Pro-Yugoslav elements, however, continued

[90] Details for the CPM in FO 371/78684, R934, enclosure from Peake to Bevin, 19/1/1949; see also FO 371/78333, R6531, Peake to Bevin, 29/6/1949.

[91] Cf. Chapter 6. The official Macedonian account on the Cominformists in the Republic, given in Dec. 1948, listed only 'six former members of the party'. FO 371/72567, Weekly Summary of Events, ending 10/12/1948, quoting the Macedonian Minister of the Interior.

[92] FO 371/78684, R934, Charles Peake to Bevin, 19/1/1949.

[93] FO 371/72192, R9169, 2/8/1948, and R8449, 13/7/1948, for such statements.

to make their presence felt and this led to a purge of communist cadres in Pirin: more than a dozen party members were publicly denounced as 'slanderers' and were dismissed. Reporting from Sofia, John Sterndale-Bennett regarded the pro-Yugoslav feeling in the area as 'fairly strong', and noted that his legation had learned from the personal assistant of Vasil Kolarov that the Bulgarian Ministry for Foreign Affairs was particularly concerned over that matter.[94] Despite Bulgarian efforts in 1948, the purges were not very effective, for until October 1949, the Southern Department continued to receive reports on 'expulsions of Vardar Macedonians' from Pirin.[95]

By the end of 1948, amidst a series of propaganda attacks between the former 'brothers', the Macedonian Question appeared to recede into the background of Balkan politics. Its epilogue, however, was written in the beginning of February 1949—in Greece. In February the Bulgarian paper *Trud* published a resolution of NOF, which advocated the union of Macedonia within a Balkan 'People's Republican' federation, and in March the resolution was broadcasted by the Greek Communist radio. The old communist slogan was thus ventilated again, but, as it was endorsed by the Cominformist KKE, it had lost its old meaning. Sir Charles Peake argued, and the Foreign Office agreed, that this time the objective was to detach Vardar Macedonia from Yugoslavia, for Yugoslavia—under the Tito leadership—was not counted among the 'People's Democratic' forces.[96]

The resolution provoked a fierce response from Pijade, and nervousness in the Yugoslav government. Bebler himself took the matter up in London with Geoffrey Wallinger, head of the Southern Department, where he was evidently disturbed and 'betrayed considerable uneasiness'.[97] The reason, apparently, was that the Vardar Macedonians might have rejected Sofia's direct rule, but a Balkan federation could lure many

---

[94] FO 371/72192, R10222, 15/10/1948.

[95] FO 371/78260, R9912, minute by A. J. Grant, dated 15/10/1949.

[96] Peake's despatch in FO 371/78333, R6531, from Peake to Bevin, 29/6/1949.

[97] For the KKE's slogan of Macedonia within a Balkan federation, endorsed by the Fifth Plenum of the Party (31/1/1949) and the Feb. Decision of NOF (4/2/1949) see Evangelos Kofos, *The Impact of the Macedonian Question on Civil Conflict in Greece, 1943–1949* (Athens, 1989), 27–8. For Peake's view see FO 371/78333, R6531, Peake to Bevin, 29/6/1949. Kofos has plausibly argued that the KKE's decision was not caused by a Soviet diktat, aiming at detaching Yugoslav Macedonia from Belgrade. It was rather a miscalculated move by the party's secretary general, Nikos Zachariadis, to enlist the support of Slav-Macedonians in Greek Macedonia, at a time when manpower for the Democratic Army of Greece was in very short supply. See Kofos, *Impact*, 32–3.

of them, mitigating the consequences of Belgrade's control. The Greek government was also disturbed, fearing that her northern provinces were again in danger, and the Greek ambassador in London communicated his concerns to the British on 3 March. But the Foreign Office saw little more than 'a war of nerves against Tito'. As a result, the only thing the Greeks were in need of was 'a little soothing syrup'. Sir William Strang was accordingly instructed to administer the remedy to the Greek ambassador.[98]

This new twist, however, did not last for long. The KKE repudiated it very soon, followed by NOF. The only result of this ill-fated resolution was to facilitate further an understanding between Tito and the British for the cessation of the Yugoslav aid to the KKE. The border was closed in the summer, and the KKE's army, the Democratic Army of Greece was defeated in the Gramos-Vitsi mountains shortly afterwards.[99] As far as Sofia and Belgrade were concerned, neither side was prepared to rekindle old flames any longer. Koliševski, in a speech in April 1949, conveniently put the blame on the 'imperialists', who 'cleverly injected [the federation slogan] into the ranks of our critics'. It is certain that Kolarov would not agree with such an interpretation, and for this reason he was more reserved, although by no means less unequivocal; in a press conference in Budapest in March, he just said that 'for us the slogan for a Balkan Federation does not exist . . . we have already outgrown this'.[100] Indeed, by the summer of 1949, they all had.

Between March 1945 and July 1948 the British saw a course of events they had tried so hard to prevent a few months earlier. Their primary objective in the Balkans remained unaltered: to safeguard Greece's territorial integrity, in order to protect vital British communication lines in the eastern Mediterranean basin. Unfortunately for them, the Balkan Slavs appeared not to have changed their own aim: to create a South Slav federation under Soviet patronage, which would possibly exert severe pressure on Greece to surrender her own part of Macedonia.

---

[98] The administering of the 'syrup' is recorded in the file FO 371/78396.

[99] In May 1949, Maclean had a long talk with Tito. The Yugoslav Marshal, anxious to conclude a trade agreement with Britain, told Maclean that no help would be given to the Greeks, but asked him not to make this public, for this would 'greatly embarrass him'. See Elisabeth Barker, 'Yugoslav Policy towards Greece, 1947–1949', in L. Baerentzen, J. Iatrides, and O. Smith (eds.), *Studies in the History of the Greek Civil War, 1945–1949* (Copenhagen, 1987), 290–1.

[100] FO 371/78333, R3434, 16/3/1949 (Kolarov's speech); FO 371/78333, R4190, 20/4/1949, (Koliševski's).

The spectre of a United Macedonia, however, did not flicker with the same intensity for all. Undoubtedly, the Southern Department could not reach concrete conclusions on the matter easily, due to lack of information concerning the deliberations between the Balkan communist parties. On the other hand, the Greeks were very keen on furnishing them with 'reliable' information, to the effect that Stalin had been keeping himself busy with Macedonia. In any case, neither the Foreign Office, nor Bevin, regarded the Macedonian threat as being substantive until the beginning of 1947. At that time, Yugoslav pressure on Bulgaria, indiscretions coming from Belgrade and Sofia alike, and the Bled–Evksinograd agreements, gradually convinced the British that the Bulgar–Yugoslav federation was imminent. Even then, however, the British legations at Belgrade and Sofia were not inclined to attach much importance to these schemes, pointing to the disagreement between the two parties over the fate of Pirin. Although information is scanty, what was made known after the 1948 split, confirmed their views. Pirin continued to be a source of friction, despite the enormous amount of official communist rhetoric.

If the Bulgar–Yugoslav intrigues puzzled the British, the clarification of Soviet motives appeared to be no less easy. Although sober voices were not absent, the perception of the Kremlin as the patron of a Balkan federation was dominant in the Foreign Office. This was only one of the many British misperceptions regarding the international role of the Kremlin, and its relations with the Balkan communist parties. The Soviets themselves, however, refuted it spectacularly in 1948.

The objectives of the Kremlin's are directly linked to the British involvement in the Macedonian Question. In the period under consideration the British did not intervene, as they had done in the beginning of 1945. Their determination to preserve the territorial integrity of Greece remained strong, but their position in the Balkans at the time, offered them limited room for manoeuvre. So they just tried to alarm the Americans, the new patrons of Greece. It can be argued, however, that the constant monitoring of Tito's moves, and their incessant warnings, persuaded the Soviets, if not Tito himself, that another attempt to establish a Balkan federation would be met with the same Western resolve to prevent it as it had in 1945.

Indeed, it can be argued that it was the action taken in the winter of 1945, and not the realities of 1948, that contributed to the expulsion of Tito from the Cominform, and the abandonment of federation plans. Although this argument is conditioned by the lack of Soviet sources, it has been established that Stalin was much more concerned by Western reactions to Tito's moves, than the Yugoslav Marshal. The example of Trieste and Carinthia is quite telling, not to mention the Greek Civil War and Albania. Thus, the prospect of another complication with the British (and the Americans), and not British strength, can be counted among the reasons that prompted the Soviet Marshal to punish his undisciplined pupil. Yet again, the Macedonian Question was shaped by perceptions.

8

A Loveless, but Necessary, Entanglement

Throughout the period under consideration here, Britain would have preferred to be left out of the Macedonian squabbles of the Balkan Slavs. Macedonia, like the Balkans in general (but with the notable exception of Greece), was a rather distant land for London, with no visible British interests at stake. In the interwar years, few things reminded the British public even of the very name Macedonia, apart from the occasional article in the British press, narrating the latest IMRO murders in Sofia, or its raids in Yugoslav Macedonia. Unfortunately for the British, the small, impoverished, and unhappy Yugoslav province offered the Foreign Office much cause for alarm. Initially, it was the possibility that Macedonia might trigger a wider Balkan conflict which prompted Britain to keep abreast of the developments in the region, while, at the end of the Second World War, the spectre of a united Macedonia under Russian domination, and the menace that such a development represented for Greece, forced them to make their presence felt. In fact, had it not been for its notorious ability to create instability in the Balkans, Macedonia would have not avoided the road to oblivion.

In the interwar years the British were already well acquainted with the complexities of the Macedonian Question. Yugoslav Macedonia, called by the Serbs 'Southern Serbia' and after 1929 'Vardarska Banovina', was fiercely contested by both Sofia and Belgrade, not to mention Petrich, which served as headquarters of a declining but not yet eliminated IMRO. The revisionist ambitions of a resentful Bulgaria, the heavy-handed attitude of an insensitive Belgrade, and continuing raids by IMROist gunmen were regarded by Britain as a more serious threat to European security than the ugly sight of dead Serbian gendarmes or Bulgarian politicians seemed to indicate at first sight. Fully aware of the potentially explosive character of the Macedonian Question, the British spent the interwar years trying to let 'sleeping dogs' lie. Having conferred on itself the role of an 'honest broker' between the two contenders of the region, the Foreign Office tirelessly offered advice for moderation and restraint, while, at the same time, working to prevent the 'internationalization' of the issue, which would inevitably have exposed sharp differences within the League of Nations. All these years, the cornerstone of British policy remained the preservation of the status quo. The peace settlements might have not produced the best of all worlds, but they did produce a more or less viable one. Moreover, it was argued that there was no need for 'self-determination' or 'adjustment' of frontiers, for the Macedonians had no national identity of their own. As far as the Foreign Office was concerned, Yugoslavia was their homeland, and it should remain so in the future.

The implementation of such a policy was a thankless task, which irritated Belgrade and Sofia, no less than some British ministers in the Balkans, who did not fail to openly accuse the Foreign Office of taking sides. Despite these attacks, however, the Foreign Office stood firm: revisionism, however small, was a menace, not a remedy. As a result Britain should steer clear of it. Although the extent to which British advice for moderation prevented a 'hot incident' between Bulgaria and Yugoslavia is difficult to gauge, it may safely be said that it contributed significantly to maintaining peace in the Balkans during the interwar years. The Macedonian 'sleeping dogs', however, were not to lie still for long.

The Second World War forced Britain to tackle the Macedonian Question again, as part of an effort to bring about a rapprochement between Bulgaria and Yugoslavia, thus creating a 'neutral bloc' against the Axis. This time, the British tried to temper their dogmatism as regards revisionism, and did not oppose the transfer of Southern Dobroudja from Romania to Bulgaria. As far as Macedonia was concerned, however, the Foreign Office continued to advocate the preservation of the status quo, despite some suggestions to the contrary. Nonetheless, it is almost certain that the failure to establish the Balkan bloc was not solely due to the British anti-revisionist agenda. Naturally, many Bulgarians resented (and were alienated by) the fact that Britain seemed to be so obsessed with sanctioning the gains of the victors of the Balkan Wars of 1912–13. But it was also geopolitics, and not just nationalism, that forced the Bulgarians to side with the Axis in 1941. Clearly, Britain was too far away from the Balkans, and it is more than doubtful whether the cession of Macedonia to Bulgaria (even assuming that Britain was prepared to agree to such a move, which she was not) would have brought her much closer to Bulgarian concerns. Such a move could, perhaps, have enabled Britain to enjoy some sympathy in Bulgaria, but in the context of 1940–1 it would have been little more than an empty gesture. The choice for Bulgaria was between Germany and Russia, and, although the Bulgarian king himself conceded that his decision to side with Germany was rational, and not emotional, it remained, nevertheless, the only possible one.

The war years, apart from unleashing all sorts of forces in the Balkans, also set free the British strategic imagination. Between 1941 and 1943, the Foreign Office, assisted by the Foreign Office Research Department based at Balliol College, Oxford, created on paper a brave new Balkan world, from which Bulgaria would have been unable to escape, and in which Macedonia could at last rest in peace. Thus, a Balkan federation was envisaged, and an attempt was made to use a Greek–Yugoslav agreement as a nucleus around which Balliol's Balkans would revolve. But Greek and Yugoslav interests (more precisely the interests of their exiled governments) were not as similar as the British would have wished them to be, nor were the Russians prepared to acquiesce in a bloc aimed at preventing the expansion of their influence in an area they had traditionally considered their own. As a result, Balkan realities coupled with Russian refusal to lend their support ensured that British plans remained what they really were: 'acres of paper'.

While the British were busy planning the future of the Balkans, others had already shaped it. By the last quarter of 1944, the communists were the indisputable rulers in Yugoslavia, and were working hard to become so in Bulgaria too. Tito had turned the old 'Southern Serbia' (and 'Vardarska Banovina') into the 'People's Republic of Macedonia', without taking the trouble to consult his Bulgarian comrades, let alone the Greeks, and was perceived as entertaining designs for the incorporation of all parts of Macedonia into his new (and increasingly impatient) federal unit. Although the clarification of his actual intentions is hindered by the distracting noises of Macedonian guerrillas and politicians, it was Tito's Macedonian designs and his plans for a Balkan federation that activated the British factor.

The British had always been supporters of the status quo, but in late 1944 they had an additional reason not to want any change of borders. Many in the Foreign Office perceived with apprehension the erection of a monolithic Slavdom, plotting to detach Greek Macedonia from Athens, and to establish a united Macedonia, which would inevitably pose a grave danger to their lines of communications in the eastern Mediterranean basin. Evidence from Greek Macedonia pointed to the close collaboration between the communist-led ELAS forces and

Slav-Macedonian guerrillas, while extreme nationalist rhetoric reigned supreme in the Yugoslav part. These indications, combined with the fact that all Balkan communists appeared to be Moscow's pawns, fanned British fears. These fears, it has to be added, were also due to the belief, evident in the Foreign Office already in the interwar years, that the Balkan Slavs were bound to coalesce, sooner or later. It was thought that racial affinities, religion, and a more or less common cultural outlook had been pulling the Slavs together, despite a historical record of friction and mistrust. As a result, communism, and Moscow's open support, was only the most recent of the forces that had been working towards a Balkan federation.

In October 1944, the British received a worrying sign of Slav intentions on Macedonia: Bulgarian troops, who had occupied Greek and Yugoslav Macedonia, not only seemed to be quite unwilling to evacuate these areas, but also participated in the war against the retreating Germans in Yugoslavia; clearly a Soviet initiative. This development, however, alarmed the British, no less than Tito's Macedonian Partisans, who had to welcome former occupiers as allies. As the Bulgarians were buying time in Greece, and were driving the Germans out of Yugoslav Macedonia (only to hand it over to fiercely anti-Bulgarian Partisans), the British did all they could to persuade the Russians to pull them out. In fact, the question of the Bulgarian army in the Balkans become the first test of the Percentages Agreement concluded in October in Moscow. The result of the British efforts was not completely unsatisfactory but, nevertheless, suggestive of the developments to come: the Bulgarians were told to evacuate Greece, which they duly did by the end of October, but were allowed to stay in Yugoslavia, from where they left some six months later. Undoubtedly, this meant that only the Greek percentage was destined to last; and indeed it was the only one that did.

Undeterred by the outcome of this first skirmish with the Russians, the British made a more decisive intervention shortly afterwards. In late 1944, as the Yugoslavs were stepping up their pressure to drag Bulgaria into a federation where she could enjoy the status of Montenegro or Slovenia, the British were led, by fragmented and not always reliable information, to believe that they were witnessing the resurrection of a most dreaded ghost: Tito's plans included the creation of a united Macedonia within the envisaged federation. British officials dealing with the Balkans had not the slightest doubt about the repercussions of such a move, nor did they need much time to draw the necessary conclusions. A united Macedonia would inevitably strive to annex northern Greece as well, thus diminishing Greece, the sole bastion of Western influence in the Balkans, and rendering British lines of communication indefensible.

This was not a novel conclusion. During the interwar years, and according to the ups and downs of Bulgar–Yugoslav relations, the Foreign Office had reckoned with the danger a united Macedonia represented for Greece, and did not fail to register their disapproval of the idea. True, some British officials had expressed views in favour of a united Macedonia, but only within a British-sponsored Balkan federation, or under a Balkan king. In 1945, however, this was not the case, for the driving force behind this undertaking was Tito. As a result, in January 1945, the British notified all those concerned, including the Russians, of their opposition to a Balkan federation. Stalin promptly agreed, and the matter was let drop. It should be stressed that it was preoccupation with the fate of Greece, not that of Macedonia, that prompted the British to intervene in 1945.

The interwar years had also witnessed a lively debate within the Foreign Office about the 'nationality' of the Macedonians, their national affinities, and their language, the conclusion being that they possessed none of the elements that could make them qualify for 'nationhood'. During the 1940s, however, there was little such discussion. It was evident that the Southern Department had neither the time nor the willingness to discuss such largely academic questions. The only thing that remained unaltered was a commitment to preserve the pre-war boundaries in the Balkans. Within this framework, the Foreign Office was prepared to let Tito handle the Macedonian Question as an internal Yugoslav problem. He could name his southernmost region as he pleased, but he should observe the existing borders. Consequently, when Tito decided to violate this rule, the British made sure he retreated.

It is beyond doubt that this intervention was successful because Stalin thought it wise to take into account British susceptibilities, and temper the impatience of his most distinguished disciple. Clearly, Stalin did not want an unnecessary confrontation with the British (and the Americans) over Macedonia, and, throughout the war, he had been at pains to teach Tito the subtleties of international politics, often to the irritation of the Yugoslav Marshal. The federation plan, no less than Trieste, was a case in point. Given that Britain had few ways of enforcing her will, it was Stalin's pragmatic approach rather than British strength, that halted Tito's drive. As far as Britain was concerned, their action reaffirmed their commitment to the security and territorial integrity of Greece. It is perhaps of interest to note that they felt that the possible threat to

Greece, arising from the Balkan federation, was so imminent that there was no need to waste time by consulting the Americans about their plans. At a time when British troops defeated ELAS forces in Greece, during the *Dekemvriana* civil strife in December 1944, their rush to block Tito's plans was indeed matched only by their determination to keep Greece out of the Soviet orbit by all means necessary.

With the coming of the Cold War, Britain's position in the Balkans became even more precarious than it had previously been. The consolidation of Tito's regime in Yugoslavia dashed their hopes of maintaining some influence through the exiled government, while the reign of communist terror in Bulgaria meant that the Bulgarians could be allowed to remember Noel Buxton, but should forget Bevin or Eden. Even Greece had, by that time, become a heavy burden to bear, and the Americans duly stepped in with the Truman Doctrine in 1947. Forced by the realities of the post-war Balkans, and despite some lonely voices advising the Foreign Office to do the opposite, between 1945 and 1947 Britain quietly extricated herself from the Balkans.

Yet again, the Macedonian Question continued to preoccupy the Foreign Office. Tito's renewed drive for federation, no less than the Yugoslav connection of the Greek civil war, alarmed the British as seriously as his previous bid had in late 1944. In 1947, Britain's determination to prevent the creation of a Balkan federation and a united Macedonia remained unequivocal, but the situation had changed. Britain could not intervene as she had in 1945, nor was she in a position to make Stalin more sensitive to her susceptibilities. This notwithstanding, the British kept up their pressure on Tito to respect the territorial integrity of Greece, although in less confident language than that used by Maclean in 1945, and called on the Americans to prevent the Macedonian Question from entering the international agenda. Britain's role, nevertheless, was limited to that of a distant, if concerned, observer. This time, however, it was Stalin that undertook the task of restraining Tito; and he did so spectacularly in 1948. That year marked the disappearance of the Macedonian Question from the arena of international politics. The brief twist in that problem, when the KKE, in desperate need of recruits, again endorsed Macedonian independence in 1949, receded shortly afterwards, after having provoked little more than anti-communist hysteria in Greece and some apprehension in Yugoslavia.

Overall, it could be said that the British connection with the Bulgar–Yugoslav dispute over Macedonia had nothing to do with the region itself. In this, Britain was not alone, for all the powers concerned with Macedonia had used the Macedonian Question to meet their own ends: Italy funded IMRO in the interwar years in order to destabilize Yugoslavia; Soviet Russia tried to achieve the same objective by forcing the CPY to accept the 'right' of the Macedonians to secede from Yugoslavia, while Germany, during the Second World War, used the Macedonian carrot to lure Bulgaria into the Axis. What mattered for the British was the preservation of the status quo, thus maintaining a balance of power in the Balkans, which would not prejudice the territorial integrity of Greece. From this, it followed that the Balkan Slavs should not be allowed to form a federation. The fact that British policy was successful both in 1944–5 (when they intervened) and two years later (when they could not) was due to Stalin's desicion not to offend British (and American) susceptibilities regarding Greece. In fact, by the end of the 1940s the British would have been amused to notice that Stalin had as many reasons to prevent Tito's plans as they had.

Bibliography

PRIMARY MATERIAL

Unpublished Archival Sources
Britain
Public Record Office. Kew, London. Class: Foreign Office (FO) 371, Files: 9659, 9719, 10667, 10793, 11221, 11405, 12091, 12092, 12855, 12856, 12864, 13571, 13572, 13573, 13710, 14135, 14314, 14315, 14316, 14317, 14318, 15174, 15273, 15895, 15896, 16649, 16775, 16828, 16830, 16859, 18369, 18370, 18373, 19489, 20434, 22129, 23724, 23727, 23728, 23733, 24870, 24877, 24880, 24881, 24887, 24902, 24891, 25030, 29729, 29785, 29786, 29838, 33123, 33128, 33133, 33134, 33135(A), 35261, 37153, 17173, 43335, 43583, 43608, 43646, 43649, 43665, 44270, 44331, 44395, 48137, 48181, 48183, 48184, 48185, 48209, 48219, 48220, 48284, 48826, 48833, 58466, 58487, 58513, 58519, 58527, 58540, 58572, 58612, 58615, 58629, 59461, 66905, 66909, 66957, 66958, 66985, 67072, 67140, 67383, 72160, 72162, 72163, 72192, 72586, 72620, 78260, 78333, 78347, 78396, 78676, 78684.

Class: FO/800. Private papers of Sir Orme Sargent, vol. 272.

Class: FO/536. Files: 3148(7), 3150(4), 5384(19).

Class: War Office (WO). Files: 201/1617, 204/9677, 208/2028, 202/1209, 201/209, 201/1122, 201/1600, 204/404, 201/1618, 202/1256, 208/113B, 201/1612A, 201/967A, 201/1622, 201/1617.

Greece
Archeion Ypourgeiou ton Exoterikon [Archives of the Ministry for Foreign Affairs], (AYE) Athens. Files: 1904/Proxeneion Thessalonikes [Thessalonike Consulate], 1905/Proxeneion Thessalonikes, [Thessalonike Consulate], A.A.K./B.

Published Documents
Britain
Cooch G. P., and Temperley, Harold (eds.), *British Documents on the Origins of the War, 1898–1914*, v. 5 *The Near East: The Macedonian Problem and the Annexation of Bosnia, 1903–1909* (London, 1928).
———— *British Documents on the Origins of the War, 1898–1914*, ix. *The Balkan Wars*, pt ii. *The League and Turkey* (London, 1934).
Foreign and Commonwealth Office, *Documents on British Policy Overseas,* ser. i, vol. vi, ed. M. E. Pelly, H. J. Yasamee, and K. A. Hamilton, assisted by G. Bennett (London, 1991).

Royal Institute for International Affairs, *Documents on International Affairs, 1947–1948* (London, 1952).

United States of America

Foreign Relations of the United States, Diplomatic Papers, *The Conferences at Malta and Yalta, 1945* (Washington, 1955).

People's Republic of Bulgaria

Press Department [of the Ministry of Information and Arts], *The Trial of Traicho Kostov and his Group* (Sofia, 1950).

Bulgarian Academy of Sciences, *Macedonia: Collection of Documents and Materials* (Sofia, 1978).

People's Republic of Macedonia

University of Kiril i Metodij, *Documents from the Struggle of the Macedonian People for Independence and a Nation State*, ii (Skopje, 1981).

SECONDARY SOURCES

Aarbakke, Vemund, *Ethnic Rivalry and the Quest for Macedonia, 1870–1913* (Boulder, Colo., 2003).

Alexander, George M., *The Prelude to the Truman Doctrine: British Policy in Greece, 1944–1947* (Oxford, 1982).

Alexander, Stella, *Church and State in Yugoslavia since 1945* (Cambridge, 1979).

Ancel, Jacques, *Peuples et nations des Balkans: Géographie politique* (Paris, 1930).

Anderson, Benedict, *Imagined Communities: Reflections on the Origin and Spread of Nationalism* (London, 1983).

Anderson, M. S., *The Eastern Question, 1774–1923: A Study in International Relations* (New York, 1978).

Apostolski, Mihailo, 'La Guerre de la libération en Macédoine', *Revue d'Histoire de la Deuxième Guerre mondiale*, 87 (1972), 15–32.

Arnakis, George, 'The Role of Religion in the Development of Balkan Nationalism', in Barbara and Charles Jelavich (eds.), *The Balkans in Transition: Essays on the Development of Balkan Life and Politics since the Eighteenth Century* (Berkeley and Los Angeles, 1963), 115–44.

Auty, Phylis, *Tito: A Biography* (London, 1970).

Avakumović, Ivan, *History of the Communist Party of Yugoslavia* (Aberdeen, 1964).

Baerentzen, Lars, 'The Demonstration in Syntagma Square on Sunday the 3rd of December, 1944', *Scandinavian Studies in Modern Greek*, 2 (1978), 3–52.

Banac, Ivo, *The National Question in Yugoslavia: Origins, History, Politics* (Ithaca, NY and London, 1988).

____ *With Stalin Against Tito: Cominformist Splits in Yugoslav Communism* (Ithaca, NY and London, 1988).

—— (ed.), 'The Communist Party of Yugoslavia during the Period of Legality, 1919–1921', in id.(ed.), *The Effects of World War I: The Class War After the Great War: The Rise of Communist Parties in East Central Europe* (Brooklyn, NY 1983), 188–230.

—— *The Diary of Georgi Dimitrov, 1933–1949* (New Haven and London, 2003).

Barker, Elisabeth, *Macedonia: Its Place in Balkan Power Politics* (London, 1950).

—— *British Policy in South-East Europe in the Second World War* (London, 1976).

—— 'Decision Making over Yugoslavia, 1941–1944', in Phylis Auty and Richard Clogg (eds.), *British Policy towards Wartime Resistance in Yugoslavia and Greece* (London, 1974), 22–58.

—— 'Yugoslav Policy towards Greece, 1947–1949', in L. Baerentzen, J. Iatrides, and O. Smith (eds.), *Studies in the History of the Greek Civil War, 1945–1949* (Copenhagen, 1987), 263–95.

—— 'Problems of the Alliance: Misconceptions and Misunderstandings', in William Deakin, Elisabeth Barker, and Jonathan Chadwick (eds.), *British Political and Military Strategy in Central, Eastern and Southern Europe in 1944* (New York, 1988), 40–53.

Barros, James, *The League of Nations and the Great Powers: The Greek–Bulgarian Incident, 1925* (Oxford, 1970).

Bell, John D. *Peasants in Power: Alexander Stamboliski and the Bulgarian Agrarian National Union, 1899–1923* (Princeton, 1977).

Bérard, Victor, *La Turquie et l'Hellénisme contemporain* (Paris, 1897).

Brailsford, H. N., *Macedonia: Its Races and their Future* (London, 1906).

Brown, J. F., *Hopes and Shadows: Eastern Europe after Communism* (Durham, NC, 1994).

Brown, Keith, *The Past in Question: Modern Macedonia and the Uncertainties of Nation* (Princeton, 2003).

Bulgarska Akademiya na Naukite [Bulgarian Academy of Sciences], *Makedonskiyat Vŭpros: Istoriko-Politicheska Spravka* [The Macedonian Question: Historical and Political Information] (Sofia, 1968).

Burks, R., *The Dynamics of Communism in Eastern Europe* (Princeton, 1961).

Carabott, Philip, 'Aspects of the Hellenisation of Greek Macedonia, ca.1912–ca.1959', *ΚΑΜΠΟΣ*: *Cambridge Papers in Modern Greek*, 13 (2005), 21–61.

Carnegie Endowment for International Peace, *Report of the International Commission to Inquire into the Causes and Conduct of the Balkan War* (Washington DC, 1914).

Carr, E. H., *International Relations since the Peace Treaties* (London, 1906).

Čepreganov, Todor, *Velika Britanija I Makedonskoto Nacionalno Prašanje, Avgust 1944–1948* [Great Britain and the Macedonian National Question] (Skopje, 1997).

Chrysochoou, Athanassios, *I Katochi en Makedonia* [The Occupation in Macedonia], vols. i–iv (Salonica, 1950–51).

Ciano, Galeazzo, *Diplomatic Papers*, ed. Malcolm Muggeridge (London, 1948).

Clayton, G. D., *Britain and the Eastern Question: From Missolonghi to Gallipoli* (London, 1971).

Clissold, Stephen, *Whirlwind: An Account of Marshal Tito's Rise to Power* (London, 1949).

——— *Yugoslavia and the Soviet Union, 1939–1973: A Documentary Survey* (London, 1973).

Clogg, Richard, *Anglo-Greek Attitudes: Studies in History* (London, 2000).

Colokotronis, V., *La Macédoine et l'Hellénisme: Étude historique et ethnologique* (Paris, 1919).

Crampton, Richard, *The Hollow Détente: Anglo-German Relations in the Balkans, 1911–1914* (London, 1979).

——— *Bulgaria, 1878–1918: A History* (New York and Boulder, Colo., 1983).

——— *A Short History of Modern Bulgaria* (Cambridge, 1989).

Crawley, C. W., *The Question of Greek Independence, 1821–1833* (Cambridge, 1930).

Cristowe, Stoyan, *Heroes and Assassins* (New York, 1935).

Cvijić, Jovan, *Remarques sur l'ethnographie de la Macédoine* (Paris, 1907).

——— 'The Geographical Distribution of the Balkan Peoples', *Geographical Review*, 5/5 (1918), 345–61.

Dakin, Douglas, *The Greek Struggle in Macedonia, 1897–1913* (Salonica, 1963).

Daskalov, Georgi, *Bŭlgaro-Iugoslavskite Politicheski Otnosheniya, 1944–1945* [Bulgar–Yugoslav Political Relations, 1944–1945] (Sofia, 1989).

Deakin, F. W., *The Embattled Mountain* (Oxford, 1971).

Dedijer, Vladimir, *Tito Speaks* (London, 1953).

——— *The Battle Stalin Lost: Memoirs of Yugoslavia, 1948–1953* (New York, 1972).

Djilas, Milovan, *Conversations with Stalin* (London, 1962).

——— *Memoirs of a Revolutionary* (New York, 1977).

——— *Tito: The Story from Inside* (New York and London, 1980).

Dontas, Domna, *I Eellas kai Ai Dynameis Kata ton Krimaikon Polemon* [Greece and the Powers during the Crimean War] (Salonica, 1973).

Dragoytseva, Tsola, *Macedonia: Not a Cause of Discord but a Factor of Good Neighbourliness and Cooperation: Recollections and Reflections* (Sofia, 1979).

Drezov, Kyril, 'Macedonian Identity: An Overview of the Major Claims', in James Pettifer (ed.), *The New Macedonian Question* (London, 1999).

Dumont, Paul, 'Une organisation socialiste ottomane: La Fédération ouvrière de Salonique', *Éetudes balkaniques*, 11 (1975), 76–88.

Eden, Anthony, *Memoirs: The Reckoning* (London 1965).

Filipova, Lilia, Introduction, in Institut za Voena Istoriya [Institute of Military History], *Vardarska Makedoniya, 1941–1944, v Iugoslavskata Istoricheska*

Literatura [Vardar Macedonia, 1941–1944 in the Yugoslav Historical Literature] (Sofia, 1992).

Filov, Bogdan, 'The Diaries of Bogdan Filov', ed. and trans. Frederick B. Chary, *Southeastern Europe*, 1 (1974), 46–71; 2 (1975), 70–93; 3 (1976), 44–87.

Fleischer, Hagen, *Stema kai Svastika: I Ellada tis Katochis kai tis Antistasis, 1941–1944* [Crown and Swastika: Greece in Occupation and Resistance] (Athens, n.d.).

Fosteridis, Antonios, *Ethniki Antistasi kata tis Voulgarikes Katochis, 1941–1944* [National Resistance Against the Bulgarian Occupation, 1941–1944] (Salonica, 1959).

Frazier, Robert, *Anglo-American Relations with Greece: The Coming of the Cold War, 1942–1947* (London, 1991).

Gellner, Ernest, *Nations and Nationalism* (Oxford, 1988).

Georgević, T. R., *Macedonia* (London, 1918).

Gounaris, Basil, 'Greco-Turkish Railway Connection: Illusions and Bargains in the Late Nineteenth Century Balkans', *Balkan Studies,* 30/2 (1989), 311–32.

Gounaris, Basil, et al. (eds.), *The Events of 1903 in Macedonia as presented in European Diplomatic Correspondence* (Salonica, 1993).

—— 'Social Cleavages and "National Awakening" in Ottoman Macedonia', *East European Quarterly*, 29/4 (1995), 409–26.

Gueshoff, Ivan, *The Balkan League* (London, 1915).

Haddad, Robert M., *Syrian Christians in Muslim Society: An Interpretation* (Princeton, 1970).

Helmreich, E. C., *The Diplomacy of the Balkan Wars* (Cambridge, Mass., 1938).

Henderson, Sir Nevile, *Water under the Bridges* (London, 1945).

Heuser, Beatrice, *Western 'Containment' Policies in the Cold War: The Yugoslav Case, 1948–1953* (London, 1989).

Hibbert, Reginald, *Albania's National Liberation Struggle: The Bitter Victory* (London, 1989).

Hobsbawm, Eric, *Nations and Nationalism since 1780* (Cambridge, 1990).

Hoppe, Hans-Joachim, 'Bulgarian Nationalities Policy in Occupied Thrace and Aegean Macedonia', *Nationalities Papers*, 14/1–2 (1986), 89–100.

Hoptner, J. B., *Yugoslavia in Crisis, 1934–1941* (New York and London, 1962).

Hristov, Alexander, *The Creation of Macedonian Statehood, 1893–1945* (Skopje, 1972).

Iatrides, John, *Revolt in Athens: The Greek Communist 'Second Round', 1944–1945* (Princeton, 1972).

Ilcev, Ivan, 'Great Britain and Bulgaria's Entry into the First World War, 1914–1915', *Bulgarian Historical Review*, 10/4 (1982), 29–48.

Ivanoff, Iordan, *Les Bulgares devant le Congrès de la Paix: Documents historiques, ethnographiques et diplomatiques* (Berne, 1919).

Jelavich, Barbara, *Russia's Balkan Entanglements, 1806–1914* (Cambridge, 1991).

Kakavos, Dimitrios, *Apomnemonevmata* [Memoirs] (Salonica, 1972).

Karpat, Kemal, *An Inquiry into the Social Foundation of Nationalism in the Ottoman State: From Social Estates to Classes, From Millets to Nations* (Princeton, 1973).

Kazamias, George, ' "The Usual Bulgarian Stratagems": The Big Three and the End of the Bulgarian Occupation in Greek Eastern Macedonia and Thrace, September–October, 1944', *European History Quarterly*, 29/3 (1999), 323–47.

Kent, Marian, 'Great Britain and the End of the Ottoman Empire, 1900–1923', in ead. (ed.), *The Great Powers and the End of the Ottoman Empire* (London, 1984), 172–205.

Kerner, R., and Howard, H., *The Balkan Conferences and the Balkan Entente, 1930–1935* (Berkeley and Los Angeles, 1936).

Kitromilides, Paschalis, ' "Imagined Communities" and the Origins of the National Question in the Balkans', in T. Veremis and M. Blinkhorn (eds.), *Modern Greece: Nationalism and Nationality* (Athens, 1990), 23–66; repr. in id., *Enlightenment, Nationalism and Orthodoxy: Studies in the Culture and Political Thought of South-Eastern Europe* (Aldershot 1994), study xiii.

——— 'Balkan Mentality: History, Legend, Imagination', *Nations and Nationalism*, 2/2 (1996), 163–91.

Kofos, Evangelos, 'The Making of Yugoslavia's People's Republic of Macedonia', *Balkan Studies*, 3 (1962), 375–96.

——— *Nationalism and Communism in Macedonia* (Salonica, 1964).

——— *O Hellenismos sten Periodo 1869–1881* [Hellenism during the Period 1869–1881] (Athens, 1981).

——— 'The Macedonian Question: The Politics of Mutation', *Balkan Studies*, 27 (1986), 157–72.

——— *I Valkaniki Diastasi tou Makedonikou Zitematos sta Chronia tis Katochis kai tes Antistases* [The Balkan Dimension of the Macedonian Question in the Years of Occupation and Resistance] (Athens, 1989) Also published in H. Fleischer and N. Svoronos (eds.), Ellada 1936–1944: Diktatoria-Katochi-Antistasi [Greece 1936–1944: Dictatorship-Occupation-Resistance] (Athens, 1989) 418–71.

——— 'National Heritage and National Identity in Nineteenth- and Twentieth-Century Macedonia', in Thanos Veremis and Martin Blinkhorn (eds.), *Modern Greece: Nationalism and Nationality* (Athens, 1990) 103–41.

——— *The Impact of the Macedonian Question on Civil Conflict in Greece, 1943–1949* (Athens, 1989); also published in John Iatrides and Linda Wrigley (eds.), *Greece at the Crossroads: The Civil War and its Legacy* (University Park, Pa., 1995), 319–30.

Koliopoulos, J. S., *Brigands with a Cause: Brigandage and Irredentism in Modern Greece, 1821–1912* (Oxford, 1987).

——— *Plundered Loyalties: Axis Occupation and Civil Strife in Greek West Macedonia, 1941–1949* (London, 1999).

Konortas, Paraskevas, *Othomanikes Theoriseis gia to Oikoumeniko Patriarcheio: Veratia gia tous Prokathimenous tis Megalis Ekklisias, dekatos edvomos—arches eikostou aiona* [Ottoman Views of the Ecumenical Patriarchate: Berats for the Leaders of the Great Church, 17th to early 20th Centuries] (Athens, 1998).

———'From Tai'fe to Millet: Ottoman Terms for the Ottoman Greek Orthodox Community', in Dimitri Gondicas and Charles Issawi (eds.), *Ottoman Greeks in the Age of Nationalism: Politics, Economy and Society in the Nineteenth Century* (Princeton, 1999), 169–80.

Kotzageorgi, Xanthippi, 'Population Exchanges in Eastern Macedonia and in Thrace: The Legislative "Initiatives" of the Bulgarian Authorities, 1941–1944', *Balkan Studies*, 37/1 (1996), 133–64.

Kousoulas, D., *Revolution and Defeat: The Story of the Greek Communist Party* (London, 1965).

Kŭnchov, Vasil, *Makedoniya: Etnografiya I Statistika* [Macedonia: Ethnography and Statistics] (Sofia, 1900).

Ladas, Stephen, *The Exchange of Minorities: Bulgaria, Greece, Turkey* (New York, 1932).

Lalkov, Milcho, *Ot Nadezhda kum Razocharovanie: Ideyata za Federatsiata v Balkanskiya Iugoistok, 1944–1949* [From Hope to Disillusionment: The Idea of Federation in South-East Balkans] (Sofia, 1994).

Lange-Akhund, Nadine, *The Macedonian Question, 1893–1908 from Western Sources* (Boulder, Colo., 1998).

Laquer, Walter, *Guerrilla Warfare: A Historical and Critical Study* (London, 1976).

Leontaritis, George, *To Elleniko Sosialistiko Kinima kata ton Proto Pangosmio Polemo* [The Greek Socialist Movement during the First World War] (Athens, 1978).

———*Greece and the First World War: From Neutrality to Intervention, 1917–1918* (Boulder, Colo., 1990).

Livanios, Dimitris, 'Conquering the Souls: Nationalism and Greek Guerrilla Warfare in Ottoman Macedonia, 1904–1908', *Byzantine and Modern Greek Studies*, 23 (1999), 195–221.

Mach, R. von, *The Bulgarian Exarchate: Its History and the Extent of its Authority in Turkey* (London and Neuchatel, 1907).

Maclean, Fitzroy, *Eastern Approaches* (London, 1949).

Manchev, Krŭstiu, 'Natsionalniyat Vŭpros na Balkanite do Vtorata Svetovna Voyna' [The National Question in the Balkans until the Second World War], in Institut Po Balkanistika Pri BAN, *Natsionalni Problemi na Balkanite: Istoriya I Sŭvremenost* [National Problems in the Balkans: History and the Current Situation] (Sofia, 1992), 9–64.

Marriott, J. A. R., *The Eastern Question: An Historical Study in European Diplomacy* (Oxford, 1967).

Mavrogordatos, George, *Stillborn Republic: Social Coalitions and Party Strategies in Greece, 1922–1936* (Berkeley and Los Angeles, 1983).

Mazarakis-Ainian, K., 'Anamniseis' [Reminiscences], in *O Makedonikos Agonas: Apomnemonevmata* [The Struggle for Macedonia: Memoirs] (Salonica, 1984), 165–265.

Mazower, Mark, *Salonica, City of Ghosts: Christians, Muslims and Jews, 1430– 1950* (London, 2004).

Medlicott, W. N., *The Congress of Berlin and After, 1878–1880* (London, 1938).

Meininger, T., *Ignatiev and the Establishment of the Bulgarian Exarchate: A Study in Personal Diplomacy, 1864–1872* (Madison, 1970).

Michev, Dobrin, 'Bŭlgarskata Komunisticheska Partiya I Makedonskiyat Vŭpros do 9 Septemvri 1944 godina' [The Communist Party of Bulgaria and the Macedonian Question until 9 September 1944], in *Voenoistoricheski Sbornik*, 6 (1986), 3–28.

_____ 'Makedonskiyat Vŭpros v Bulgaro-Iugoslavskite Otnosheniya na Sŭvremenniya Etap' [The Macedonian Question in Bulgar–Yugoslav Relations in the Contemporary Stage], in L. Panaiotov, K. Paleshutski, and D. Michev, *Makedonskiyat Vŭpros I Bŭlgaro-Iugoslavskite Otnosheniya* [The Macedonian Question and Bulgar–Yugoslav Relations] (Sofia, 1991), 98–124.

_____ *Makedonskiyat Vŭpros I Bŭlgaro-Iugoslavskite Otnosheniya, 9 Septemvri 1944–1949* [The Macedonian Question and Bulgar–Yugoslav Relations, 9 September 1944–1949] (Sofia, 1994).

Micheva, Zdravka, 'Balkanskiyat Pakt I Bŭlgaro-Iugoslavskite Otnosheniya, 1933–1934 Godina' [The Balkan Pact and Bulgar–Yugoslav Relations], *Istoricheski Pregled*, 4 (1971), 3–30.

Miller, Marshal Lee, *Bulgaria during the Second World War* (Stanford, 1975).

Milman, R., *Britain and the Eastern Question 1875–1878* (Oxford, 1979).

Minchev, Dimitŭr, 'Formirane i Deynost na Bŭlgarskite Aktsioni Komiteti v Makedoniya prez 1941 Godina' [Formation and Activity of the Bulgarian Action Committees in Macedonia in 1941], *Izvestiya na I.V.I.*, 50 (1990), 39–93.

Nesovic, Slobodan, *Yugoslav–Bulgarian Relations, 1941–1945* (Skopje, 1979).

O'Mahony, Anthony, 'The Christian Communities of Jerusalem and the Holy Land: A Historical and Political Survey', in id. (ed.), *The Christian Communities of Jerusalem and the Holly Land: Studies in History, Religion and Politics* (Cardiff, 2003).

Oren, Nissan, *Bulgarian Communism, 1934–1944: The Road to Power* (New York and London, 1971).

Paleshutski, Kostadin, 'Iugoslavskata Komunisticheska Partiya I Natsionalniyat Vŭpros, 1924–1934' [The Yugoslav Communist Party and the National Question, 1924–1934], *Izvestiya po Istoriya na B.K.P.*, 45 (1981), 121–59.

_____ *Makedonskiyat Vŭpros v Burzhoazena Iugoslaviya, 1918–1941* [The Macedonian Question in Bourgeois Yugoslavia] (Sofia, 1983).

_____ *Iugoslavskata Komunisticheska Partiya I Makedonskiyat Vŭpros, 1919–1945* [The Yugoslav Communist Party and the Macedonian Question, 1919–1945] (Sofia, 1985).

Palmer, Stephen, and King, Robert, *Yugoslav Communism and the Macedonian Question* (Hamden, Conn., 1971).

Pano, Nicholas, *The People's Republic of Albania* (Baltimore, 1968).

Papastratis, Prokopis, *British Policy towards Greece during the Second World War, 1941–1944* (Cambridge, 1984).

Pavlowitch, Stevan, *Unconventional Perceptions of Yugoslavia* (New York and Boulder, Colo., 1985).

_____ *Tito: Yugoslavia's Great Dictator* (London, 1992).

Paximadopoulou-Stavrinou, Miranda, 'To Foreign Office kai to Makedoniko to 1925', [The Foreign Office and the Macedonian [Question] in 1925], *Valkanika Symmeikta*, 10 (1998), 225–42.

Pentzopoulos, Dimitri, *The Balkan Exchange of Minorities and its Impact upon Greece* (Paris, 1968).

Perry, Duncan, *The Politics of Terror: The Macedonian Liberation Movements, 1893–1908* (Durham, NC and London, 1988).

Petrovich, Michael Boro, *The Emergence of Russian Panslavism, 1856–1870* (New York and London 1956).

Popović, Pavle, *Serbian Macedonia: A Historical Survey* (London, 1916).

Rachev, Stoyan, *Anglo-Bulgarian Relations during the Second World War, 1939–1944* (Sofia, 1981).

Reis, A., *The Comitadji Question in Southern Serbia* (London, 1927).

Rendel, Sir George, *The Sword and the Olive* (London, 1957).

Robbins, Keith, 'British Diplomacy and Bulgaria, 1914–1915', *Slavonic and East European Review*, 49/117 (1971), 560–86.

Roberts, W. R. *Tito, Mihailovic and the Allies, 1941–1945* (New Brunswick, 1973).

Rossos, Andrew, 'The Macedonians of Aegean Macedonia: A British Officer's Report, 1944', *Slavonic and East European Review*, 69/2 (1991), 282–309.

_____ 'The British Foreign Office and the Macedonian National Identity, 1918–1941', *Slavic Review*, 35/2 (1994), 369–94.

_____ 'Macedonianism and Macedonian Nationalism on the Left', in Ivo Banac and Katherine Verdery (eds.), *National Character and National Ideology in Interwar Eastern Europe* (New Haven, 1995), 219–54.

_____ 'Incompatible Allies: Greek Communism and Macedonian Nationalism in the Civil War in Greece, 1943–1949', *Journal of Modern History*, 69/1 (1997), 42–76.

_____ 'Great Britain and Macedonian Statehood and Unification, 1940–1949', *East European Politics and Societies*, 14/1 (2000), 119–42.

Rothschild, Joseph, *The Communist Party of Bulgaria: Origins and Development, 1883–1936* (New York, 1959).

Rothschild, Joseph, *East-Central Europe between the Two World Wars* (Seattle and London, 1990).

Rothwell, Victor, *Britain and the Cold War, 1941–1947* (London, 1982).

Roux, Michel, *Les Albanais en Yougoslavie: Minorité nationale, territoire et développement* (Paris, 1992).

Sfetas, Spyridon, 'Autonomist Movements of the Slavophones in 1944: The Attitude of the Communist Party of Greece and the Protection of the Greek–Yugoslav Border', *Balkan Studies*, 36/2 (1995), 297–317.

Shoup, Paul, *Communism and the Yugoslav National Question* (New York and London, 1968).

Smith, Anthony, *The Ethnic Origins of Nations* (Oxford, 1985).

Sowards, Steven, *Austria's Policy of Macedonian Reform* (Boulder, Colo., 1989).

Stavrianos, L., *Balkan Federation: A History of the Movement toward Balkan Unity in Modern Times* (Northampton, Mass., 1944).

—— *The Balkans since 1453* (New York, 1958).

Stavropoulos, V., 'Apomnemonevmata' [Memoirs], in *O Makedonikos Agonas: Anamniseis* [The Struggle for Macedonia: Memoirs] (Salonica, 1984), 383–465.

Stephanove, Constantine, *The Bulgarians and Anglo-Saxondom* (Berne, 1919).

Stojanovic, Mihailo, *The Great Powers and the Balkans, 1875–1878* (Cambridge, 1939).

Sumner, B. H., 'Ignatyev at Constantinople, 1864–1874', *Slavonic and East European Review*, 11/32 (1933), 341–53; 11/33 (1933), 571.

—— *Russia and the Balkans 1870–1880* (Oxford, 1937).

Swire, J., *Bulgarian Conspiracy* (London, 1939).

Terry, G. D., 'The Origins and Development of the Macedonian Revolutionary Movement, with Particular Reference to T.M.O.R.O. from its Conception in 1893 to Ilinden Uprising of 1903' (Unpublished M.Phil. thesis, Nottingham University, 1974).

Terzioski, Rastislav, 'The Bulgarian Institutions in Occupied Macedonia, 1941–1944', *Macedonian Review*, 1 (1976), 72–8.

—— 'I.M.R.O.-Mihajlovist Collaborators and the German Occupation: Macedonia, 1941–1944', in Pero Morača (ed.), *The Third Reich and Yugoslavia, 1933–1945* (Belgrade, 1977), 541–603.

Todorov, Kosta, *Balkan Firebrand: The Autobiography of a Rebel, Soldier and Statesman* (Chicago, 1943).

—— 'The Macedonian Organization Yesterday and Today', *Foreign Affairs*, 6/3 (1928), 473–82.

Tomasevich, Jozo, *War and Revolution in Yugoslavia, 1941–1945: The Chetniks* (Stanford, 1975).

Troebst, Stefan, *Mussolini, Makedonien und die Mächte, 1922–1930: Die 'Innere Mekedonische Revolutionäre Organisation' in der Südosteuropapolitik des Faschistichen Italien* (Cologne, 1987).

_____ 'Yugoslav Macedonia, 1943–1953: Building the Party, the State, and the Nation', in Melissa Bokovoy, Jill Irvine, and Carol Lilly (eds.), *State–Society Relations in Yugoslavia, 1945–1992* (New York, 1997), 243–66.

Turlakova, Tanya, 'Balkanskata Komunisticheska Federatsiya I Natsionalniyat Vŭpros na Balkanite, 1920–1931 Godina' [The Balkan Communist Federation and the National Question in the Balkans], in *Problemi na Politikata na Balkanskite Komunisticheski Partii po Natsionalniyat Vŭpros* [Problems of the Policy of the Balkan Communist Parties on the National Question] (Sofia, 1987), 5–75.

Tyler, Mason Whiting, *The European Powers and the Near East, 1875–1908* (Minneapolis, 1925).

Ulam, Adam, *Titoism and the Cominform* (Harvard, Mass., 1957).

Van Creveld, Martin, *Hitler's Strategy, 1940–1941: The Balkan Clue* (Cambridge, 1973).

Vasilev, Vasil, 'Maiskiyat Manifest na Ts.Ka. na V.M.R.O., 1924g. Obstanovka, Pregovori, Poslednitsi' [The May Manifesto of IMRO, in 1924: Setting, Negotiations, Consequences], *Istoricheski Pregled*, 5 (1984), 39–63.

_____ 'Velikobritaniya I Makedonskiyat Vŭpros, 1924–1929g' [Great Britain and the Macedonian Question], *Istoricheski Pregled*, 11 (1985), 20–41.

Veremis, Thanos, 'From the Nation State to Stateless Nation, 1821–1910', in id. and M. Blinkhorn (eds.), *Modern Greece: Nationalism and Nationality* (Athens, 1990).

Vlahov, Dimitar, *Govori i Statii, 1945–1947* [Speeches and Articles, 1945–1947] (Skopje, 1947) [Greek trans., deposited at the Institute for Balkan Studies, Salonica, Greece].

Vucinich, Wayne (ed.), *At the Brink of War and Peace: The Tito–Stalin Split in a Historical Perspective* (New York, 1982).

Vukmanović, Svetozar (General Tempo), *Struggle for the Balkans* (London, 1991).

Weber, Eugene, *From Peasants into Frenchmen: The Modernization of Rural France, 1870–1914* (Stanford, 1976).

Wheeler, Mark, *Britain and the War for Yugoslavia, 1940–1943* (New York and Boulder, Colo., 1980).

Wilkinson, H. R., *Maps and Politics: A Review of the Ethnographic Cartography of Macedonia* (Liverpool, 1951).

Wolff, Robert, Lee, *The Balkans in Our Time* (Harvard, Mass., 1956).

Woodhouse, C. M., *Apple of Discord: A Survey of Recent Greek Politics in their International Setting* (London, 1948).

Woodward, Sir Llewellyn, *British Policy in the Second World War*, iii (London, 1971).

Xydis, Stephen, *Greece and the Great Powers, 1944–1947: Prelude to the Truman Doctrine* (Salonica, 1963).

Zalar, Charles, *Yugoslav Communism: A Critical Study* (Washington, DC, 1961).

Index